Where Did the Revolution Go?

Where Did the Revolution Go? considers the apparent disappearance of the large social movements that have contributed to democratization. Revived by the events of the Arab Spring, this question is once again paramount. Is the disappearance real, given the focus of mass media and scholarship on electoral processes and "normal politics"? Does it always happen, or only under certain circumstances? Are those who struggled for change destined to be disappointed by the slow pace of transformation? Which mechanisms are activated and deactivated during the rise and fall of democratization? This volume addresses these questions through empirical analysis based on quantitative and qualitative methods (including oral history) of cases in two waves of democratization: Central Eastern European cases in 1989 as well as cases in the Middle East and Mediterranean region in 2011.

Donatella della Porta is Professor of Political Science and Dean of the Institute for Humanities and the Social Sciences at the Scuola Normale Superiore in Florence, where she directs the Center on Social Movement Studies (Cosmos). Among her very recent publications are *Social Movements in Times of Austerity* (2015); *Methodological Practices in Social Movement Research* (2014); *Mobilizing for Democracy* (2014); *Can Democracy Be Saved?* (2013); *Clandestine Political Violence* (Cambridge University Press, 2013); and *Blackwell Encyclopedia on Social and Political Movements* (2013).

Cambridge Studies in Contentious Politics

Editors

(continued after index)

Where Did the Revolution Go?

Contentious Politics and the Quality of Democracy

DONATELLA DELLA PORTA

Scuola Normale Superiore

CAMBRIDGE
UNIVERSITY PRESS

CAMBRIDGE
UNIVERSITY PRESS

One Liberty Plaza, New York NY 10006, USA

Cambridge University Press is part of the University of Cambridge.

It furthers the University's mission by disseminating knowledge in the pursuit of education, learning and research at the highest international levels of excellence.

www.cambridge.org
Information on this title: www.cambridge.org/9781107173712

© Donatella della Porta 2016

First published 2016

Printed in the United States of America by Sheridan Books, Inc.

A catalog record for this publication is available from the British Library

ISBN 978-1-107-17371-2 Hardback
ISBN 978-1-316-62596-5 Paperback

To Sid, friend and mentor

Contents

Figures

Acknowledgments

I asked myself the question "Where did the revolution go?" in 1990 in Berlin, where I was working at the Social Science Center. Just a few months after the excitement of the "peaceful revolution" of 1989, the streets seemed empty and the hopes fading away. At the same time, however, it was my impression that those events had provided some long-lasting empowerment capacity for the citizens. It was only many years later that I formulated that question in more scientific terms and tried to address it through empirical research. In the meantime, the very same question was asked, over and over again, after another wave of mobilization for democracy in the Arab Spring in 2011.

For the opportunity to develop a cross-national, cross-area, and cross-time empirical research project, I am most grateful to the European Research Council, which financed the project on Mobilizing for Democracy with a generous Advanced Scholars' Grant. In this project, I aim at analyzing the forms and effects of social movements on democratic politics in transitions to democracy, as well as in democratic consolidation and deepening. While the results of the research on different paths of transition have been published, among others, in my *Mobilizing for Democracy* (2014) and those on democratic deepening in, among others, in my *Can Democracy Be Saved?* (2013) and *Social Movements in Times of Austerity* (2015), I look in this volume at the impact of different paths of transition on the democratic qualities of the ensuing regimes.

I am also grateful to the research collaborators who helped me enormously throughout the research, by conducting the in-depth oral history interviews as well as the protest event analysis. For their care and commitment, I am most grateful to Kivanc Atak, Matteo Cernison, Teije Donker, Milan Hrubes, Joachen Kleres, Hugo Leal, Grzegogz Piotrowski, Simon Teune, Lili Torek, and Jana Warkotsch.

I was able to present and discuss research results during conferences and lectures in St. Petersburg, Bremen, Jyvaskyla, Berlin, Oxford, Cambridge, Prague, and Porto Alegre, as well as at the Cosmos that I directed at the Political and Social Science department at the European University Institute (EUI) and now direct at the Scuola Normale Superiore in Florence.

For extremely helpful comments on a previous version of this manuscript, I am particularly grateful to Sidney Tarrow and Ondrej Císar, as well as three anonymous referees. At Cambridge University Press, I am grateful to Lew Bateman, who believed in this project.

My utmost gratitude goes to the dozens of activists and former activists who have struggled for justice and democracy, and who were willing to share their memories with us. In this volume, I have aimed at giving them voice, as I believe their testimonies are precious for us not only as scholars but as citizens of the world.

As ever, Sarah Tarrow, my editor in chief, helped me to communicate my ideas in a foreign language.

Where Did the Revolution Go? The Outcomes of Democratization Paths

Where Did the Revolution Go? An Introduction

Where did the revolution go? The main puzzle – revived by the recent events of the so-called Arab Spring – is the apparently sudden disappearance from the political sphere of the large social movements that contributed to episodes of democratization. Media, activists, and scholars have often used terms like Velvet Revolution or Jasmine Revolution – but also Carnation Revolution or Orange Revolution – to describe regime transition involving massive participation from below. However, with the emergence of political liberalization or even the installation of a democratic regime, observers are often surprised to note the sudden emptiness of the once-full streets, and even the rapid loss of influence of the oppositional leaders, once the new regime has been installed. Even more, those who fought for democracy seem quickly disappointed by the results of their own struggles, and choose to exit the movement. But is the disappearance real, or just an optical illusion, given the focus of mass media and scholarship on electoral processes and "normal politics"? Does it always happen, or only under some circumstances? Are those who struggled for big changes bound to be disappointed by the slow pace of transformation? And which mechanisms are activated and deactivated during the rise and fall of episodes of democratization?

These questions – which have rarely been addressed in the social science literature – refer, in their essence, to the effects of transition processes on consolidated democracy. The main theoretical frame of the research presented in this volume builds upon reflections on outcomes in the cognate fields of democratization and social movement studies, although read through the lens of an approach that aims at reconstructing processes rather than identifying causes. I also bring in studies on revolutions, even if to a more limited extent. I do this because, although it would be inappropriate to define the episodes mentioned above as revolutions, some of them imply sudden breaks through mass mobilizations that can indeed be illuminated by that field of study. I believe, in fact, that there is much to gain in this theoretical endeavor in order to move toward systematic models for understanding social movements' impacts in terms of big transformations. While social movement studies have systematically addressed the crucial issues of their effects at the structural, political, and cultural levels, they have mainly adopted static models, singling out correlations but not causal mechanisms. Moreover, they have focused mainly on incremental changes in "normal" times. In contrast, democratization studies, even if largely overlooking social movements in favor of the elites, have focused on the strategic choices of the different actors, linking them to their preferences and interests. Finally, recent studies of revolutions have contributed to our understanding of moments of (big) changes through attention to the emergence of new actors and to their coalition-building, internal divisions, and dilemmas within a context of rapid transformation.

In combining these literatures, I aim at providing an understanding of the effects of mobilizations for democracy on social movements' actual and potential characteristics – an understanding that is dynamic, recognizing the relational nature of contention; constructed, stating the importance of cognitive assessments of a situation; and emergent, looking at the transformative emotional intensity of some events. My main assumption is that the forms and paths of mobilization during the episodes of mobilization for democracy have an effect on some of the qualities of the ensuing regime. In particular, I expect the participation of social movements in democratization processes to have important consequences in terms of specific civil, political, and social rights – as the call for a break with the past and increased rights for the citizens will be louder than in regime transitions that happen mainly through elite pacts. Episodes of mobilizations for democracy in fact represent critical junctures, which then affect democratic developments toward a higher or lower quality of citizenship rights. This means that even when these movements disappear from the mass-mediated public sphere, and even when they are mourned by their former activists as being in decline, we can still find traces of their effects on the recognition of citizens' rights to protest, the presence of channels of institutional access, and sensitivity to social justice.

This approach implies some caveats vis-à-vis existing literature that aims at explaining democratization and its quality, on the one hand, or rapid, revolutionary changes, on the other. First of all, my aim is not to assess democratic qualities in general – other researchers have already done so, using a variety of qualitative and quantitative techniques. Moreover, I do not aim at providing general explanatory models (parsimonious or otherwise) of the success or failure of democratization processes, with or without mass mobilization, as other literature on democratization does. Admittedly, there are therefore many conditions that affect the quality of democracy that I do not address. Rather, I would aim at singling out some causal mechanisms that, in the cases I studied, intervened on both the evolution of protest waves and their legacies. While democratization studies as well as studies of revolutions tend to neatly distinguish positive cases from negative ones, I address much more fuzzy evolutions. As social movement studies have often suggested, the effects of contentious waves are complex, never fully meeting the aspirations of those who protest, but rarely leaving things unchanged. In addition, while effects can happen at the policy level, they often develop first in terms of culture, evolving in the long term, with jumps and reversals. This is all the more relevant when looking at democratization – an extended process that in other epochs required many steps in a long process, but today is often expected to happen in a few short weeks.

While social movement studies allow for useful reflections on the long-term and complex assessment of movement outcomes, I would also like to go beyond some expectations present in that literature. First and foremost, I will not just look at protest as contributing to explaining policy or cultural changes. Rather, I want to investigate how protest actors – particularly social movements – also develop their own resources in action, not only using previously accumulated resources but also acquiring new ones; and not only exploiting existing opportunities but also opening new windows by breaking former alliances and by challenging the expectations upon which they were based. Protests, particularly the intense moments of mobilization for democracy, are therefore understood as eventful, given their capacity to transform structures through relational, emotional, and cognitive mechanisms (Sewell 1996; della Porta 2013b, 2014a;). As I argued in a previous work (della Porta 2014a), the transformative power of protest can be seen when analyzing episodes of democratization, defined, following Ruth Collier (1999), as moments toward a process of democratization, rather than necessarily bringing about a transition to democracy.

Without assuming that democratization is always produced from below, I have singled out – in the cases I have analyzed and without pretense of being exhaustive – different paths of democratization by looking at the ways in which masses interact with elites, and protest with bargaining. In all of these paths, social movement organizations are considered among the important actors in a complex field: they stage protests that have an impact in steering the change. Their relevance, however, lies in the fluid processes of breaking and recomposing, mobilizing and negotiating (Glenn 2001). In particular, I identified *eventful democratization* as defining cases in which authoritarian regimes break down following – often short but intense – waves of protest. Recognizing the particular power of some transformative events (Sewell 1996), I have addressed them as part of broader mobilization processes, including the multitude of less visible, but still important, protests that surround them (della Porta 2014a). While protests in eventful democratization develop from the interaction between growing resources of contestation and closed opportunities, social movements are not irrelevant players in the other two paths I singled out. First of all, when opportunities open up because of elites' realignment, *participated pacts* might ensue from the encounter of reformers in institutions and moderates among social movement organizations. Although rarely used, protest is also important here, as a resource to threaten on the negotiating table.[1] If participated pacts occur in relatively strong civil society that meets emerging opportunities, more *troubled* democratization paths develop in very repressive regimes that block the development of autonomous associations. In these cases, escalation of violence often follows from the interaction of a suddenly mobilized opposition with a brutal repressive regime. Especially when there are divisions in and defections from security apparatuses, skills and resources for military action fuel coups d'état and civil war dynamics.

Comparing eventful democratization with participated pacts, the claim I discuss in this volume is that the different forms and degrees of participation of social movements during transition, and their positions during the installation of the regime, have an impact on some of the qualities of the ensuing regime. Without taking a deterministic stance, but also without

---

[1] My typology has some resonance with the classification, widespread in research on democratization, that distinguishes transition by rupture from pacted transition according to continuity among elites. However, my typology has a different focus, being built upon two dimensions that are related with social movement participation: strength of civil society and amount of protest (della Porta 2014a, chap. 1).

decontextualizing agency, I will suggest some specific mechanisms that link protest for democracy to democratic qualities. This will require us to look at the evolution of the waves of protest that accompany episodes of democratization, singling out relational, affective, and cognitive dimensions in the periods before, during, and after regime transition.

I address these tasks via a research project based on a mixed-methods research design, combining in-depth interviews oriented to an oral history of contentious events in transition and post-transition with protest event analysis, as well as extensive use of secondary sources. Within a most-similar research design, I conduct an infra-area comparison of Central Eastern Europe (CEE) (in particular, contrasting Czechoslovakia and the German Democratic Republic [GDR] as cases of eventful democratization, with Poland and Hungary as cases of participated pacts). Additionally, I broaden the scope of the comparison in space and time by looking at two eventful episodes of mobilization for democracy in the Mediterranean and North African region. For this part of the analysis, Tunisia and Egypt will be compared with two purposes in mind. First, looking for similarities within a cross-area, most-different research design, I will examine the extent to which some mechanisms identified in the CEE region are robust enough to travel to the MENA (Middle East and North Africa) area more than twenty years later. Second, a within-area comparison will allow me to shed light on the different outcomes of those mobilizations, with apparently more positive results in terms of citizens' rights in Tunisia than in Egypt.

THE THEORETICAL FRAME: HOW MOBILIZATION FOR DEMOCRACY AFFECTS ITS QUALITIES

How to understand the trajectory and effects of social movements mobilizing for democracy, as they interact with other actors in complex fields? How to make sense, then, of the results of transition paths on the quality of democracy? In addressing these questions, the focus is on the *how* rather than the *why*. In particular, I do not aim at developing a powerful but parsimonious model to explain democratic qualities, as other scholars have done with large numbers of cases and quantitative indicators. Instead, in the search for causal mechanisms that allow understanding how movements for democratization affect the movements to come, I looked for inspiration in three cognate areas of study that have often looked at the same events, but using different analytic lenses: democratization studies, revolution studies, and social movement studies.

Democratization studies have traditionally focused on the successes and failures of attempts to democratize, often searching for scientific law-like statements that might allow identification of the general conditions for democracy. Ever more complex models have been built in an attempt to explain the maximum of variance in the success and failure of democratization attempts. In criticism of a deterministic approach looking for contextual causes, a more strategic orientation looked at the ways in which influential actors played the game of democratization. While social movements and protests tended to be dismissed as of little relevance, or even as dangerous for democracy, the literature on democratization has provided important theoretical and empirical contributions to understanding critical interactions between (mainly elite) actors (for a critical assessment, see Bermeo 1997).

Revolution studies were initially focused on social revolutions, which affected also the political and economic regimes, thereby transforming relations between the state and the market. Distinguishing neatly between successful and failed cases, studies on revolutions – social ones, at least – define them as "basic transformation of a society's state and class structures," "accompanied and in part carried through by class-based revolts from below" (Skocpol 1979, 4–5). Success is usually understood as "coming to power and holding it long enough to initiate a process of deep structural transformation" (Foran 2005, 5). While a deterministic approach initially dominated here as well, a violent break was also considered as a determinant of change. Broadening the field of studies to include a (somewhat stretched) definition of revolution as nonviolent and nonsocial, scholars of revolution also started to address the strategic choices of various actors, including those who claimed to represent the masses. Even if definitional issues are still debated, studies on revolutions contributed to challenge democratization studies through their attention to the conflictual dynamics before, during, and after revolutions, considered as breaking points.

As mentioned, while both fields of study tend to neatly distinguish successes and failures – positive and negative cases – as their explanandum, social movement studies have looked at the effects of mobilization as more ambivalent, complex, and long term. It has long been common to state that the effects of social movements have rarely been addressed in social movement studies, especially given the difficulty in assessing multicausal and long-lasting processes. In particular, the recognition that social movements have often utopian aims has made it difficult to find measures of the degree of success. This narrative is, however, less and less apt to describe a field of research in which outcomes appear more and more as relevant objects of investigation. The very interest in social movements as agents of change has in fact focused attention toward those effects, with much reflection on the possible solutions to methodological challenges. While I built upon these assumptions in the search for the consequences of episodes of mobilization, I also tried to innovate on explanatory approaches that I found either too deterministic or too agency oriented, through an analysis of the more dynamic aspects on the path toward democracy.

In this introductory chapter, I aim at building a theoretical framework that might help readers in understanding the effects of social movements in transition on democratic qualities in consolidation. I attempt to do this by bridging social movement studies with the literatures on democratization and on revolutions, which have indeed looked for the causes of the success and failure of efforts to bring about political and social change. These social science fields have rarely been linked to each other and/or with the social movement theory that, I argue, can provide new lenses to explain how movements' characteristics at the time of transition might affect the qualities of the ensuing democracy and therefore the future dynamics of protest itself. At the same time, looking at the effects of social movements in terms of democratization (or, sometimes, revolutions) can help to enrich social movement studies, which have rarely addressed these types of effects, focusing instead on long-lasting democracies. Following the contentious politics approach, rather than emphasizing structural determinants, I concentrate on the mechanisms that mediate between structures and action (McAdam, Tarrow, and Tilly 2001). I attempt in fact to bring into focus the actors' agency, without losing awareness of the environmental constraints on their desires. In particular, I give leverage to the actors' perceptions, focusing on social movement activists, as I believe they influenced the movements' effects as they intervened between the external reality and the action upon it.

What Do We Want to Understand: Institutional Effects of Democratization Paths

My central assumption is that the role of social movements varies in different paths of transition, with consequences for the democratic qualities of the ensuing regimes (della Porta 2014a). In particular, it might be expected that eventful democratization, through social movement participation, enlarges the range of actors that support the new regimes, while pacted transitions remain more exclusive toward citizens' demands, focusing instead on elite interests.

In order to look at the effects of social movements' participation in transition on the eventual democratic institutions, we must first conceptualize these effects. The social science literature on democratic quality (or, better, qualities in the plural) has made an important contribution in mapping the specific dimensions on which democracies should be assessed. Summarizing various reflections, Leonardo Morlino (2012, 197–8) distinguished procedural and substantial dimensions. Procedurally, quality of democracy implies rules of law, including the following:

1. Individual security and civil order.
2. Independent judiciary and a modern justice system.
3. Institutional and administrative capacity to formulate, implement and enforce the law.
4. Effective fight against corruption, illegality and abuse of power by state agencies.
5. Security forces that are respectful of citizen rights and are under civilian control.

To these procedural dimensions, Morlino added two substantive ones: freedom (as translated into political and civil rights) and equality (as translated especially into social rights). In particular, political rights encompass the right to vote, to compete for electoral support, and to be elected to public office (ibid., 204). Civil rights encompass

personal liberty, the right to legal defense, the right to privacy, the freedom to choose one's place of residence, freedom of movement and residence, the right to expatriate or emigrate, freedom and secrecy of correspondence, freedom of thought and expression, the right to an education, the right to information and a free press, and the freedoms of assembly, association and organization, including political organizations unrelated to trade unions. (Ibid., 206)

Finally, social rights include

rights associated with employment and connected with how the work is carried out, the right to fair pay and time off, and the right to collective bargaining . . . the right to health or to mental and physical well-being; the right to assistance and social security; the right to work; the right to human dignity; the right to strike; the right to study; the right to healthy surroundings, and, more generally, to the environment and to the protection of the environment; and the right to housing. (Ibid., 206)

We can rephrase these dimensions in terms of sets of citizenship rights. In historical sociology, democracy has been linked to the extension of citizenship rights, typically broken down into categories of civil, political, and social rights. In Marshall's influential account (1992), civic rights were the first to be achieved, followed by political rights and, with them, the possibility to create pressure for social rights as well. However, more recent analyses have stressed the various possible timings in their development, both for specific social groups and for specific countries (della Porta 2013a). In this sense, they are not necessarily moving in the same direction, as in fact an increase in political rights (and formal democracy) can accompany a decline in social rights. As democratic states do show different achievements on all these sets of rights, an analysis of democratic qualities must first assess and then explain those differences. While various indicators (or proxies) have been chosen (and their own quality discussed) in order to measure democracy, qualitative investigations are also important to complete and understand those data.

Without pretending to assess, let alone explain, all dimensions of democratic quality in all the selected countries, in this work I aim instead at identifying some specific effects that the paths of transition have on the development of the civic, political, and social qualities of the emerging regimes. Following leads from studies of social movements, of revolutions, and of democratization, I want to move, in my argumentation, from structures and strategies to relational dynamics. Charles Tilly has suggested categorizing the scholars working on political violence as *idea* people, who look at ideologies; *behavior* people, who stress human genetic heritage; and *relational* people, who "make transactions among persons and groups much more central than do ideas or behavior people" (2004, 5). So, he continues, relational people focus their attention "on interpersonal processes that promote, inhibit, or channel collective violence and connect it with nonviolent politics" (ibid., 20; see also McAdam, Tarrow, and Tilly 2001, 22–4). This also applies, as I will argue in what follows, to research on contentious politics, more generally, which has considered structures and agency and is now moving toward a more relational perspective – a perspective that is not separate from the first two, but can use some of their insights in order to understand the contextual constraints as well as actors' strategies within relations.

How to Explain: Structural Constraints and Outcomes

For some time, research on democratization, revolutions, and social movements has stressed the structural conditions for their development.

Various approaches have searched for causal explanations, citing socio-economic, cultural, and political conditions.

The literature on democratization has looked at regime consolidation, linking democratic qualities to some of the characteristics of the previous regimes, as well as at the dynamics of transition. In general, it has singled out several favorable or unfavorable conditions, in some cases extending the reflection to conditions of nonconsolidation. If economic and social factors were initially emphasized, researchers tended to add more and more explanatory dimensions. In a broad synthesis of the determinants of democratization, Jan Teorell (2010) suggested that, if economic crises, peaceful protests, media proliferation, neighborhood diffusion, and membership in democratic regional organizations contribute to democratization (and foreign interventions work only sometimes), socioeconomic modernization and economic freedom tend to prevent downturns, while volume of trade is negatively linked to democratization. While modernization helps regimes to survive, economic crises trigger democratization processes as they (and, especially, the connected recessionary policies) divide elites, with ensuing private sector defection as well as mass protests on social issues. Failed democratization has been predicted not only by structural conditions of a socioeconomic nature but also by political factors such as the longevity of statehood or the degree of power of the legislative branch, as reversed liberalization is linked to the intervention of a strong executive. The position of the military is especially relevant. Military dictatorships, multiparty autocracies, military regimes, and single-party regimes have different likelihoods and dynamics of democratization (Bratton and van de Walle 1997). External powers are also seen as acting to facilitate or jeopardize democratization (Fish and Wittenberg 2009). Falling dominos have been singled out, as membership in regional organizations as well as diffusion from neighbors promotes democracy, while foreign intervention is only sometimes effective. Military intervention is also of varying influence. More specifically with reference to 1989, reflections addressed the specific difficulties of double or triple transitions, looking at the complications that emerge when a change in political regime overlaps with one at the socioeconomic level and, in some cases, also with transformation in the definition of the nation-state (Linz and Stepan 1996; Offe 1996).

Structural conditions have also been a main focus for the literature on revolutions. Even without referring much to each other, scholars in the fields of democratization and revolution have built mirrored images of what facilitates democratization and what instead supports revolutions, which were initially conceptualized as involving broad and abrupt social changes, often through violent means. Influentially, Theda Skocpol (1979) has linked successful social revolutions to some particular socio-economic and international challenges that the state is not able to address. In her view, the great revolutions in France, Russia, and China emerged when the regime in power could not face external threats, given internal constraints in terms of economic system and elites' constellations. Research on revolutions has also linked them to accelerated shifts from traditional to modern society. According to Jeff Goodwin (2001), revolutionary movements are especially powerful in peripheral societies, when they build large coalitions with strong international allies. They tend to emerge where regimes are weak (in terms of policing capacity and infrastructural power), unpopular (because of the economic and social arrangements they support), and using high levels of repression (indiscriminate, but not overwhelming). They are more likely to prevail when corrupt and personalistic rules divide the incumbent elites. In general, in fact, people do not support revolutions if they believe that there are alternative paths, but do engage in them if they see no other way out (ibid., 25–6). Looking for necessary and sufficient causes, Foran (2005, 14) suggested that successful revolutions require dependent development, repressive exclusionary and personalist regimes, and economic downturn, as well as the specific political culture of the opposition, defined as "the diverse and complex value systems existing among various groups and classes which are drawn upon to make sense of the 'structural' changes going on around them" (ibid., 18). While these analyses focus on revolutionary success in terms of achieving and keeping state power, the democratic qualities of the ensuing regimes have been addressed by research on nonviolent revolutions (or civil resistance), which pointed at the distribution of power within the elites –the military in particular – in determining the chances that a democratic regime will unfold (Nepstad 2011).

Explanations on the policy effects of social movements have also looked at structural stable conditions (such as opportunities in politics and in the administration) as well as at the (more conjunctural) availability of allies. Social movements are supposed to be more successful in reaching their aims when they have more channels of access to decision makers, thanks to a high degree of functional distribution of power or territorial decentralization, as well as availability of instruments of direct democracy (Kriesi 1991). It has been also observed, however, that all of those channels are also available for social movement adversaries, with the possibility then to oppose or reverse social movements' successes (Kitschelt 1986). Besides obtaining favorable laws, implementation of the decisions is a most fundamental step, in which the characteristics of the public administration also play an important role. Finally, having sympathetic parties in power is said to improve the chance that social movements will achieve their goals (Tarrow 1994; della Porta 1995). From an economic point of view, not only are times of economic growth of course more favorable to the concession of social rights than are times of economic crisis, but the type of relations between the state and the market also sets constraints upon movements' achievements (della Porta 2013a, 2015). Specific traditions embedded in existing institutions (such as the citizenship regime or welfare institutions) also affect responses to movement demands (Giugni, Bosi, and Uba 2013).

While, as we will see, my research tends to confirm that some of the mentioned – socioeconomic, political, cultural – conditions are indeed structuring actors' choices as well as the effects of those choices, it would be too deterministic to consider them as either unchangeable or unaffected by the strategies that different actors adopt during critical moments, and/ or by broader relations in the social and political arenas. Instead, it is often under harsh conditions or closed opportunities (defined as threats) that people find the energy to mobilize. Rather than seeing preconditions as fixed, then, one should consider them as part of a contextual background that constrains but also motivates action. Combining the insights from the various fields of research, one can expect democratic qualities to be higher when socioeconomic conditions are improving and political structures are open and autonomous from powerful external actors (such as the military).

How to Explain: Strategic Choices and Democratic Consolidation

Uneasy with a deterministic view, all three areas of study I have mentioned have indeed moved toward a recognition of the role of agency as shaping the structures themselves. In this turn, scholars of democratization, revolutions, and social movements have elaborated some concepts that might be usefully integrated within a relational perspective, with a focus on the dynamic process of interactions between different actors rather than on static causes.

A structuralist bias in the traditional vision of democratization has been strongly criticized by the *transitologist* approach, which stresses instead the dynamic nature of the process, while focusing on elite strategies and behavior (O'Donnell and Schmitter 1986; Higley and Gunther 1992). With this turn, social science reflection on democratization processes has indeed pointed at the importance of actors' strategies, choices, and actions, especially in moments of transformation when contingency plays a role, solutions are open-ended, and social dynamics are underdetermined (O'Donnell and Schmitter 1986; Beissinger 2002). This explains the expectation that, especially in these moments, historical processes tend to be more sensitive to individual agency. In times of uncertainty, the predispositions of elites, in particular their concern for their future reputation, are seen as determining whether democratization occurs at all. In this narrative, "Individual heroics may in fact be key: the 'catalyst' for the process of democratization comes, not from a debt crisis or rampant inflation or some major crisis of industrialization, but from gestures by exemplary individuals who begin testing the boundaries of behavior" (Bermeo 1990, 361). Through game theory, negotiations toward democracy are explained by the attitudes of defenders and challengers of the regime, the preferences of the public as well as the positions of actors such as the military or the church, and international pressures (Casper and Taylor 1996). Of utmost importance are considered the attitudes of elites, their availability to encapsulate conflicts, and their capacity to work within democratic institutions. Relevant factors for consolidation include the extent to which the military feels threatened; the attitudes of the judiciary; and the position of public service and civil society (Bratton and van de Walle 1997).

Opinions diverge, however, on the role of movements in the beginning of the consolidation phase. In fact, literature on transition has traditionally pointed at the importance of an agreement between moderate forces, among both challengers and incumbents, with a privileged role recognized to institutional actors. According to the moderation thesis, consolidation is easier when civil society is not mobilized (or at least demobilizes), leaving space for the emergence of representative institutions (Huntington 1991, 589). Moderation was therefore seen as a positive evolution, as the attitudes and goals of the various actors change along the process. In a comparison of democratic consolidation in southern Europe, Leonardo Morlino (1998) observed, in particular, the need to strengthen political parties, rather than social movement organizations. However, in other analyses, protest, especially if multiclass, is considered as important in promoting democracy (e.g., Bratton and van de Walle 1997; Bermeo 1997).

In comparison to mainstream democratization studies, research on revolutions tends to develop different expectations in terms of the role of pressures from below, as a revolutionary break is often considered as a necessary condition for social and political change. Looking at strategic choices in long-lasting processes and criticizing the structuralism of Skocpol's model, a new generation of scholars of revolution stressed the role of actors' strategies in determining the forms and outcomes of political processes. In particular, attention developed on "issues of agency, political culture and coalitions, and the dimensions of ethnicity (or 'race'), class and gender" (Foran 2005, 13). These researchers analyze the specific preferences and capacities of social classes such as, for example, the unwillingness of the bourgeoisie to modernize or the availability of peasants and workers to build coalitions (e.g., Paige 1997). Ideology is considered as playing a central role in the stabilization of revolutionary coalitions (Parsa 2000), which are expected to be particularly successful when they oppose authoritarian states that adopt exclusive strategies even toward the middle and upper classes (Goodwin 2001, 27). With the broadening of reflections to nonviolent revolutions, attention focused in particular on the negative effects of the use of violence on the democratic quality of the regime (Chenoweth and Stephan 2011; Nepstad 2011). Peaceful forms of noncooperation are seen instead as undermining the rulers without threatening the security force, and therefore facilitating their defection from the regime.

If social movement studies have long shied away from explaining protest effects in terms of the strategic choices of various actors, preferring more structural types of explanation, there has been, however, some debate on the role of the opposition's organizational strategies in facilitating or thwarting success. In particular, scholars have focused on organizational dilemmas, as a certain level of organizational resources seems necessary for collective mobilization (McCarthy and Zald 1977). Thinking small, and a moderate repertoire of protest, have been proved effective in achieving specific aims (Gamson 1990). However, organizational trends such as professionalization and bureaucratization are considered dangerous for a social movement, alienating rank-and-file supporters and reducing the disruptive capacity of poor people's movements (Piven and Cloward 1977). Particularly relevant here is the issue of how social movement organizations address strategic dilemmas (Jasper 2004). Here as well, the use of violent repertoires is seen as risky in terms of alienation of potential allies as well as public support (della Porta 1995, 2013b).

In sum, combining the three fields, one could expect democratic qualities after transition to be higher when elites and challenges cooperate in a peaceful way. However, the development of strategic preferences toward moderation or radicalization, compromising or breaking up in itself needs to be explained. Often, the effects of specific strategic prefer-ences are in fact influenced by the context, with violent rebellions leading to democracy under conditions of high exploitation (Wood 2000). Focusing attention on the contrast between structure and agency can in fact be misleading if we do not consider the relations between the different actors.

Consolidation and Protest: A Dynamic Approach

Following a relational perspective, I shall suggest that forms of action emerge, and are transformed, in the course of physical and symbolic *inter-actions* between social movements and their opponents, but also with their potential allies. Changes take place in encounters between social move-ments and authorities, but also in countermovements, in a series of recipro-cal adjustments. Within this relational perspective, I suggest that the types of interactions that develop during transitions have an impact on the evolution of protest during consolidation. Regime transitions, as critical junctures, bring about important changes that then, path-dependently, structure the characteristics of the new regime. The characteristics of social movement participation have a specific relevance for the development of inclusive forms of democracy. In this research, I am in fact especially interested in reflections (and empirical evidence) on the effects in terms of democratic qualities of paths of democratization, as influenced by social movements' participation in them. I suggest that this assumption is relevant from the theoretical point of view, as well as being backed by some – admittedly not systematic – empirical evidence.

Although with different emphases and in different combinations, the three fields of knowledge I have reviewed so far have in common an increasing interest in agency over structure, as well as a growing preference for processual rather than deterministic explanations. The capacity of collective actors to strategize and make rational decisions in times of intense transformation has been challenged, however, by a relational vision that considers the complex dynamics of interactions between different actors and their mechanisms. Looking from the macro perspective, democratiza-tion processes have indeed been considered as underdetermined moments, as they fell out of routines and institutional arrangements. From both the meso and the micro perspectives, assessments about other collective and/or individual actors' behavior are difficult to make. Decisions are therefore made – as some protagonists have mentioned – "on the run" (rather than allowing time for pausing and thinking) and "betting" on (rather than predicting) other people's behavior (Kuran 1991; della Porta 2014a). For O'Donnell and Schmitter, transitions from authoritarian rule are indeed illustrations of "underdetermined social change, of large-scale transformations which occur when there are insufficient structural or behavioral parameters to guide and predict the outcome" (1986, 363). In fact, their influential collection of research on the transition from authoritarian rule emphasizes its *structural indeterminacy*.

Contentious politics during transitions can be seen as eventful moments in which actions change structures (Sewell 1996): influencing the relations between elites and challengers, they can be expected to have durable effects (della Porta 2014a). In these critical junctures, in which change is produced not by slow adaptation but by brisk turning points, resources for mobilization are created in action, as emotional, cognitive, and relational processes develop quickly, changing actors' perspectives and forging new collective identities.

As critical junctures, transitions are therefore turning points that pave the way for changes, which then tend to become resilient. Later, consolidation phases build upon founding moments in which institutional and normative codes are established, with long-lasting effects. Different degrees and forms of contention could develop from specific processes that originate in transition phases. In this vision, in fact, "instead of connecting initial conditions to outcomes, events carry the potential to transform the X–Y relation, neutralizing the reversing effects that initial conditions would have otherwise produced" (Collier and Mazzuca 2008, 485).

Once changes are produced via critical junctures, they impact on the relations that are established in new assets (or new regimes). While I do not assume deterministic and unmutable effects of transitions upon consolidation, I expect, however, transition paths to constrain consolidation processes, as "what has happened in an earlier point in time will affect the possible outcomes of a sequence of events occurring at a later point in time" (Sewell 1996, 263). So, once a particular outcome occurs, self-reproducing mechanisms tend to cause "the outcome to endure across time, even long after its original purposes have ceased to exist" (Mahoney and Schensul 2006, 456). It has in fact been observed that transformations tend to stabilize, as "Once a process (e.g., a revolution) has occurred and acquired a name, both the name and the one or more representations of the process become available as signals, models, threats and/or aspirations for later actors" (Tilly 2006, 421). After a critical juncture stabilizes, changes over time become difficult (Mahoney and Schensul 2006, 462) – unless there is a new rupture or disruptive event.

Critical junctures are forms of change endowed with some specific characteristics. As Kenneth Roberts (2015, 65) noted, "critical junctures are not periods of 'normal politics' when institutional continuity or incremental change can be taken for granted. They are periods of crisis or strain that existing policies and institutions are ill-suited to resolve." In fact, he stated, they produce changes described as abrupt, discontinuous, and path dependent:

Changes are abrupt because critical junctures contain decisive "choice points" when major reforms are debated, policy choices are made, and institutions are created, reconfigured, or displaced. They are discontinuous because they diverge sharply from baseline trajectories of institutional continuity or incremental adaptation; in short, they represent a significant break with established patterns. Finally, change is path dependent because it creates new political alignments and institutional legacies that shape and constrain subsequent political development. (Ibid.)

If critical junctures are rooted within structures, they are however open-ended. In this vision, critical junctures are structurally underdetermined as they are characterized by high levels of uncertainty and political contingency. During these periods of crisis, "the range of plausible choices available to powerful political actors expands substantially" (Capoccia and Kelemen 2007, 343). As Roberts (2015, 13) noted with reference to the neoliberal critical juncture in Latin America,

citizens and social actors influenced outcomes through various types of political mobilization, inside and out of the electoral arena. The complex and contingent political realignments produced by neoliberal critical junctures, then, were not straightforward crystallizations of strategic choices or institutional innovations adopted by political leaders; societal resistance and reactive sequences produced myriad unintended consequences that pushed institutional development (and sometimes decay) along unforeseen paths.

Choice points are particularly important in this sequence since, as exogenous shocks are introduced, the responses by different actors to specific challenges tend to reconstitute relations.

If these are theoretically relevant reasons to focus on eventful protest in the democratization process, empirical research has collected some scattered evidence that justifies a systematic focus on the consequences of choosing particular paths of transition on democratic qualities. Without assuming that transition forms determine once and forever the potential for consolidation as well as the democratic quality of a regime, I argue that moments of fluidity and uncertainties such as transitions shape in fact the access to democratic institutions by different groups in democracy

(O'Donnell and Schmitter 1986; Shain and Linz 1995). Different modes of transition can indeed be expected to have different effects, related to the continuity/discontinuity of the mobilized actors – whether institutional or noninstitutional, incumbents or oppositional actors, or a mix of those. The characteristics of the actors who drive the transition – elites, counter-elites, or a combination of the two – have in fact been singled out as having an impact on the development of the transition as well as on the next steps in democratization processes, with higher expectations for cases of transitions by rupture (Munck and Skalnik Leff 1997).[2] While some scholars tend to consider mass mobilization as potentially dangerous in moments of transition, as it places a higher expectation on the emerging regime, others have suggested that pressures from below can instead improve the quality of life of affected citizens by bringing about deeper democracy (Anderson 2010), more gender equality (Viterna and Fallon 2008), a more progressive welfare state, more effective land distribution and educational policies (Foran and Goodwin 1993), and more efficient agrarian development (Bermeo 1986). When transitions derive from pacts among elites that control the agenda on issues to be addressed, this might instead be expected to increase inequalities among the citizenry (Schmitter 1984, 366). In fact, more inclusive coalitions of opponents are then expected to be more conducive to democracy, as they will exert pressure to accommodate a broad range of claims. In this direction, it has been concluded that "transitions from below have better chances of installing a new government which has fewer nondemocratic elements because fewer, if any, promises have to be made to the authoritarian regime to get it to exit, allowing the new democracy more leeway to introduce reform" (Casper and Taylor 1996, 10).

Particularly relevant for the analysis of the effects of paths of transition on democratic qualities is Robert Fishman's comparative work on the

---

[2] Munck and Skalnik Leff's (1997) comparative analysis covers cases of revolution from above (Bulgaria), social revolution and reform from below (Chile), reform through rupture (in Czechoslovakia and Argentina), reform through extrication (in Hungary), and reform through transaction (in Poland and Brazil). In this vision, the strength of old elites in Chile thwarted the opposition to accept undemocratic features in the constitution, while in Brazil and Poland, long periods of liberalization explain the stronger support for democracy among incumbent elites and, therefore, a less authoritarian constitution. In Hungary, the September 1989 agreement reflected an equitable distribution of power, resulting in a complex, mixed electoral system (majoritarian electoral law, parliamentary system). Argentina and Czechoslovakia, both cases of rupture, are presented as the least problematic forms of transition in terms of their outcomes, as rupture allows for deeper transformation.

Iberian Peninsula. Considering the role of civil society in democratization, he suggested that paths of transition have an effect on whether predominant forms of democratic action incorporate the voices of low-income and socially marginal sectors. In particular, pathways into democracy are expected to hold enduring consequences, as "the legacies of democratization scenarios take the form not of fixed states but instead of ongoing approaches to a wide range of political matters. Regime transitions hold the ability to change not only the basic rules linking governmental institutions to the broader populace, but also a variety of social practices and understandings" (Fishman 2011, 4). Civil society and the emerging regimes "are mutually constitutive, developing in a dynamic and iterative series of interactions" (Fishman 2013, 3), as the "forms taken by civil society and its action in the context of democratic transition carry large and enduring consequences for the type of democratic practices that dominate after transitions" (ibid., 4).

Building upon these theoretical and empirical suggestions, I expect the role of social movements in transition to be reflected in their post-transition relations with the state, with more recognition of civil, political, and social rights in regimes that emerge from eventful democratization rather than participated pacts. My assumption is that if participated pacts are based on compromise within elites, eventful democratizations should instead leave more space for in-depth, unconstrained transformation. In fact, despite the relative brevity of those periods, "Decisions made during revolutionary moments about future institutions can structure political competition in the short to medium term by defining who is permitted to participate in the polity and on what terms" (Glenn 2001, 11). The mentioned path-breaking research on the Iberian Peninsula, based on a comparison of Spain as a case of participated pact and Portugal as a case of eventful democratization, has shown indeed how the path of transition influences the interactions between power holders and protestors in the ensuing regime – particularly with regard to democratic practice, defined as "the way in which actors within a democracy understand and make use of opportunities for political action and influence, and interact with other participants in the polity" (Fishman 2013, 5). This refers not only to emerging institutions but also to implicit cultures that define shared norms; so action affects the recognition of civil society voices, beyond their strength and resources. As Fishman noted, cultural processes working in times of flux have an impact on practices by reconfiguring fundamental elements of national identities and the public rituals that affirm them.

Considering the theoretical and empirical literature, we can therefore expect that paths of transition might influence the consolidation phase through mechanisms of *legislation*, that is, through the making of law and regulations, particularly on the issues that are central for the movements, as well as *legitimation*, as the recognition of some actors and forms of action. These mechanisms affect civil, political, and social rights.

As we will see in what follows, Czechoslovakia as a case of eventful democratization and Poland as a case of participated pacts tend to confirm the trend that emerged in the Iberian Peninsula. However, by extending the number of cases beyond a binary comparison, I can not only control the robustness of the results of previous studies but also expand and complexify our theorization on the effects of social movements' participation in transition phases by looking at potentially disturbing factors in the moments of installation and consolidation. In particular, I will suggest two specifications.

First of all, it will emerge (in particular through a comparison of Czechoslovakia and the GDR) that besides the strength of the social movements and of the mobilization from below, external factors can intervene during the installation phase that thwart the movements' capacity to affect consolidation. Modes of installation differ, in fact, in terms of duration and the constellation of the civil (and sometimes military) actors that participate in them as well as in the degree of inclusiveness and the forms of conflicts involved.

Second, as the extension of case studies from CEE to the MENA region will make clear, considering mobilizations for democracy as critical junctures does not imply the expectation that movements' victories are either straightforward or durable. As research on revolutions has pointed out, the battles between revolutionary and counterrevolutionary, new and old elites, moderates and radicals last well beyond highly symbolic moments of change. While social movements might continue to be important actors in democratic installation and initial phases of democratic consolidation, empowered by their successes, their adversaries often reorganize to reduce the amount or reverse the direction of the social and political changes. Critical junctures transform some things, but they do not change everything, and they are not irreversible. To be sure, I do not suggest that the transitional critical juncture determines once and forever the quality of democracies but rather aim to trace back and discuss some of these effects in terms of citizens' rights and social movements as well as civil society characteristics. I will argue, however, that power relations within and outside movements, even if reshuffled, nevertheless continue to affect postrevolutionary process.

In order to understand these complex developments, we need in fact to look in-depth at the evolution of the waves of protests that, I suggest, accompany eventful democratization. Besides expecting a tide of contention that advances, peaks, and retreats, I look inside protests in order to trace the ways in which cognitive, affective, and relational mechanisms evolve along the waves of contention, seeing them as a necessary step in order to understand their effects. While I consider democratic qualities as explananda, I do not aim at a complete assessment of civil, political, and social rights, or at identifying all possible causes for them. My purpose is rather to link some specific democratic qualities to social movements' participation in the paths of transition. In this sense, using the language of Mahoney and Goertz (2006), I will not pretend to provide a complete causal explanation of democratic qualities (by identifying the causes of an effect) but rather investigate the effects of some specific mechanisms – singled out in each chapter – that I see as being at work in the evolution of the various processes of democratization I address.

Causal preconditions might indeed not be the most pertinent questions to address phenomena that develop in time, interacting with different structural conditions and changing structures. This is why, in my cross-national comparison, I am not interested in discovering general laws and invariant causes that could explain all the cases at hand. Rather, I want to identify some dynamics that are present in the evolution of these different cases. In this sense, I have built upon a research design that allows me to move beyond the analyses that trace dissimilarities between similar types, and look instead for similarities in the causal mechanisms through which different types of democratization unfolded (see also McAdam, Tarrow, and Tilly 2001).

In recent years, the language of mechanisms has become fashionable in the social sciences, signaling dissatisfaction with correlational analysis (Mahoney 2003). The concept of the causal mechanism has been used, however, in different ways: to refer to (historical) paths, with a search for events that are observable and context dependent; or to address micro-level explanations, with a search for variables at the individual level. In macro-analyses, causal mechanisms have been linked to systematic process tracing through a causal reconstruction that "seeks to explain a given social phenomenon – a given event, structure or development – by identifying the process through which it is generated" (Mayntz 2004, 238). In micro-level explanations, instead, the theoretical focus is on "detailing mechanisms through which social facts are brought about, and these mechanisms invariably refer to individuals' actions and the relations that link actors to one another" (Hedstrom and Bearman 2009, 4). In my own understanding, mechanisms are categories of sequences of action that filter structural conditions and produce effects (see della Porta 2013b, 2014a). Following Tilly (2001), I conceptualize mechanisms as relatively abstract patterns of action that can travel from one episode to the next, explaining how a cause creates a consequence in a given context. I would not restrict capacity of action to individuals, however, instead including collective actors as well. Adapting Renate Mayntz's (2004, 241) definition, mechanisms are considered in my research as a concatenation of generative events linking macro causes (such cycles of protest) to aggregated effects (such as democratic qualities) through the relations between individual and organizational agents.

The focus on causal mechanisms has been connected with the so-called processual turn in social movement studies, which in fact shifted attention from static variables to the processes connecting them (McAdam, Tarrow, and Tilly 2001). In a similar vein, in my work on political violence (della Porta 2013b) and on democratization from below (della Porta 2014a), I suggested an approach that is, first, *relational*, as it considers social movements within broader fields that see the interactions of various actors, institutional and noninstitutional. Second, the approach is *constructivist*, as it takes into account not only the external opportunities and constraints but also (and especially) the social construction of reality by the various actors participating in social and political conflicts. Third, the approach is *dynamic*, as it recognizes that social movement characteristics develop in intense moments of action and aims at reconstructing the causal mechanisms through which conflicts develop.

I will in particular address cognitive, affective, and relational mechanisms. At the cognitive level, protest cycles involve a mechanism of *framing in action* as, especially in the ascending phase of the protest and at its peak, some visions of participatory and deliberative democracy develop. Notwithstanding contextual changes, there are then mechanisms of *framing consolidation* that also sustain those visions during the low ebb of the protest, contributing to disengagement from institutional forms of participation.

Cognitive mechanisms are accompanied by emotional ones, with a transformation in the dominant emotional climate. As protest grows, mechanisms of *emotional prefiguration*, as emotional work oriented to control fear and engender empowerment, develop in action. In the declining phase, mechanisms of *emotional adaptation* accompany a general

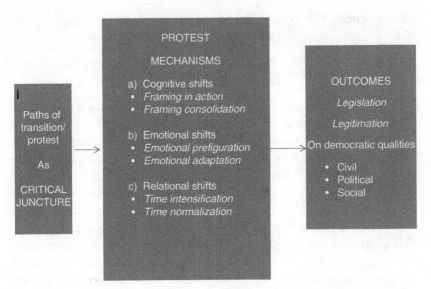

FIGURE 1.1 From Critical Junctures to Outcomes: The Theoretical Model

mode of disillusionment, which however does not cancel the experience of empowerment.

Finally, I will look at the relational resources produced in intense time, as well as the shift in normalized time. During the emergence and growth of protest activities, both individual and organizational ties increase at high speed through a mechanism of *time intensification*. Protest decline is then reflected in a reconsolidation of the net of interactions (and expectations), through mechanisms of *time normalization*.

In particular, I expect that in the eventful path of transition, horizontal conceptions of democracy are supported "in action," hope is fueled by clear victories, and time is perceived as moving at a particularly intense pace (see Figure 1.1). While cognitive visions, emotional feelings, and relational expectations change at the end of the eventful democratization, I expect that the democratic framing developed in action, the feeling of empowerment, and the impressions of intense time will remain relevant experiences for those who lived them.

The interactions of relational, emotional, and cognitive mechanisms bring about an increased capacity to affect the institutional process in a moment of opening opportunities, as well as establishing a more inclusive culture. While this does not automatically translate into more protests, it does create more favorable conditions for the development of civic, political, and social rights. Once again, however, these effects are filtered through specific interactions among different actors.

THE RESEARCH DESIGN

The research is based on a comparative analysis of cases of eventful democratization versus participated pact, as defined earlier. In order to understand the effects of paths of democratization on the development of social movements and on some democratic qualities, I will first compare four countries in CEE: Czechoslovakia (and then the Czech Republic) and the GDR as cases of eventful democratization, on the one hand, and Poland and Hungary as cases of participated pacts, on the other. Within a most-similar research design, the aim is to single out robust mechanisms that distinguish the two paths. However, the two-plus-two comparison will also allow the identification of some infra-path dissimilarities and therefore the specification of causal mechanisms that intervene between transition and consolidation.

In the second part of the research, I will then perform a partial comparison between 1989 in CEE and 2011 in the Arab Spring, by replicating some of the research in Egypt and Tunisia. Through the analysis of these cases, I aim at "complexifying" my line of analysis by showing that, while some mechanisms are similar in 1989 and 2011, different conditions of installation intervene in transforming the type of processes after transition. While in both cases the outcomes of the democratization paths are still unclear, with more optimism for Tunisia than for Egypt, some information on the years immediately following the episodes of democratization in 2011 will allow further discussion of the mechanisms of demobilization of social movements after regime change, as well as on the effects of the mobilization for democracy on the further evolution of democratization processes. Besides controlling the robustness of some results of the empirical analysis of the 1989 transitions through a cross-time as well as cross-area comparative design, this further comparative element will allow some reflections within cases of eventful (episodes of) democratization that had different outcomes in terms of consolidation.

As it is often (and increasingly) the case in comparative politics (Schmitter 2009), we cannot assume that countries as units of analysis are independent from each other. This is all the more the case in waves of democratization during which the involved countries are intensively related to each other, with frequent learning by both the movements and the regime (e.g., Beissinger 2007; Bunce and Wolchik 2010). Rather than assuming independence of countries, I recognize the cross-national influences, addressing them during the analysis.

All in all, I do not aim at theory testing but rather at theory building, within a logic of discovery that I think is appropriate to the state of knowledge in the field and the aims of my research. Keeping an interest in the historical events that I analyze, I compare by cases rather than by variables, through an in-depth analysis of complex systems of relations that cannot be fragmented into their main components (della Porta 2008). While using secondary literature as well as documentary sources to reconstruct some aspects of the democratization process, given the already mentioned importance I give to the construction of the external reality, the research considers as most relevant the activists' perceptions of the historical events of which they have been part.

These preferences and choices are reflected in the methods used in the empirical research for data collection and data analysis.

Protest Event Analysis

From the methodological point of view, part of the research is based on protest event analysis as a way to single out some main characteristics of contentious politics in the period of transition as well as in the ensuing years. Using existing databases, but recoding the data when necessary, attention focuses first on three years including transition in Poland, Hungary, GDR, and Czechoslovakia, also adding Romania, Bulgaria, and Albania. Moreover, in order to be able to investigate long-term developments in more depth, I used the Prodact database on protest in Germany within a comparison of the eastern and western regions in the country. Post-reunification Germany offers an experimental setting in which to note both the adaptation to protest waves in established democracies and the resilience of democratization politics. In particular, the comparison of the former Federal Republic of Germany in the west and the former German Democratic Republic in the east can be particularly telling, allowing for the observation of cross-regional similarities and differences in terms of the amount, aims, and forms of protest. Similar original data are presented for Egypt and Tunisia.

Protest event analysis is a much-used quantitative methodology to study the dynamics of protest in time and space. First employed by Charles Tilly and his colleagues during the 1970s to shed light on the historical transformations in repertoires of collective action, it later inspired other important studies on the American civil rights movement

(McAdam 1982), the Italian cycle of protest during the 1970s (Tarrow 1989), new social movements in Western Europe (Kriesi, Koopmans, Duyvendak, and Giugni 1995), and the transformations of environmental activism in Europe (Rootes 2003). As synthesized by Koopmans and Rucht, protest event analysis "is a method that allows for the quantification of many properties of protest, such as frequency, timing and duration, location, claims, size, forms, carriers, and targets, as well as immediate consequences and reactions (e.g., police intervention, damage, counter protests)" (2002, 231). In general, daily press represents the source for the analysis, where articles on protest are found and coded following specific methods of content analysis (Lindekilde 2014) with a focus on protest (Kriesi et al. 1995; Hutter 2014). In this process, the primary unit of analysis is the protest event, and information is collected on indicators that usually include the actors who protest, the forms they use to protest, their claims, and their targets (as well as place, time, and immediate outcome).

While extremely helpful in defining broad trends in protest, protest event analysis must be handled with care (Hutter 2014). In fact, the reporting of protests is quite selective, and selectivity is often a source of bias, as the portion of the universe of protest events that is reported is never a representative (nor a random) sample but rather – *pour cause* – influenced by the logic of the media. This affects tendentially all main dimensions of the analysis, as we can expect that some actors (either more endowed with institutional resources of access to media or more "scandalous" per se), forms of action (those involving more people, more violence, or more innovation), and issues (those with high news value within specific issue cycles) are more likely to be reported (McCarthy, McPhail, and Smith 1996; Fillieule and Jimenez 2003; Hutter 2014). Reporting can also be more or less detailed and neutral according to the characteristics of the actors and forms of actions. Additionally, the more frequent the protest becomes, the more selective will necessarily be its reporting.

In addressing these biases, two observations have to be taken into account. First, we can assume that as protest is an act of communication, protest event analysis captures those events that have already overcome an initial important threshold to influence public opinion and policymakers: being reported upon (Rucht and Ohlemacher 1992). In this sense, Biggs (2014) suggested a focus on large events, which are both covered in a more reliable way and analytically important. A second caveat is that, as for any source, we need to be self-reflexive, acknowledging and considering bias when interpreting the results as well as triangulating newspaper-based protest event analysis with reporting of protests in other sources.

For this research, data on Eastern European countries shortly before, during, and after transition come from the European Protest and Coercion 1980–1995 Database,[3] covering twenty-eight countries in Europe. Based on news reports on domestic conflicts, it comprises all reported protests and repressive events for which a date and a location could be identified. Data were coded for each day/event, by one expert coder per country. The primary source of the data base was LexisNexis, accessed through Reuters textline library, which provides access to over 400 wire services and online newspapers and magazines, choosing the highest quality sources in case of divergent reports.

For part of the research on Germany, I used the Prodat dataset that emerged from the research project *Dokumentation und Analyse von Protestereignissen in der Bundesrepublik*. Protest events were extracted from the coverage of two high-quality newspapers (*Frankfurter Rundschau* and *Süddeutsche Zeitung*) from 1950 to 2002. It is important to note that only a sample of the coverage was searched and coded, namely every Monday's edition plus Tuesday through Saturday every fourth week. Thus, the database does not report all protest events to be found in both papers, but only those reported in the selected issues. For the comparison between East Germany and West Germany, the data subset includes only protests taking place in the territory of eastern and western Länder, respectively. Cases of protests in Berlin (where it would be difficult to distinguish between protest in the East and the West) and nationwide protests are excluded from the analysis or presented separately.

For Egypt and Tunisia, we relied mainly on LexisNexis as much as possible using similar strategies to the ones developed for the CEE countries. For Tunisia, in the first stage, we opted for "search for content type" and then clicked on "newspapers" in advanced options to determine the source type. Then, we entered "protest! OR strike! OR demonstration! w/25 protest!"[4] into the search engine, and sorted the news by date (from oldest to newest for each month in each year). As a second step, we asked LexisNexis to browse news only from the following sources with reasonably high coverage for international

[3] The project was funded by the National Science Foundation (SBR-9631229) and a General Research Fund grant from the University of Kansas.
[4] The keywords "protest," "strike," and "demonstration" are searched within the first twenty-five words (w/25) of the news text.

audiences: *BBC Monitoring International, Agence France Press, Associated Press, Agency Tunis Afrique Press,* and *Xinhua.* The resulting articles were then coded. For both Tunisia and Egypt, we also utilized supplementary material from the *Global Database of Events, Language, and Tone* (GDELT) and the Integrated Crisis Early Warning System (ICEWS). Created by Kalev Leetaru from Georgetown University, GDELT is a project that brings together online records of social and political events since 1979 from a variety of news sources around the globe, such as *Agence France Press, BBC Monitoring,* and the *New York Times.* It transforms them into a computable format, and is automatically updated every fifteen minutes (Leetaru and Schrodt 2013). The GDELT Event collection[5] contains more than 250,000 records (originally retrieved from LexisNexis) covering three decades of political events (from January 1, 1979, to the present) coded across fifty-nine variables. For this study, we query the entire GDELT database, pairing Google BigQuery cloud-based analytical service and the statistical analysis software Tableau, and extract the subsets deemed relevant for the analysis. The most used variables are: "ActionGeo" (location of the event), "Event Code" (type of event), "Actor1*" (type and country affiliation of the initiator of the action), "Actor2*" (type and country affiliation of the target of the action), and "Quad Class" (an aggregation of the CAMEO event codes into four categories ranging from Verbal Cooperation to Material Cooperation, Verbal Conflict, and Material Conflict).[6]

For the protest event analyses, the codebook included the following core variables: date, form of action, target, issue, number of protestors, and number of persons arrested/injured/killed.

---

[5] See URL: http://data.gdeltproject.org/events/index.html.

[6] Egypt is selected as event location and actor affiliation, and we set the Event Base Code to the "14" range, the raw CAMEO action code identifying the general category "Protest" and respective subcategories (141 = Demonstration; 142 = Hunger Strike, etc.). Thereafter, we plot these variables against the number of records according to our time frame, from 2010 to 2012, using the date field "Year Month(proper)." According to the numbers released, ICEWS incorporates more than six thousand news sources and thirty million stories (retrieved from aggregators such as FACTIVA) (Ward et al. 2013, 3–4). ICEWS is more parsimonious in the way it deals with the information glut, thus less prone to false positives. For this reason, we use it to trace the longitudinal evolution of protest events, quantify their forms, and calculate the reported repression. GDELT works better for the Actor-Target-Location triplet, and we use it to analyze these variables. Given its recognized superior geolocation range, we employ it for the geographical distribution of events. Additionally, the original implementation of the "quad class" variable allowed us to extract data on repression.

Oral History

Protest events data are triangulated with in-depth interviews with activists of the movements for democracy in Czechoslovakia, Hungary, GDR, Poland, Egypt, and Tunisia. In the study of activism, historians have long experience with oral history, used either to collect information on events or groups for which archives are particularly poor or as materials for the study of mentalities and culture. In both types of contribution, individual activists are considered as central sources for their capacity to act beyond existing external constraints (Balan and Jelin 1980), as "attention shifts from laws, statistics, administrators and governments, to people" (Thompson 1978, 223). Against a vision of history as created by the elites, oral history places normal people as important actors in the making of history (Barkin 1976; Bertaux 1980; Buhle 1981; Passerini 1981). By giving normal people a voice, and thus going beyond official documents, "these studies emphasize the importance of understanding the way in which history is transformed in individual cognition, how public events intervene into private life, how perceptions of the world influence action" (della Porta 1992, 173). The use of oral sources thus responds to "the need to analyse every aspect of everyday life to restore sense to activities that seem to be losing it, sucked out by current, alienated uses" (Passerini 1978, XXXVII). In this conception, normal people play a vital role in giving history sense, direction, and an ultimate goal (Buhle 1981, 209).

In social movement studies, oral history has been considered as particularly suited "for researchers interested in generating rich and textured detail about social processes, understanding the intersection between personal narratives and social structures, and focusing on individual agency and social context" (Corrigall-Brown and Ho 2013, 678). The narratives of the events convey contextual information (Reed 2004, 663) but, what is more, the stories people tell about their personal experiences reveal how subjective meanings are attached to the unfolding of eventful protest.

As with protest event analysis, the researcher must be aware of the potential bias of this type of source as well. Concerns have been expressed, in fact, about their reliability, as individuals are said to be the worst narrators of events in which they have been involved, insofar as they have a direct interest in them. Memory implies creative acts of imagination; the truth is often manipulated through narrative ability; people also tend to forget, confound, and lie. Literary ambitions or economic interests are seen as incentives to present one's own life as more dramatic and one's own role as more influential (Faris 1980; for a summary, della Porta 2014b).

Oral historians have successfully defended life histories against this criticism (della Porta 2014b). First of all, they have employed various devices in order to increase the reliability of the information collected orally: for instance, by discussing the internal incongruities of the narration with the interviewees themselves; comparing different biographies with each other (Poirer and Clapier-Vailadon 1980); using an interdisciplinary approach in order to separate the "real" from the interpretation (Grele 1975); applying communication theory in order to control the interactions between interviewee and interviewer (Clark, Hyde, and McMahan 1980); and checking information from interviews with those from other sources such as mass media accounts, movement documents, interviews with experts, police statistics, and trial records. In addition, distortions have become the focus of the analysis, whose aim is singling out some systematic evolution in the description of reality in terms of prevalent cultural myths and individual preferences (Grele 1979; Gagnon 1980; Hankiss 1981). The reaction to all these limitations in terms of source reliability is to place the form of the interview at the center of the investigation: "The question is not directed at the facts, but at the nature of individual memory and historical conscience" (Faris 1980, 172). Research is not therefore oriented to control the reliability of the source but rather to reveal the broad lines along which human memory is organized. As Luisa Passerini notes, "all autobiographical memory is true; it is up to the interpreter to discover in what sense, where, for what purpose" (1989, 197).

In the present research, I have chosen oral history mainly as a way to collect information on the activists' perceptions, their account of emotions, and cognitive mapping. As Bosi and Reiter (2014, 129–30) observed, "The 'new' data obtained with oral history techniques can clarify, elaborate, re-contextualize or even challenge previous understanding based exclusively on documentary sources," as oral history enables "the researcher to analyze the subjectivity and agency of voices that in archival records to a large extent are represented only through the lens of state agencies or of main social movement organizations."

In fact, my use of oral history aims not only at reconstructing some aspects of the history of social movements of the past but also at reconstructing their memory, considering oral history as "a methodology about subjectivity that recognizes that memory stories are contingent and often fluid" (ibid., 131). In this way, as Portelli suggested, "oral sources tell us not just what people did, but what they wanted to do, what they believed they were doing, and what now they think they did. Oral sources may not add much to what we know, for instance, of the material cost of a strike to the workers involved; but they tell us a good deal about its psychological costs" (Portelli 1991, 50).

In this project, oral histories have been collected, mainly in the activists' mother languages, by research collaborators in the Czech Republic, former GDR, Hungary, Poland, Egypt, and Tunisia. In each country, the sampling of interview partners (between twelve and fourteen per country) was of course not random but rather followed a logic of theoretical sampling, with the aim of covering a broad range of positions during the mobilizations for democracy. As random sampling was not possible,[7] we instead followed the suggestions of a diversification of the sample (Bertaux 1980) through the choice of interview partners that represented the diverse components of the social movements we had selected. Some main "types" – social groups, generations, gender categories, political affiliations, forms of participation in the movements – were represented in the sample. Interviews lasted about two hours on average; they were carried out either at the home of the interviewee or in public places. All interviews were recorded and transcribed in full.

A common outline, translated into the different languages, was used in the interviews. After presenting the aim of the research as an investigation on what happens to civil society organizations once democracy is formally achieved, the interviewers asked for a periodization of the different phases of social movement participation during the protests against the previous regime, locating its beginning, peak, and decline, with particular attention to the evolution (peaks and low ebb) of mobilization as well as to the organizational transformation within social movements. Another set of questions addressed the perceived motivations of the participation in protest and the reasons for the eventual decline in commitment (from frustration to fatigue, from repression to co-optation). Interviewers also solicited assessments about the achievement and nonachievement of social movements' mobilization for democracy as well as potential strategic mistakes. Finally, conceptions of democracy as well as of the conditions of transition were investigated.

---

[7] Besides the obvious problem of research on social movements related to the fact that the universe of activists is rarely known, there are problems specific to oral history research, from the very problem of finding enough activists available to tell their biographies to the time-consuming and labor-intensive nature of interviewing, transcription, and analysis.

Comparative Historical Analysis

Acknowledging the limitations of protest event analysis and oral history, I have triangulated them – within a comparative historical analysis perspective – with existing research and statistical databases. As with protest event analysis and oral history, comparative historical analysis based on secondary sources is also certainly not free from potential bias: knowledge is in fact extracted from a selective reading of an often partial source.

Without aiming at strong testing of hypotheses, however, the use of secondary sources is certainly useful to contextualize and double-check both protest event analysis and oral history accounts. As Daniel Ritter (2014, 107) noted, most often

the objective is not to discover new facts, but to provide a new interpretation with the help of "old" evidence. As a consequence, comparative historical researchers depend especially on the meticulous work done by historians and area specialists, but also on that produced by sociologists, political scientists, anthropologists, psychologists, diplomats, and journalists. As a rule of thumb, anything written from a social scientific or professional perspective could constitute evidence. The comparative historical scholar's task is in part to evaluate the credentials of other authors, and thus the credibility of the sources.

The relevance of moments of transition ensures the existence of abundant social science literature, also often allowing for triangulation of accounts by different authors. Indeed, following Ritter's lead, I used all three categories of secondary sources: historical accounts of a country, texts focusing specifically on the research topic, and texts dealing more specifically with factors considered as causally relevant (ibid., 108).

In sum, I do not aim at a systematic assessment of the quality of democracy in the selected countries. On this, there are many studies to which I indeed refer in what follows; but I also differentiate my own perspective from theirs, as I aim at singling out activists' subjective perspectives on their specific visions of "Where did the revolution go?" rather than obtaining an objective assessment of the quality of democracy. As this is a main aim of the analysis, I give emphasis to the activists' voices, their values and principles, and their memories of their (more or less distant) past. As such, I am not so much interested in how realistic their hopes were, but rather in the discrepancies between those hopes and what they see as the development of democratization that indeed accounts for their disappointment and, at times, disengagement. Nevertheless, as much as possible, I also make large use of secondary sources and some statistics to contextualize the activists' perceptions.

THE STRUCTURE OF THE VOLUME

Most of the following chapters are devoted to a comparative analysis within CEE, the results of which are then contrasted with the two North African cases.

A first step in what follows is to assess some trends in terms of both protests and social movement infrastructures. This will be done in the next chapter, based on protest event analysis on CEE, with a specific comparison of East and West Germany during and after transition. Mainly a descriptive chapter, it aims at empirically substantiating the claim about the more significant eventfulness of some transitions when compared with others. The size and frequency of protest events vary in fact among the analyzed cases, with cycles of protest emerging in cases of eventful democratization, while protests remained more sporadic in the participated pacts. After transition, protest did not disappear in any of the countries involved – rather, it "normalized" in terms of its forms and scope.

In Chapters 3, 4, and 5, three main sets of mechanisms are singled out as mediating between paths of democratization and quality of democratic consolidation in CEE. At the cognitive level, I focus on a sort of misalignment in the conception of democracy between the movement activists and the institutional actors (Chapter 3). While, in action, participatory and deliberative conceptions had in fact developed in the opposition – not only meeting some specific contextual constraints but also developing into a normative preference – the changing conditions with democratization made those very conceptions somewhat problematic. A limited adaptation then occurred, with various strategic dilemmas to address. This shows, however, some differences in diverse paths of transition.

At the emotional level, I will look at the shifting moods during and after mobilization for democracy (Chapter 4). Emotional work is analyzed by looking at the ways in which the fear of repression is transformed into outrage, through chains of moral shocks. Hope then develops at the peak of the mobilization, making participation a happy experience and contributing to transform the very identities of the individuals involved. Finally, satisfaction and disillusionment follow transition, although with cross-country differences, contributing to micro-level dynamics of withdrawal from protest. Relying on previous research on passionate movements, I bridge collective emotions to protest, looking at them as some of the conditions activists aim at changing, but also as a constraining power on protest action. The intensity of the emotions that emerge during the process is fundamentally different in eventful democratizations versus participated pacts, but also varies within each path, with potential implications for the democratic quality of established democracies.

At the relational level, I will reflect on how time is experienced as affecting the interactions among different actors (Chapter 5). As we will see, the perception of time shifts in the various steps of mobilization for democracy: after a slow start, events take on a very fast pace, followed by a return to normality. This shifting perception of time is linked to the development of very different forms of relations – which move from rarefied in the beginning, to accelerated at the peak of the protest, and eventually to normalized. The perception of intense time is accompanied by an emphasis on the contingent, the unexpected, and the unpredictable. Looking at the activists' perception of time, I will analyze the different rhythms of the relations within emerging actors as related to the overcoming of routines and the search for signals.

In Chapters 6, 7, and 8, I will focus on the outcomes of the democratization process in CEE in terms of civil, political, and social rights. In fact, while transition to democracy is a success for the human rights organizations that mobilized against the authoritarian regime, it presents challenges as well. Chapter 6 addresses civil rights. While civil rights were basically respected in the four cases I analyzed in CEE, the former activists judged the support for civil society as not satisfactory. Policies about associational rights as well as the very definition of them are in fact criticized as not welcoming for the social movement activists that had grown during the struggle for democracy. If part of the so-called civil society develops as externally funded by donors, mainly top-down, depoliticized, and quite isolated from a potential basis, there is however also a sort of adaptation of various social movements from the more liberal environment. Although there are cross-issue and cross-country differences, social movement organizational formats do survive, normalizing and in part adapting to the different paths of transition.

Chapter 7 then moves to political rights and their quality. Research has often pointed at the low degree of institutional participation in the CEE area in terms of party membership, voting rates, institutional trust, and the like. Paradoxically, activists seem the most dissatisfied with the political results of the transition. The founding elections are thus often perceived as a burden rather than an achievement by those who struggled for democracy and who find themselves abruptly marginalized. Political parties are stigmatized as divisive and often unethical. However, together with the criticism of the electoralization of politics and partitization, there is also participation in institutional politics, with different forms and effects in the different paths of transition, with participated pacts versus eventful democratization.

Chapter 8 addresses quality of democracy from the point of view of social rights. In CEE, the double transition not only from authoritarian regime to democracy but also from "real socialism" to "embedded neoliberalism" is a source of bitter disappointment for the population at large, but even more so for those who struggled for democracy and are then considered, and perceive themselves, as the social losers of the changes to which they had contributed. In fact, even if socioeconomic transformations were barely thematized during the struggle for democracy, large parts of the opposition, rooted within the Left, assumed a development toward freedom – but not at the price of social inequalities. If activists tended therefore to be frustrated by the socioeconomic development, in cases of eventful democratization there was more attention to social rights than in cases of participated pacts.

Chapters 9 and 10 expand the analyses to the Arab Spring, addressing Egypt and Tunisia as cases of eventful episodes of mobilization for democracy – although with less success than their CEE counterparts (especially in Egypt). The first of these two chapters looks in fact at the protest waves and their dynamics, also analyzing what I defined as cognitive, affective, and relational mechanisms.

As in the CEE region, in the MENA region as well protests increased slowly but surely throughout the decade before the uprisings, which in fact grew out of those developments, as spin-off mobilization. Differently from the CEE countries, protests involved here a much more multiform range of actors, including, in particular, labor, precarious workers, and poor people, with somewhat more organizational capacity in Tunisia than in Egypt. While contacts increased rapidly during the mobilization, in contrast to the CEE region, protests continued unabated after the ousting of the dictator, through competitive dynamics that took different forms. At the cognitive level, here as in the CEE region, participatory and deliberative conceptions of democracy developed during protest and were opposed to the minimalistic visions of electoral accountability. Emotional dynamics were extremely relevant, as the very use of the term "revolution" was charged with feelings of outrage and hope, but then also disillusionment. Finally, the shifting perceptions of time – from slow to intense to normal – affected the development of relations within and without the oppositional movements.

Finally, in Chapter 11, I look at the civil, political, and social qualities of democracy in the two countries, Egypt and Tunisia, especially – but not only – through the perceptions of those activists who had struggled against the dictators. While in the CEE region eventful protests appeared to have produced higher-quality democracy than did participated pacts, Egypt and Tunisia, both cases of eventful (episodes of) democratization, achieved (at least initially) much lower qualities in terms of civil, political, and social rights. From the point of view of civic rights, there was certainly an increasing presence of autonomous civil society organizations, often developing from within the protest. This was allowed by some liberalization, but also by the sense of empowerment that the revolution had produced and that kept mobilization alive, even in the face of heavy repression. Of similarly low quality are political rights (even lower in Egypt than in Tunisia): political institutions are in fact perceived as still in continuity with the old regime, while activists stress the importance of remaining in the street in order to try to maintain ownership of a revolution that is perceived as ongoing. Finally, the situation was perceived as extremely negative in terms of social rights. Disappointment is all the more serious as, in contrast to the CEE countries, protestors' claims had addressed both justice and dignity, after decades of neoliberalist policies.

In the conclusion, the empirical findings are summarized with particular attention to their contribution to studies of democratization and revolution as well as social movements – and to their bridging.

2

Cycles of Protest and the Consolidation
of Democracy[1]

In 1990 there were some protests and ... they were around things that are characteristic to a free country ... and they were closer to what we call political tensions that are typical to a free country more than to a totalitarian country. So it was a completely new type of tension. (PL1)

Protest today has a different form. In the GDR period, protest was always protest against dictatorship, against the leading role of the SED. So all short-comings that existed with respect to education or health care, it was the SED's fault. So the enemy was very much in focus. ... Today, we don't have one enemy but we have a swarm of enemies: in the banks, in insurance companies, in hospitals, in the health care system, in the education system at universities ... and then there is a swarm of relatively small groups. (GDR10)

Especially December was crucial. It culminated with Havel being elected president. ... The following six months until the first regular elections were accompanied by high activity of civil society. After the first regular elections the situation stabilized because the goal of the revolution – transformation of the system – had been achieved. Plurality had been achieved. ... Political parties were emerging, and it all culminated with the first regular elections held in June 1990. Then it all became normal and the reconstruction started. ... I would say that protests have a different character in democratic conditions. They are focused on some particular problem of the society. ... There was some wave of protest during Nečas' [former prime minister] government. These protests were aimed against social reforms. It was mostly organized by trade unionists ... there were several activities aimed at corruption ... I think there have been more protests since 1989. I think that this is a normal element of civil society. (CZ14)

---

[1] For their collaboration with data collection and data analysis of protest events, I am grateful to Matteo Cernison and Simon Teune.

Cycles of Protest and Democratization Processes: An Introduction

Protest is important in transition and – as the three quotes in the incipit assess – it does not disappear thereafter. Rather, it "becomes normal": less radical, more focused, and less visible.

Research on social movements and research on democratization have barely communicated, developing quite different expectations about the evolution of protest in democracy. For a long time, the former focused on the West, under the assumption that political opportunities must be sufficiently open to enable protest. Paradoxically, after transitions, the assumption is that opportunities are too open, as former oppositional leaders find space to enter parliaments and governments. The latter assumed that democratization processes, although sometimes foreseeing mobilization from below, are mainly moments for constitution of formal political institutions. Mass protest has indeed been considered as dangerous for democratic consolidation, potentially disturbing the establishment of those institutions – read political parties – that are usually seen as the main carriers of democracy. As Sidney Tarrow observed long ago, "Most scholars of democratization have either ignored movements altogether or regarded them with suspicion as dangers to democracy, while most students of social movements have focused on fully mature democratic systems and ignored the transition cycles that place the question of democratization on the agenda and work it through to either democratic consolidation or defeat" (Tarrow 1995, 221–2).

Studying contentious politics in East Germany, Hungary, Poland, and Slovakia between 1989 and 1993, during consolidation stages, Grzegorz Ekiert and Jan Kubik (1998) noted that consolidation has been explained by elite pacts (O'Donnell and Schmitter 1986), especially by elites' skills, values, and preferences (Diamond and Linz 1989). They wrote, "existing literature has accorded more prominence to certain dimensions of consolidation and neglected others: institutional choices of governmental structures and electoral institutions as well as the formation of party systems, are usually viewed as the most important elements in the stabilization and consolidation of democracy" (Ekiert and Kubik 1998, 550). In fact, "The preoccupation with (1) elites, (2) institutional choices concerning governmental and electoral systems, (3) party systems, and (4) the relationship between political and economic changes is responsible for a considerable gap in the democratization literature. We know very little about the activities of nonelite actors and how these activities shape the processes of democratization" (ibid., 550–1). In addition, the study of the role of citizens in democratic transitions has too often been reduced to an examination of political attitudes, conducted on representative samples of the population (ibid., 552).

The impression, widespread in democratization studies, that protest declines as democratic institutions develop has been challenged theoretically and empirically. From the theoretical point of view, as social movement studies suggest, the opening up of political opportunities should in fact increase, at least up to a certain point, the potential for contentious politics. First, under authoritarian regimes, opportunities are certainly rather closed, but at the same time the threat of nonaction is high (Goldstone and Tilly 2001). Further, besides domestic opportunities, international prospects could become favourable for movements active in authoritarian regimes, either in the form of potential international allies (Keck and Sikkink 1998) or through shifting positions in international systems. Protest movements themselves can promote this change by forcing democratic allies of authoritarian regimes to withdraw their support – what Daniel Ritter (2014) has called the "iron cage of liberalism."

The idea that consolidation processes require social acquiescence in order to be successful has been disputed. First, Nancy Bermeo (1997) and others noted that consolidation of democracy often happens during moments of continued high mobilization, which might even take radical forms. Second, democracy itself brings about the conditions for the flourishing not only of political institutions but also of citizens' participation in unconventional forms. Third, while post-1945 and early 1970s' waves of democratization saw much emphasis by democracy promoters on the construction of political parties, with party legitimacy challenged even in consolidated democracies, especially since the 1989 wave of democratization in Eastern Europe, the belief has spread that democracy needs civil society organizations (della Porta 2014a).

From the empirical point of view, various studies showed the importance of social movements in the various steps of a democratization process. In fact, during the *transition*, various social movements have been noted as relevant participants in large coalitions asking for democratic rights and social justice (Jelin 1987; Tarrow 1995). Protests can then be used by modernizing elites to push for free elections (Casper and Taylor 1996, 9–10; Glenn 2003, 104). Social movements are also important in the *consolidation* phase, which opens up with the first free elections, the end of the period of uncertainty, and/or the implementation of a minimum quality of substantive democracy (O'Donnell 1993, 1994; Linz and Stepan 1996). The presence of a tradition of mobilization and of political allies can in fact help to maintain a high level of protest, as with the shantytown dwellers' protests in Chile (Schneider 1992, 1995; Hipsher 1998), the peasants' and labor movements in Brazil (Branford and Rocha 2002; Burdick 2004), or the environmental movements in Eastern Europe (Flam 2001). Later in the consolidation phase, movements' alternative practices and values have often helped in sustaining and expanding democracy (Santos 2005; della Porta 2009a). Keeping elites under continuous popular pressure after transition can be important for a successful consolidation (Karatnycky and Ackerman 2005). For Central Eastern Europe (CEE), Ekiert and Kubik (1998) have shown indeed that contentious politics was also relevant after transition. Movements then call for extending rights to those who are excluded by low-intensity democracies and target authoritarian legacies (Eckstein 2001; Yashar 2005; della Porta 2013a).

We can, however, expect that waves of protest after transition will be subject to oscillation, growing under some social and political conditions, and declining in others. While protests might decline around the first election, as attention focuses on more conventional politics, it can grow again later on. In general, one could expect a sort of normalization, with cycles of protest following the dynamics and characteristics proper to those in established democracies, driven by the presence of some grievances as well as some organizational resources and political opportunities. We also expect that organizational resources must be mobilized and resonant frames articulated. In addition, we can expect some peculiarities in cases of democratization processes that developed through eventful democratization. In fact, we can assume that, in the struggle against the authoritarian regime, citizens might have learned specific skills in contentious politics. Additionally, we can suspect that the very hopes for a better life developed during the turbulent days of regime change, are bound to be frustrated and that protest can ensue. We might also expect that as some components of the movement for democratization are co-opted into institutional politics, others may radicalize.

Comparing 1989 in Eastern Europe and 2011 in the Middle East and North Africa, I have suggested that even within the same wave of democratization, social movements might play different roles in different paths of transition to democracy, distinguishing eventful democratization, participated pacts, and troubled democratization (della Porta 2014a; see also Chapter 1 in this volume). In all paths, mobilization of resources, framing processes, and appropriation of opportunities develop in action, but in different combinations. The extent to which these different combinations play a role in the steps immediately following transition is a question to be addressed empirically. One way to do this is to examine how protest events evolve before, during, and after transition; I will show that there were different types of mobilization waves in the three paths, but only in the eventful democratization path there was a cycle of protest.

In social movement studies, research on protest events developed around the concept of cycle of protest, under the assumption that, as political opportunities open up, causal mechanisms tend to produce a condensation of protests in time, with imitation and competition among different groups (Tarrow 1989). For various reasons, however, protest cycles tend also to decline, as aims are either achieved or proved impossible to achieve; opportunities close down under the pressure of countermovement; and private commitments take activists back to normal routines (Hirschman 1982). Throughout the cycle, some characteristics of the protest are expected to change, with parallel moves toward moderation and radicalization (della Porta and Tarrow 1987). It has been observed that protest events tend in fact to cluster in time, as "events and the contention over identity which they represent are not distributed randomly over time and space. Their appearance is structured both temporally and spatially" (Beissinger 2002, 16). So, protests come in chains, series, waves, cycles, and tides, "forming a punctuated history of heightened challenges and relative stability" (ibid., 16).

In what follows, I will first use data on protest events during the late 1980s and early 1990s in Eastern Europe, looking for similarities and differences in cases belonging to the eventful protest path (specifically, the German Democratic Republic [GDR] and Czechoslovakia), to the participated pact path (specifically, Hungary and Poland), and to troubled paths (Albania, Romania, and Bulgaria). Second, I will compare – over a longer time perspective – data on protest in the west and east parts of the Federal Republic of Germany.

PATHS OF TRANSITION AND PROTEST EVOLUTION: COMPARING WITHIN CEE COUNTRIES

Social movement studies have considered the dynamics of protest cycles as influenced by both contextual changes and endogenous relational mechanisms. Protest cycles are usually expected to be linked to the opening and closing of political opportunities, but also to mechanisms of emulation (imitating other groups that have been successful) and competition (fighting against other groups). In cycles around transition, we can expect opportunities to be extremely fluid. As Ekiert and Kubik (1998)

observed, there is a difference between the structure of political opportunities in stable polities and the unstructured opportunities that characterize transitory, open polities. In fact,

in transitory polities this underlying cultural matrix of allies and foes takes on an
ambiguous character: former oppositional activists take over the state apparatus
and it is no longer clear who is us and who is them. Such conditions, which we will
call unstructured opportunity, offer protesters considerable freedom of action:
there are few established organizational boundaries that should be abolished;
there are no predefined agendas whose expansion may be demanded; ruling
alignments change often; there are potentially many available allies; and
cleavages within and among elites are fluid and poorly identified. The state
manages to maintain order within the public domain, but it offers little
resistance to nonviolent protest actions and it seems to ignore protesters.
Additionally, state functionaries do not know how to deal with protesters, as
formal and informal procedures through which protesters are either marginalized
or included in the policy-making processes are poorly developed. (Ibid., 43)

Protest Frequency

I suggest that these "unstructured opportunities" are affected by the
specific paths of intervention taken by social movements in transition
processes. Overall, we expect protest to grow in eventful democratization,
as elites react in exclusive ways to first mobilization. This means that
protests then increase in number, reaching a peak before the fall of the
regime. There are some rival hypotheses about what happens later on: one
expects a sharp decline as democracy is achieved and activists often enter
institutions; another, a radicalization due to the frustration of the hopes
raised during the transition; a third, a sort of normalization, with protest
becoming a regular feature of democratic politics. In participated pacts, in
contrast, we would expect no cycle, but rather a sporadic increase of
protest in some difficult moments in the negotiations, when challengers
need to put pressure on incumbents. As pacted democracy is established,
protest should remain low, as the nature of the pact itself is often based on
the marginalization of the non-moderate wings for both incumbents and
challengers. Finally, we expect quick explosions of protest in troubled
democratization, with waves of brutal repression but, at the same time,
moments of quickly spreading radical protests (della Porta 2014a).

If we look at the protest event data (see Figures 2.1a–g), we can see indeed
that both cases that I defined as eventful democratization – Czechoslovakia
and GDR – are characterized by proper cycles with beginning, peak, and

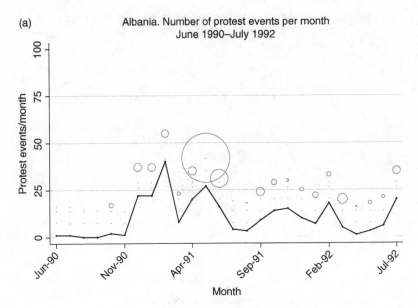

The dimension of circles varies in relation with the number of protesters/month.

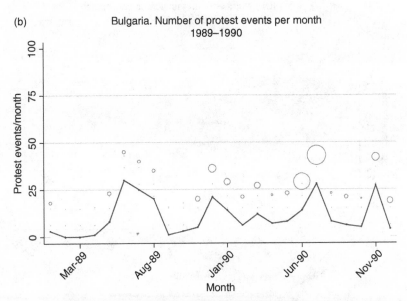

The dimension of circles varies in relation with the number of protesters/month.

FIGURE 2.1 Protest Events (Number and Intensity) in Selected East European Countries

(c)

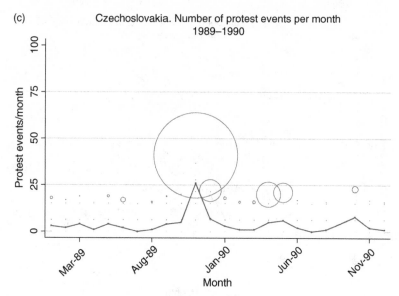

The dimension of circles varies in relation with the number of protesters/month.

(d)

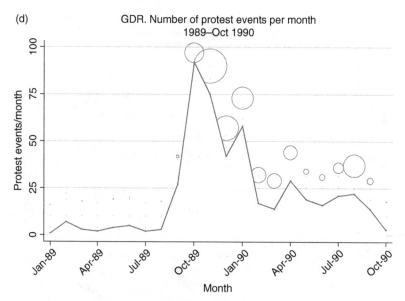

The dimension of circles varies in relation with the number of protesters/month.

FIGURE 2.1 (cont.)

(e)

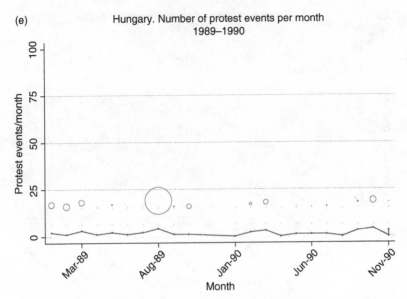

The dimension of circles varies in relation with the number of protesters/month.

(f)

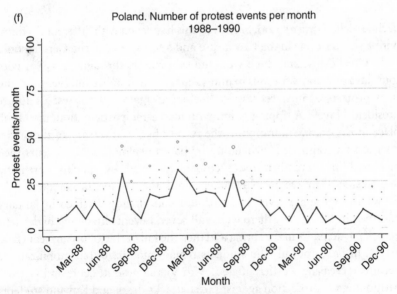

The dimension of circles varies in relation with the number of protesters/month.

FIGURE 2.1 (cont.)

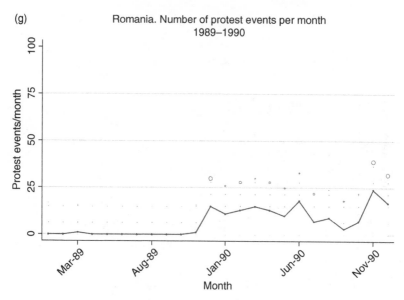

The dimension of circles varies in relation with the number of protesters/month.

FIGURE 2.1 (cont.)

decline (della Porta 2014a). However, this happened with different rhythms, with a shorter cycle in the Czech case and a longer one in the German one.

In Czechoslovakia, there were indeed protests throughout 1989, with four days of demonstrations in mid-January, harsh police intervention, and then protests against repression (including against the arrest of future president Havel). A tipping point, with increasing participation, then took place at the commemoration of the twenty-first anniversary of the Soviet invasion on August 21, broken up by baton-wielding police. Events then increased in September and October, followed by quickly spreading marches and strikes in November, until the regime broke down. As shown in Figure 2.1, even if the protest had already declined in January and then in December, there were still several events involving high numbers of participants in the spring and then the fall of the following year (Eyal 2003). In fact, not only did students remain mobilized, but mobilizations became increasingly differentiated, with Vietnamese students and Gypsies petitioning for protection against racist attacks, Iraqi and Kuwaiti students protesting the invasion of Iraq, marchers calling for Slovak sovereignty or supporting Polish women denied abortion, brewery workers striking for independent company status, and hunger strikes celebrating the Chinese students who fought in Tiananmen. At the same time, protests pushed for deepening democracy through calls for freedom and human rights, for the withdrawal of Soviet troops, for Havel, or against communism (for example, for investigation into the communist party or the return of public buildings used by it). Thus, a short cycle was punctuated by a few very large events, peaking in November 1989 and declining later on.

Protests indeed continued, going in waves, with a remobilization in the midst of the privatization process. In the Czech Republic, activities developed in the middle of the 1990s, also on social issues. As an activist recalls, "there are marches organized by trade unions where 800 000 people gather. This was inconceivable at the end of December 1989 – that one day I could see a march of trade unionists protesting against capitalism" (CZ5). Protests, even massive ones, emerged when there was the perception of a particular danger. This was the case in the 1990s and early 2000s for the "Thank You, Time to Go" Initiative; the defense of the public television station (ČT, Czech Television) against plans to privatize it; and the mobilization against the agreement between the social democrats and the civic democrats, accused of limiting political competition. As an interviewee noted, "It was interesting how everything that existed in the society during that year was exploding, smouldering, exploding, smouldering and now ... we managed to defend ČT" (CZ1).

There was also protest against the new government, and the marginalization of the group of former dissidents built around Havel. Some of these mobilizations addressed corruption – this also happened at the beginning of the 2010s, when Veřejnost Proti Korupci (Public against Corruption) was officially founded. A former activist recalls, "We connected it all into Give Us the State Back – a broad platform comprising about 100 NGOs" (CZ1). So, former activists assess that waves of protest reemerge when needed to defend democracy. In the Czech Republic, the perception was widespread that

after November 1989 people didn´t have any need to demonstrate their opinions or protest against the way we managed it here, against political transformation of the system. ... This was ten years after revolution: there were big protests and partially thanks to these protests people managed to stop some bills that were proposed by parties of Opoziční Smlouva, e.g. changes to the electoral law, changes to the constitution etc., taking Česká Televize away from public control and placing it under control of political power. That was at least partially successful: we managed to stop these attempts. (CZ3)

If Czechoslovakia is particularly striking for the large size of some protests (as indicated by the size of the "moons" in the figure), in the

GDR protests were much more numerous throughout the cycle. The first half of 1989 was characterized by protests on issues of rights to migrate and respect for human rights, which is indeed the main slogan of the path-breaking demonstration of September 18. Calls for political reforms characterized the fall of 1989, until the end of the authoritarian regime (Dale 2005). The protest curve indicates in fact a sharp rise of activity in September and then in October, with numbers remaining high in November. In December, a 600-mile human chain across the country was organized in order to call for deep and permanent reforms.

Although at a lower intensity in terms of quantity, protest events were still frequent and, often, highly participated until the fall of 1990. After transition, in fact, protestors continued to raise their voices for the punishment of former corrupted elites, the dissolution of the regime party, the Socialist Unity Party of Germany (Sozialistische Einheitspartei Deutschlands, SED), and the clearing of secret services' activities. Demonstrations followed for German reunification, sometimes with counterdemonstrations for keeping two Germanys instead. Racism also became a divisive issue, with the radical Right staging protests against Jews and migrants, and the Left countermobilizing against discrimination. Throughout 1990, moreover, protest also developed on the quickly evident downsides of unification: against unemployment, for the one-to-one exchange rate of the East German Mark against the West German Mark, for compensation of losses due to price increases, and for equal income between east and west. While brewery workers blocked roads against plummeting sales after the economic merger, peasants protested (even taking pigs and cows in front of parliament or dumping milk outside state offices) against unregulated imports and called for measures to safeguard farm products and service cutbacks, asking for better pay and emergency measures to cope with the negative effects of the free market. Even if protest events declined in quantity, they still mobilized large numbers of participants.

If mass protest was cyclical in cases of eventful democratization, no cycle is visible in the two cases of participated pacts, although with noticeable differences between Hungary and Poland. In fact, from protest event analysis, Hungary emerges as the least contentious case, with a flat line and small circles, indicating relatively low numbers of participants – with the sole exception of the August 1989 protests. Indeed, no cluster of events is visible in mobilizations on topics ranging from environmental issues to solidarity with the Chinese or Czech oppositions or for the rights of Hungarian minorities abroad, from denunciation of the Soviet invasion in 1956 to demands of punishment for officials but also for better pay and guaranteed jobs.

Also in Hungary, however, some protests were organized to defend democracy as well as to oppose economic transformations and their social effects. Some main protests are remembered by former members of the opposition as following a competitive logic:

When the first right wing government, technically going against the consensus of the late 1980s, showed restorative and anti-democratic features, there were symbolic events, such as the public and semi-official reburial of Miklós Horthy. ... There were very strong nationalist and anti-Semitic tendencies. The new regime showed several authoritarian traits and certain members of the government wished to curtail the freedom of speech and pluralism, or used anti-Semitic language. In response, the Democratic Charter, a mass movement emerged from civil society, maintained the excitement with mass demonstrations and other protest actions. Following the fall of 1991, there was an ongoing universal political battle, between the Right and then the liberals, they hadn't started calling themselves Left yet. (HU5)

A first protest after transition was the so-called taxi-drivers' blockade, a "genuinely grassroots" action that paralyzed most of the country for three days. While "hard to define ... whether that was a food rebellion or a social movement coming from the lower-middle class because the government lied about the price of petrol," the blockade is described as having

a moral aspect and a social aspect as well ... So those who a year before were making the revolution found themselves on the other side of the barricade all of a sudden. ... This later ended in an average trilateral negotiation between employers, employees and state representatives: the government retreated and cab drivers set free traffic back to normal ... later they received amnesty. The blockade was a huge shock. It was probably then that the population realized that with the end of the era of set prices came inflation, and there would be not only democracy, but also capitalism. ... This can be framed as an early anti-capitalist protest. (HU9)

Protests later more explicitly addressed the sudden deterioration of the economic situation. So, the perception is that "the transition did not bring peace: the street was very much present in politics in the years after 1989, in the form of an increasingly radical right on the one hand, and a democratic movement then still capable of mobilizing masses" (HU1).

In comparison with Hungary, protests were more frequent in Poland but also involved small numbers in sporadic ups and downs, with no visible cyclical dynamics. Throughout 1988, protest emerged in (relatively small) events promoted by students and workers, with some repression, followed by protest against repression. As a wave of strikes seemed on its way to spreading, however, Lech Walesa and the official leadership of Solidarity, the oppositional organization, actively pushed for demobilization, with the union leader directly calling for halting strikes as negotiations developed at the roundtable. In protest accounts, in fact, a contestation against Solidarity emerged, with anti-Walesa youth fighting with police on the streets and disrupting Walesa's rallies, calling him a traitor. Young people mobilized for more freedom, and also against the once-glorious Solidarity. Politicization of claims emerged around issues of repression, but also in demands for deeper democracy, with calls for the Soviet troops to go home, hunger strikes for amnesty, and demands for media pluralism. Mobilizations also spread to a heterogeneous list of claims: from opposition to nuclear power plants to calls for rights for German minorities, along with actions against the repression of Chinese students or the Wall in Berlin, or freedom in Laos or Lithuania. However, contentious politics developed especially on socioeconomic issues, with peasants, miners, telephone workers, postal employees, bus drivers, and coal workers asking for pay raises and subsidies. Thus, in Poland, the flat trend was often punctuated by occasional events, with peaks in September 1988 and then in March and September 1989, and with ups and downs throughout the 1990s.

Also in Poland, there were moreover moments of intense labor mobilization, as the frequency of strikes ratcheted up by about 350 percent in 1991 and 450 percent in 1992, falling afterward (Kramer 2002). Since 1991, there were in fact mass demonstrations by agricultural workers, teachers, and farmers who organized roadblocks. About 2,000 protest events were counted in 1989, 1,680 in 1990, 3,350 in 1991, 3,530 in 1992, and 4,380 in 1993, with increasing magnitude and growing approval of protest as a form of collective action (Ekiert and Kubik 1999, 115). There was a spread of not only strikes but also demonstrations; not only economic demands (57 percent) but also political ones (30 percent), with the state as the main target. Protest brought about little repression and frequent negotiation. In fact, the year 1993 was defined as a new "spring of the people," with increasing resistance to neoliberal reforms. A sharp rise in political criticism was expressed in highly polarizing frames used by radical political fringes, with increasing politicization in the early 1990s. In sum, civil society was not demobilized – rather, "Poland turned out to be an excellent example of the disjointed and chaotic development of the institutional realms of the polity during a period of transition" (ibid., 195). At times, civil society organizations grew political and challenging.

Troubled democratization paths, as repression and protests alternate, are also characterized by a sequence of waves rather than a proper cycle. Here as well, we note relevant differences between the short moment of contentious politics in Romania and the longer one in Albania. In Romania, protests against the regime emerged and peaked quickly in December 1989, with no proper protest events registered in the remainder of the year. While about a week of protests accompanied the regime change, some mobilization followed the death of Ceausescu, contesting the decision by the successor of the regime party, the National Salvation Front (NSF), against election. Protestors called for the punishment of communist leaders and members of the *securitate*, removal of symbols of the past (including a statue of Lenin), abolishment of media censorship, and greater minority rights. While some protests also addressed social issues (e.g., against the abolition of price controls) as well as environmental pollution, the more political calls against the resilient power of old incumbents were at the core of contentious politics, although involving small numbers of participants.

In Albania, protest event analysis points at the presence of quite a lot of protest, although without a cyclical shape. While clearly influenced by the democratization waves in other Eastern European countries, the protests here were delayed, with some peaks in December 1990, March 1991, and (especially large in) May 1991, but also later on in February and July 1992. According to the protest event analysis, the years 1989 and even 1990 remained quite calm, although marked by several instances of citizens escaping from the country until April 1991, as well as some mobilization around the newly founded Democratic Party at the end of 1990. However, protests spread throughout the following two years, with antigovernment rallies and strikes by workers asking for higher pay and students calling to remove Hoxha's name from the university in Tirana. Strikes continued to spread, often met by brutal repression. While protestors stigmatized the continuous power of the old oligarchy and symbols of the old regime were verbally and physically attacked, claims were pushed forward on human rights. As the economic crisis deepened, however, protests often took the form of crowds looting food warehouses (as repeatedly happened in February 1992).

Unachieved transition in Bulgaria also saw no cycle of protest, but rather some peaks in June–August 1989, and then in December of the same year and in July and November of 1990. After daily instances in which Bulgarians of Turkish origins fled the country to avoid forced assimilation from May to August 1989, protests spread on demands for

free speech and the right to assembly, as well as the end of forced assimilation, with counterdemonstrations calling for "Bulgaria for Bulgarians"
and against the persecutions of Bulgarians in Ukraine and Moldova. The
following year protests proceeded in short waves, addressing a growing
number of issues: from opposition to toxic fumes from lead and zinc
complexes, to human chains around a nuclear plant and a demonstration
on the anniversary of the Chernobyl accident, as well as to demands for
US troops to leave the Persian Gulf and for a free Lithuania. Calls for the
removal of symbols of the regime (including the body of the first communist leader from a mausoleum) and for the reestablishment of truth about
the past were accompanied by demands for resignation of BSP from
government but also some demonstrations in its support. Highways
were blocked to protest shortages of gasoline and food.

In sum, while protests were present in all paths of transition, only in
eventful democratization did we find the development of cycles of protest
that lasted well beyond the collapse of the authoritarian regime.

The Forms of Action. There is another characteristic of protest during
and after transitions that varies along the different paths: forms of action.
Building upon Tarrow's seminal work on a cycle of protest in Italy
(Tarrow 1989), researchers developed the expectation of high potential
for radicalization in the declining phase of protest waves (della Porta and
Tarrow 1987). As competition among political and social groups
increases, while protest fatigue spreads, the expectation is that some of
those who remain active tend to raise the stakes in order to attract or keep
commitment by using more radical forms. As the media, public opinion,
and decision makers become accustomed to more moderate forms of
action, the need to innovate often pushes protest organizers toward
more radical events. Moreover, as the number of participants at demonstrations declines, radicalism could be seen as an alternative logic in order
to attract media attention. Finally, frustrated by the paucity of results
from more moderate forms, some activists can test new ones. This trend is,
however, not confirmed in general by our data, as radicalization happened
only in the third, troubled, path (see Figure 2.2).

In the eventful path, at least in this wave of democratization, the forms
of action remained moderate, mixing protest and negotiation (Glenn
2003). Beginning with acts that required a small number of participants
(such as letters to the press, petitions, vigils, or theatrical action), forms of
action then usually moved toward massive marches, with strikes sometimes punctuating moments of more intense contention. In several early

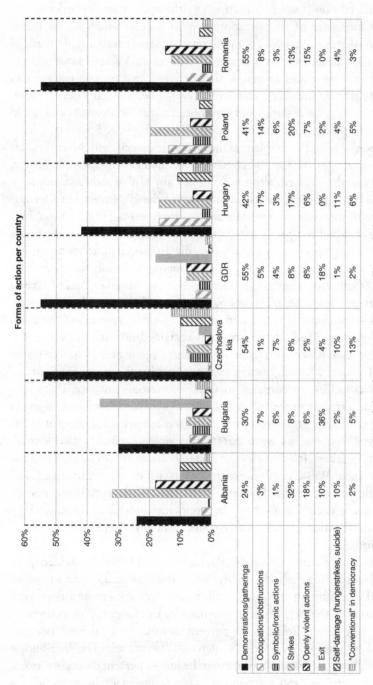

Forms of action per country

	Albania	Bulgaria	Czechoslova kia	GDR	Hungary	Poland	Romania
■ Demonstrations/gatherings	24%	30%	54%	55%	42%	41%	55%
▨ Occupations/obstructions	3%	7%	1%	5%	17%	14%	8%
▥ Symbolic/ironic actions	1%	6%	7%	4%	3%	6%	3%
▨ Strikes	32%	8%	8%	8%	17%	20%	13%
▨ Openly violent actions	18%	6%	2%	8%	6%	7%	15%
Exit	10%	36%	4%	18%	0%	2%	0%
▨ Self-damage (hungerstrikes, suicide)	10%	2%	10%	1%	11%	4%	4%
▤ "Conventional" in democracy	2%	5%	13%	2%	6%	5%	3%

FIGURE 2.2 Mobilized Participants per Million Inhabitants

cases, official events were "squatted" by the opposition, in order to use allowed moments of mobilization and to exploit attention to them. In Czechoslovakia, in 1989, demonstrations were indeed a main form of action, with leaders such as Alexander Dubcek or Václav Havel addressing the crowds (Innes 2001). A sign of intensified protest emerged as marchers grew in numbers, and protest events became daily occurrences. The two-hour general strike on November 27 was considered as a critical juncture in pushing for the breakdown of the regime. Forms of action remained stable and nonviolent in the next year as well, with several rallies and a few strikes on specific concerns. As the challengers took power, protests clearly declined, although without any visible radicalization.

In the GDR, as well, the ascending part of the cycle was characterized by peaceful forms of contentious action (Joppke 1995; Opp, Voss, and Gern 1995; Mueller 1999; Pfaff 2006). While frequent episodes of citizens illegally fleeing the country attracted media attention, marches organized by those who had applied for visas were sometimes brutally repressed, and candlelit vigils and religious services (such as the Monday Peace Prayers) put forward demands for human rights and freedom. Here, as well, marches – increasingly larger and more frequent – represented the main form of protest. While demonstrations remained nonviolent even in the face of repression, some direct action emerged against the large apparatus of secret police, with angry citizens sometimes breaking into Stasi (Staat-Sicherheit) offices. In contrast to Czechoslovakia, however, there was some radicalization in the following year, as neo-Nazis attacked migrants and left-wing activists, some of whom responded in kind. Police interventions were frequent, as were arrests and violence. Strikes also spread, however: workers felt increasingly exploited and discriminated against vis-à-vis their Western counterparts, as factories were privatized and closed down and unemployment increased. While remaining mainly peaceful, the declining part of the cycle was indeed characterized by some radicalization as well as a diversification in the repertoire of collective action.

Similarly, in participated pacts, the repertoire of protest remained quite limited both during and after the transition itself, although with a broader range of disruptive forms in Poland, where civil society had been very contentious at the beginning of the decade. In Hungary, 42 percent of actions were demonstrations, 17 percent strikes, and 17 percent occupations, with some hunger strikes (11 percent) also present. The distribution of forms of protest was similar in Poland, with 41 percent demonstrations, 20 percent strikes, and 14 percent occupations, with however also a

7 percent of violent action. Given the higher number of events, there is also more variety of forms inside those broader categories. Students climbed on roofs, while there were frequent appeals by Solidarity leader Walesa to stop strikes. Young people threw percussion grenades and stones at the police, or tried to disrupt Walesa's speeches or official parades and clashed with police. Farmers organized blockades, symbols of the regime were destroyed, and headquarters of the previous regime's institutions was occupied. Feminists organized pickets at Solidarity buildings to protest against proposals for restrictive abortion laws. Hunger strikes and street theater were also used.

In troubled democratization, protests emerged in a series of (often violent) outbursts. This is the case, with some difference in size and frequency, for Albania and Romania. In Romania, demonstrative forms of action represent more than 50 percent of the coded events, strikes are not negligible (with 13 percent), and violent events reach a quite high 13 percent. They are however concentrated in December 1989, when demonstrators often clashed with police while, after Ceausescu's violent death, direct action was limited to the storming of buildings hosting institutions of the previous regime, some disruptions at their rallies, and scuffles between dissidents and NSF supporters.

Protest forms were more numerous and varied in Albania, with the highest proportion of strikes (32 percent) but also of openly violent actions (18 percent, while demonstrations were just 25 percent of total events). Especially in the early days, violent events included the destruction of symbols of the incumbent regime or mysterious bombings at Democratic Party rallies and headquarters, as well as clashes with police when the latter intervened to disperse protest. Pro- and anti-Hoxha demonstrations as well as pro- and anti-Democratic Party supporters developed a competitive dynamic in 1991, although protests were increasingly influenced by the heavy economic crisis: strikes but also waves of riots in stores even led to occasional shootouts with police, with demonstrators killed and resulting riots, while more and more people fled the country.

While leading to unaccomplished democratization, the events in Bulgaria are significantly less radicalized, with violence present only in about 6 percent of events and, instead, a very high presence of political exiting by ethnic Turks fleeing from forced assimilation along with some highly educated Bulgarians leaving for the West. Some competition emerged here between Turks' claims to citizens' rights, often incorporated by the new governments, and calls for Bulgarian ethnic dominance.

Protest Claims. Protest waves and cycles vary also according to the types of claims that are put forward. In general, social movement scholars have observed that protest tends at first to focus on some specific issues, then grows in generality as different groups mobilize and, what is more, start to build coalitions or compete with each other (Saxonberg 2001; della Porta 2014a). In the declining phase of a cycle, we can again expect a fragmentation of the requests, with more specific demands dominating, even if on a more plural range of issues. At the same time, we can expect the degree of politicization – as indicated in particular by the chosen target and the issues addressed – to follow a similar development. In particular, if protests are often not politicized in the beginning, the very interaction with the police forces brings about some initial focus on state institutions. Furthermore, the more general the claim, the more we can expect politicization to increase in parallel. Vice versa, politicization should be expected to decrease if and when, with the decline of a cycle, more specific issues come to the fore of contentious politics.

When thinking about protests before, during, and after transition, we can modulate these expectations. First and foremost, politicization and generality increase during the ascending phase of the cycle – as contention politics focus on regime change – and then decline after transition with a pattern of protest politics more in line with the typical one in democracies. In our cases, we might therefore expect an increase in the proportion of events on specific issues over the more general ones in the second periods (in 1990). Similarly, politicization should decline in the same periods.

When comparing our three paths, we can expect these dynamics to be more evident in eventful paths of democratization, when cycles emerge in full swing. Moreover, the more moderate protest during participated pacts should leave space to less general and politicized claims. Conversely, we might expect a higher degree of generalization and politicization in troubled transitions, when episodes of brutal repression focus attention on the state.

Looking at the degree of generality (as measured by the presence of general claims addressing regime transformations or rights versus more specific ones) (see Table 2.1), we notice that, for cases of eventful democratization, protests in the GDR fit indeed our expectations, increasing in generality up to 1990 and then declining. In particular, while claims on general issues and rights dominate between October 1989 and January 1990, later on, the protest politics addressed mainly specific issues. We find a similar increase in generality in Czechoslovakia, although with

TABLE 2.1 *Generality of issues by country and time period* during the protests for regime change in seven Eastern European countries*

	Albania		Bulgaria		Czechoslovakia		GDR	
	1st Period	2nd Period	1st Period	2nd Period	1st Period	2nd Period	1st Period	2nd Period
Specific issue	42%	61%	6%	25%	7%	13%	9% (11)	32% (112)
Generic issue/right	58%	39%	94%	75%	93%	87%	91% (118)	68% (142)
Total % (No.)	100% (128)	100% (103)	100% (35)	100% (127)	100% (54)	100% (30)	100% (129)	100% (254)

	Hungary		Poland		Romania	
	1st Period	2nd Period	1st Period	2nd Period	1st Period	2nd Period
Specific issue	67%	67%	40%	49%	6%	13%
Generic issue/right	33%	33%	60%	51%	94%	87%
Total % (No.)	100% (18)	100% (18)	100% (272)	100% (144)	100% (17)	100% (147)

* The 1st and 2nd time periods represent, respectively, the first half and the second half of the months taken into account for each country. These months are not the same for every country; therefore, the time period varies. For Bulgaria, Czechoslovakia, Romania, and Hungary: 1st time period →1989‖ 2nd →1990.

For GDR: 1st time period → Jan–Nov 1989 ‖ 2nd → Dec 1989–Oct 1990 //For Poland: 1st time period → Jan 1988–Jun 1989 ‖ 2nd → Jul 1989–Dec 1990//.

For Albania: 1st time period →Jun 1990–Jul 1991 ‖ 2nd → Aug 1991–Jul 1992.

Source: Data collected and analyzed for this project by Matteo Cernison.

no sharp decline in 1990. In the GDR, in fact, protests' generality increases from 9 to 32 percent between 1989 and 1990, while protest remains general in claims in Czechoslovakia (only down from 93 percent to 87 percent).

Politicization, measured as protest targeting state institutions (such as parliaments, governments, or secret services), follows a parallel trend (see Table 2.2). In the GDR, we see in fact a sharp increase in politicization between October 1989 and January 1990, followed by a drop from 80 percent in 1989 to 44 percent in 1990. Here as well, politicization happens since the very beginning, through the chain of protest and repression, with increasing demands for release of prisoners and permission to leave the country, and for freedom, human rights, political reform, and fair elections. After transition, protests tend instead to address a plurality of more specific issues. The evolution of politicization in Czechoslovakia is only partially similar, with an increase in the proportion of protests oriented against the government until November 1989, and then a downward trend in 1990 (with a drop from 59 percent to 40 percent). Throughout the first half of 1989, politicization happens through protests against repression, including both hunger strikes in prison and demonstrations outside of the courthouse.

We see a different trend of protest claims in participated pacts, with broader issues dominating only in the spring of 1989, and more specific issues present throughout the period. In general, specific claims characterize a high percentage of protests, increasing from 40 percent to 49 percent between 1989 and 1990. Given the low number of reported events, no particular trend is visible in Hungary. As for politicization, participated pacts seem to keep protestors from targeting main state institutions: in Poland, antigovernment protests remain at a very low 15/20 percent; in Hungary, they are even less, decreasing from 11 percent in 1989 to 0 percent in 1990.

Finally, we again find differences in troubled democratization paths. In Romania, there is a low proportion of protest on specific issues, increasing only slightly (from 6 percent to 13 percent) after transition. As for politicization, the proportion of politicized events is generally high but declines from 88 percent to 52 percent after transition. In Albania, with a higher number of reported protests, more general claims dominated in the winter of 1991 and then again in the summer of the same year and the following one. In Bulgaria, we have a significant increase in the number and percentage of specific events since October 1990.

As for politicization, the percentage of protests targeting state institutions remained high in Romania, although with a decline from 88 percent

TABLE 2.2 *Politicization of protest by country and time period* during the protests for regime change in seven Eastern European countries*

	Albania		Bulgaria		Czechoslovakia		GDR	
	1st Period	2nd Period	1st Period	2nd Period	1st Period	2nd Period	1st Period	2nd Period
Not opposing gov.	48%	63%	37%	52%	41%	60%	20% (26)	56% (141)
Opposing gov. or system	52%	37%	63%	48%	59%	40%	80% (103)	44% (113)
Total % (No.)	100% (129)	100% (104)	100% (35)	100% (126)	100% (54)	100% (30)	100% (129)	100% (254)

	Hungary		Poland		Romania	
	1st Period	2nd Period	1st Period	2nd Period	1st Period	2nd Period
Not opposing gov.	89%	100%	86%	80%	12%	48%
Opposing gov. or system	11%	0%	14%	20%	88%	52%
Total % (No.)	100% (18)	100% (18)	100% (272)	100% (144)	100% (17)	100% (147)

* The 1st and 2nd time periods represent, respectively, the first half and the second half of the months taken into account for each country. These months are not the same for every country; therefore, the time period varies, too. For Bulgaria, Czechoslovakia, Romania, and Hungary: 1st time period →1989‖ 2nd →1990.

For GDR: 1st time period → Jan–Nov 1989 ‖ 2nd → Dec 1989–Oct 1990 //For Poland: 1st time period → Jan 1988–Jun 1989 ‖ 2nd → Jul 1989–Dec 1990//.

For Albania: 1st time period →Jun 1990–Jul 1991 ‖ 2nd → Aug 1991–Jul 1992.

Source: Data collected and analyzed for this project by Matteo Cernison.

during the upheaval to 52 percent after transition. Albania, although with a lesser degree of politicization, has a similar trend, with protests targeting important governmental institutions dropping from 52 percent to 37 percent after transition. Finally, in Bulgaria, the percentage of protests with high politicization drops from 63 percent to 48 percent.

In sum, a general assessment is that there is a normalization of protest. The term is used to synthesize various trends. Protest after transition tends to address several targets rather than focusing on the breakdown of the authoritarian regime; it also tends to become less political in its target and to be local in scope and fragmented.

Against a vision of exceptionalism, protest is also considered in the narratives of our interviewees as "normalized," transformed but still alive. There is more focus on specific problems – as, in the words of an interviewee, "it became normal protest culture; has become normal where it hurts particularly" (GDR8). Furthermore, mass participation in protest was perceived as less frequent. As observed for Poland,

when it comes to 1989 and after 1989 the amount of protests has increased, and was not falling, but they were not as big as they were before … Electoral mechanisms lead to the fact that huge protests are generally declining and their meaning also, because they are substituted by political elections and it is done efficiently. But in my opinion small protests can only to a certain extent be discharged by elections, because their reasons are usually smaller than the ones for the huge protests. (PL2)

Protest was indeed perceived as becoming normal. As the fear of repression declined, dissatisfaction kept mobilization alive. In Poland, as in other countries, "after the Round Table most of the protest was not tamed, but at the same time the reasons for the protests were beginning to decline. … Rather small claims could result in some street protests and social protest" (PL1). Protests were then "pushed by the feeling that now more things are allowed and more things can be done" (PL14).

Normalization also implied a perceived depoliticization and, especially, decrease in the power of protest. As a Czech activist noted, after transition, "There were more protests but they didn't cost any effort. I would even say that there was some inflation of them. … Before the Velvet revolution you guaranteed for every word you said, and you risked your safety and your career. You can say everything nowadays and nothing will happen. … Of course there are more protests today but they have more specific value" (CZ13).

Repertoires of action also became more moderate. With normalization, in the words of an interviewee, "there was a decline in spontaneous, 'explosive,' activities, and the best evidence for that were the occupations and street demonstrations and things like that." Although "since the revolution there have been no such protests. I mean such big and numerous ones," the assessment is nevertheless that "people are more active" (CZ11).

Normalization implied that the tasks temporarily taken over by the protestors were reallocated to the state. This was for instance the case in Hungary with organizations involved in the fight against poverty. In the words of an activist,

now we had the state! And we were supposed to put together our nonexistent little money . . .? Now we could count on the state to carry out its duties . . . like it hadn't in the Kádár regime, now it could, because we had a much smarter state, and I felt there was no more need. . . . I was very, very hopeful . . . because now the local governments were Communist-free . . . freely elected people who would lead their towns competently. Of course this is not what happened, but this is how we felt at the time. (HU12)

Institutionalization affected various groups, as some of their tasks were taken over by the new institutions. So, in Czechoslovakia, "the student movement transformed into academic senates. . . . As we all finished our studies, it was a completely different generation of people and they were interested in practical things, e.g. halls of residence, canteens and in fact they were not political. . . . I would say that the student movement became apolitical, it turned into interest groups of students" (CZ1). Initiatives formerly organized from below tended to become public, as, in the GDR, the environmental libraries, which "were directly taken over by municipalities . . . there are 150 *Umweltbibliotheken* now in Germany, but they have other sources for financing or are supported by municipalities or by some private persons" (GDR4).

Research on the 1990s and the 2000s confirmed a normalization of protest, with more contentious development, especially on social issues, in Poland and Hungary than in the Czech Republic, where social conflicts were better represented in the party system along the left–right cleavages (Císar 2014). Mobilizations against austerity policies (often carried out by left-wing governments) developed in all three countries: in Poland and in Hungary toward the end of the 1990s and the mid-2000s, in the Czech Republic in the second half of the 2000s.

CONTENTIOUS EASTERNERS? COMPARING WITHIN GERMANY

Allowing a comparison with the evolution of protest in the West, the analysis of protest in East Germany shows a very high degree of contentiousness. In particular, after massive participation during transition in 1989, there was only a short break, followed throughout the 1990s by a very high degree of protests that in some cases followed competitive mechanisms, targeting migrants accused of stealing welfare benefits, but were often oriented to the defense of social rights.

The Amount of Protest

The peaceful revolution in 1989 is reflected in a huge mobilization of citizens. The yearly sum of protestors registered in the Prodat database for East Germany reaches its maximum level in 1989, with a total of 3.5 million East Germans mobilized in the street. After a gradual development of the opposition during the 1980s, the year 1989 saw a rapid intensification, up to the massive demonstrations of the fall, followed by the breakdown of the authoritarian regime and, then, in 1990, the reunification with West Germany (Jessen 2009). In 1989, intense fluxes of exiters – understood as citizens who migrated or applied for migration visas – interacted with the increasingly louder calls for regime changes by those who wanted to stay (Pfaff 2006; della Porta 2014a).

With democracy and reunification, the following years experienced a steep decline in protest participation. After millions of protestors triggered the fall of the Wall and raised other issues such as civil rights and environmental concerns, the year 1990 saw protests falling to less than a third, with a further decline through the following years. The only year for which more than 500,000 protest participants were counted is 2000.[2] Western *Länder* (States), by contrast, saw a peak in the yearly sum of participants in 1992, especially thanks to the candlelight marches (*Lichterketten*) organized against a wave of racist attacks in the early 1990s. After 1992, the number of protestors declined, notwithstanding another peak in 1997 (linked to two referenda in Bavaria).

---

[2] Four-fifths of this peak in protest participation is related to a referendum in Thuringia with the aim of lowering the bar for referenda.

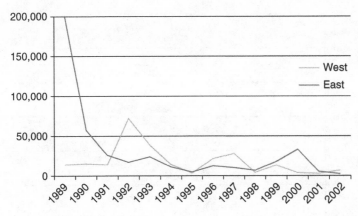

FIGURE 2.3 Mobilized Participants per Million Inhabitants in selected East European Countries

Looking at the total numbers of reported protestors tends to be misleading, however, as the population is distributed unequally between East and West. Looking at the relative number of protesting citizens per million inhabitants, the comparison shows the steep decline in the East after 1989, when more than 200,000 protestors per million were reported (see Figure 2.3). However, after the peaks in 1989 and 1992 (in the West) and, apart from the referenda in 1997 and 2000, protests in the East and the West proceeded in parallel, with the number of mobilized participants in the East sometimes overtaking those in the West.

Looking at the yearly sum of events as an indicator of their degree of activities, we note that it does not decline as drastically as the number of the people involved. In fact, the number of events, which is virtually unrelated to the number of participants, decreased in the East from around 175 events in the early 1990s to around 75 events in the later years under examination; but West Germany experienced however a comparable dynamic with high figures between 250 and 400 yearly events until the late 1990s, and later a decline that brings the yearly event count to some 150 in the last years under study. Focusing on the city of Leipzig, a protest stronghold during the revolution, the pattern is more or less the same. A remarkable drop in the number of protestors accompanies a discontinuous dynamic in the number of events. As the number of events is related to the population size, however, the initial impression of drastic decline in the East has to be corrected (see Figure 2.4). In fact, the number of events per million inhabitants is larger in the East than in the West throughout the

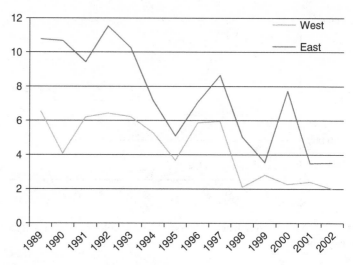

FIGURE 2.4 Events per Million Inhabitants in Selected East European Countries
Source: Data collected and analyzed for this project by Simon Teune.

examined period. Nevertheless, the declining trend is obvious for both parts of the country, at least for the years under study.[3]

Overall, in the comparison of East Germany and West Germany, similarities in the protest volume are striking. Obvious differences are visible in the maximum sum of protestors and different peaks in East and West. While the revolutionary demonstrations in the East were not met with support on the streets in the West, East Germans did not follow the call to stand up against racist violence two years after unification. Apart from these differences, the focus on the volume of protest suggests that the dynamics of mobilization harmonized quickly after the two parts of Germany merged.

The transfer of institutions and the cross-fertilization in terms of a civic culture through unification can be seen as peculiar to East Germany, if compared with other East European countries in the 1990s (Lemke 2013). However, the fact that the number of events per inhabitant is even higher in the East than in the West seems to indicate that we are not just observing a process of adaptation of the East to the West, but rather also some resilience of the contentious months of eventful democratization (della Porta 2014a).

If we look at the evolution of the type of protests, we might note the presence of both emulative and competitive mechanisms, although

---

[3] Other data indicate a new rise in both events and participants after 2002 (Hutter 2014).

within a panorama characterized by difficult economic conditions (Rink 1999). Protests of course took peculiar forms in 1989, the year of the peaceful revolution. Starting with leafleting, open letters (including to Gorbachev), and religious services, the protests moved toward more massive and public forms, especially marches since October. The aims also grew in generality and politicization. Initially focusing on specific rights, such as freedom of travel or the request for a voting booth, they moved to demands for deep social, economic, and political reforms, including criticism of police repression. Toward the end of the year, requests for open borders, the resignation of the government, the dissolution of the regime party, and reunification of Germany became audible.

Protestors usually presented themselves under the label of a citizens' movement, composed of (as listed in the foundation document of New Forum) students, workers, scientists, artists, and even party members. In fact, toward the end of the period, critical members of the regime party SED organized protests against the corruption of the party apparatus. Claims also emerged on environmental issues (especially in local campaigns against polluting carbon, chemical, and nuclear plants) and women's and gay rights. Buildings were squatted for political activities but also for housing. Especially, protests spread territorially from East Berlin, Lypsia, and Dresden to the entire country (Mueller 1999; Dale 2005; della Porta 2014a).

If contentious politics in 1989 focused on democratization, the next years saw more plurality in forms, claims, and involved actors. Protests increasingly addressed environmental pollution, targeting the import of garbage from the West and the construction of hazardous plants in the East. Citizens also contested un-participatory urban planning and the introduction of the West German law on abortion; they protested against the Soviet army and for peace. In particular, social issues very soon emerged in the protest arena. The year 1990 already saw increasing contention on the economic downside of regime transition, with citizens, students, workers, and peasants protesting against their uncertain economic future, price increases, speculation in urban restructuring, the retrenchment of the welfare state, the restructuring of the university system. On November 4, 1990, the anniversary of the big demonstration for democracy, people asked for equal social rights in the East and the West. Some sporadic violence emerged only during an occupation of the Stasi headquarters and during break-ins in other Stasi centers. In prisons, protests for better living conditions and the revision of the trials conducted under the dictatorship took the form of hunger strikes and roof occupations, but also included some more disruptive moments. Some escalation in street battles with police happened around occupied youth centers.

Especially in the second half of 1990, instead, racist attacks of the radical Right and skinhead groupings against migrants and shelter houses for refugees multiplied. This type of action escalated in 1991 and 1992 with the spreading of arsons and violent break-ins to migrants' shelters, but also in assaults against left-wing activists and punks. However, these two years were also characterized by the spreading of strikes for labor rights, occupations against factory closures, and marches against the privatization politics of the *Treuhand*, as well as house squatting in reaction to the lack of affordable housing and peasants' claims for protection. Workers mobilized not only from all industrial sectors (from textile to metallurgic factories) but also from the service sectors, from theaters to mail and transport. Still in 1994, contentious politics addressed mass unemployment, but also peace, the environment, youth culture, and gender rights. In the following years, as well, mobilization targeted austerity measures, with perceived worsening of public services, including education. The radical Right also took up social issues, calling for "work for Germans first."

Forms of Action

Research on protest cycles has often predicted radicalization during the declining phase. Some activists moderate their aims, satisfied with what they have achieved and exploiting new channels opened by the protest itself; others drop out, disillusioned with what they perceive as a lack of success. In an attempt to keep the mobilization going, and in light of signs of declining commitment, small numbers might however choose to increase militancy. While the social science literature on transitions assumes a moderation in the forms of political participation if institutions open up, the increasing tolerance for contentious politics might move in the opposite direction. In particular, if the economic conditions worsen and promises fail to materialize, some radicalization might be expected to ensue (on claim radicalization in the GDR, see Muller 1999).

Regarding forms of protest, the Prodat database for East Germany shows a significant change after unification. Categorizing protest events into six classes (appealing, procedural, demonstrative, confrontational, non-severe violence, and severe violence), the data show that moderate protests are overshadowed in the first year after unification by a steep rise in violent protests (see Figure 2.5). In 1992, as much as about 60 percent of the recorded protest events in East Germany are violent – almost exclusively attacks by right wing extremists targeting refugees and other people categorized as either non-German or even not worthy of living. After a peak in 1991 and 1992, racist attacks by the Right continue to be a constant in East Germany.

The statistics on the number of people killed in right-wing extremist attacks shows the high frequency of these incidents.[4] However, the fatal violence perpetrated by the radical Right is not a particular East German problem, but rather concerns Germany as a whole, with a maximum of twenty-three fatalities in 1993. A comparison of protest forms in East Germany and West Germany shows violent protests on the rise in both parts of the country. Such events are, however, more visible in the East, where their share of the reported protest events is larger, particularly in 1991 and 1992. Apart from the frequency of violent events in the East (roughly a quarter for the reported period), the distribution of protest forms is similar in both parts of the country. While procedural forms play a limited role, appeals and confrontational protests are constant elements in the repertoire, with occasional rises to more than a third of all protest events per year.

Related with the higher presence of violence, we also find more police intervention, arrests, and injuries in the East. In the covered period, the police intervened in 12 percent of the recorded protest events in the West, but 20 percent in the East; arrests were made in 10 percent of protest in the West versus 21 percent in the East; and people were wounded in 6 percent of the reported protests in the West, but in 13 percent in the East.

Competitive Claims

Research on protest cycles has linked radicalization with increasing competition at the social and political levels. At the beginning of a cycle of protest, some actors successfully mobilize as early risers; others follow as they aim at emulating those early risers, or at opposing them. More specifically to double transitions, both democratization and economic reforms create winners and losers who might try to gain supporters

---

[4] This is shown in the numbers drawn from the Internet portal *Mut gegen Rechte Gewalt* (Courage against Right-Wing Violence), which has documented the cases based on research by both antiracist activists and journalists. The count registers politically motivated homicides in East Germany in every year in the report period.

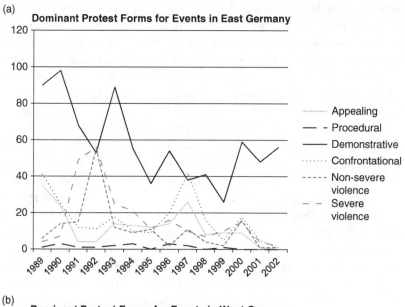

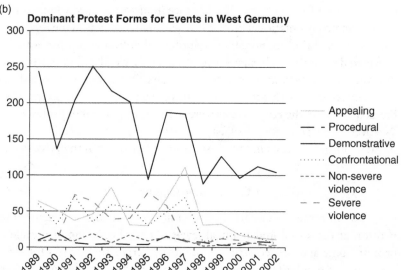

FIGURE 2.5 Forms of Protests in Germany
Source: Based on data from Prodat.

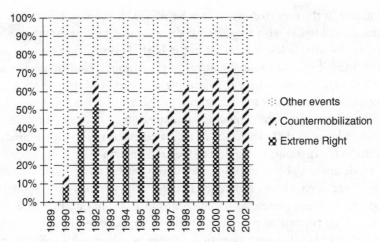

FIGURE 2.6 Share of Extreme Right Mobilization and Counter-Mobilization in East Germany
Source: Data collected and analyzed for this project by Simon Teune.

through street action. Competition can also develop among the losers, however, as different social and ethnic groups compete for scarce resources, or find scapegoats for their grievances.

The violence against refugees and migrants is indicative of the mobilization around issues that had previously been marginal in the streets. After unification, the extreme Right in fact (re)discovered protests as a political means of expression (Virchow 2007). These protests, in turn, triggered counterprotests by left-wing activists and concerned citizens. As for the claims put forward by the extreme Right, those against migration and for the defense of the nation occupy a large share of the events. However, they are frequently countered by antiracist protestors calling for migrants' rights and opposing racism and xenophobia as well as neo-Nazism in general. The comparative analysis reveals the dominance of this type of contention in East Germany (see Figure 2.6). After 1990, the protests of the extreme Right account in fact for between 20 percent and 50 percent of the events reported every year. Adding countermobilization against the radical Right, the two broad issues add up to 44 percent in the East versus (a still high) 23 percent in the West.

Apart from the domination of East German protest arenas by the extreme Right and its opponents, there is another remarkable difference between East and West. The diversity of protest issues is much broader in the West, whereas, together with migration and democracy, labor issues dominate in the reported events in East. Peace, education, and the environment – all issues with a significant share among protest events in West Germany – are far less important in the East. This distribution of claims seems indeed related to the dynamics of transition: claims on democracy are linked to struggles over the meaning and extent of democratization; protest on labor issues testifies to the problems of economic transition. While claims related to democracy remained high all along, protests on issues of labor and on social issues increased since 1990, with consistent results in the first half of the decade (see Figure 2.7a–b).

Trade unions, absent in 1989, started to be visible immediately in 1990, with quite high values especially between 1993 and 1996. Similarly, workers were not present as social groups in 1989, but participated in as much as 30 percent of protests as early as 1990, with high percentages until 1996. Until 1995, moreover, protests addressed especially the national level. Overall, workers were present in 19.6 percent of protests in the West, with a slightly lower 14.4 in the East; social issues in, respectively, 13 percent and 10 percent; the economy in 12.7 percent and 8.7 percent. Work as an issue was mentioned in 19.5 percent of the covered protests in the West and a still high 13.9 in the East (21.4 percent in Berlin).

In fact, issues of democracy and social rights emerge as especially relevant from an analysis of the evolution of protest events in Lypsia, a city that had played a most important role during the protest for democracy. In 1989, all reported protests focused on citizenship rights and political reform up to the resignation of the government, including demonstrations and religious services such as those during the protests scheduled every Monday. In 1990, protests were already more diversified, addressing not only political issues (such as reunification of the two parts of Germany and dissolution of the secret police, the Stasi) but also social issues (Grey Lions called for the rights of seniors and students opposed to the restructuration of the university system) and environmental ones (e.g., for pedestrian zones in the city center). Competition emerged on issues of national reunification as well as on migration issues, with the beginning of an escalation of demonstrations and counterdemonstrations as early as 1990.

Given the difficulties of the double transition to democracy and to capitalism (Offe 1996), in the midst of economic difficulties (Ekiert 1996), contentious politics addressed social issues. In 1991, protests developed against the privatization politics of the national government, with among others a 70,000-strong demonstration against the Treuhandanstalt (the agency responsible for privatization) and for the

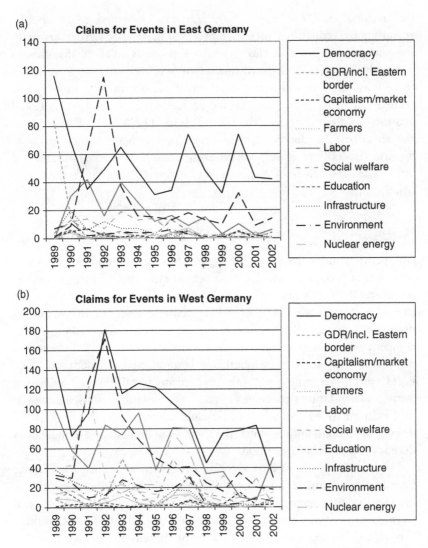

FIGURE 2.7 Issues of claims in East Germany and in West Germany

creation of jobs in the Eastern states. In the following years, as well, protests targeted declining social protection and the increase in the cost of living, with *Montagsdemos* (Monday demonstrations) once again organized by churches and trade unions. Strikes became very frequent, in particular, but not only, in the public sector. In the mid-1990s, protests targeted the *Sparpaket* (oriented to saving money) of the national and the regional governments, oriented to cut public spending by reductions in social protection. In 1998, together with the unions, religious circles organized protests against the closing down of factories and the dismissal of workers. At the same time, there was, here as well, an escalation of action on migration issues: while right-wing skinheads attacked asylum-seekers, the Left protested against racism and against the war on Iraq. The Nikolai Kirche, once the space of the democratization movement, again hosted protests against the radical Right, which sometimes attracted thousands of citizens, as the issues of human rights extended to include the rights of migrants.

Reconstructing Organizations

Competition might be linked to organizational dynamics, as cycles of protest first favor the emergence of new organizations in the ascending phase and then see a decline in participation, which pushes organizations to fight with each other in order to keep commitments and recruit among declining numbers. Radicalization can be seen as an outcome of this competition, or even of the lack of organizational resources needed to put pressure on authorities mobilizing large numbers of activism (della Porta 1995). We can expect both mechanisms to take specific relevance during consolidation processes; as preexisting organizations would not fit well in the new environment, organizational traditions in terms of the development of an autonomous civil society are limited, and mobilization declines sharply after transition.

In his panel study of East German protest participants, Karl-Dieter Opp (2004) identified integration into protest-promoting networks as the most important predictor of protest participation (Opp, Voss, and Gern 1995). While throughout the 1990s no lasting protest milieu, comparable to the new social movement milieus in the West, developed in the transforming *Länder* (Rink 1999), some institutionalization of civil society organizations has been observed in areas such as the environment or gender rights (Rucht, Blattert, and Rink 1997; Flam 2001; Rink 2001). Although with some difficulties of adaptation to a different conception of democracy, the citizens' organizations that had participated in the mobilization for democracy produced their own organizational spillover, moving in part into representative institutions, but also, in part, engaging in contentious politics (Olivo 2001). At the same time, the professionalization of social movements that was characteristic for the early phase after unification tended to decline, as less and less public funds were made available. For many of the protests in the East, the newspaper coverage does not provide information about protest organizers. Although this was also true in the West, it is even more visible in the East, with some 62 percent of the cases lacking specification of involved organizations. When protest organizations are known, there is especially one significant difference between East and West: long-standing organizations such as trade unions, churches, and interest groups play a more limited role in the East, while they are most important players in the West. In fact, unions, churches, and associations called for about 30 percent of organized protests in the West and about half of those in the East. Nevertheless, also in the East, protest by the unions on labor issues already tended to assume an important role at the very beginning of the 1990s, as privatization raised fears and opposition. If parties are mentioned slightly more in the East, this is especially due to the extreme right NPD, which is named as responsible for 41 percent of the party-led protests in the East from 1989 to 2002.

Looking at the evolution in organizations involved in protests over time, we notice obvious signs that the organizational infrastructure of the revolution in the GDR did not survive transition. After 1990, in fact, many civil rights organizations ceased to exist, as they disbanded or merged with preexisting parties and organizations. For instance, part of the leadership of the New Forum, one of the key protest organizations until 1990, joined the party coalition of the (Western) Green party and some (Eastern) civil rights organizations, Bündnis 90/Die Grünen.

Competition on conceptions of political and economic transition can also be seen if we look at the social groups mobilized. As we noted for the organizations that mobilize protests, the Prodat data are fragmentary when it comes to the social groups involved in contentious events. For two-thirds of the recorded protest events, this information is not available, either in the East or in the West. We can note, however, that about 10 percent (30 percent, if we only look at valid cases) of protests in the West and 7.6 percent (more than 20 percent of all events, without missing values) are carried out by the workers.

While broadly similar on this dimension, the comparison of East and West Germany shows two important differences. First, protests in which the presence of non-German citizens is reported are 5 percent of the total (which rises to almost 15 percent if we remove missing values) in West Germany, while only 0.5 percent in the Eastern part. These figures reflect a demographic difference: the share of non-German citizens in the East was and continues to be significantly lower (less than 1 percent in 1991) than in the Western *Länder* (up to 12 percent in 1991[5]). Not only were the communities of non-German citizens larger in the West, they were also represented by organizations that were virtually absent in the East.

Second, youth are mentioned as carriers of protest in 11 percent of the cases (about 33 percent excluding missing values) in the East, while only 3 percent of the events in the West fall into this category. This difference, again, is linked to the high share of racist assaults in East Germany. More than two-thirds of the cases in which youth are specified as protestors in this time frame go back to issues of the extreme right.

While young people had been much mobilized during the protests for democratization – against human rights violations and for political reform and freedom to travel, against police repression and for various educational policies – since 1990 reported youth protests consisted mainly of rioting against migrants, especially asylum seekers, but also homosexuals, Soviet symbols, and punks as well as left-wing radicals. Especially since 1991, forms of action moved from riots to setting fire to migrants' shelters and armed assault to shelters, with often deadly consequences. While the radical Right became more politicized, using nationalist and neo-Nazi symbols, the left-wing youth protested high rent through squatting of empty buildings and organized counterdemonstrations against neo-Nazi events. Large protests targeted youth unemployment, with 30,000 participating in a Job Parade in Schwerin, or called for reform of the educational system, with 40,000 demonstrating in Berlin. Especially in 1991 and 1992, violence took a very prominent role, covering about 60 percent of the events, while attacks on migrants by radical right activists tended to undergo a drastic drop in 1993, though remaining high in absolute numbers, not only in the East but also in West Germany. In general, extreme right protests also remained quite high, covering up to 55 percent of the sample in 1992 and 40 percent between 1999 and 2000. However, countermobilizations were also frequent and growing. While radical Right protests never involved more than a dozen people, anti-Nazi groups were able to mobilize a few hundred.

[5] www.destatis.de/DE/Publikationen/Thematisch/Bevoelkerung/MigrationIntegration/AuslaendBevoelkerung2010200037004.pdf?__blob=publicationFile.

CONCLUSION

In general, we noted that protests around transition periods meet some expectations developed in social movement studies, but also show variations between cases. These differences can in part be explained by the paths of transition. In Ekiert and Kubik's analysis, cited above, modes of breakdown of communist regimes had no noticeable impact on the magnitude of protest. They note, in fact, that "countries that experienced 'pacted transitions' (Poland and Hungary) have as much variation between themselves as do countries where 'popular upsurge' forced the removal of the communist elites from power (Slovakia and the former GDR)" (1998, 580). Our analysis shows, however, that besides the magnitude of protests, the different transition paths do show some peculiarity. While proper cyclical dynamics could be found only in eventful paths – with growth in generality and politicization in the ascending phase and a converse trend in the descending – participated pacts show more moderate forms and specific/nonpoliticized claims, while the opposite was true in troubled transitions.

Ekiert and Kubik also suggested that one can expect more protest where there are more rapid economic transformations. Their reasoning goes as follows:

(1) rapid economic reforms produce higher social costs and more dissatisfaction among the populace than slower, more gradual reforms. In turn, (2) the heightened level of dissatisfaction with the reforms and the elites that designed and implemented them results in the increased protest magnitude. Finally, (3) intense protest brings about the downfall of the reforming, neoliberal elites. (Ekiert and Kubik 1998, 565–7)

We noted, in fact, much voice on socioeconomic claims against the misery introduced by market building in the GDR, but also in dramatic protests in Albania, where the economic crisis hit hardest.

In all cases, we can also confirm that, as a trend, more and more, "protest is employed as a means of bringing forward demands for reforms and not challenging the legitimacy of the regime; its methods are recognized as legitimate by a large sector of the populace; it is channeled through well-known strategies and coordinated by established organizations" (ibid., 567). Protests remained in fact moderate in CEE, in contrast to Latin America, for instance, as CEE countries in general

experienced no massive and violent rebellions against the economic reforms, despite the deep economic recession, rapidly growing unemployment, and declining standards of living during the initial stages of the reform process. Also, despite the political turbulence and expanding opportunities for collective action, the magnitude of protest in Central Europe was lower than in the established democracies of Western Europe. Throughout the period under study these countries did not experience escalating protest activity that would constitute a significant threat to their newly established political institutions. While the employees of "losing" industries or sectors were often at the forefront of protest activities, as the Olsonian argument would predict, their organizations and leaders rarely challenged the legitimacy of the new sociopolitical order or the necessity of economic restructuring. (Greskovits 1998, 56)

The differences with Latin America have in fact been explained by the different forms of capitalism that developed in the two areas. In general, the socialist regime left societies less prone to rioting or other violent forms of collective action: "The lack of extreme income inequality, the smaller number of marginalized poor, the relatively lower degree of urbanization of the population, and the absence of recent, violent experiences with coups and riots may all have contributed a stabilizing influence under postcommunism" (ibid., 85). Additionally, "reformers in the East have not been in a hurry to eliminate the 'premature welfare states' left behind by communism. Indeed, from 1990 to 1993 social consumption increased as a share of GDP in several East European countries" (ibid., 85). Social pacts have consolidated relations between unions and governments, converging with increasing job insecurity and flight in the informal sector to explain low levels of strike activities. Especially, protest did not disappear. Rather, "in East Central Europe protest became one of the routine modes of interaction between the state and the society, a regular feature of many democratic regimes at the end of the twentieth century" (Ekiert and Kubic 1998).

Transition literature tends to predict a decline in mobilization in the street after democracy is achieved: electoral and party politics are expected to absorb the energies that were previously expressed in the streets. In terms of social movement studies, one could expect instead that the opening of conventional channels of political participation is rarely such that contention is unnecessary. In fact, we noticed that East Germany has not only experienced a revolution that was based on popular mobilization in the streets. After the fall of the Berlin Wall and after the reunification, people in East Germany also took to the street to express their concerns. In fact, former GDR citizens remained quite contentious. Although there was some obvious decline in protest participation immediately after transition, there were still mobilizations on several issues and in various forms. With regard to the volume of protest, there are in fact no striking differences between the East and the West during the period under examination. This harmonization of politics from below in both parts of the country is not what one would expect comparing the former GDR with other transforming countries of the former Soviet Bloc. We noted a similar trend in Czechoslovakia: protests did not disappear either in the cases of participated pacts or in troubled democratization processes.

As our within-Germany comparative analysis has shown, some differences can still be explained in terms of the declining phase of a cycle of protest, implying a mix of radicalization and moderation. As democracy (even reunification) is achieved, many citizens leave the streets and return to normal life. However, others are dissatisfied with the results and look for more radical means to put forward their claims. In the former GDR, the first half of the 1990s is in fact characterized by higher levels of violence than in its Western counterpart, especially in the forms of physical attacks against migrants, including arsons and murders. In the streets, radical Right activists clash with opponents on the Left and Punk youth, but also with the police, which tend to be more present during demonstrations by the radical Right, where we find also more arrests and injuries. While these actions, which follow a competitive mechanism of diffusion, usually involve very small numbers of perpetrators, they tend to dominate the protest picture in the media. In addition, these right-wing protests were met with counter-activities that, taken together, account for more than half of the protest events in this part of the country.

However, the economic and social crisis that followed the rapid transition to free market also produced other forms of action, following an emulative trend: primarily strikes but also more symbolic forms (already experimented with during transition) were used to denounce unemployment, the decline of social protections, and increases in the cost of living that privatization and austerity policies brought about.

In terms of claims, one could predict that in a declining phase of mobilization, those who remain active are the most politicized. In terms of transition studies, one might expect the radicals within both incumbent and opposition groups to attempt mobilization while the moderates negotiate. In the former GDR, politicization is indeed expressed in the dominance of conflicts between the radical Right, with its exclusive nationalism, and the left-wing anti-fascist demonstrations, both by smaller and more radical groups and by moderates. While protests in West Germany from 1989 to 2002 mirror the antecedent history of a normalization of contentious politics, with citizens organizing protests on a wide variety of issues, in the East, by contrast, migration issue dominates street politics. In times of economic stress, competitive claims in fact emerge, with calls for excluding migrants (in particular, refugees and asylum seekers) from restricting rights, but also protests against racism. At the same time, however, we see the emergence of more traditional forms of social and economic conflict, such as those opposing the decline of social rights and increasing unemployment, the privatization and closing down of factories, and the declining quality and increasing costs of everyday life.

This is also somewhat related to developments with regard to the social and political actors that mobilize in the street. Literature on democratization in general expects a weak civil society in new democracy, with lack of traditions in free social organizations and a tendency to privilege parties and institution building. Even when democratic promotion favors the creation of civil society organizations, these are noted to be quite elitist and professionalized, not oriented toward the use of protest as a form of advocacy (Beichelt and Merkel 2014; Hahn-Fuhr and Worschech 2014; Schimmelfenning 2014; Wolff 2014). In terms of social movement studies, we could indeed expect instead mobilizable resources to develop with expanding rights, rooted in the empowering experiences of mobilization. Indeed, in the German case, we noted that established actors such as churches, interest groups, and trade unions were among the main carriers of protest as a means to attract public attention in the western part of the country, while remaining less visible in the East. Much more than in the West, protest politics in the East have been dominated by the activity of the right-wing groupings, dangerous but quite small. However, there is also a quite rapid construction of organizational resources, especially, but not only, in union politics. If political opportunities initially tended to be quite closed for those calling for a different economic and social vision, it was the protests themselves that pushed for some changes in the social and economic policies.

3

"How Great That You Exist . . ."

Shifting Conceptions of Democracy

Two young people came into the church, that was in 1983 at the beginning of February; they looked so untypical, so a mo[hawk], spiky bracelets, much leather and metal, so to speak, the contrary of what was somehow allowed in the GDR. And I thought, "gee, what do they want here?" Went up to them, "so, friends, do you like our church?" "Great here, we could sing sometime." ". . . you want to sing? are you a band?" "Of course, we are the band Fit of Rage." I said, "That's a fresh name. Maybe I can hear what kind of music you make." And they gave me an address in our demolition area. . . . I went there: a completely ramshackle house, no doors, no windows: luckily the staircase was still holding up. They were under the roof, in three rooms, mattress from the trash, six guys. And when I came up, they said, in Saxon, "now we start." I was quite happy that there were no doors and windows. They had good equipment, you have to grant them. . . . when they stopped abruptly, after ten minutes, and I came back to consciousness, ten seconds later, they gave me a booklet written in pen: "our text booklet. We also have something against the pope and against the church, can we sing that too?"; I said, "guys, that doesn't make me exactly happy, but there is no censorship with us. If you think you need to sing this, then you just have to sing it; if you can do without, you probably have something else too. Then, the idea of Fit of Rage in the Nikolai church is also quite o.k. with me."

The state called with great concern: "Mister reverend, if you let them into your church, chaotic people will come from everywhere and beat your church to trash." I thanked them many times, for the care of the socialist state for the church, and said, "you have enough worries of your own, we'll take care of it ourselves." That evening approached, the youth chapel had never been that full: you could not even bend over, you stood tightly next to one another – you could only jump up to move. Then they started, and after a short time they all realized what they wanted: they wanted to draw a circle around themselves, and say "I don't let you strangle me with your blue cloth." . . . I thought, "gee, guys: how great

that you exist!" – that you have the courage and the talent for your own
lyrics and sounds; but it is just as great that the church exists, for that's
the only place where you can bring that into the public, otherwise you
can only whisper it into each other's ears at night in bed, and nobody
benefits from it. Everybody understood that: that the church was the
great opportunity to come together in order to discuss the hot issues, to
get counselled by others too. For instance, conscientious objection was
a big issue: officially that didn't exist in the GDR. And environmental
issues were of course all secret: the data was not available, a terribly
filthy and dirty and contaminated country ... they could only (gather) in
the church, so we had the absolute monopoly for freedom.

The next big thing was in 1986: this company of twenty people came up to
me, it was after the Wednesday service, they said, "Mister reverend, we filed
a demand to emigrate; do something for us." I set up a group for people
wanting to emigrate and then we came into the central crosshairs of
the GDR observation, because each one willing to emigrate was, so to
speak, the incarnate critique of the state, and they now also found refuge
with us in the Nikolai church. ... One didn't know how many, but there
were a hundred thousand in the country. Everyone had heard of someone
and everyone knew someone in his family or among his friends and so on.
They brought the mass base, and here in particular one thing should be
mentioned: in 1988, that circle kept growing continuously, ... they sat on
packed suitcases full of despair, without knowing what their fate would be.
I said then, people, listen, if you sit on your packed suitcases and get ever
more depressed and you really come to the West and arrive that feeble and
can't cope with that free society ... and then not fifty came, but six hundred.
That was on February 19, 1989, and this evening had an incredible effect
in the long run. First, the people felt comfortable and safe in the church.
At the exit, they said, "Mister reverend, we are not members of the church,
but can we too attend your peace prayers?" and I said, "outside it's written,
Nikolai Kirche open for all, that goes of course for you too."

This February 19, 1989 was a Friday, and as of the following Monday, ever
more people came from this gigantic pool of those willing to emigrate. They
experienced the peace prayers as the contrary to how they were treated by the
state, like a piece of dirt ... come ... here you could bear witness to being
affected, you could say what depressed you, what you have difficulties with
right now, and you could also talk about one's lack of resort or hopelessness:
one could simply bring that out. What depressed you most: those were
elements that were so important for the people that it became known, and
ever more people now came to Leipzig to the peace prayers and now we had
this group, it brought the mass potential, and the critical grassroots group of
people, they were so to speak the intellectual head. ... They had power but
were few, really few, and the others: they were many. Both now, as a critical
mass under the roof of the Nikolai church, and then the affair peaked.
(GDR7)

As this long excerpt from an interview with a pastor of the Nikolai Kirche in Leipzig so well illustrates, experiences of democracy developed during mobilization. It shows, first of all, that democracy, conceived as dialogue, happens (also or mainly) outside of the official political institutions. Even in authoritarian regimes, free spaces are often carved out where normal citizens can meet and talk about the public good. These spaces have an important function in socializing the individuals within the community, as participatory and deliberative visions are framed in action. As we will discuss in what follows, the frames of democracy, conceived in action, were then consolidated, emerging at odds with the institutional forms that were implemented after transitions.

In this chapter, I will in fact focus on a specific cognitive aspect, conceptions of democracy – as they were theorized by the opposition, but also how they were practiced during the struggle for democracy, especially in cases of eventful democratization where political opportunities for the prefiguration of different forms of democracy were created in action. This brought about resources for further mobilization, but also disappointment with the representative democracy that developed at the institutional level during consolidation. In what follows, I will first review general conceptions of democracy and then focus on the characteristics of the oppositional conceptions, as elaborated in the theoretical visions of some of the movements' leaders, but even more during the mobilization for democracy. I shall then discuss the strengths and limitations of these conceptions and practices in order to address regime change, considering perceptions and memories of former activists.

CONCEPTUALIZING DEMOCRACY: AN INTRODUCTION

The conception of democracy developed during the oppositional period certainly had an effect on post-transition. But a positive or a negative one? As we will see, especially within democratization studies, the idea is widespread that a stress on "democracy from below," or an "ethical civil society," can jeopardize the development of a political society and a "normal" democracy. Vice versa, social movement studies would suggest that the presence of multiple conceptions enriches democracy, allowing not only for the control of the elected representatives but also for the socialization of the citizens and the development of innovations toward a participatory and deliberative vision (della Porta 2013a).

In normative theory, two main democratic dimensions have been discussed: one refers to delegation versus participation, and the other to decision making through (majority) voting or (broad) consensus. On the first dimension, the challenge for liberal conceptions that stress delegation is the recognition of participation as an integral part of democracy; on the second dimension, the main challenge refers to the construction of political identities endogenously (rather than exogenously) to the democratic process.

First of all, while the ideal of democracy as government of, by, and for the people locates the source of all power in the citizenry at large, *representative* institutions drastically restrict the number of decision makers. Electoral accountability is considered to give legitimacy to the process, by allocating to the citizen-electors the power to periodically assess those in government. Considering electoral accountability as an insufficient means, participatory theorists of democracy have instead stressed the need to create multiple opportunities for participation (Arnstein 1969; Pateman 1970). Elections are not only considered as too rare to grant citizens control of the elected but they moreover offer only limited choices by leaving several themes out of the electoral debate. What is more, elections are more and more manipulated, given the capacity of some candidates to attract licit or illicit financing or to command privileged access to mass media. A multiplication of channels of participation is instead praised as capable of creating schools of democracy and, with them, better citizens. In this perspective, social movements are considered as guardians of democracy, by improving permanent accountability of the delegates in a "counterdemocracy" in which surveillance happens from below (Rosanvallon 2006). Legitimacy derives therefore from the possibility for the citizens to participate in multiple ways in the decision-making process, bringing in their demands and knowledge (della Porta 2013a).

Together with delegation, the value and legitimacy of the majoritarian decision making that dominates formal democratic institutions have also been contested. A "minimalist" view of democracy as the power of the majority has been considered as risky, not only in terms of jeopardizing the rights of the minorities but also in reducing the quality of decision making. As there is no reason to attribute superior wisdom to preferences that are (simply) more numerous, other decision-making principles are needed to temper at least the majoritarian one. In normative debates, deliberative theorists have in fact promoted open spaces for the exchange of arguments, the construction of shared definitions of the public good, and therefore a legitimation of public decisions (among others, Dryzek 2000; Cohen 1989; Elster 1998; Habermas 1981, 1996). By relating with each other – recognizing the others and being recognized by them – citizens should be able to understand the reasons of the others, and to assess them against emerging standards of fairness. Communication would thus allow for the development of better solutions, by increasing pluralism of knowledge and expertise; what is more, it would help in transforming the perception of one's own preferences, making participants less concerned with individual, material interests and more with collective goods.

Participation and deliberation are in fact democratic qualities in tension with qualities of representation and majority decisions, and together with those, in various precarious equilibria in the varied conceptions and institutional practices of democracy. In social movements, qualities of participation and deliberation have also been combined in what I have defined as a participatory–deliberative model of democracy, including the following elements (della Porta 2009a, 2009b, 2013a):

(a) *Preference (trans)formation*, through interaction (Dryzek 2000, 79)
(b) *Orientation to the public good*, as moving citizens' interests and identities toward the construction of public goods (Cohen 1989, 18–19)
(c) *Rational argumentations*, based on the force of the better argument (Habermas 1981, 1996)
(d) *Consensus*, in different degrees, as decisions should be approvable by all participants
(e) *Equality*, as involving "free deliberation among equals" (Cohen 1989, 20)
(f) *Inclusiveness*, as giving voice to all those who have a stake in the decision
(g) *Transparency*, as deliberative democracy is seen as "an association whose affairs are governed by the public deliberation of its members" (Cohen 1989, 17).

These seven elements might be distinguished in terms of conditions, means, and effects: we have participatory–deliberative democracy when, under conditions of equality, inclusiveness, and transparency, a communicative process based on reason (the strength of the better argument) is able to transform individual preferences and reach decisions oriented to the public good (della Porta 2009a). With different nuances and balances, all of these elements have been addressed in various social movements, including those for global justice (della Porta 2009a, 2009b; della Porta and Rucht 2013) and extending to the ones against austerity in various parts of the world (della Porta 2015).

As we will see in what follows, in Central Eastern Europe (CEE), as well, oppositional thinkers had indeed developed conceptions of democracy, linked to those on civil society, that stressed participation and consensus. These democratic qualities had been learned throughout the mobilization for democracy, remaining particularly rooted in those countries in which there had been an eventful path to transition (but less where there was a participated pact). As frames of democracy, constructed in action, did consolidate, they constituted benchmark values against which the practices of representative democracy had been assessed and, often, criticized. As we will note, however, differences in the assessments of current and desired situations existed, related to the degree of fit/misfit between conceptions of democracy in the opposition to the authoritarian regime and institutionalized forms of democracy after transition.

THE OPPOSITIONAL CONCEPTION OF DEMOCRACY

Existing research on the ideological construction of democracy has pointed at some peculiarity in the oppositional vision in CEE countries, often characterized as "anti-political," horizontal, ethical, and the like. However, this type of definition fits some countries better than it does others, with a clear distinction – once again – between cases of eventful democratization and cases of participated pacts. In fact, eventful democratization allowed for more participatory and consensual conceptions to spread, especially where experiences of mobilization from below were stronger, with effects on the next steps of the democratization process. This was less the case in participated pacts, where alternative democratic practices had not had the time to develop or had been repressed long before.

Some social science research on conceptions of democracy in CEE has focused on theorizations of democracy among the leaders of the opposition. The most influential among them was the leader of Charta 77 and future president of Czechoslovakia and then the Czech Republic, Václav Havel. His reflection developed around the concept of an "anti-political politics," which he defined "not as the technology of power and manipulation, of cybernetic rule over humans or as the art of the utilitarian, but politics as one of the ways of seeking and achieving meaningful lives, of protecting them and serving them" (cit. in Renwick 2006, 289). Havel thus rejected power as manipulation, stating that the phenomenon of dissent grows out of an essentially different conception of the meaning of politics than that prevailing in the world today. That is, the dissident does not operate in the realm of genuine power at all. He does not seek power. He has no desire for office and does not woo voters. He does not attempt to charm the public; he offers nothing and promises nothing. He can offer, if anything, only his own skin – and he offers it solely because he has no other way of affirming the truth he stands for. His actions simply articulate his dignity as a citizen, regardless of the cost. (cit. in Renwick 2006, 289)

Stressing the importance of politics as recognition of human dignity, Havel in fact supported a participatory vision of democracy. In his famous speech to the Czech Parliament on December 9, 1997, he presented civil society as

characterized by a systematic opening of a room for a most diverse self-structuring, and for the broadest possible participation in public life. This kind of civil society brings with it, essentially, a twofold impact: firstly, it allows a human being to develop all of the facets of human personality, including that which makes a person a social animal, desirous of taking part in the life of his or her community; secondly, it constitutes a true guarantee of political stability. (cit. in Myant 2005)

A participatory view of democracy goes together with a preference for devolution of decisions to the civil society, following visions of self-government. So Havel supported "the progressive creation of the space for a diversified civil society in which the central government will perform only those functions which nobody else can perform, or which nobody else can perform better" (Myant 2005, 248). Similarly, dissident Václav Benda promoted the development of a "parallel polis," as creation of

parallel structures that are capable, to a limited degree at least, of supplementing the generally beneficial and necessary functions that are missing in the existing [state] structures. Such structures would follow the model of the "parallel culture" – notably pop culture – that already existed in Czechoslovakia. They would encompass a parallel education system, parallel information networks, parallel political discussion fora, and a parallel economy. (cit. in Baker 1999, 4)

The deliberative value of dialogue and consensus building is also embedded in the conception of politics as a search for truth, bridged with respect for the other. The moral emphasis of this conceptualization of political participation has been very much stressed as, in Havel's definition, "politics outside politics" is ethical and existential (Flam 2001). Against a politics pursuing specific interests, Havel in fact promoted an ethical civil society – so, for instance, in his first New Year's Address as president, he stated: "It is not really important now which party, club, or group will prevail in the elections. The important thing is that the winners will be the best of us, in the moral, civic, political, and professional sense, regardless of their political affiliations" (cit. in Renwick 2006, 304). Among the promoted values are in fact solidarity, tolerance, compassion, humility, and respect for one another. As dissidents linked the importance of possessing the truth about oneself to dignity and morality, stressing the value of an authentic life of sacrifice, their frames were said to resonate with new social movements' criticism of political power as oppressive and their appeals to moral resistance as a duty against the state's interference in everyday life (ibid.).

In this vision, against the routinized, bureaucratic institutions of Western democracy, expected to become corrupted by power struggles, Havel defended the idea of a community, based on participation of its members and moral human relations, built from below. "There is no real evidence," he wrote, "that western democracy ... can offer solutions that are any more profound [than those of communism]. ... It would appear that the traditional parliamentary democracies can offer no fundamental opposition to the automatism of technological civilization and the industrial-consumer society" (cit. in Renwick 2006, 308). Emphasis on self-determination goes together with a criticism of representative democracy as, dissident Konrad observed,

workplace and local community self-government, based on personal contact, exercised daily, and always subject to correction, have greater attraction in our part of the world than multi party representative democracy because, if they have their choice, people are not content with voting once every four years. ... When there is parliamentary democracy but no self-administration, the political class alone occupies the stage." (cit. in Baker 1999, 4–5)

This conception of politics as a search for truth is often contrasted with the idea, more widespread in Poland, of the opposition as a pressure group with the aim of exercising influence on the regime in order to obtain reforms. In fact, Solidarity presented itself as a trade union pressuring the state from outside, with support for a conception of politics as based on a plurality of interests (Renwick 2006). Here, after 1989, nonparticipatory elements came to dominate as, after transition, the political participation of groups of citizens was "banned under the liberal theory of democracy except for political parties, which ought to mediate between the state and the individual citizen, theoretically conceptualized as having been atomized." In the struggle for power within the Solidarity milieu that followed (but in part also preceded) the transition, parties in parliament in fact converged in their attempts at limiting civil society groups' access to power by introducing rules to safeguard the predominance of the parties. Similarly in Hungary, "the political oppositionists were consequentialist and spoke of pursuing particular goals, including group-specific interests" (Renwick 2006, 313).

After the regime change, the oppositional visions of civil society as fundamental actors of democracy were then contrasted by the conceptions of democracy promoted by the institutions. The cleavage between communitarian views and interest views of politics is synthetized in the debate in the Czech Republic between Prime Minister Václav Klaus and President Václav Havel. In the words of one of the founders of the student organization STUHA (Studentské hnutí – Student Ribbon), what was mainly at stake was the moral dimension of the conceptions of democracy, as

the most important and crucial thing that failed ... was moral cleansing. And the Velvet Revolution was ethically loaded, so it was not just about getting rid of communists, but it concerned moral cleansing as well. That means: return to the truth, because the previous regime was based on lies: people lied in the schools, we lied to our children, parents lied to their children because they were afraid that their children might say something. Lying was a modus operandi. The Communist party lied to almost everyone and they even lied to themselves, quite often. So it was: back to truth, I mean to truthfulness, morals. ... And these ethical aspects have been lost in the clash of conceptions, which can be in a simplified way described as a clash between Havel and Klaus – that means between ethics and economics – and ethics lost. (CZ4)

Promoting a neoliberal conceptualization of civil society, Klaus suggested in fact an individualistic value system, rejecting "Havel's sense that citizenship requires a collective conscience – a commitment to the larger society and its well-being." Therefore, Klaus' argument was that

the market would be the harbinger of citizenship – property and profit energize and enable people to care and participate in the public political sphere. These views, much as John Locke envisioned, mean democracy and free market are inseparable, and no non-profit, non-governmental sector is needed to mediate between the state and citizens. Individual interests, pursued via profit and the market, are (to Klaus) the best guide for citizenship. (Nelson 1996, 350)

In this way, Klaus "tried to build a united political party around a narrow base of social interests. Those using the term civil society appeared to him as opponents of his project and he subjected their views to powerful polemical attack" (Myant 2005, 248). Supporting the classic form of representing public opinions through elections, the expectation was that autonomous civic society associations should develop without any state support, as "societal interests are best expressed through periodic elections, for groups distort information about what society truly wants" (Green 1999, 219).

Also after democratization, Dryzek and Holmes' (2000) research on CEE noted the presence of various discourses on democracy, with surviving cross-country differences. In the Czech Republic, while "civic enthusiasts" believed in democracy as the only guarantee for freedom, human rights, and the rule of law, "disaffected egalitarians" did not believe that true democracy exists, given the widening social inequality:

> Yes, we have more "freedom," but only those who have money and power can rule. ... An ordinary citizen cannot effectively exercise his rights, because he is struggling for economic existence, does not know how to influence politics, and thinks it is useless anyway. ... Politics is full of careerist and corrupted politicians who do not give a damn about ordinary people. ... We need more participation of all people in direct democracy. (Ibid., 1059)

In Poland, democracy was instead mainly identified with election and parties, even if a discourse of civic republicanism survived, with a conception of democracy as not identified with the majority rule or political power, but open to all citizens (ibid.).

In sum, conceptions of democracy emerged as framed in action, with the development of participatory and deliberative visions, especially in cases of eventful democratization.

PROTEST AS SCHOOL OF DEMOCRACY

> They relearned self-confidence in the church, at the microphone of affectedness. You know if you get up from your safe bench and walk up to the reading desk, church full up to the roof, and you stand there on your own, and you are not used to standing in front of so many people to speak and you did have the courage to say what you had to say: that gave such self-confidence. We then lit candles during the prayer, and said, "Whoever wants to light a candle for something or someone can come up, but doesn't have to say anything." So anyone who was shy just put a candle down and that was so wonderful. (GDR7)

Thus, a German pastor described participation in the peace prayers as acts of protest, but also as an open space for learning to communicate with others. While the conceptions of participatory and deliberative democracy theorized by the opposition thinkers were certainly influential, norms and beliefs about democratic qualities emerged at least as much from action as from reading. In fact, when talking about their conceptions of democracy, our interviewees refer especially to direct experiences with mobilizing. In general, lacking other experiences, the very activities in the oppositional civil society organizations mobilizing within the authoritarian regime provided rare occasions for individual socialization. In action, participants framed participatory and deliberative visions, with an emphasis on direct experience within civil society as educating to a specific conception of politics and the public good.

Especially some forms of protest during the authoritarian regime contributed not only to overcoming fear but also to spreading awareness of citizens' skills and rights to take part in public decision making. Conceived as spaces for debate among equal participants, oppositional groups adhered to an ideal of an open discourse, free from domination (Preuss 1995, 108). In fact, they built upon a moral opposition to the vanguard politics associated with communism (Goodwin 2001, 277). The preference for grassroots democracy was fueled by the direct experience of opposition to the authoritarian regime. Horizontality was in symbolic contrast to the verticality of the regime, as "voices are horizontal because they offer an alternative to 'vertical voice,' that is, to the communication of petition and command that dictatorships prefer. ... the aspiration to reject the system's opacity, to be public and transparent, was powerful" (Di Palma 1991, 71). As we will see, deliberation and participation were embedded in the practices of many of these groups.

First of all, participation was seen as a way (if not the only way) to empower the citizens. Oppositional groups stressed horizontality to express their refusal of power – in the words of a German activist, "the opposite force to power is a grass-roots movement" (Poppe 1995, 261). A socialization process to alternative values of participation unfolded within the informal oppositional groups, which were indeed "a training field for social relations. Peaceful attitudes, tolerance and solidarity can be practiced in the groups" (Fehr 1995, 315). In an original conception of civil society, informal "micro-groups" allowed for the spreading of a "horizontal and oblique voice," with "the development of semantically coded critical communication" (Di Palma 1991, 71). One of the leaders of New Forum thus declared, "We do not want to make the mistake of ... trying to lead other people, when we know quite well that we do not have the solution ... it is important to analyse the situation together ... that's a path from below to above, in contrast to what otherwise happens in parties" (Pfaff 2006, 96). In the words of a member of Peace Circle, participation in these types of initiatives is conceived as taking responsibility rather than seizing power: "we want to exert influence on society, we want to take on political responsibility . . . not with the objective . . . to gain power but to simply assume responsibility, to participate" (GDR8).

Groups within which democracy was experienced tended to be informal, characterized by "a very low degree of organization: no real membership but you joined in and then you were there" (GDR2). As social movement organizers imagined "a fully open citizen movement in the grey zone of legality in the SED state," they "did without formal membership" (Olivo 2001, 94). Not by chance, at its founding conference, New Forum adopted non-centralized but rather grassroots structures – as an activist declared, "there should be no group of elites; there should be no circle of specialists who instruct the rest of the population on what should be done" (Pfaff 2006, 198). The role of personal network is also stressed, as "A lot happened in groups of friends who were active in a variety of circles, and a lot of things were done together besides the political. One did not sit in darkened cellars and promote 'the revolution'; we laughed and partied together. Many people shared apartments" (Pfaff 2006, 94).

Deliberation was strongly emphasized as a democratic value and practice. This is particularly visible in the German Democratic Republic (GDR) in the peace prayers that, with their emphasis on good communication, stimulated participants to think and talk about various topics. Initially addressing issues of peace, over time the range of the topics expanded to war and military service to "education, alternative pedagogical concepts, . . . or same sex groups . . . human rights as well" (GDR11). This broadening was facilitated by the way in which the prayers were organized; as a human rights activist and pastor noted,

each single group always alternated with doing a peace prayer, and through that the different groups of course then also learned from each other . . . for me it was important that in this work you are *learning democracy to begin with*, how you deal with one another, . . . and that no one group works covertly, and no one is the dictator, but to the contrary in what you want to do, you have to learn: to learn while doing it. (GDR11, emphasis added)

In the memory of the pastor who coordinated these activities, participants learned to feel responsible, and to "to take responsibility in public for all you are doing." In these occasions in the churches, open also to nonbelievers, high-quality communication oriented to the public good was indeed actively promoted.

Attention to democracy as dialogue allowed for networking in action, through the encounter of different social and political actors.

Particularly telling is the narration of the encounter, in the GDR, between pastors and young people, considered as disruptive elements by the socialist apparatus. So a pastor recalled it, stressing the opening to reciprocal learning:

an important point was a crucifix meditation with teenagers. ... I was totally surprised: it started at ten p.m.; I thought, well if ten, fifteen people come. ... It was 130 people. Unusual hairstyles, unusual clothes; ... the state was scared of them and called them "elements"; so, 130 elements in the altar room of our church ... and the teenagers took a seat; the entire altar room was full with 130, up to the altar, and the "elements" filled up the space. I put a basket of candles next to the crucifix and said, "now, people, let's see who wants to say something about it, Christians can include a prayer, non-Christians just say it." And then the big surprise came: they all did it, and it became an endless process ... not a proposition written down from a book but firsthand: what freedom means; here you can speak, say what you think, and ... That never became boring, they all really had something to say, ... With every candle that was put on it, the sight of the crucifix changed from this brutal wooden crucifix into a crucifix of light; like the resurrection overcomes the crucifixion: a wonderful sight. When we were finished, it was long after midnight. There was this incredible atmosphere of freedom that was tangible, and the young people sat there, like it had always been their place ... for Jesus lived for those who were pushed to the margins, the dulled and the silenced, the people who couldn't talk or weren't allowed to, or from whom the right was taken to assume a respected position in society... many of them had never seen a church from the inside, and that didn't matter at all. (GDR7)

It was thanks to this openness that some churches became free spaces even for nonbelievers, as they "got an incredible attraction, as a place of free speech, of exchange about taboo topics, that you are not reprimanded here, that you cannot be punished here, that you are not somehow limited here, but you can let out what's on your mind, and then it can be talked about and we then look for answers from the bible" (GDR7).

Transparency was also a main value in the opposition, allowing for broadening informal participation. The idea of publicity, pluralism, citizens' and human rights, autonomy, self-organization of society, and tolerance gained relevance in opposition to a monocentric and hierarchical structure of power. The strategy evolved to openly developing collective action, in public (Fehr 1995). In fact, "In their activities, the groups tried, differently than in the 1970s, to stay open and visible, to all" (Poppe 1995, 257). Transparency was in fact a rooted value against the shortcomings of a clandestine opposition.

The values of consensus building and good communication were broadly stressed, against the idea of politics as power, spread by the authoritarian regime. The visions activists defended were therefore oriented to "talking about different ways of life, about lesbian and gay relationships, about breaking away from two-person-relationships, it was about education ... the primary focus was not 'we want free elections' or something like that" (GDR1). The liberalization and then transition phases thus "broadened the political spectrum" through "the possibility to get in touch and to learn that elsewhere there were others" (GDR1). Horizontal visions were facilitated by the fact that the groups in the opposition were kept small by repression: as an activist synthetized, groups involved "many sympathizers, few members" (GDR9).

Later on, it was especially during the exceptional moments of the transition that spaces for learning democracy opened up. This was particularly intense in the GDR where, from late 1989 to mid-1990, an unexpected institutional vacuum opened, in particular during the new government led by reformist leader of the regime SED party Hans Modrow. Given the weakness of state institutions as well as a widespread sense of uncertainty, with the regime party having lost power and the parliament lacking legitimacy, "the entire administrative and judiciary apparatus from the national to the local level was in a state of confusion and disarray" (Rucht 1996, 40). It was then that citizens' committees started to participate in roundtables and local and national parliaments.

In this situation, the experience of the roundtables was particularly important. Their aim was in fact presented as empowerment of the people, rather than a move toward taking power, proposing a vision of citizens' democracy as horizontal, among equal partners, oriented to consensus. Perceived as alternative to parliamentarianism, roundtables reflected moreover a mistrust in central structures and delegated democracy, and a preference instead for informal groups as well as a strong moral discourse (Haufe and Bruckmeier 1993). Also important were the *Burgerkomitees*, conceived to represent the political will of the people, creating a public sphere through consensus building (Haufe and Bruckmeier 1993). Formed by citizens who occupied public buildings, they were "forums for direct democratic participation in public matters" (Preuss 1995, 112), oriented at fostering a plurality of ideas.

In and around the roundtables and citizens' committees, a conception of consensual democracy was nurtured, with praise for the capacity to produce open discussion rather than voting on preexisting positions. As a German gender rights activist explained, while in "normal politics," the basic denunciation of the political opponent always played a role, that was not the case at the round table. It could not have been the case either, since it could happen that, on the next item on the agenda, you had to form quite different alliances ... or wanting to form them, which is hardly possible if you consider the other as politically off or something like fundamentally devalued, as is unavoidable in a party system – that makes reciprocal understanding difficult to develop. (GDR1)

In these experiences, transparency in fact goes together with openness, understood in terms of the capacity to change one's own opinion by listening to others. In the roundtables, which worked as sort of ad interim governments, in fact, "the majorities were not set from the beginning and also the decision about certain questions was not predictable, simply because people had to come to an agreement with each other, and ever changing majorities were being formed" (GDR1).

Similarly, the reformed Volkskammer, the GDR parliament in which representatives of the opposition were co-opted, was praised as an open space, facilitating deliberation. One of its members remembered the experience as "incredibly lively" and "vital" and contrasted it with the rigidity of the federal parliament of the unified Germany, in which he was later elected:

we were twenty people, but a nice composition ... The media wrote that we were amateurs in the Volkskammer, that we didn't master that democratic vocabulary or the technique, and it was like that, but on the other hand it was incredibly lively. It happened so much differently than in the Bundestag where everything is prepared for a long time, first maybe in a small circle, then in the parliamentary parties, then later in the parliament, and then there were also the committee sessions and then it went back to the parliament and so on: that was all completely different in the Volkskammer: the committees hardly played a role ... the plenum sometimes lasted twelve to sixteen hours until late into the evening, and then simply through motions for the rules of procedure still other points could be put on the agenda which were initially not planned at all. There was changing vote, ... which you have very rarely in the Bundestag.... The whole thing was perhaps all a little bit chaotic but it was a piece of vital democracy after a forty-year phase of one party rule and undemocratic procedures. I believe that really had a sustained effect. (GDR12)

Openness was also valued in terms of participation of citizens as equals. The roundtables were perceived as experiments with alternative forms of decision making, open (and visible) to all. Filling the space left empty given the declining power of the regime meant the development of new expectations among the citizens about what democracy is. Political decisions had, first of all, to become really public. As a former dissident explained, the great experience with the round table for the population was that for the first time politics was negotiated openly, and the media filmed everything. Then, it was possible: the entire population could witness how there were arguments about the pathway into democracy and that was of course something completely new. The round table got many, many letters with conceptual proposals and so on. (GDR2)

The civilizing power of publicity (Elster 1997) is explicitly proclaimed, as the fact that the sessions of the main roundtable were broadcast on television "had at least at the time an incredibly disciplinary effect because people then said, why are you fighting . . . one really debated on a rational level in a way that I later didn't experience anymore in politics to that extent" (GDR1).

Several interviewees emphasized the importance of devising democratic formulas that could be legitimated in the process, given the immediate needs of the transition period. As the Volkskammer "was practically paralyzed" and "the round table thus should make decisions which we could not fully grasp, also economic decisions and such," it was all the more important to single out procedures people could accept as just. In fact, there was the perception that the discursive quality of the process had important legitimizing effects. As one of the founders of Women for Peace noted:

the credibility of the decisions at the round table or the acceptance of the round table decisions in the population depended significantly on how we debated and how we were able to pick up what the population wanted and direct it into orderly trajectories, and in all of that a priority for us was to avoid violence. So the acceptance came through transparency of decision making, through the credibility of the people sitting at the round table. (GDR2)

During the phase of the transition, the gap in power pushed citizens to enrich their capacity to participate in public discussion and even in the management of common goods, developing a sense of a community and acting upon it. In the narration of a member of the opposition, a participatory afflatus grew among the population, in large cities as well as in the countryside, where citizens' initiatives were built in order to work as a "counterpart to the lacking city parliament." In many places, in fact, a German environmentalist noted,

the mayor had stepped down then, with all of his other figures as well . . . via the round table, people were named to take on these functions, and there we also tried again to realize a certain co-operation. We as the citizens' committee got offices in the new city hall, telephones and office space, we could introduce visiting times. We published this telephone number and then the citizens also came. (GDR6)

Therefore, given the intensity of the short moment of the transition, participation fed further participation, through a sense of empowerment. In the GDR, a member of the opposition defined as "a fundamental need that you as a citizen want to have a say about and to co-determine the things which interest you, affect you" (GDR10). The impression is recalled of a spontaneous but steady increase in the citizens' availability to participate in decisions that affected them. In the few months of the transitional phase, "it happened in a fantastic way, without anybody organizing it, simply out of the atmosphere. From the villages to the cities and the counties, in the regions, up to Berlin, round tables were constituted addressing different fields: the health care system, economic issues, all fields which were worthy of discussion at the time" (GDR10). Through participation, many people invested their own specific commitment and knowledge in the search for solutions to common problems. This showed that, according to a founder of the New Forum,

the people had some expertise: those who were interested in it sat together, and thought about it, how they had an influence and could change something, how you could improve the situation. There were incredibly many people ... practically coming out of nowhere ... and you started to think very concretely about what you should change in what ways. That was fantastic: so much was being debated there ... so many ideas were brought to the fore like never before and also never after. (GDR10)

Common knowledge was, thus, produced and reproduced.

As in the GDR, in Czechoslovakia, as well, during eventful democratization the organization of oppositional activities went hand in hand with the experimentation with various democratic practices, even though a much shorter transition time, and no visible power vacuum, reduced the space for experimentation. As explained by one of our interviewees, a member of Charta 77, socialization to democracy was, there as well, conceived as an exchange of opinions – in his words, "we learnt democracy, and I'm very glad for the period when I was at Charta ... we learnt to communicate with people of different opinions. ... Democracy is a dialogue, democracy is the art of accepting the difference of the other. ... It is positive, looking for the way with someone who thinks differently than I do" (CZ2). In this vision, participation was praised for giving normal citizens the possibility of taking responsibility (CZ11).

The situation was at least partially different in the recollections by activists who had lived through pacted transitions, where intense phases of collective mobilization or (perceived at least) self-government had not been experimented with in the years around 1989.

The need for learning democracy through mobilization is stressed by some Polish activists, although they also emphasized the brisk interruption of civil society development during transition. The experience with democracy in the heat of mobilization is here located in 1980–1981. As a former activist, publisher of an underground journal, recalled: "During the first Solidarność we had discussions on what democracy is and there was a learning process: we were learning what compromise is and how to transfer ideas into action" (PL1). Debates on democracy developed, here as well, in action: "within underground journals and magazines, flying universities, endless meetings to a larger extent than later when changes took place. . . . There was a discussion about different visions of the society" (PL6). In cases of participated pacts, however, there is a widespread perception that "afterwards, it all ended up unfortunately" (PL6). What is perceived as a main achievement of the civil society is, in fact, action per se – "For sure this simple activity of the people" (PL10), "that we showed that we are capable of self-organizing" (PL8). As one of its first activists stressed, the first Solidarity is indeed presented as having allowed for "taking responsibility as a citizen" (PL8). The interviewees identified the "biggest thing of this movement" in the fact that "it actually became the civil society for the first time in the history of Poland after the war, actually after 1939" (PL8). In 1980–1981, the presence of a common enemy seemed in fact to have increased the sense of identification and group belonging:

the enemy was clear, it was the reds and their allies. . . . Ten million people signed the declaration to become members of the union . . . it shows that in such situations people are trying to be good together, and that they are trying to organize themselves to be good together . . . those feelings of the group and a unity amongst us: that was completely amazing in the relations between the people. (PL8)

Here as well, conceptions of self-governance were indeed embedded in the repressive atmosphere; as a publisher of samizdat during the martial law recalled, "its goal was to achieve these changes within the system. And in the long run it will lead to the overthrow of the system, but the main goal was to democratize the remaining within its boundaries" (PL11). Democracy was also understood as a peaceful way of addressing conflicts. In this sense, an activist who had participated in the 1980–1981 protest noted,

Solidarność between 1980 and 1989 was . . . teaching the people what democracy was supposed to be, theoretically, and how to struggle for democracy through peaceful means; it never told people how to overthrow power by force. When it was talking about demonstrations, these were peaceful demonstrations. Demonstrations were not supposed to burn buildings down. If it was talking about producing something, it was talking about producing books and pamphlets and not producing bombs or grenades or bottles with fuel. ... And it was petitioning that a piece of paper that is printed with words that speak the truth is more efficient than bombs or Molotov cocktails. (PL8)

If democracy was therefore experienced in action in Poland as well, this happened in the beginning rather than at the end of the decade. While in fact an activist who had participated in the mobilization presented 1980 as the year of "the biggest explosion of social activism" (PL12), in 1989 the negotiations are instead perceived, by those who had lived the martial law, as deriving not from the strength of the movement but rather from a double weakness, as "the roundtable negotiations were the result of the weakness of the authorities. ... And the strike of 1988 was very weak and the roundtable negotiations took place because the authorities were even weaker then ... there was also no social energy" (PL11). The strong repression during the martial law was seen as having thwarted any further democratic learning. As a former activist of the first Solidarity in the 1980s explained,

it's hard to have discussion when democracy is pushed into the underground. ... Underground resistance kills democracy ... the tradition of the sixteen months of democracy. ... It is also a huge virtue and this is transferred into the underground. But could you really discuss such issues as democracy when you're in prison? Can you think about it in the categories of the future of the state, in a prison cell? Not really. (PL3)

Those experiences of repression indeed summed up with other historical memories in developing some skepticism toward mobilization and a preference for negotiation instead. In an activist's recollection,

this is something in you and in the whole history of Poland because we had uprisings; we usually lost all these uprisings. And here the lesson of history has reached a young generation ... they had the consciousness that the Warsaw uprising [in 1944] was spectacular, but that it ended with a disaster, and that actually almost every uprising, armed uprising, ends with a disaster (PL3).

In Hungary, as well, interviewees' accounts have pointed at experiences within protest campaigns under dictatorship as moments of learning democracy, as socialization to politics happened before, during, and after democratization, particularly around the opposition to the dam to be built on the Danube. Within a horizontal conception, the workers' council, based on traditions of 1956, was in fact revitalized as an organizational model. So, in the memories of an activist member of the oppositional Alliance of Free Democrats (SZDSZ),

these civil society movements were structurally, as well as in terms of their programs, methods, conduct, and mentality autonomist and sovereignty oriented, with the characteristics of participatory democracy ... strongly anti-hierarchic. Obviously, since it was all in the context of a dictatorship, they would have to be, but these movements were very strongly anti-hierarchic in nature, regardless of their objectives ... there were a million movements like these, all of them pluralist, anti-hierarchic, and democratic, emphasizing popular participation, and it had a drive towards some sort of participatory model. (HU5)

So, also in Hungary, the perception was of a demobilization before transition. In fact, "Up until 1988, there were some remnants of the new left in these notions, there were more participatory elements ... it was present at least in the slogans of civil society if not in its realities. This democracy would be more plebiscitary and participatory had those notions remained" (HU5).

But here, as in Poland, the search and justification for compromise through formal negotiations were stressed as characterizing 1989 much more than experiences with horizontal forms of democracy did. As a former dissident recalled, more traditional forms of parliamentary democracy tended to dominate, as "in the democratic opposition we had a consensus on the duplicity expressed by Michnik, of what we wanted and what was possible ... that we should distinguish between the things we would imagine to be optimal and those that can be subject to negotiations" (HU1).

So, the belief is expressed that, while under authoritarian regimes, "There was no other way, but to protest," later on "in the context of a democratic system, you can have parties in the opposition, and you have an institutionalized form of political debate, and you don't have to resort to protest and demonstration, or not as a primary means of expression" (HU10).

These differences between cases of eventful democratization and cases of participated pacts, as we will see in the next part, had an effect on activists' assessments of the representative institutions that democratization brought about.

OUR DEMOCRACY, YOUR DEMOCRACY

Although it is labeled democracy, it has virtually nothing to do with the will of the people ... a small club governs in the parliaments – just as few people as those making decisions in the GDR, under the dictatorship. You cannot get into that from the outside, and the decision making is in the hands of very few people. (GDR10)

In comparison to participatory and deliberative conceptions of democracy, the liberal democracy, in a neoliberal version, appeared as unsatisfactory to many of those – like the just-cited founder of the German New Forum – who had fought against the authoritarian regime. As Eastern Europe's new elite agreed in 1989 on a minimalist definition of "democracy," given that "the international bodies they wanted to join insisted on it as a condition of entry" (Ost 2005, 9), many activists felt betrayed. The frames they had developed in action then consolidated into a different idea of democracy from the institutional one.

During transition, the oppositional movements had indeed contrasted their own conceptions of democracy as "from below," participatory and deliberative, with the criticized representative democracy "from above," delegated and majoritarian. Western democracy was identified with parliamentarianism, which went against "the growing political competences of a broad, not party-member basis, and therefore the need for grass roots democracy" (Poppe 1995). As an activist observed, "For us, parliamentary democracy was only one possibility, perhaps an intermediate step, but certainly not a model to strive for" (Pfaff 2006, 199). As activists perceived democracy as an open dialogue, the representative forms achieved after transition were seen as highly problematic.

While democracy was conceived first and foremost as participatory, with particular attention to open discussion, political parties were also criticized as too elitist and too closed. This happened in particular in the GDR, where, in several interviews, party politics was criticized as closely resembling the one-party regime:

These grassroots democratic citizens' movements, they had the ideal notion that the problems are to be discussed at the bottom, by the rank and file, that then propositions are made on the next level, and the people up there were more or less meant to implement the decision of the grassroots. With parties it was the other way around: up there, in some back rooms, something was concocted and then the machinery was started in order to align the party ... and if you see how parties work today, it doesn't differ significantly from how the SED worked, so the party of the dictatorship. It is clearly going top down, and what the population would like to have, that doesn't matter at all. (GDR10)

So, for many, the disappointment with the institutional evolution, and a refusal to take part in it, is linked to the fact that "the kind of politics in the parties established doesn't match this notion of relatively direct democracy" (GDR11). As a human rights activist and then member of the federal parliament for Bund 90/Greens observed, parties tended indeed to be identified with the bureaucratic structures of the regime – which also had multiparty systems and local, regional, and national parliaments – so that *"we said, for god's sake, not immediately parties again, we have had enough of them"* (GDR12, emphasis added).

Together with parties, parliaments were also feared as places that discouraged not only participation but also dialogue. In the words of the same activist,

there was always a certain skepticism too about parliamentarism in the West ... because we saw that the parliament too, to a certain extent, is dominated by the parties. In the parties, way too much is predetermined ... we had a somewhat independent notion of democracy. It was always of course about co-determination, but there was a lot of talk about grassroots democracy or co-participation rights, co-determination rights. (GDR12)

Representative institutions were criticized as places for power games, while activists described themselves as rather shy toward taking power – as observed by one of them, who had been active in the oppositional group Democracy Now, "when we ... thought about which of us would sit at the round table, it is not like today or like in the West: nobody wanted to ... the people from the opposition didn't long for power" (GDR2). They remembered that their aim was instead, an environmentalist observed, "well, just that we take responsibility, in the representation of the people and also in the administration ... it was about quite concrete things ... the citizens' movement wanted to overcome party democracy in general" (GDR4).

Even those who initially agreed to participate in the institutional game often expressed frustration at what was perceived as a useless form of parliamentary democracy. As a human rights activist and later member of the regional parliament in Berlin noted,

even if you are a member of the parliament and you are in an opposition party, there is virtually no possibility to achieve anything. You pedal like mad and keep the seat warm, and see to it that you are reelected next time, but you virtually cannot do anything against the policy of the government. That is quite depressing: I experienced this in the parliament for several years. I will never become a member of a parliament again. (GDR10)

In addition, existing channels of participation for citizens in governing institutions are seen as, in the word of a cofounder of the Green Party, "fake participation," as "There is citizens' participation, especially regarding large construction projects, but also with land-use plans and such, that all goes according to the law, but in the end it hardly takes place. The people are frustrated or out of their depth, and it is too complex, they cannot actually really participate" (GDR3).

Given the consolidation of participatory and deliberative frames, electoral politics is thus perceived as pushing the citizens away from decision making – "so that was a rude awakening and then in the end we had hardly any time to continue working programmatically because . . . it was about the next elections . . . that went so far that the dissolution of the state security was to be controlled and guided without the citizens' committee" (GDR3). The very values spread through electoral politics are criticized as oriented toward individualization, rather than community building. So, for instance, a feminist remembered her shock when, on the occasion of the first national elections for the federal parliament,

somebody from the Greens in the West said, "many people vote according to tactical considerations, and they vote following their personal interests." I was completely shocked: what is that? What is that kind of picture of society? I vote according to my personal interests, that is, material interests was implied: so I vote for those who promise the lowest taxes. What bullshit! As long as people act like this, you cannot talk of democracy. Or how you can vote tactically, like . . . I don't actually like her, but I just vote for her so that this and that constellation comes out: what kind of reasoning is that? If, so to speak, the purely personal, material, egotism determines the voting decision? (GDR1)

For those who perceived politics as commitment to a community, the representation of individual interests appeared illegitimate.

Similarly, in Czechoslovakia, the critique of party democracy is linked to a lack of attention to what the opposition had considered as a most fundamental actor: civil society. Recalling Havel's essay "The Power of the Powerless," one of the founders of Charta 77 noted,

He thought that political parties should not have played such an important role in the society and that the development of civil society which enters politics outside the elections should have been much stronger. The result didn't prove his idea right, but the role of the civil society could be bigger and the role of political parties, which nowadays represent partial and private interests and not the public sphere, could be weaker. (CZ3)

Skepticism toward political parties is also fueled by the belief that rooted parties are difficult to establish in Eastern Europe, and that powerful but unrooted parties are at risk of corruption. As observed by one of the promoters of Charta 77 and a future minister, political parties can be healthy only when they emerge from civil society: "This is what Havel said. He was absolutely right. ... Anyway, political parties are drying out and they will keep drying out ... Dahrendorf says: 'We need sixty years to build civil society.' Attention! In the meantime the parties atrophy, get bureaucratized and transform into clientelist structures" (CZ13). Corruption is indeed criticized as one of the evils of the new, democratic phase. In Czechoslovakia, activists

simply imagined democracy as a set of rules, where there was freedom ... we had no idea that corruption and money would play such an important role: it spoiled the milieu, it spoiled the relations and functioning of the state, so that people were interested only in money and they were capable of doing everything to get it. This concerned even politicians. We didn't realize that power corrupts and that new politicians, some of them would have the tendency to be corrupted. We didn't know it or we didn't think of it. (CZ4)

This was seen as in bitter contrast with a conception of politics as highly moral service to the community. As one of the speakers of the University Strike Committee in 1989 remembers, their vision of politics was "very naïve, idealistic, nice, so nice that one was willing to sacrifice his own career and take risks" (CZ1).

Criticisms of minimalistic representative conceptions and practices of democracy were also present in cases of participated pacts, but these critical voices were less audible there. In Poland, too, some who had experienced radical, direct democracy saw it as superior to the representative version; this tended to discourage some from direct involvement with party politics. Here as well, one activist who had organized clandestine publishing during the martial law saw individualization as linked to the disappearance of interest in the common goods, the discovery that "there were more and more positions that were focused on particular branches and were not based on collective good, instead they were focused on the well-being of the particular group. Or even individuals" (PL1). Some disappointment then developed in reaction to a perceived marginalization of civil society, with interested and selfish conceptions prevailing, as:

in 1989, we thought that, after all the evidence of this potential that is in the society, it turns out that it completely stops being used, that if they engage, they don't think about others – they think of their own interest. If they are active, they are active for their own, narrowly interpreted group. ... Often I witness the situation that people are not listening to each other. There is barely an exchange of arguments and nobody's analyzing the arguments of their opponents, it is supposed to be as I want it to be. (PL1)

From the political point of view, there is also the perception, at least among the young generation, that "after the elections everything stopped" (PL9). As an interviewee of the Orange Alternative recalled:

I was born in 1970. Being so young, I still believed in this very utopian vision of direct and radical democracy, and I remember that we hesitated to go to the first elections in 1989. It was a big problem for me because at that time I already knew that this democracy, this representative democracy, it's not the way I want to go because it has nothing to do with real power, with real democracy. (PL4)

As observed by a former member of Solidarity, who had then joined Walesa's citizens' committee, pragmatism tended to prevail:

This feeling of liberty and freedom threatened by communist oppression was once something that created this big unity within the society and this unity ... well maybe in people's thoughts it is still needed, but in my opinion it's impossible to achieve. Because you cannot live throughout your life, for the whole of your life, rejecting all other issues or other needs and focus only on a few. ... that is just impossible. It is very beautiful, this feeling of unity, and I understand people's need for this unity, but you cannot live your whole life rejecting some needs and focusing only on the ones that unite you with other people. (PL2)

Pragmatic acceptance of a party politics – with parties weak in members but rich in patronage power – also spread in Hungary. Here, the legacy of the left-wing opposition, which had emerged already in 1956 and was brutally repressed by the Soviet army, played an important role in the development of a conception of an informal society. As a former activist, founder of the National Trade Union of Scientific Workers, reminded us,

It is hard to understand the intellectual life of Budapest without this group of people, which contained the 1956 "counterrevolutionaries" who were in prison, and without work on the peripheries of society, the Lukacs school of philosophers, the ones who stayed in Hungary, the young intellectuals, sociologists, economists. ... This was a very small circle until the beginning of the eighties ... it was restricted by a lot of things. (HU7)

However, since the very beginning of the transition, also in Hungary the focus was instead on the creation of political parties and institutions. In sum, disappointment with the delegated and majoritarian conceptions of democracy emerged especially where eventful democratization had contributed to the framing in action and then the frame consolidation of participatory and deliberative visions of democracy.

FIT OR MISFIT?

I remember someone raised his hand in Špalíček: "Shouldn´t we think more about programme aspects?" We haggled over who would lead this or that ministry or over ambassador positions. But there was no time for it. I was at the Civic Forum´s programme commission, and if this commission had met at least five times. ... And my proposal for education or foreign policy was: "Come on, there is no time for that, when we are at the ministries we will prepare it." When they were at the ministries – there was Burešová at Ministry of Justice, Dienstbier at Ministry of Foreign Affairs, Ruml at Ministry of Interior – they did not have even the little time to meet. In fact they did not have time to talk about what they would like to do. (CZ1)

The lack of time for thinking and planning during the intense day of the revolt is lamented, among others by the speaker of the University Strike Committee in Prague. While the mentioned conception of democracy seemed quite adapted to protest in the authoritarian regime and during regime changes, some observers have stressed its lack of fit in times of democratic consolidation. As noted by Dieter Rucht, for instance, while apt to resist repression in an authoritarian GDR,

the groups' organizational structures no longer served their instrumental purposes, however, when repression ceased and the masses poured into the streets and many people joined the opposition groups. At this point the groups were overwhelmed with the parallel tasks of breaking the remaining powers of the regime, integrating new adherents into existing or newly formed groups, and developing a convincing strategy for political change within a constantly changing environment. (Rucht 1996, 48)

Additionally, the strong moral orientation of the oppositional groups is considered as limiting the capacity to adapt to the new context, as "due to their conception of grass roots democracy, their holistic approach, and their naive vision of a politics ruled by moral principles, the groups were reluctant to seize power and compete with other actors who, for the most part, ... had fewer problems playing an instrumental power game" (Rucht 1996, 51). Civil society is seen as made up of "courageous individuals asserting their independence, but they operated in a world of limited contacts and organizational experience. ... the organization element that was expected to achieve that function was missing" (Myant 2005, 252).

The former activists we interviewed stressed indeed their limited capacity for adapting to the new context, citing their surprise at the degree of change as well as the high speed of the transformation, which did not leave any time to ponder the various alternatives. This was felt in particular in the GDR, where activists lamented that, after the sudden and dramatic fall of the Wall, the participatory dynamics were broken and the civil society organizations emerged as unprepared to address the shifting mood. The perception was widespread that, in the words of a founder of Democratic Beginning, "in an immensely short time an incredible amount of things were achieved ... the goals of the revolution were changed in a very fast period of time. ... Basic elements of democracy were introduced, but just based on the proven West German model, and relatively little of what we initially wanted in the way of experimental forms or such was included then" (GDR8). A sudden break is also presented in the narrative of a founder of New Forum, who bitterly recalled that "with the fall of the Wall on the 9th of November all this interest in co-shaping society fizzled out from one day to the next. Then it was only a question of how you get into the West as fast as possible, going shopping and getting Western money and such" (GDR10).

Indeed, activists often pointed at their lack of preparation for the deep changes to happen. Self-critically, the fact that "we just ignored the fall of the Wall and continued like before" is mentioned, as

in retrospect completely incomprehensible to me, because in the midst of the fall of the Wall it was clear that it would march with express speed in the direction of Federal Republic West. The GDR simply gets collected in a colonial fashion: that was clear, we lost a lot of time by simply continuing to practice this democracy or to try alternatives at a time when we should have prepared for the reunification, for the modalities of reunification. That was a tactical mistake ... so the propaganda phrases that were introduced from the West German side at that time also had an effect. (GDR8)

The shift from the movement slogan "We are the people" to "We are one people" is thus conceived as "really the end of the emancipatory movement in East Germany, that was bitter for us, but that's how it was. The mass base which we had in the fall of 1989, that was then gone from one day to the other, within minutes" (GDR10).

The fast changes did challenge the need for the long learning processes of democratic practices. In particular, among GDR activists, with the fall of the Wall, a certain victory for the movement paradoxically started to be perceived as a bitter turning point. So, as noted by a peace activist and later MP,

we had all kinds of utopian things in there: starting with the right to labor, right to housing, right to self-determined dying and so on. ... We had no idea of real democratic processes. We first had to learn all of that, of course, quick and dirty ...

suddenly we all had political mandates, which we were not prepared for, and we had ... to learn how you do it well. (GDR5)

The bitter conclusion is that the "blooming dreams of democracy didn't mature, especially direct democracy, and many who realized how quickly citizens were gone again, and participation was gone, then withdrew" (GDR4).

The lack of historical experience with democracy is also seen critically, as it made reflections on the possible institutional evolution more difficult, while authoritarian regimes produced misleading visions of a socialist democracy. In the words of one of the founders of Women for Peace,

we didn't know any democracy, we hadn't experienced any democracy. The special thing in Germany is perhaps that our parents' generation also didn't experience any democracy, but instead just grew up in national socialism. Maybe the grandparents still had recollections of the Weimar Republic, but for many these were not particularly positive recollections: economic crisis and many lost everything and such. In that time, our image of democracy came via the media, from what we knew about the West and learned about western countries. (GDR2)

This lack of experience facilitated the import of representative models from abroad. Yet, again in the GDR, the initial offer of support by the FRG was indeed perceived as turning into the imposition of a different conception of democracy from the one for which the activists were struggling. Disappointment was especially linked to the refusal to discuss a new constitution at the federal level. All ideas and projects developed during the short intense moment of the transition were seen as rejected without any consideration during installation and consolidation. In this vision,

the perspective of reunification meant that we practically don't have to build up the new political order by our own means, but that we are supported in that by the West, or that the West sucks us up ... we saw the need for reforms in the West as well, not only for us, because we found, for instance, that in the West there is not enough grassroots democracy. (GDR2)

Along the same line, a lack of professional expertise is often lamented, together with the opportunities it offers for patronizing by the Westerners. In GDR, the perception is widespread that

there were few people in the GDR who had enough experience on how to build up an administration, for instance, and all had to go relatively fast. One needed a new police, and one needed administrative structures in order to get a constitutional system governed by the rule of law, in which the citizens also have the possibility to defend themselves against administrative decisions, for instance; and that all had to be staffed by people who had the requisite training. Those people were not available in the GDR, and in that sense it was also consistent that the Western experts came first, but that also led to withdrawals by some who felt patronized and who said, "well, actually we wanted self-determination and now come the *Wessis* and patronize us": so there was an atmosphere like this sometimes. (GDR2)

In Czechoslovakia as well, the accelerated speed of the transition was perceived by the activists, ex post, as thwarting strategic thinking. As one of the founding members of Civic Forum explained,

Everything we had not done before we missed during the time when everything was in process, and we did not have any time to think anything over. Every organizational and ideological work that had not been done by Charta 77 – hard to reproach us for that because we were 22 years old at the time of revolution, but maybe we had to press more. ... The dissent was somehow tired when we entered, everything was upon us. You cannot expect 22- or 23-year-old people to have some prepared programme. Instead we had the ideals, and then everything went so quickly. (CZ1)

Here as well, lack of experience was perceived as a limitation. As a former activist and later member of the government recalled, "at that time it was people without any political experience, total outsiders, e.g. me, who didn't think politically. I can think revolutionary, I can change anything quite quickly or so. To think conceptually and politically requires experience" (CZ11). Lack of expertise is also identified as the consequence of the dictatorship by another future member of parliament as well: "We have to acknowledge that there were not many professors to replace the profaned ones because of forty years of decimation and the unwillingness of the ones who were abroad to return. Two generations of elites were totally devastated or expelled. It is difficult then" (CZ7).

Idealism is also perceived as a handicap, once democracy is achieved, and with it a system that is oriented to pragmatic achievements. So, a Czech activist and playwright recalled that "movements' members were quite often idealists. They were not practitioners. They didn't know how to handle the power, and most of them even didn't want to know. They were interested in the reform of the society, in their visions, and this was not everyday politics. The others were practising everyday conceptual and maybe not very fair politics meanwhile" (CZ8).

In contrast to the GDR, the effect of the transfer of some leaders into the institutions as reducing the strategic capacity of the movement was dramatically felt in Czechoslovakia. With Havel as president, the former opposition "lost its most important brain. ... Perhaps he was really irreplaceable. Havel said he wanted to be a non-party president (president for all) and unfortunately only we – students – were the ones who tried to persuade him not to do that. The others felt relieved when he left Špalíček: everybody was in a good mood" (CZ1).

While in eventful democratization, framing in action had produced participatory and deliberative conceptions, which had then consolidated, the situation was only partly similar in the cases of participated pacts, although the institutional path was already prepared and the dream of a democracy from below had been shorter. In Poland, activists criticized inexperience, stating that "what was lacking was a preparation for what will happen later. ... Preparation was insufficient, because even if we assume that there will be some kind of democratization, then so what? The system would be liberalized and a new reality will be formed, what to do next with it? Such preparation, even the simplest, was lacking" (PL12). A pragmatic view of democracy spread, however, with an acceptance of a compromise toward representative democracy, with limited participation.

In Hungary, as well, the opposition's lack of reflection on the future of democracy was linked to the accelerated timeline and its unexpected outcomes. Even though the dissident movement had started there quite early, as one of the founders of the Hungarian Helsinki committee observed, this "did not deal with what should happen after the transition, because before 1988 no one thought that the regime could collapse like this" (HU1). Different positions were also present, with a tendency toward a democratic compromise. As "the sheer fact you could demand democracy and that you could set achievable political goals was new," the need to act quickly did not allow for a synthesis to emerge:

there were a lot of different notions around, up until the establishment of the Roundtable, ranging from a minimum of an alternative political sphere ... everybody thought in terms of political liberalization, which was imagined entirely within the framework of the Communist party state ... to establishing some kind of semi-democratic system, like the Polish had in the eighteenth century with a House of Commons that you could elect with free elections, with the Central Committee of the Party sitting on top like some sort of House of Lords. In between the two were all kinds of notions regarding what the political goals should be. (HU7)

The perception was so widespread that the accelerated timeline of the transition had jeopardized the possibility of developing alternative ideas that would have helped to adapt the oppositional conception of democracy to the new conditions. The pacted transition brought about a sudden

stop to the elaboration of alternative forms of democracy, as, an oppositional unionist observed, "in March 1989 the whole thing stopped just
like that. Bam. From then on the objectives were free elections" (HU7).

In sum, in eventful democratization we saw the framing in action and,
then, frame consolidation of participatory and deliberative visions of
democracy. Although these did not automatically facilitate interactions
with institutions, they kept alive the memory of a possible alternative.
This was less the case for participated pacts.

CONCLUDING REMARKS

Conception and practices of democracy were linked to the different
moments of the struggle for democracy.

First of all, we noted that the democratic opposition against the authoritarian regimes expressed a criticism of liberal democracy, instead favoring participatory and deliberative democratic qualities. The memories of
our interviewees are confirmed by other research. While not aiming at
conquering state power, dissidents wanted to build autonomous spaces to
develop what they defined as "a culture of dialogue," "a culture of
plurality and the free public domain" (cit. in Olivo 2001, 14). Also
confirmed is a commitment toward a politics of consensus, which is
"not based on partial interests, because tackling an issue without the
consent of the opponents would only bring harm" (Joppke 1995, 180).
The groups that formed the citizens' movement were in fact characterized
by values such as "openness and publicity ... grassroots democracy,
rejection of patriarchal, hierarchical, and authoritarian structures, nonviolence, spirituality, unity of private and public consciousness" (Joppke
1995, 88). The citizens' movement (calling for "democracy now") aimed
at constituting public forums for deliberation, open to all citizens, self-
organized, and committed to participatory democracy (Joppke 1995, 92).
Local roundtables and citizens' committees allowed for the framing in
action of this conception. In these free spaces, in the words of dissident
activist Ulrike Poppe, "members learned to speak authentically and to
relate to each other ... to engage in social matters and to put up resistance" (in Joppke 1995, 180).

While clearly no new ideology was created in 1989, the framing of the
"self" of the oppositional groups was quite innovative. These movements
did not try to impose a common will of the people, but rather promoted
the principle of self-government, building upon "the idea of an autonomous civil society and its ability to work on itself by means of logical

reasoning processes and the creation of appropriate institutions" (Preuss 1995, 97). The organizational format and style of the oppositional groups in authoritarian regimes were indeed influenced by the need

to cope with a hostile institutional environment. Keeping a low organizational profile was a necessary means of survival. Consequently, the groups were relatively small, informal, and only loosely coupled with one another, if connected at all. They had learned to live in a marginal and constantly endangered position, one in which they were stigmatized, controlled, and repressed by a clear-cut opponent. (Rucht 1996, 48)

Our research went beyond these observations by noting, first, how framing of democracy developed in action. While the intellectuals' theorizations of civil society and self-government were relevant points of reference, also cited by some of our interviewees, the most important experiences happened during the mobilization, as oppositional groups and protest actions (such as the Monday prayers) functioned as schools of democracy, encouraging dialogue and participation. Referring to the concept of deliberative and participatory democracy, I noted how equality, inclusiveness, and transparency became important participatory values, bridged with deliberative values such as the emphasis on consensus building, preference transformation, good communication, and orientation to the public good. The "anti-political politics" was therefore declined as another politics – more ethical and grassroots – rather than a refusal of politics.

As those frames consolidated, in comparison to those conceptions and practices, representative democracy appeared insufficient. In fact, parliaments, parties, and elections were seen as wanting when weighed against the norms of participation and deliberation. This was all the more the case where eventful democratization had happened – and even more so where a few months of power vacuum during the agony of the regime allowed for citizens' mobilizations in various experiments with democracy, as was the case in the GDR. Here, in fact, the quick reunification with the western part of Germany was perceived as a brisk halt to the possibility of developing another democracy, more resonant with the experiences of citizens' participation and deliberation. Disillusionment in Czechoslovakia was limited by, at the same time, the perception that an ownership was maintained by the civil society on the outcome of the Velvet Revolution, as well as by the shorter and narrower direct experiments with alternative forms of politics and democracy.

The research confirms that, if participatory and deliberative conceptions and practices of democracy supported the mobilization against the regime, they also appeared problematic to sustaining mobilization after the transition to democracy. The grassroots view of the civil society that had developed in the opposition in CEE was "tamed" after the transition, when a liberal conception of democracy prevailed. As Baker summarized, "For the opposition theorists of the 1970s and 1980s, civil society was an explicitly normative concept which held up the ideal of societal space, autonomous from the state, wherein self-management and democracy could be worked out. That is, the idea of civil society was political and prescriptive" (Baker 1999, 2). Civil society theorists "saw civil society originally in the more positive, or socialist, terms of community and solidarity. Indeed, for many such theorists civil society indicated a movement towards post-statism; for control of power, while not unimportant, would be insufficient for the fundamental redistribution, or even negation, of power itself. If this was to be achieved, self-management in civil society was necessary" (Baker 1999, 15). The activists' appeal for the construction of a community from below did not resonate, however, with mainstream institutional conceptions of delegated and majoritarian democracy. The consolidation of a liberal model of democracy, relying on elected elites, tended to deny civil society the political role, which was monopolized by political parties. Procedural democracy appeared then to obscure the claims of a radical conception of civil society, thus contributing to limit the participation of the citizens.

Confirming the difficulty to adapt "maximalist" (or as someone wrote, idealistic) conceptions of democracy to the "minimalist" one promoted by the institutions, activists point at the limits imposed by the quick pace of the transition, the lack of experience and expertise from democracy, and the promotion of Western visions of democracy by powerful external actors. Especially but not only in the cases of eventful democratization, interrupted experiences with other conceptions and practices of democracy often left activists frustrated and demotivated. However, the presence of those experiences also left memories and practices that could be reactivated later on.

4

"It Was a Tsunami"

Shifting Emotions

In September, October, Mejstřík and I went on a spying trip to East Germany. We were surprised how it was there. At that time, their Mondays [protests] in Leipzig, Halle, and Magdeburg were established. We were surprised because in East Germany it was worse than in ČSSR and now, at that time, they were willing to gather in front of Saint Thomas Church and protest. We could not believe it. We stayed there with my friends who were from the Evangelical church in Leipzig and we asked them how they had managed to persuade people to come in such huge numbers. And they said: "It must be permitted, it must be permitted. It was an officially permitted demonstration. We were allowed to protest in front of the church after the Mass." When we went back by train, we were racking our brains over how anybody could permit us any demonstration. When we returned, we immediately presented the idea on Thursday; we used to meet every Thursday . . . in Bílý Koníček – a restaurant on Staromák (Old Town Square), down in the cellar. We presented it there. We also showed photographs from the trip to East Germany; we presented the interviews we did there, and especially the innovative idea of allowed demonstrations. Everybody burst into enormous laughter when they heard it and laughed at us, that we had to travel to East Germany to get this idea, and they asked how we wanted to do it.

However, the occasion for a legal demonstration unexpectedly emerged on November 17, 1989, as, for the anniversary of the killing of students during the Nazi occupation, the youth organization of the regime party gave availability to co-organize a demonstration – an authorized one, which people should not fear to participate in. In fact, as a student activist recalled,

About ten days before the demonstration, Daňhel was his name I think, visited the Benda family. He was an SSM [Czechoslovak Socialist Union of Youth, the official student union] city committee emissary and offered us that if the demonstration were organized together and if the SSM city committee and SSM university council representatives could speak there as well, then they would arrange for the demonstration to be allowed. We debated a lot about it within STUHA [an oppositional student organization], but pragmatism later won. The fact that the demonstration was officially permitted was a very important factor, which freed people from fear. We could stick up the posters at universities and halls of residence. This was even new to us, because nothing like this had ever happened before. We had no Internet. And thanks to this communication, perhaps, not perhaps but surely, 40,000 people gathered there. Until that date it was an unprecedented number. The rest is quite well known. (CZ4)

In fact, the oppositional students had been strategic in advertising the march as a permitted one. A member of the University Strike Committee in Prague recalled,

they came to visit us and asked if we could organize it together. There were people who knew each other, e.g. the Benda family, the Němec family, the Karasek family, I have known them since childhood because of my parents, who were part of that society, but on the other hand, there were people who, when they heard it for the first time, were close to a heart attack. That we should have organized such a huge event together with Charta; they saw themselves being fired from the school and even imprisoned. So there were two of us authorized, me from STISK and Benda from STUHA, to go to universities and persuade people that this was a good idea, that we should organize it together, so they should come and participate and not be worried, because it was permitted, official. And finally we succeeded. (CZ1)

This narrative points at the importance of cross-national learning for devising strategies to combat fear, an emotion that jeopardizes much of the public expression of opposition in authoritarian regimes. As we will see in this chapter, indeed, emotional work and shifts in the emotional atmosphere have effects on the various steps of contention in democratization processes. The type and intensity of felt emotions are one level of transformation that occurs between the moments of the struggle for democracy and after its achievement through mechanisms of *emotional prefiguration*, defined as the construction of an excited feeling of empowerment, and *emotional adaptation*, defined as the return to a normal emotional state.

As we will see in the first part, in order to mobilize in authoritarian regimes, one must first overcome the *fear* of repression that usually constrains mobilization – and, possibly, transform it into feelings of *anger* against the regime. In the second part, in contrast, we will observe that actors stressed the role that *hope* played in pushing them to mobilize.

As we will see in the third part, *satisfaction* and *disillusionment* are both
cited – but with cross-country differences – to explain the micro-level
dynamics of withdrawal from protest. The intensity of emotions that
emerge during the process is fundamentally different in eventful democratization versus participated pacts, but some diversity also emerged within
each path, with potential implications for the democratic quality of established democracies. Building upon a growing literature on passionate
movements, I shall link collective emotions to the dynamics of the protest,
considering them as part of the conditions activists aim at changing, but
also as having a constraining power on protest action.

EMOTIONS IN MOVEMENT: AN INTRODUCTION

Transition times are intense times, ripe with emotional feeling. In fact, as
Reed (2004, 660) noted, in order to explain the mobilization contexts, we
have to examine "the actual 'conditions of protest mobilization' as
'microevents' with their own distinct 'effect.' Political actors can 'suddenly' assume a new and radical orientation under the dynamics of contention." Specific moments of some intensity can produce an "explosion
of consciousness" (Mann 1973, 45), becoming redefining events that
signify something unexpected, pushing for the development of visions of
an alternative society. These events are emotionally intense: they provide
for a space in which some emotions are triggered and others controlled,
thus changing the ways in which actors construct their selves (Reed 2004,
663). In this process, the emotional responses that emerge within these
contexts set in motion and keep alive some attribution of meaning to
specific events (ibid., 663). In this sense, "emotions ... give direction
to action when an individual's sense of social reality is challenged or
open to interpretation. Emotions, because they presuppose an historico-
cultural context, therefore help diagnose the severity and urgency of
a given 'problem,' facilitate understandings of the efficacy and feasibility
of actions, and ultimately, help embody an active or otherwise course of
transcendence" (ibid., 666). They are transformative, constituting collective identities.

When recognizing the importance of micro-level explanations, transi-
tology has tended to look at various groups of incumbents and opposition
as strategic actors, rationally acting on their own purposes (see
Chapter 1). In social movement studies, instead, the importance of questions about the types of emotions that develop during collective action has
increasingly been recognized. This implies, first of all, a redefinition of

emotions themselves not as irrational, but rather as cognitively driven, as well as a recognition of emotions as collective phenomena and an awareness of their contextualized location.

While for some time research on social movements has shied away from emotions, stressing instead the normality of movement participants, more recently there has been a growing recognition of social movement politics as passionate politics (Goodwin, Jasper, and Polletta 2001). Indeed, social movements are rich in emotions, as "anger, fear, envy, guilt, pity, shame, awe, passion, and other feelings play a part either in the formation of social movements, in their relations with their targets ... in the life of potential recruits and members" (Kemper 2001, 58). Emotions that are often mentioned in relation to social movements also include grief, anger, joy, pride, love, and indignation (Gould 2004).

Various typologies have been constructed, distinguishing emotions that address a specific object from those with a more generic target, short-term versus long-term ones, reciprocal versus shared ones (Goodwin, Jasper, and Polletta 2001), and emotions of trauma (grief, shame, helpless anger) from emotions of resistance (pride, happiness, love, safety, confidence, righteous anger) (Whittier 2001, 239). Particularly relevant are "'High order' emotions (evaluative emotions) such as hope and moral outrage, which require a greater degree of evaluation processing, are often fueled by such primary emotions as anger and fear" (Reed 2004, 668). These (and other) emotions can play a different role at different times: emotions such as anger, outrage, or fear can be particularly important in recruitment; indignation, pleasure, or pride can enforce commitment (Goodwin, Jasper, and Polletta 2001).

The tendency to oppose emotions to interest, ideas, and cognition has been criticized (Goodwin, Jasper, and Polletta 2001), as "participants in rituals communicate whole complexes of ideas and embodied feelings" (Barker 2001, 188). Emotions instead contribute to the ways in which people make sense of things; feeling is part of thought and moral shock alters ways of thinking (Gould 2004).

Emotions do not emerge naturally, but are worked upon. Rituals fuel collective effervescence, group solidarity, emotional energy and identities. They help to transform shame into pride, as it happened in the gay and lesbian communities (Gould 2001), or shame into self-realization, as in the Christian Right antigay activism (Stein 2001). Especially, social movements tend to transform emotions by changing the everyday relations to which the "old" emotions were attached (Calhoun 2001, 55; Kane 2001).

Emotions are embedded in social relationships (Kemper 2001), which imply a need for researchers to specify better "the conditions in which particular emotional dynamics are more likely to occur" (Polletta and Amenta 2001, 306). The Western culture of modernity, with its tendency to stigmatize emotion, favoring interests over passion, has affected social movements, which often prefer to spread a self-image as reasonable and rational actors (Dobbin 2001). However, some movements or movement organizations are seen as more prone to showing (some) emotions than are others (see Whittier 2001). Some groups nurture specific master emotional frames (or habitus) that define appropriate emotions (della Porta and Giugni 2009). Social movement organizations tend to stimulate emotions of sympathy, in different forms (Allahyari 2001; McAllister Groves 2001).

Activists also tend to assess the different emotional cultures present in the different environments in which they participate, developing a (conscious or unconscious) emotional labor oriented to keep some emotions under control and stimulate others (Whittier 2001). Emotions are transformed, indeed, in interactive settings, as specific types of emotions are considered as appropriate in meetings, others in demonstrations (della Porta and Giugni 2009). Social movements as well as protest events also tend to transform emotions (e.g., from shame into solidarity), or to intensify them (Collins 2001, 29).

In this chapter, I will point at the ways in which emotions are linked to cognitive assessments of the situation, how they are worked upon at the collective level, and how they are culturally embedded in a broader environment. In analyzing the sequence of emotions that are produced by and, in turn, fuel the protest waves, I will point at mechanisms of emotional prefiguration as well as emotional normalization. I will first discuss how fear was addressed through emotional work by the movements targeting authoritarian regimes building up a mechanism of emotional prefiguration. Repression then backfired, producing anger rather than fear and then more long-lasting moral outrage at what was considered as socially unjust, as well as unbearable. As fear gave way to outrage, mobilization happened and, with it, hope, with the related pleasure of empowerment. These emotions contributed to fuel rebellion, up to the breakdown of the regimes. Finally, I will argue that excitement tended to normalize into either satisfaction or, more often, disillusionment, as the emotion of frustration spread during the early years of consolidation, triggering demobilization. In line with evolution in conceptions of emotion in social movement studies, I will look at how emotions are linked to cognition, and embedded in collective processes. As we will see, the narrative reconstruction of events emerges as more passionate in cases of eventful transition than in participated pacts, with the effect of leaving at least a memory of empowerment.

OVERCOMING THE BARRIER OF FEAR

The last big wave of people from the entire republic came to us and, that is important for me, that was not only Leipzigers or Saxons and Thuringians, but people from the entire republic.... Ninety percent non-Christians: ... so many that the people then didn't fit into the church anymore; they stayed on the square outside ... in the meantime they had enforced three police cordons; the trucks for arrested people stood ready. Two thousand people fit into our church (so in the aisles sitting and standing); then we reached perhaps 2,400 ... full up to the roof. We only had a small side entrance because the main portal was blocked due to construction work.... We had no intervention team, we had no security guards, nothing. We had two toilets for those masses: completely, absolutely unfit ... and we never had any damage in the church.... In the new testament it says, the peace of God is higher than all reason and reaches deeper than all fear. That was in the church – whoever made it into the church was safe: nothing could happen to him, no matter what horror scenario they built up on the outside.... I was always very happy if a deaconess was recognizable, with her habit, or a Catholic nun or simply old people with a cane who could hardly walk and who struggled through those masses. I asked a grandma, ... "tell me, how do you do it?," ... she said, "you know, reverend, I have such anger: if I sit in the tram, what we put up with, such cowards, all of them, going along with everything, accepting everything, but those in the Nikolai church they do something; you have to go there, you must be part of it." And she said, "When I leave the church I have gained such strength and such confidence that I can really get out there without fear of those outside." (GDR7)

Thus a German pastor vividly recalled the ways in which some churches functioned as spaces where fear was controlled and transformed into positive sentiments. Fear of repression is indeed often evoked as thwarting mobilization, but what emerges is also the awareness of the problem by organizers as well as attempts to overcome this barrier, through various strategies of "emotional work." For the activists, the challenge is to transform fear of repression into moral shock against it. As noted by a Polish activist who had been active since the late 1970s, "Every movement aiming at changing a totalitarian system, every oppositional movement has to break down the barrier of fear" (PL12).

A paradox often noted in research on repression – which described the so-called dilemma of the dictator (Francisco 2005) – is indeed that it can scare people away from the street, but it can also catalyze protest by producing moral shocks. The effects of repression on mobilization then remained a discussed, but undetermined, issue (della Porta 2013a, chap. 2, 2014a, chap. 5). In our narratives, a perceived need to rise up against injustice is often recalled as being at the basis of the initial individual path of rebellion against unjust authority. As a Czech worker activist, and later minister, recalled,

I started to do something on Monday morning after the police intervention on Národní Street. *I thought it was enough.* . . . Later on Monday when I saw the TV news and the way they talked about it, the arguments they used, I picked up the phone and it started. I was in, and in a moment everything went automatically. You call someone, someone calls you, and suddenly there is no way out. (CZ11, emphasis added)

At the collective level, these individual acts of breaking down barriers of fear happen along long relational chains of reciprocal adaptations and provocation between elites and challengers, with moments of liberalization but also returns to brutal repression that are then perceived as all the more outraging. This alternation emerges, for instance, in the account of protest and repression, as the latter became a cause for outrage, or it broke with expected higher degrees of tolerance. Spirals of repression developed with anti-repression protests, as even smaller acts of repression were perceived as outraging.

The collective elaboration of fear within protest activities allows for its transformation into a will to resist. This is what happened in 1988 in Czechoslovakia, as illustrated in this excerpt from an interview with a Czech actress, who recalls the intense emotional atmosphere during a performance at her Prague theatre after an act of police repression: "People who came were trembling, and police cars full of arrested people were passing by the theatre. Then Roman Poláček, our colleague's husband, came with someone. We . . . took them on the stage and we interviewed them in front of the audience, because they were hit by the police" (CZ8). After this experience,

People from theatres met and talked about the situation. . . . The pressure had reached the limits and we talked about if we were going on strike or not. Honza Nebeský, who is a director, came in as he had participated in the demonstration, and told us about it. Then we debated the possibility of going on strike, whether yes or no. Someone said: "we have to. . . . We are from theatres and our duty is to play." . . . There were several crucial moments. One of them was when Kodet [a famous actor] stood up and said with his characteristic way of speaking: "We played 40 years as idiots and, if we are not going on strike now, then we will play another 40 years as idiots." I think this influenced the atmosphere in the room. (CZ8)

In a relational trend, courage is then presented as contagious, as more and more people emulate others in challenging the regime, spreading signals that resistance is possible. An activist of Charta 77 thus recalled this perception of increasing courage among the citizens:

My address was publicly known and we published it in *samizdat*. We signed it with our names, not pseudonyms. We even published our addresses. It was in the year 1988, maybe a year earlier, and people started to come. I was used to expecting secret police when the doorbell rang; usually detention followed. But now it was students who came to pick up *Revolver revue* on the way to the university. Some were even very courageous. They were publishing a magazine at the Faculty of Medicine and they came and asked me for an interview or if I could arrange a meeting with Havel, if he could write anything for them. So it was all gradually breaking down. The first public demonstration in August 1988 helped a lot. (CZ6)

Reactions to repression thus take the forms of further marches, symbolic action (such as the releasing of soap bubbles in the main squares), and old "charivari" acts of public denunciation such as "to sing under the windows where disciplinary proceedings for someone who was detained during the last demonstration were taking place" (CZ4). A former student activist thus recalled the chain reactions to repression in 1988–1989, fueled by the feeling that "the regime cannot do it this way." In fact, in the fall of 1989,

It's the first time when the demonstration is dispersed, and *people have the feeling that the regime cannot do it this way, that they cannot use water cannons against people when it is −10°C and that they cannot use police in full gear*. In this way, a week of unrest takes place in Prague. It ends up with the imprisonments of Havel, Vondra, and Čarnogurský in Slovakia. ... Then we have a candle demonstration ... in connection with the police intervention during Palach's week. ... A new petition ("A Few Sentences") is signed not just by the notorious signatories but also by people from the cultural sphere. Students are starting to gather, at least part of them, and there are events. Then we have the petition to the Ministry of Education. It states that the representatives of schools and universities should not only be members of the Union of Socialist Youth. It was signed by 170 people. This number is ridiculous if you compare it to nowadays, but in that time when everybody has to come to school or university to sign it and when everybody was checked, the number was really powerful. ... *There are more and more people participating and they are less and less frightened*. (CZ7, emphasis added)

Emotional work was in play when activists succeeded in carving out spaces of protest where fear was easier to control. Remaining with the history of Czechoslovakia, the possibility of holding a legal demonstration, mentioned in the incipit of this chapter, is a main move in overcoming fear. The first permitted demonstration occurred on November 17, 1989, following complex negotiations within the student movement. The permission was given once the dissident students agreed to organize the protest together with the official student union, the SSM. This was presented as "the biggest gathering if we compare it to the previous ones. It is so because it is permitted and very peaceful and calm. At the same time everybody feels that the atmosphere is combative and optimistic – something has moved" (CZ7). The overcoming of fear is visible as the SSM speaker is then shouted down, as "To the rhetorical question: 'What can SSM municipal university council do for students?'": "the crowd spontaneously chants: 'Resign, resign, resign . . .'" (CZ7).

Acts of repression work in fact as catalysts for outraged protest, as short- and long-term development of repressive strategies intertwine. A virtuous circle thus developed: as liberalization certainly allowed a broadening of the bases of mobilization, since people were ever less afraid of the consequences of their action, it also made relatively minor episodes of repression – if compared with the past history of the country – appear unbearable. A Czech student activist thus describes long-term changes in the level and forms of repression, and their effects on the mobilization, as in the 1980s, "the regime was not as repressive as it used to be in the 1970s. When someone was detained, usually firing from school/university or some disciplinary proceedings followed, but rarely arrest" (CZ4). The softening of repression was then considered as a sign of weakening of the regime, which, in turn, reduced fear – as a former student activist observed, "Simply, the regime was weakening. And because it was weakening, the fear from the regime weakened as well, and this led to the fact that more and more people were willing to show up in public" (CZ4).

International developments, through comparison and emulation, contribute to setting the cognitive context for the development of emotions – again in the words of a former student activist, "with the easing of the situation in the whole of Eastern Europe – something is happening in Poland, there are roundtables, in Russia, there is Perestroika and Glasnost – there is a huge activation and mobilization of the movements. They act publicly and they have lots of new activities" (CZ7). So, while international changes, especially Gorbachev's turn in the Soviet Union, spread the impression that more was allowed, the very retreat of the regime from repressive activities was taken as a sign of weakness (CZ7).

In this heated atmosphere, contingent acts of repression can also fuel impressive, massive reactions. This was the case on November 17, as part of the march deviated from the planned route and was brutally attacked by police. The repression of that protest is presented as, at the same time, a non-reflected reaction by the regime, and a trigger for indignation – as a former student activist recalled,

The march was stopped, because it was permitted only for Prague 2 – Vyšehrad and Albertov, but it continued to the city centre. Most of the people from the apparatus who could make any decisions left for the weekend because it was Friday, and the ones who were monitoring the demonstration had only one order: "Don't allow the demonstrators to continue to Wenceslas' square": and they didn't know how to deal with the situation. That means that it was a blocked situation. That's why they used force. Obviously it was the only thing they knew how to use. (CZ4)

Outrage at repression was then linked to the cognitive assessment of the situation – as the (weakened) regime was no longer able to portray the student demonstrators as enemies, and the citizens perceived them as "our children" rather than as dangerous troublemakers. So, November 17 became

the key catalysing moment which brought several thousands of people to the streets, because the communist propaganda had no longer been able to sell this demonstration of a few thousand people in the city centre as a gathering of pro-Western subversives and other disreputable down-and-outs who disturbed the peace needed for working. ... At that time, it was thousands or tens of thousands of students. ... The fact that the police acted quite brutally and the special forces acted brutally against children, or at least still almost children, changed the assessment of the situation. The anger and the irritation – how dare they – and the emotions connected to the dispersion of the demonstrations in Národní street – this was one of the strongest catalysing moments that explains why suddenly a hundred thousand people met on the square. ... The strike at Prague universities started on Monday 20 November and was spreading gradually outside Prague, to Bratislava and further and further ... within three or five days all universities across the republic were on strike. Demonstrations had been called since Sunday 19 November and grew stronger in the first week. Then there were demonstrations on Letná on Saturday and Sunday, where there were three quarters of a million people, and the general strike followed on Monday 28 November. (CZ4)

Protests against repression thus spread and politicized, as

they massacre it... and the shock is really enormous. ... Monday there are 100, 150, even 200 thousand people on Wenceslas square and it ends with demonstrations on Letná. These demonstrations are really massive. People from the countryside come. ... The famous Petr Miller comes with *kováci* [workers from the ČKD engineering company] to the Old Town Square, other workers start to come as well. We organize information campaigns during the whole week. Students, dissidents and actors visit the countryside to persuade more and more people outside Prague to participate. (CZ7)

At a certain point, therefore, repression no longer seems to work to slow down mobilization; to the contrary, it seems to accelerate it. In some narratives, we even find a reverse fear, as members of the military or the police started to be afraid – or to be perceived as being afraid – of various forms of punishment if the opposition was successful. This was the case with the Velvet Revolution, as members of the army, as recalled by one of the founders of the group Bridge,

were indoctrinated by the Great October Socialist Revolution and they couldn't have imagined any other form of coup d'état than the bloody one. They were afraid of being hanged on a lamppost. The word lamppost was one of the *most* used ones. They were really afraid of being hanged. . . . [we] had never held a rope in our hands and we didn't even think about it, not even for a second. But they were really obsessed with it because they were told so in Moscow. We made use of it because we realized that they were really afraid of it. We told them that we would try to do our best to stop the worst. In fact we laughed at it because we knew nothing like that would happen. It's not anything that would be present in Czech nature. I mean to hang someone on the lamppost. (CZ10)

A similar emotional work and shift in the emotional context were at play in the German Democratic Republic (GDR). Similarly, memories of state repression were strong in the GDR, where the state security apparatus played an important role in infiltration and provocation; but here as well, at a certain point, fear gave way to moral shock. The narratives point, indeed, at an alternation of mobilization and demobilization, and of repression and liberalization, that tended eventually to encourage protest, also bringing about more radical claims for democracy. So, a peace and human rights activist since the late 1960s recalled that:

In 1965, the writers were criticized. Biermann was not allowed to perform anymore . . . Havemann was removed from the university . . . he was also kicked out of his institute. Also other authors were criticized: censorship increased. Then there were in-between phases again, in which the extent of this censorship or the repressive dealing with opinions decreased somewhat. . . . And then comes the next break: it is then 1968, Prague. . . . Large parts of the population . . . reacted with great sympathy . . . it was said socialism with a democratic countenance and well . . . we hoped that something like that could exist at that time. . . . It was brutally repressed. . . . Then 1976 came, and it was also again a decisive point, once more . . . this harassing of the artists and writers and so on increased. And then Biermann's expatriation in 1976 in November was basically the trigger for the exodus of writers, artists, theater directors, actors and so on . . . those are people

I would put into a similar category, with their political ideas: they also believed somehow in reform coming from the left but hated that SED regime. ... 1978–79 ... : that is the time when those many people disappeared into the west ... who were important to us. Also, two thirds of my circle of friends was suddenly gone. (GDR12)

Repression also continued in the 1980s, as an independent peace movement developed. Surveillance was then a main means of coercion, followed as it was by various forms of harassment. Activists recalled how they were intimidated through threats of social marginalization rather than brutal use of physical force. As the state security infiltrated the groups, harassment followed. So an environmental and human rights activist recalled:

if you were an academic, you could assume there would be an employment ban – I got an employment ban in 1983 – which means you were not allowed to work in the academic occupation that you had anymore, but you also had difficulties finding a different job. The paragraph on asocial behaviours hovered above such people like a sword of Damocles: it stated that, if you don't have regular work for more than six weeks, you can be subjected to reeducation through work [*Arbeitserziehung*]. So the employment ban, travel bans (we were no longer allowed to visit the few socialist countries that were open for us), home raids – official ones and unofficial ones. The official ones looked like that: a raiding party of the state security stood at the door at six in the morning and then searched the apartment for incriminating evidence. The unofficial ones like that: one day I left the apartment in bright daylight in order to shop for groceries, upon return the apartment door was open ... everything rummaged through, the books pulled off the shelves and so on; nothing was missing, that was not the intention, but that was like the signal that you have no refuge, are safe nowhere. They enter everywhere, even in broad daylight. (GDR5)

However, liberalization was also very vividly perceived by the activists when comparing these forms of harassment in the 1980s – when "we were always controlled, but we were never beaten up" (GDR12) – with the much more brutal ones of the 1950s, when "if people turned against the SED or also to a larger extent wanted to enlarge their own free spaces, then the pressure was a lot stronger, also the incarceration much quicker, the sentences much higher" (GDR12).

Here as well, given the increasing internalization of the right to protest, the alternation between liberalization and de-liberalization contributed to decreasing fear and increasing outrage at repression, as everyday repression was perceived as more and more unbearable. This was the case, in particular, regarding the constraints on freedom of movement such as the

Berlin Wall, which was often felt as an unfair instrument of oppression –
a "massive form of restriction," a feeling of "being locked up" (GDR9).

During mobilization, the control of fear was thus embedded in some
strategic choices by the organizers regarding the format of the mobilization itself. Exploiting some legal opportunities, free spaces were carved
out in Protestant churches, which enjoyed some degree of protection from
state repression. Especially in the 1980s, when the regime violated the
church prerogatives that allowed them to offer spaces for oppositional
activities, the religious leadership protested, and the opposition organized
vigils such as the one at the Zionskirche in Berlin. As an environmentalist
recalled,

we had found out that not only was the church a free space, but also a bit of land
around it belonged to each church, was church-owned property, where the state
security was not allowed to take down posters and so on. We made use of this for
the first time in the Zionskirche: we put our protest poster on the outside of the
church and in front of the church, and held that vigil at the gate of the church: so
not inside the church anymore but outside, and that caused an enormous stir. ...
Apart from many, many people, the western journalists also came, and it was the
first big showdown between opposition and Stasi, and it ended up to our
advantage: after four days they had to give in, release the guys, return the
printing machines. (GDR5)

An important move was to organize protests in permitted spaces –
through a tunneling-under sort of mechanism – where critical voices
could be heard publicly. This was the case, for instance, with the demonstration in honor of Karl Liebknecht and Rosa Luxemburg, which was
always organized in Berlin in January. As an activist recalled,

Since we couldn't register a demonstration, the idea was to go to a demonstration
organized by the SED. ... We wanted to go there with our own posters; the most
well-known slogan was a quote by Rosa Luxemburg that one of us had found in
her unpublished writings: "freedom is always the freedom of the one who thinks
differently." On my poster ... was "each citizen of the GDR has the right to voice
his opinion freely and publicly"; it was the first sentence of article 27 of the
constitution of the GDR. I participated in this action only because I was sure
I could not get arrested for this, because it was an official SED demonstration and
my poster had a sentence from the GDR constitution. (GDR5)

Specific strategies are also devised in order to, simultaneously, overcome fear but also control the explosion of rage. In the GDR, given the
mentioned role of some free spaces related to the Protestant church, and
the involvement of some pastors, this happened especially through social
appropriation via the mobilization of religious rituals (McAdam, Tarrow,

and Tilly 2001). This theme emerges in particular from this account of the Monday prayers, as recalled by a pastor of the Nikolai Kirche in Leipzig:

On May 8, 1989, they started to surround the Nikolai church with police in all access roads, quite casually, without weapons, without clubs, without dogs. ... The policemen were in a difficult position: their 16-year-old son or 17-year-old daughter could have been among those who went into Nikolai church or, even worse, their own wife. We talked about that in the peace prayers: de-enemification, in the sense of the sermon on the mountain of Jesus. ... The policemen are not our enemies; because, once you have an enemy in your head, it is not far to violence. (GDR7)

The same pastor remembered the calls against violence:

And always when we then wanted to leave the church, I said, "folks, take the nonviolence with you onto the street: to be without violence here in the church is hopefully the norm, but outside, given this clubbing violence of the police, those arrests without reason ... there, it will be difficult to remain without violence and, so to speak, to secure nonviolence. Make an effort, folks, because inside and outside are inseparable, praying and acting are inseparable, altar and street are inseparable." And then the people went outside and the only violence was from the state organs. (GDR7)

Methods of controlling group dynamics were developed in order to learn "how you can diminish fears, how you can learn to be self-confident" (GDR11). Humor was also used, based on the conviction that "if you are in a situation where you are that despairing or sad or depressed, if you can smile or even laugh: that is more liberating than a good argument" (GDR7).

Within spirals of opportunity and threats (McAdam, Tarrow, and Tilly 2001), over time, instances of brutal state repression in the GDR started to trigger, rather than jeopardize, protests, with campaigns developing against repression, in a (for the opposition) virtuous circle. The first victories encouraged people to oppose a repression that was considered as not only less and less justified but also less and less efficient – thus favoring mobilization. In 1988, protests in the GDR had shown that "a lot of people became more courageous in the meantime"; so, one of the most influential civil right activist remembered, "when our six people were arrested there were similar protests in twenty, thirty cities in the GDR, the biggest ones in Berlin. There, we had the Gethsemane church ... almost three thousand people in there" (GDR12). When more than 100 activists were unexpectedly imprisoned by the government and its secret police after the mentioned demonstration in honor of Karl Liebknecht and Rosa Luxemburg, massive protests developed. An environmentalist recalled, we know, since the opening of the Stasi files, that they assumed that there would be protests, but they were sure that after three days at the latest, protests would be finished. What they didn't consider was that, for every day we were in prison in over thirty cities of the GDR, three hundred protest events took place every evening for our release. In Berlin, the biggest one was attended by thousands of people and also by the Western journalists who were accredited in the GDR. Every day we were also a topic in the Western media. Political pressure became so strong that after about sixteen days Erich Honecker, the party and state leader at the time, had to summon a press conference to announce that all civil rights activists would be released within ten days. (GDR5)

The definition of those who protested was relevant in producing waves of support. It was as repression hit the peaceful protest prayers in Leipzig that, a pastor stressed, solidarity spread:

At the Schkeuditz freeway intersection they didn't let people without a Leipzig license plate drive into the city Monday afternoon. They also checked on the central station, didn't let people in who didn't have an address in Leipzig, ... [This] led to a lot of anger, and those who didn't know until then what was going on at Nikolai church, on Monday at 5 P.M., learned about it now at the latest. There was an enormous wave of sympathy, which was directed at us from the population. (GDR7)

If repression was perceived by the activists as backfiring in the two cases of eventful democratization, in Poland it was instead considered as particularly disruptive for the development of the opposition. An activist of underground Solidarity, often imprisoned by the regime, thus describes the demobilizing and demoting effect of the martial law that followed the strike waves of 1980–1981:

what Solidarność lost was the result of repression, because Solidarność after December 13 was destroyed. ... During the martial law, through prisons and arrests or some kind of imprisonment, more than ten thousand people went through it. That is a lot within the society. And the main strike of the martial law was directed against the young workers, because the main engine in this Solidarność in 1980 was the new working-class. ... Tens of thousands of people who are going through prisons, hundreds of people who are leaving and they are the best ones, the ones who are leaving, the leaders of trade unions, of the ones who were leading the strikes in 1980, they are leaving. This, in my opinion, led to breaking of the spine of Solidarność. (PL7)

In fact, of the thousands who went to prison, most "were not coming back to their working places or were emigrating, or if they were coming, they wanted to have a peaceful life, they were not professional revolutionaries" (PL7). Here, the decline of mobilization was therefore related to the introduction of martial law, which remained as a threat to the opposition as, at the same time, the potential mobilization of workers pushed the incumbents toward a compromise. The compromise of 1989 was therefore based on the fear of tanks returning to the streets. So, according to another member of the underground Solidarity, "Besides the two months of preparations for the semi-free elections, in 1989 there was not such an energy as you could see in 1980 when you were walking on the streets. . . . *The people were becoming more frightened of the changes rather than becoming energized by them*" (PL11, emphasis added).

Repression is perceived as backfiring in Hungary as well, particularly around the resistance against the building of a dam on the Danube. In the memory of an activist of this massive protest,

they tried to intimidate the participants with the involvement of the police, but here in Hungary this is not advisable. So, whoever did this did not know the Hungarian psyche. So then the Danube movement turned into a mass movement, and by the very end, at the end of the 1980s, when the government was reluctant to retreat, the Danube circle's enraged leaders initiated a referendum about the construction of the dams. . . . From then on . . . the dams issue turned into some kind of a symbol. The symbol of the impotence of the Communist regime, its impotence and its aggressive character. So an immense social movement unfolded from this. (HU3)

Here as well, however, negotiation was preferred to protest, and the fear of potential repression helped in maintaining law and order.

In sum, where eventful protest spread, this came with a transformation of fear into outrage, in a context characterized by an alternation of liberalization and de-liberalization in which exceptional episodes of repression appeared as less and less bearable to a broad public. Emotional work was embedded in specific choices and rituals oriented to overcome fear, but at the same time channel outrage. While the increasing impression that courage was spreading brought about more participation, this was taken as an indication that repression was not working. As courage was, that is, perceived as contagious, each new action of repression mobilized new people who felt solidarity and even identification with those who protested – increasingly seen as "some of us."

HOPE IN TRANSFORMATIONS, SATISFACTION WITH THE CHANGE

We always needed some naiveté. You can't plan any revolution, if you think you cannot win. . . . If you count all the military, police and militia it means you will never think you can win. (CZ10)

The naiveté referred to by this Czech activist, who played a pivotal role with the group Bridge as well as in Civic Forum, is linked to the perception of a moment of madness (Zolberg 1972), when mobilization itself raises big expectations. Hope has been cited in fact as most important to trigger protest. As activists from all countries explained, the first experiences of mobilization were imitated when people thought they had shown a possibility for change. As they say, without hope, there would have been no mobilization. At the same time, it is important to note that hope develops with the mobilization itself, with its various moments of trials and errors. In this sense, hope might be triggered by small acts of resistance that acquire high symbolic value and emotional impact.

This is particularly true in one of the eventful democratization: Czechoslovakia. There, a member of Charta 77 recalled, "There were mass protests ... mainly in November. There were protests almost every day. It was amazing what the society achieved. ... There were 250,000 people on Wenceslas square and about 500,000 people on Letná" (CZ14). Excitement is thus recalled as bringing about an enhanced feeling of empowerment. As a participant remembered, "it was a wonderful time in our lives. It was like a miracle. And we were full of euphoria and full of optimism. And we were thinking you can move the world. It was beautiful. I'm very happy I was there" (Long 1996, 71). Similarly, another former dissident recalled the "Initial euphoria, the enthusiasm of the whole society, the goodwill – is something that lasts a certain limited time period. Then things have to go back into their track, and that's another story" (Long 1996, 87). As a founder of the oppositional group Most noted,

I realized it at that time ... "When you don't have any hope, then people don't do anything to change the situation." They want to get used to it, usually. When you don't have any hope, when you live in a police state where the regime controls everything concerning power, when the regime has got nomenclatural lists of people who are allowed to do something, and you are not on the list, then you don't bother about it. Because why you would bother; you could only hang yourself in that situation. But when *the little crack that shows possible change appears*, then everybody's feeling unites, people unite, and that is why the huge gathering on Wenceslas square was possible. That is quite a usual thing. It's becoming unbearable when it seemed that change was possible. ... As the people saw that it was growing, first a few hundreds, then a few thousands, and suddenly people said to themselves: "I think it might make sense." And they joined spontaneously. ... These were normal people and they said: "Watch out, there is a hope that it could be changed." It was real action; it was about what to do. ... It was important that people gathered together. (CZ5, emphasis added)

Hope was also mentioned in other cases to explain mobilization for democracy. It was considered a necessary condition for protest in the GDR, even though the perception by most of our interviewees is that expectations were subsequently betrayed. As a peace activist explained,

I was surprised in 1989 by the potential that was suddenly there, within the GDR population, because I would have never expected it that way ... however it disappeared relatively quickly, also because of the fast reunification: people were thrown back into their mainly economic problems, unemployment, orienting yourself in the new society, and stood up less for democracy and human rights and freedom rights and civil rights. (GDR8)

Hopes go together with the perception of high energy. In many activists' narratives, "there was really an energy of ideas, ... the energy was completely free, there was ... an intelligence in the air" (GDR11). Thus, energy was perceived as highly contagious, as "indeed so many people took to the streets and stood up for democracy and civil rights who before never concerned themselves with [those topics]" (GDR9). In this energetic atmosphere, opportunities are perceived as opening up. In the words of a German activist, 1989 was "a very special situation," as "everything is in transition and everything is questioned, everything is debatable, everything has to be newly negotiated. That is an experience that makes you very, very happy, because it seemed possible to exercise influence ... everything was possible" (GDR1).

In the cases of participated pacts, hope in broad changes is cited, but with much less emphasis, while expectations seem to focus more on the negotiations. In Hungary, 1988–1989 is remembered as a joyful period – in the words of a member of the liberal organization SZDSZ and a member of parliament,

In 25 years' retrospect ... this era was the most positive in my opinion. This is when the great demonstrations took place against the destruction of villages in Romania, and the protest against the dams, with the torches ... at this point everyone was only hoping, no one thought of what it would be like when it has happened and people would start thinking in strategic, power-related terms. Lots of people joined the movement in those days, really the middle class, secondary school teachers and honest manufacturers. .... They stood up for themselves: intelligently, beautifully and courageously, they talked about what should be done. (HU2)

However, the impression is of a very short moment, as "This very promising company disappeared in half a year after 1990. Very early on they felt that the ensuing order wasn't their world, and so these genuine civil peoples disappeared terribly fast. What followed was again, something completely different" (HU2). After the hope in mobilization, therefore, came rapid demobilization as, according to an interviewee from the Hungarian Democratic Forum parliamentary faction,

> you had to oust a dictatorship and you couldn't have that without social mobilization. . . . The segment of society that was mobile and devoted to public affairs felt that there was room for changing the unbearable conditions and for mobilization . . . and that was their only means to achieve change. So these people realized that there was a chance on the one hand, and realized that there was a need for mobilization in order to make use of that chance. Because the methods otherwise used in a democracy for public participation, social change, or influencing public outcomes were missing. So this was the only way to go. And after the transition the legitimate ways to change were established. (HU10)

In the memory of several Hungarian activists, "social movements played a much greater role in the transition process than is acknowledged today" (HU1). Protest is in fact remembered as happening during the transition, but it accompanied the negotiations rather than taking the lead: "the trilateral negotiations had already begun, the oppositional roundtable had been set up. The preparations for the democratic elections had already been taking place, but in the meantime . . . the opposition tried to increase the pressure on the government through protest actions" (HU6).

In Poland, as well, the end of the 1980s saw a renewed hope after the years of martial law, but this was mainly not oriented to mobilization. Many narratives therefore converge in defining a search for security, rather than the expectation of a sudden break. In the account of the publisher of an underground journal,

> 1989 was important for me because hope was reborn. And this hope was supported by some events and some facts that allow for hope that freedom and sovereignty will be regained and that we will start changing the reality in the way we wanted to, that our voice, the social voice is beginning to be maybe not decisive, but it is being heard and that the leaders are beginning to take it into account. (PL1)

Hope notwithstanding, in Poland as in Hungary, feelings of uncertainty are perceived as a cause of demobilization. In the words of a former unionist who had joined the first Solidarity, "in 1989 people had the conscience that things are changing and it will be irreversible. . . . People had no idea, what is free market economy, democracy, what will be the costs of transformation for the society. There were a lot of question marks. And this uncertainty did not benefit organizing protests, I would say on the contrary" (PL3). So, in Poland, the year 1989 is seen as a period characterized by "no chance for such massive protests of a revolutionary type" (PL12). The timid expectation that "the new government will change everything and will change the system for the better" was soon disappointed, as "it was like believing in a miracle that you can have social benefits like in Scandinavia, salaries like in the United States and still work like in Poland. But it wasn't for long, this hope. . . . Frustration and fatigue came when people realized that the changes are not the way they have imagined them to be" (PL13).

In sum, during eventful protests, as fear was transformed into outrage, hope emerged as sustaining the wave of protest, at the same time being fueled by the excitement of participation in historical moments. In participatory pacts, hope also emerged, but more in negotiation than in mobilization.

A "STOLEN REVOLUTION"? DISENGAGEMENT BETWEEN FRUSTRATION AND SATISFACTION

One had to do some things around the clock, and had to make one's living too and if you then lost your job or did a retraining and all these things. . . . Many didn't manage that right . . . personal exhaustion too . . . people were out of their depth because of their own personal circumstances: so work, perhaps also housing, rent increases, retraining, and all those things. Partnership stress also increased, . . . because the (expectations) of a relationship are quite different and people had to figure out how to deal with that with the new times. (GDR3)

If hope sustained mobilization, demobilization instead ensued, this German environmentalist recalls, when hope gave way to frustration. Notwithstanding the end of the authoritarian regime, former opponents declared a lack of satisfaction with what they had achieved. Disappointment is explained by too high expectations, but also by the negative assessment of the events that pushed for an emotional adaptation, with declining investment in politics.

Part of the reason for withdrawal from public life is seen in the need for personal adaptation to the difficult challenges of a changed situation. Such a sentiment emerges, for instance, in the words of a German activist, who singled out "a withdrawal step by step," linked to the fact that

A completely new life situation was suddenly in the foreground too, that everybody really had to earn his own bread every day now. . . . That was a complete reorientation. Who told me how a tax declaration works? Nobody: I had no clue at all about what I must do to fill a tax declaration. . . . Frustration is surely a great part of it because if you didn't adapt to that immediately, which then so to speak washed over you like a tsunami wave, then you were an outsider of course. . . . I also had to have my daily bread, I had to orient myself. (GDR8)

While in the Czech path of eventful democratizations, the perception was, as we will see, initially of success, many GDR activists lamented instead a deep failure of the "peaceful revolution" – as "a lot developed the wrong way" (GDR9). They are in fact adamant in presenting the transition as "a great beginning which finally ended up to be a tremendous disappointment" (GDR1). This disillusionment was fueled by a narrative of colonization by the West – as "there is someone coming from the west and promising us blooming sceneries . . ." (GDR4). This is expressed, in a very bitter way, in this account of the fall of the Wall by one of the founders of New Forum:

I remember exactly when we heard that the Wall was being built on the 13th of August 1961. We were on holidays on the beach, and the neighbor came and told us about it, and I felt really nauseous because it was immediately clear what it meant. . . . I remember exactly the feeling in my stomach, and I had the same feeling when the journalist told me that the Wall is open, because it was clear immediately that it meant that all ideas about how you turn the GDR into a decent country would be at once hollow words. (GDR10)

Colonization by the West is in fact a widespread framing of the first years after transition. In the process of reunification, the activists felt bitter as the GDR was, from several points of view, colonized. So, in a broadly shared account, East Germany was bound to fail, as

it was a minority in the midst of transition; it was the minority in terms of numbers, that means in all negotiations and such the GDR was at a disadvantage from the beginning. . . . It was mainly a matter of the insufficient willingness by the West German partners too, to adopt something of the experience, also the newest experience, of the peaceful revolution, for instance, or the experience of the citizens' rights movement, which could have been done very easily, which surely would have benefitted the democracy in the whole Germany too. (GDR9)

The feeling toward the achievements of democratization is thus particularly negative in the GDR, where a New Forum cofounder observes: "I took to the streets for democracy for years; what we ended up getting in my experience doesn't have much to do with democracy. . . . We thought, well the *Wessis*, surely they are sometimes a little pushy, but with one thing they are ahead of us, they can deal well with money: you see what is happening with the money, right?" (GDR10). Feelings of frustration therefore spread and, with them, demobilization. As a feminist remembered, after 1989, "there was for at least half a year almost depression; everything a waste of time. But also just the hope for a societal alternative, that was for now buried ... and then it started that also, most women lost their work and so on" (GDR1).

In the narratives of former activists, the acceptance of the ready-made Western model is also linked to the spreading fear of insecurity and a related search for pragmatic solutions against the dreams of another democracy. In the GDR, given the widespread exhaustion, after the intense moments of transition,

> many were glad that it was leading up to reunification ... one underestimates how much need for security there is in the population, to somehow come back onto a secure track. So, this anarchy is ... an incredible instance of insecurity, because you never knew what would happen tomorrow. There are I believe personalities who like that, but there are also many ... it scares them a great deal and they are happy when everything is orderly again, and is calculable and predictable. (GDR2)

Given the intensity of the transition time, there is thus a widespread perception of the need for emotional normalization. In the words of a German founder of Women for Peace, as the situation was perceived as leading to the reunification between the East and the West,

> some were also tired and then said, it is nice in the West, then we simply get incorporated, and then everything is fine. ... Many were happy that they finally suddenly had the opportunity to study or to learn an occupation or like all that they had been denied in the GDR. Precisely because they were politically active, because they were oppositional, many couldn't do the occupational trainings that they wanted, or they were not allowed to work in their occupations, and then some reoriented themselves again ... also had a right to somehow withdraw again into the private sphere. (GDR2)

Transition is then perceived as a chance to return to "normal life," even if keeping an active interest in social and political activities. So, former activists

> founded publishing houses, they founded newspapers, they joined the broadcasting houses ... people who really completely withdrew, there are several, but I think this is really a minority. And that is often underestimated: the extent of building up work achieved in the trenches, the really back breaking work that was done by people who up till then had no administrative experience at all, who had learned it by themselves: how you lead an administration, how you lead a government or a ministry. Those are really quite magnificent achievements. (GDR9)

In Czechoslovakia, the initial emotional outcome of the protest was instead satisfaction, given the widespread perception that the movement had fully won its battle, entering the institutions of government. Satisfaction is in fact cited as a main sentiment toward the new regime in the first years in which the Civic Forum leaders were in power. Activists from the different organizations we interviewed converged in the assessment that, for a long period,

people were in a good mood. ... When something is successful. ... Frankly, in the beginning people got it rather for free. The regime collapsed into itself, international circumstances were favourable and then there was a group of people which showed some leadership, effort and courage. The majority was satisfied because their dreams had come true and everybody thought it would be easy since that time. (CZ6)

Hopes seem indeed to have lasted for a time, pushed by the belief that those who had led the Velvet Revolution were now in power. So, here, "for quite a lot of years ... people believed that this process will be easy, ... new possibilities opened for people. They could travel, they could get acquainted, lots of people started their businesses. ... It was a guarantee for people that morally clean persons were assuming office" (CZ2).

In the narrative of another activist, "Nobody had the feeling it was unsuccessful here. Everybody felt it was heading somewhere and that we could influence it" (CZ3). In fact, an activist remembered that

People were full of energy, they wanted to do anything. They were entering Civic Forum and it was a time when people felt they could influence the society somehow. ... The atmosphere of early 1990 was like, we finally could do anything we wanted and do whatever one wished to do. People didn't feel they needed to protest against anything. (CZ9)

The impression of achievement prevailed. The feeling was widespread that "it's done": "presence in the streets was not needed anymore" (CZ3), as "there wasn't anything to protest against. We reached the goal" (CZ5), "There was no need to protest because the fight had already been won" (CZ10). The euphoric atmosphere was fueled by the belief of having reached what had been considered as impossible only a few months before.

Protest therefore declined when other channels were perceived as opening up, as

people felt that there was somebody they could approach and they didn't have to deal with it in the streets because their people were in the right positions ... can communicate with authorities and the authorities are listening to them, . . . they are trying to meet their demands. . . . There is no need to call for a demonstration to force someone to talk to me. (CZ7)

So, in the words of an activist, the decline in protest meant, "The meal has been cooked. Let's move to the dining room to eat it" (CZ10). The perception was then that it was like running in a marathon: "The winner is rewarded with huge applause. Spectators are in raptures and the winner deserves the applause. Well, and you ask me why does the applause weaken? It weakens because you cannot clap your hands all the time. We won and we got the applause" (CZ10). Another concurred: "It surpassed our expectations, our dreams: nobody thought it would change so dramatically and substantially at the beginning of November. . . . We protested a bit, then we celebrated it, and finally we went back to work" (CZ5). This is explained as *"It's not possible to live in euphoria for a long time,* and new possibilities appeared. I remember very well how people were enthusiastic and how they had no need to protest. Injustice emerged later" (CZ2, emphasis added).

In a situation in which the impression of a victory was widespread, activists also felt they could go back to normal life, after a quite exacting period. As one of those who had mobilized for democracy explained, there was an optimistic feeling of possibility for the new life:

some of them wanted to study, to publish; others wanted to run their own business. They came with excellent ideas, and now it was possible. So there was no reason to protest and nobody to protest against. Protests are the result of frustration but in the beginning of 1990s there was no frustration. . . . It's like: we succeeded, we celebrated, and finally started to pursue our interests. People grew mature, they finished their studies, ran businesses, travelled, whatever. Simply, they were doing what they had not been allowed to do before. (CZ5)

Feelings of satisfaction interacted with a need for normality, as "people went back to their normal life as they were rather exhausted by the ongoing revolution . . . they were on Wenceslas square or on Letná all the time. It was the time of constant activism, so people were tired. But it was positive fatigue because everything was moving in the right way. We felt euphoric" (CZ10). In another account, "it started to decline because the goal was reached. Such a tense situation cannot be held for a long time" (CZ14). Another concurs, "They achieved what they wanted and they didn't need to continue. I think that their expectations were met. . . . You cannot protest and demonstrate until the end of the world. . . . If the protest fulfils what you want, you don't protest anymore" (CZ11).

Activists only later regretted having shared the "naïve idea that democracy has been built once for all." As one of them synthetized, "I thought: 'I'm returning to journalism, diplomatic service. I don't have to care anymore. It's done.' And now, mainly after ten years, ... 'Jesus, that's catastrophe, how could it happen. It was built once and for all'" (CZ1). A main failure is later singled out in

the fact that civil society in the broadest meaning, i.e. nongovernmental organizations, active people, had the feeling that the main had been done. That means that communism collapsed and we had freedom, and we thought that everything was going to be better: people who would govern would strive for the common good and the situation would improve. So the failure was some naïveté or resignation to watch new elites. (CZ4)

The lesson is that "we should have remained active, entered politics, tried to understand what was going on and not had the feeling that when the communists were gone and Havel was president everything was done" (CZ4).

Although there was a longer period of satisfaction during the first years of democracy, frustration also emerged in the Czech case, as "The disillusionment rose when these people felt that the revolution was thwarted." In particular, student activists started to speak about a "stolen revolution," as – they declared – "We thought it would be different" (CZ12). Personal difficulties in adapting to the new system were described here as well. In the words of one of the ministers in the very first government after transition, citizens were "frustrated by some circumstances they weren't prepared for" (CZ9). Insecurity was fueled by the discovery that the state was no longer protecting citizens from aggressive ways to make profits. An activist and member of parliament recalled citizens who went to complain to him:

"Look, it is really bad here. I wanted to build a house. There was a company that dealt in house building and they offered really nice terms. We signed the agreement and they wanted one million CZK deposit. I gave them the money and nothing happened. I wanted to visit the company's office. When I got there the landlord or the receptionist told me that they weren't there anymore. I asked where they were. He told me he didn't know and that they left because they hadn't paid the rent. ... It was all lost. I lost one million CZK, sir. What shall I do, sir?" I told him: "First of all you should search your conscience. You have lost your family's savings, one million CZK. It is the same as giving the money to people in the street. You acted as if someone on the street stopped you and offered you to build a house for one million. You would give him/her the money and he would promise that he would bring the plans of the house next week to the nearest café so you could check them. You did exactly the same." He asked:

"Doesn't the government guarantee for it?" and I told him: "The government doesn't guarantee for private companies." He replied: "So what is this government for? There must be some justice here, am I right?" ... This was typical. I experienced a lot of similar cases. People were trusting because during the communist regime nobody had escaped. They caught everyone – every fraudster they wanted to catch. And now, everyone was supposed to be responsible for his/her money. (CZ12)

The frustration is perceived as increased by the high expectations raised by the very use of the term "revolution." As the future head of the first government after transition observed, frustration was bound to follow the expected revolutionary catharsis, with "some separation of the good from the evil, the guilty ones from the innocent ones." In this situation, "The frustration came from the feeling that somebody stole from them the catharsis" (CZ13).

Frustration was also present in the cases of participated pacts within, however, a situation in which emotions had been kept at bay. In Hungary, indeed, the disappointment with the effects of the transition produced frustration mixed with apathy – as a founder of the oppositional group Fidesz noted, "Frustration was characteristic of course of the entire society ... disappointment with the transition was already sizable in 1992 ... the loss of illusions ... but instead of resulting in a political backlash, I would rather say it resulted in exhaustion" (HU11). Similarly, in Poland, frustration was felt in particular by those who had been nearer to the original claims of Solidarity and who compared them with what they perceived as a weak democracy. The new regime's betrayal of the value of Solidarity is particularly stigmatized: as early as 1990, an increasing number of strikes signaled the dissatisfaction of those who, having fought for change – as an activist of Solidarity since the early 1980s observed – had gotten "the bill for the reforms they supported, meaning that the factories are bankrupting, there is a growing pauperization of the society due to reforms introduced that liquidated subventions and financial support to factories. And at that moment politicians who have their own ideals leave Solidarność and these are some sorts of leftist ideals" (PL8).

Summarizing, after protests declined, whether satisfied or frustrated, citizens tended to demobilize, pushed by a general search for normality after the emotionally heightened moments of the regime change. Stronger emotions fueled eventful democratizations, while they were kept more at bay in participated pacts.

CONCLUDING REMARKS

Looking at the micro level, research on democratization has often stressed interests and rationality. Without considering activists as irrational, recent works in social movement studies as well as on revolutions have reevaluated emotions as resources for and constraints upon mobilization.

The narratives of the activists who struggled for democracy in Eastern Europe were full of emotion – fear, outrage, hope, satisfaction, and disappointment. While fear, satisfaction, and disappointment discouraged some from further protest, outrage and hope were positively linked to contentious politics. Indeed, the recognition of emotion has also been explicit in other research on democratization movements in Central Eastern Europe. In the Solidarity movement in Poland, contrasting emotions such as fear and courage, anger and pride, nervous breakdown and solidarity were observed, especially in the very intense seventeen days of protest in Gdansk in 1980 (Barker 2001). In the civil rights movements in East Germany, as in the United States, emotions such as fear, sadness, and anxiety developed together with those of anger, happiness, outrage, surprise, agitation, fearlessness, excitement, togetherness, pride, and anxiety (Goodwin and Pfaff 2001, 286).

To these observations, I added an analysis of a sort of sequencing of emotions (and emotional work) during the ups and downs of the protest wave. Keeping the focus on what have been defined as "high order" emotions (Jasper 1997; Reed 2004, 668), I reconstructed in this chapter sequences of moral outrage, hope, and frustration. In sum,

- Under authoritarian regimes, activists needed to control fear and transform it into outrage. This happened when repression produced moral shock – given not only its level of brutality but especially its assessment as unusual, inappropriate, and incongruous, as well as "against us."
- Hope, we saw, is a main feeling in triggering protest. In phases of high mobilization, hope is also linked to intense sentiments – such as excitement – that are not sustainable in the long term. Hope emerged as particularly strong in eventful democratization.
- Frustration was especially visible after transition, with a demoting effect on mobilization. It was not so much linked to high or unrealistic or irrational expectations, but rather rooted in cognitive assessments of achievement. However, satisfaction can also justify disengagement if those in government are trusted to implement the movement's claims.

In line with recent literature in social movement studies, I observed in this chapter that emotions developed in context, not just as individual feelings but rather as collective moods, influencing the Zeitgeist of the different moments in the waves of mobilization for democracy. In particular, mobilization grew as negative emotions of trauma (such as grief or shame) could be transformed into emotions of resistance, such as righteous anger and hope (on this distinction, see Whittier 2001). Later on, however, demobilization tended to overlap with an emotional climate dominated by frustration. Emotions did not function on their own, but were embedded in the shifting relations produced by protests. Especially, emotional work was needed to overcome fear, and mass mobilization empowered citizens, increasing hopes that were, however, not sustained in the long term.

Far from being spontaneous, emotions were influenced by activists and their organizations, as well as by their opponents in an important emotional work, oriented to generate positive sentiments in collective action (della Porta and Giugni 2009). Emotions were in fact linked to cognitive assessment of the context, opportunities, and constraints (see Goodwin, Jasper, and Polletta 2001). Through various devices, emotions could be transformed – for example, fear could develop into anger and, then, moral outrage, which facilitated protest, which in turn spread hope. As activists encountered what Elisabeth Wood (2004) defined as a pride in collective rebellion, participation in opposition produced joyful and positive feelings. In our cases, activists carved out free spaces where fear could be controlled through appropriate techniques, while spirals of indignation followed episodes of repression that were considered as unfair. Also important in the spreading of moral shock was the cognitive work around the definition of those who protested as "part of us."

This does not mean that emotions are easy to manipulate; rather, they often present strong constraints to contentious politics. Indeed, narratives describe a widespread mood of disappointment, up to depression: not only was there no "revolutionary catharsis," with the related search for a neat distinction between the good and the evil, but even everyday life conditions turned from rosy to grey. A need for security and normality also followed.

As emotional feelings are also linked with different assessments of reality, they remained more positive in Czechoslovakia, where activists expressed their ownership of the revolution, than in the GDR, where with reunification the narrative of a lost, or aborted, rebellion spread. Moreover, the sense of hope was weaker in transitions characterized by participated pacts than in eventful ones. Indeed, emotions are not detached from cognition, as appreciation of the external reality as positive or negative is reflected in emotional responses. If frustration follows rising expectations, this is not related to an irrational reaction. Instead, activists seemed quite able to point at specific sources of disappointment, even if feelings simultaneously influenced their thinking.

Notwithstanding the return to normality, the experiences of intense emotions in collective action can be expected to have long-lasting effects. As Perrot noted about the workers' community of the nineteenth century,

Revolt is not instinctive. It is born of action, and community in action. The strike, in this view, offers a remarkable occasion for basic training, an antidote to isolation, to the mortal cold that the division of labour reduces workers to. With its leaders, its assemblies, its demonstrations, its language, sometimes even its financial organization, it forms a community with Rousseauian aspirations, anxious for direct democracy, avid for transparency and communion. (Perrot 1974, 725)

In its everyday dimension of celebration and words, the long strike was "experienced as a liberating force, able to break the monotony of the days and force the retreat of the bosses' power, it crystallized an ephemeral and often-regretted counter-society. Strike nostalgia carries the seed of its recommencing" (ibid., 725). Similarly in our cases, the experience of empowerment, as the memory of the positive feelings that accompanied it, was not forgotten.

5

"Like a House of Cards"

Time Intensity and Mobilization

What happened in November 1989 was a culmination of the protests. Basically all the civic activities came together in Národní Street and this is how the revolution started in the year 1989 ... people were prepared to declare that they were not satisfied with the past era of the communist system on a mass scale after November. ... there were big demonstrations on Wenceslas square, then there were big demonstrations on Letná, these were really demonstrations of nearly a million participants and they broke the regime's neck, because the regime saw that it remained alone. It was all people's declaration of disagreement with the communist regime. These activities ended about ten days after November 1989 with the general strike, when almost the whole nation took to the streets for an hour with the national flag to declare, basically, the takeover by the whole society. (CZ3)

The old town of Leipzig is surrounded by this ring ... six thousand people started walking ... at the end of the ring it was nine and a half thousand at the next Monday prayer. It was then sixty thousand, at the next a hundred and twenty thousand. The result is well known: within two weeks of the first Monday prayer, there were these demonstrations in more than thirty cities of the GDR. (GDR5)

Thus a former Czech activist and a former East German activist described, with words resonant with the narratives of many of their comrades, the intensification of events in 1989, and its consequences. A shifting perception of time accompanied the various steps of the mobilization for democracy, from a slow start, to a very fast, extraordinary pace, and then a return to normality. This is linked to very different forms of relations – rarefied in the beginning, accelerated at the peak of protest, and eventually normalized. The perception of an intensification of time goes together with an emphasis on the contingent, the unexpected, and the unpredictable.

It has been often noted that protest campaigns linked to episodes of democratization often appear as sudden. Tocqueville observed about the French Revolution, "Never was any such event, stemming from factors so far back in the past, so inevitable yet so completely unforeseen" (1955, 1). Surprise, excitement, and innovation are indeed terms that often emerge to describe regime change as exceptional moments during which a power vacuum is filled by the energy of mobilized citizens, with large space for agency. As mentioned in Chapter 1, time can be analyzed in different ways. In social movement studies, Sewell (1996; see also McAdam and Sewell 2001) has suggested the concept of eventful temporality as characterized by the capacity of events to affect structures, Beissinger (2007) has singled out some extraordinary times in the development of nationalism, and I have looked at eventful protests as able to transform relations (della Porta 2004, 2014a).

In this chapter, after looking at the ways in which time has been addressed from a micro and macro perspective, I will single out the impact of some time-related relational mechanisms of time intensification and then time normalization. I will do that through the analysis of activists' perception of time, from the slow motion in the building up of an opposition, to the accelerated time of the transition period, and then the normalized, or lost, time of the consolidation. In particular, I will assess the different rhythms of the relations among emerging actors and with their environment as linked to the overcoming of routines and the search for signals.

TIME AND DEMOCRATIZATION: AN INTRODUCTION

Time has mostly been a silence in sociologic and political science analyses, although some attention has been paid to the impact of events and time horizons on social processes (Abbott 2001). Even if time is often considered as objective, there is a growing recognition of the importance of subjective temporality. While theories of causality tend to see bits of time as independent from each other, studying causes as mainly synchronic issues, time-conscious narrative has been proposed as the foundation of a sociological methodology that sees processes (or stories) at the basis of social reality, as "sequences of action located within constraining or enabling structures" (Abbott 1992, 428). In fact, "the times they are a-changing" is a statement that could be theoretically supported at micro, meso, and macro levels.

A shifting conception of time and the relations within it have been discussed at the micro level, especially within game theoretical perspectives. In particular, in the literature on transitions, scholars singled out a shift in the very "game" played by actors – from a prisoner's dilemma, which discourages cooperation, to "a coordination or even an assurance game in which individuals' incentives to contribute and collective benefits reinforce each other in a virtuous circle" (Kitschelt 1993, 416). Changes include a different matrix of risks and benefits in expressing anti-regime preferences in public. The assumption is that there are "behavioral cascades," as the net benefits of each individual choice are influenced by the number of people who make that choice (Granovetter 1978), and mobilization is fueled by the action of a "critical mass" (Marwell and Oliver 1993).

In his analysis of events in 1989, Kuran linked the sudden increase in protest to the decreasing risks for participants when the number of participants increases. In his approach, while private preferences are fixed, the decision to express them in public is affected by a calculation of the risks it brings (Kuran 1991, 17). When the dissidents in Eastern Europe were few, they did not enjoy public support, as even those who agreed with them were afraid to express their opinion in public. There was therefore broad ignorance about the spread of anti-regime positions, as people "could sense the repressed discontent of their conformist relatives and close friends; they could observe the hardships in the lives of their fellow citizens; and they could intuit that past uprisings would not have occurred in the absence of substantial discontent. Still, they lacked reliable, current information on how many of their fellow citizens favored a change in regime" (Kuran 1991, 30). The risks of repression decline, however, as the number of protestors increases, as "the smaller the individual dissenter's chances of being persecuted for his identification with the opposition, the fewer hostile supporters of the government he has to face" (ibid.). As protest against the regime spreads, fewer people are available to collaborate with the state repressive apparatuses, which additionally have more difficulty in effectively repressing the unfamiliar phenomenon of a mass mobilization. Moreover, the higher the number of people participating in protest, the higher the symbolic rewards in terms of societal recognition, and the higher the sense of personal integrity (Kuran 1991, 17–18).

Still within a micro perspective, other authors have also noted a sort of revolutionary bandwagon that follows the overcoming of some threshold of participation, as it becomes easier to convince those with private preferences against the government to mobilize, but also to change the preferences of others. Some incidents might trigger imitation, as unambiguous signals "reassure potential participants that there will be others present in sufficient numbers to reduce the individual risk of participation" (Pfaff and Kim 2003, 409). Regime repression and the action of countermovement also have an impact on turnout (Chong 1991). Not only are negative incentives reduced by the number of participants but positive incentives also increase, as participation is expected to be praised in the individual's circles of recognition (Chong 1991; Goodwin and Pfaff 2001). In a similar perspective, James De Nardo (1985) links the individual decision to participate in a mobilization to the distance between movements' claims and regime policies: while reform can reduce that distance, this choice is constrained when the movement reaches a revolutionary threshold. In fact, spreading knowledge of shared grievances enhances social recognition, as people receive the unmistakable message that they are all against the regime.

According to signaling theory, this mobilization process has an effect as senders (who have information) distribute information to receivers (who make decisions). The assumption is that each individual is imperfectly informed and that no one can individually decide to overturn the status quo (Lohmann 1994). In this sense, political action is a way to express dissatisfaction with the regime, the public looks for information about the size of protest, and the regime risks losing power if communication cascades are successful (Lohmann 1993, 1994). Each individual can undertake action in order to give a signal to large numbers, and the public is especially sensitive to the size of the aggregate turnout when deciding whether to make a private experience with the regime public. In short, as "people are limited in their abilities to articulate their personal experiences and opinions on complex policy issues or to understand other people's communications," "the masses take an informational clue from this simple signal: aggregate turnout" (Lohmann 1994, 50). In East Germany, the increasing number of those who had applied for permission to migrate was in itself taken as a signal of growing dissatisfaction but, at the same time, reduced the number of potential protestors: "Exit as crisis signals the extent of grievances against the state, reveals publicly falsified preferences enabling mutual recognition of discontent, and increases the pressure for voice. Yet exit is also capable of undermining the relational foundation of protest movements by siphoning away prospective movement participants" (Pfaff and Kim 2003, 438).

Policy preferences intervene in this process, as the receivers could also have different preferences from the senders in terms of moderate versus extremist positions, so that "protest activities have little impact and quickly evaporate if demonstrators' opinions are relatively extreme compared with those of the population at large. Further demonstrations are triggered only if some people with relatively moderate opinion participate in the initial stages of mass protest movements" (Lohmann 1994, 53). Applied to East German protest in 1989 and the following years, this signaling approach aims at explaining success in the increase of protest, but also demobilization or lack of mobilization.

The rapid increase in oppositional behavior has also been explained at the macro level. As Guillermo O'Donnell and Philippe Schmitter (1986, 363) have noted, transitions from authoritarian rule are examples of "underdetermined social change, of large-scale transformations which occur when there are insufficient structural or behavioral parameters to guide and predict the outcome." While previous approaches searched for the preconditions for democratization, their transitologist approach focuses instead on the dynamics of interactions between and within different actors, in the incumbents as well as in the oppositional fronts. During these intense moments, the fast interactions between many different and differentiated actors are not governed by normal capacity of assessment, which usually provides some predictive leverage. This leaves the outcome underdetermined at both structural and strategic levels.

Going beyond the individual level and systemic perspective, the analysis of eventful democratization at the meso level points at the power of action itself in creating and recreating environmental opportunities and organizational resources that influence the strategic interactions of various actors (della Porta 2014a). Within accelerated time, protest events tend indeed to fuel themselves, as action produces action. As indicated by the use of terms like "protest cycles," "waves," "or tides," they cluster in "a punctuated history of heightened challenges and relative stability" (Beissinger 2002, 16). Protests fuel each other as they are linked "in the narratives of struggle that accompany them; in the altered expectations that they generate about subsequent possibilities to contest; in the changes that they evoke in the behavior of those forces that uphold a given order; and in the transformed landscape of meaning that events at times fashion" (Beissinger 2002, 17). Structural conditions change during protest campaigns that are eventful, as they produce new relations that favor mobilization, rather than being a simple product of external and internal conditions (della Porta 2014a). As Mark Beissinger observed, indeed, "the spectacle-like quality of the event makes it an important site of cultural transaction at which national identities are potentially formed" (Beissinger 2002, 22).

In the following analysis, I stress the emergent nature of protest in 1989. Notwithstanding the relevance of protest events for social movements, they have mainly been studied as aggregated collective action (for example, in protest cycles). In social movement studies, in fact, protest has principally been considered as a "dependent variable" and explained on the basis of political opportunities and organizational resources. In my conception of eventful democratization (see also Chapter 1), looking at waves of protest for democracy, my assumption is instead that eventful protests have relational impacts on the very actors that carry them out, by intensifying and transforming interactions. Through these events, participants experiment with new tactics, send signals about the possibility of collective action, create feelings of solidarity, and consolidate organizational networks.

In what follows, we will see how a perception of time acceleration affected the process of transition, through increasing interactions between different actors. Not only did interactions intensify, but they are also described as being of a different nature from those in "normal" times: surprising, open-ended, not based on routine. Differences then emerge, once again, between eventful democratization and participated pacts, reflecting eventually on the expected consequences of these dynamics in the phase of democratic consolidation and, therefore, time normalization. The different paths of transition have an effect on this process, as time intensification is perceived especially in cases of eventful democratization, and much less in participated pacts.

EVENTS AS TURNING POINTS

We thought that November 17 would be a dress rehearsal before the Palach's week in January, and we did not count on it: I wonder if you could find just one person who did think that it would erupt on November 17. We organizers did not think that. We thought that it would be a test of how many people we would be able to gather and if they were able to act in a disciplined way ... we managed to ... turn the huge crowd of several tens of thousands of people at Macha's grave to the centre. That was a great success, and as we walked along the waterfront people joined us, so that when we arrived at Národní the crowd was enormously huge. ... It came earlier than we expected. ... Everything was much accelerated. (CZ1)

This emphasis on turning points that transformed the perception of time is common in the narratives of the transition phase. One important characteristic of this sense of accelerated time – especially in eventful democratization – is its unexpected nature. The acceleration of time in fact makes events difficult to predict, producing the mentioned widespread "surprise." As for 1989, "before the demise of communism made the front pages around the world, few if any of the revisionist students of communism were betting on it" (Di Palma 1991, 52). Not only were Western scholars stunned, but the sudden change surprised East European dissidents as well: for instance, as late as the end of 1988, Czech dissident Václav Havel had expected the opposition to remain "for the time being merely the seed of something that will bear fruit in the dim and distant future." According to an opinion poll conducted in Czechoslovakia a few months after the transition, only 5 percent answered affirmatively to the question, "A year ago did you expect such a peaceful revolution?" (cit. in Kuran 1991, 10–11).

Our interviewees also often expressed surprise about the regime collapsing "like a house of cards." In the German Democratic Republic (GDR), many activists mentioned their astonishment as

this SED, which defended its power so massively with the help of the Soviet Union, ... *nevertheless collapsed like a house of cards* ... nobody expected that, nobody could expect that. ... Obviously this party system of bloc parties, and with all those organizations around it, was *so rotten and in itself so fragile that a relatively small pressure was enough.* (GDR9, emphasis added)

The very history of New Forum shows how the surprise caught the same activists. In the words of one of its founders:

we were invited to come to the premises of Robert Havemann; he wasn't alive anymore, but his wife was living there ... we met there and for a weekend discussed the problems, thought about what to do, and one page of text emerged – the first text of New Forum, we all signed it and then we agreed to meet on the third of December ... in the meantime basically the entire GDR turned over. (GDR10)

In Czechoslovakia, as well, activists recalled their surprise about what they did not expect to happen, but did happen, as they "really didn't think that the regime would change so quickly" (CZ14). As oppositional activists recalled, "frankly speaking, we didn't believe that it would suddenly collapse like a house of cards. It was a big surprise" (CZ6); as "The Berlin Wall fell and it was obvious that something was going to happen, but one didn't think that it would be so fast" (CZ6). The pace of the mobilization accelerated indeed, exceeding anyone's highest expectation.

Accelerated times are based on turning points, which are often narrated with reference to the rapidly increasing numbers of participants. This was the case in Czechoslovakia for the demonstration on November 17. Thus, when the idea of calling for a public demonstration emerged in August, a member of Charta 77 remembered this "spark off":

> half of us was against organizing the demonstration, because we were afraid of brutal dispersion; the others wanted to organize it. It was quite unsure in that time, anyway people came even though we didn't call it. ... Anyway it was a big surprise that so many people came, and this was the spark off for me. We marched down the waterfront and we couldn't see the end of the march. After this it was only about the numbers of people who came to the Wenceslas square – *when there were a hundred thousand people it was not possible to disperse them.* (CZ6, emphasis added)

During intense episodes of protest, acceleration happens in the course of few hours. Thus, a Czech member of oppositional Most recalled the demonstration on Letná as "the biggest one in Czech history. There were three quarters of a million people there who came to say that they didn't want the regime anymore. This was an enormous impulse, of course" (CZ5). The massive participation in the demonstrations of November 17 was taken, in fact, as a signal that "dissatisfaction is so enormous," that protest "cannot be compared to anything. ... It was gigantic. ... It was unbelievable. ... Wenceslas square was crowded all the time. There were hundreds of thousands of people all the time. I would say that, *if the dissatisfaction is so enormous, it cannot be solved any other way than via some huge, mass action*" (CZ10, emphasis added). Increasing participation thus makes protesting no longer a cost, bringing instead the seeds of intrinsic benefits. The attribute of "beautiful" is often paired with that of demonstration – as "the atmosphere of the big demonstrations in 1989 was really beautiful and people liked it a lot. So ... would like to repeat it" (CZ9).

In this situation, some moments produce big changes, as people become more courageous, as they are reassured and stimulated by the courage of the others. Expressing private preferences against the regime becomes public criticism and, indeed, a testimony to the widespread dissatisfaction. Intensification of protest in Czechoslovakia is thus linked to the fact that, as noted by a bishop who had participated in the Committee for the Defence of the Unjustly Persecuted in the 1970s, "people spoke relatively openly when they met mostly in restaurants, they became braver" (CZ2). Eventful protest is thus seen as producing that "little crack" that seems destined to push down the entire wall. This is very clearly expressed in this interview, which also stresses how collective identification might be triggered in such circumstances: As "when *the little crack that shows possible change appears, then everybody's feeling united*: people united and that is why the huge gathering on Wenceslas square was possible. . . . It's becoming unbearable when it seemed that change is possible" (CZ5, emphasis added).

Activists often remember their reading of some individuals' behavior as signals of growing support for the opposition. This emerges clearly in Czechoslovakia, where several interviewees recalled when they started to perceive the possibility for change by considering the type of person who joined the protest. Signals of change are in fact offered by the joining of unexpected personalities, such as former regime supporters. Defection by this type of individual sends a strong signal about the difficulties of those in government. This is well illustrated by the following quote, referring to the signatures on the *Několik vět* petition, by one famous Prague actress:

She had always been known as the author of the exclamation marks that followed regime activities: "Yes, the Government is doing well! Doing so is right and our commitments are valuable!" . . . and this lady had arrived from her cottage in the countryside and learnt that this initiative had been launched. She wanted to sign it immediately: "Who collects the signatures?" she asked. They told her: "Wait till Monday. It is a weekend. We don't know if they are at home now. It is a weekend." She said: "No, no, I have to get there. Tell me where it is." She arrived there at 9:30 P.M. and signed it. She didn't want to wait because she was worried she would miss it and she didn't want to be a second-wave signer. *Based on this event I realized that the sympathy of the pro-regime prominent persons was changing in the opposition's favour and that the rats were leaving the sinking ship.* I say it quite harshly but it was like that. (CZ11, emphasis added)

Although this quote refers to a famous person, similar clues on growing support are offered by the (re)mobilization of normal people. Thus, an interviewee recalled his impressions about the changing position of his dentist, who was critical of the regime but did not express it in public:

She had been harmed by the regime in 1948 . . . at that time she belonged to the group of politically unreliable medical university graduates who obtained empty tubes at the graduation ceremony (that is, there was no diploma inside the tubes). Well, some of them got the diploma but she belonged to the group that didn't get it. It was a group of tens of people. These people were told: "The working class doesn't trust you. You may be given the diploma only if you prove your good behaviour at work, or you may be not given it, and then you cannot work as a dentist." Well and once, it was in 1986, she asked me: "When your friend Mr. Havel calls Mr. Tigrid in Paris, how does he do it?" I said: "Since it is automatic it is sufficient to know the phone number. You dial it and if your phone is not blocked for calls abroad, it is done. You can try it." She replied: "No, I won't try it. I have suffered enough but I am happy the others try." . . . She

kept a close watch on the situation: "I won't participate. I have suffered enough."
Well, then these people changed their minds and started to participate. (CZ11)

ENLARGING CIRCLES

We were really surprised that people, who had not been willing to come to
a demonstration a year or two before that spring, signed it at that time. ...
This spring was really successful. And this was perhaps the start that could
have not been stopped. (CZ1)

The mobilization process itself increases moral satisfaction by showing
broadening support for the oppositional ideas. The number of participants is not the only important signal: The diversity of the groups involved
is also considered as an important indicator of the spreading of dissatisfaction and, especially, the availability to express it through protest.

The expansion of the oppositional relations beyond the core group is
taken as a particularly encouraging sign given the "new quality" of the
relationship. As a GDR environmentalist recalled:

This knowledge of each other, that you were not there alone, either as a person or
as a single group ... had a new quality, because that gave moral support too,
because that gave encouragement: if you realized you were not alone, if you were
at one of those networking meetings and there were suddenly hundreds of people
or even more, that bolstered up and encouraged further activities. (GDR6)

During accelerated times, turning points might in fact be produced by
the sudden intensification, but also the interactions, of some specific
conflicts. This is for instance the case of "exiters" and oppositors in East
Germany. The ways in which exit and voice interacted in East Germany
has been stressed as "contrary to the presumption that 'exit' (or, emigration) is inconsequential in contentious politics, the revolution in East
Germany was begotten of the mass exodus of its citizens to neighboring
countries" (Pfaff and Kim 2003, 402). In fact, the wave of exits expanded
the awareness of widespread grievances, functioning as signals of disaffection, along with increasing inclinations by others to speak up. Substantial
exit can facilitate voice, as a sign of defection from the regime; but if it is
too high, it can also negatively affect the oppositional networks by disrupting important nodes (ibid.). In fact, in the GDR case, the interaction
of exiting and voice introduced a series of vicious circles and points of no
return for the regime. As a human rights activist recalled,

many who were active came under pressure, and they preferred to move to the
West. So, they applied for emigration or escaped into the West; especially the

oppositional politically active had it relatively easy to get into the West, because the state had an interest in getting rid of these people and therefore it bled the oppositional movement to death, while the threshold to leave the country was much higher for the Czechs, the Poles, the Russians. (GDR2)

Especially the exiting of young and skilled citizens revealed the weakness of the regime, as

it became clear that the economy was totally down, the infrastructure is ramshackle, and the welfare provisions cannot be financed. The mass scale leaving the GDR, on the one hand, and the inability of the state to respond to it appropriately, on the other hand, made it all escalate so much that now the small opposition groups became bigger mass movements, which then were one of the driving forces for the revolution. (GDR2)

Similarly, in Czechoslovakia, it was not just the sheer number of participants but also their diversity that was perceived as encouraging people to join. So, a speaker of the University Strike Committee noted,

The years before, 1988 and 1987, were only attempts. We used some dates, like September 28, August 21, we went to some demonstrations, ... they dispersed us with water cannons and we did not have really good feeling from it. As I said, it was still the same people. But in 1989 we had the feeling that in *the Palach week* and mainly concerning *Několik vět*, that the group of people was extending and that people who had been afraid to even meet us on the street before were willing to talk to us. (CZ1)

As the numbers increased, so did the variety of people involved. From the small core, contentious politics reached to the larger number of those who were dissatisfied, but had not mobilized earlier. Actions expanded mobilization as they reached what Czech activists called a "grey zone," made up of people who were discontented but passive. Indeed, when "people from the grey zone appeared there," "it was absolutely obvious that the regime was intolerable at that time, even for communists" (CZ5). So, the success of the mobilization came from this growing capacity to mobilize the grey zone – as, when oppositional activities moved to the public, "people tried to show via different public performances, spontaneous as well as organized, that the regime is not democratic and that part of the society was not willing to accept it"(CZ3).

Thus, thanks to the signals given by the increasing mobilization of different social groups, public support for civil resistance expanded. From the small ghetto of dissenters, mobilization spread in fact to students and artists. In Czechoslovakia, the mobilization of the workers, who had been the reference group of the regime and often loyal to it, was considered particularly important. As an activist since the 1970s observed,

The breakthrough came in November 1989 and I consider it very important that the intelligentsia joined forces with workers. The substantial breakthrough, I think, was on Wednesday in that November week, when ten thousand ČKD (the engineering company) blacksmith labourers came into Wenceslas square. Because Communists governed in the 'divide and rule' way and it turned out that workers are well aware of the changes needed. (CZ2)

Acceleration is also related with the entry of new generations of activists who introduce new energy, as "each generation has to learn it anew" (GDR11). This is particularly visible in Czechoslovakia, where a generational cleavage was noted within Charta 77, as the students who mobilized "were mostly sons and daughters of dissidents" (CZ13). The involvement of the students in the opposition also represented, to a certain extent, a generational rebellion against their parents, accused of being too timid in their own mobilization. In fact, in Charta 77, as a cofounder of Civic Forum noted,

Younger generation felt that there was a need to attract younger elements and also to spread Charta's activities beyond the Prague ghetto. ... Moreover, they wanted to address the public and put it into practice instead of only speaking about it. They wanted to go into the streets. ... part of the society, e.g. students, was losing the fear of the regime or inhibitions. I felt it. (CZ6)

Indeed, the younger generation's criticism of the older one stigmatized a "generational fatigue" that affected their parents' cohort. In the words of a student activist, "We perceived them – they were about the same age at that time as we are now – as tired out, passive, not willing to work on any programme about what was going to happen afterwards, not willing to participate in an open conflict with the then power" (CZ1). So, another interviewee since the late 1970s noted, "this had been a long lasting debate within Charta during 1988–89. Some said: 'Look, let it be, don't organize anything. Charta is not a political organization.' The younger ones said: 'No, no, people are willing to demonstrate and we have to demonstrate with them' " (CZ12). Indeed, young people adopted a much more open and confrontational style of mobilization, and, as "the tension and courage was growing," "some followed up the students."

At the same time, however, the mobilization of the young catalyzed the mobilization of the parents as, a then student activist remembered,

we were young, we all had parents and grandparents who were worried about us, and we managed to mobilize people who had not said a word since the year 1968.

These people were completely decimated, I mean *šedá zóna* [the grey zone], they were, figuratively, death. And these people were pulled together at the moment, when their kids were beaten, the poor students at universities, where they were able to study only because their parents made a huge effort to get them to the universities anyhow ... and now, there was a serious threat that not only would they not finish their studies, but moreover they would be imprisoned and their lives would be ruined. (CZ1)

In the words of another activist, "it was mostly the way that we all worked parallel and this was the thing that brought the people to the streets in the first weeks, that persuaded our parents to join us" (CZ4). Ties between the students and the rest of the opposition were indeed formed, bridging different generations. For the young people, in fact, an important oppositional activity related to rock culture, in particular the oppositional band the Plastic People of the Universe (CZ1).[1]

The signals of an increase in support are all the most relevant when they involve the state apparatus. So, examples of the disassociation of police from the regime are publicized during demonstrations. Here as well, signs of defection seem to be particularly needed given the intensity of time, where constructing expectations based on "normal" rules of behavior no longer seems possible. As recalled by the leader of the oppositional organization Bridge (Most), set up to facilitate negotiation between the opponents and the incumbents,

Two policemen came once. They were members of the special corps. Both of them were dressed in plainclothes and both were nearly tearful. ... They told us they really felt sorry for what happened on November 17, and that they would have liked to disassociate from the police intervention. They also wanted to tell us that not every policeman is a bad one and they both had hearts in the right place, and that they support the revolution. We told them to think it through, pluck up courage and appear at the demonstration which would be on Letná on December 5. "No, No, No," they said. But two days later they came .... It was really nice, and we got to like them because they risked everything in that moment. I told them to come dressed in uniforms. ... It was a really big turn and since that time the police was ours. (CZ10)

Various hints are thus interpreted as encouraging, indicating a weakening in the repressive capacity of the regime. Still in Czechoslovakia, an interviewee explained how the forms of repression were perceived as softening, indicating that the regime had become a dog that no longer

---

[1] After transition, as well, youth subcultures developed around alternative music; in particular, punk is identified as an "important influence" on the rebirth of Czech anarchism (Císar and Koubek 2012; Williams and Lee 2012).

bites (see also Chapter 4). Expectations were in fact that, with members of the opposition, "They would have interrogated him/her and frightened him/her. They may have sued you. They would have brought charges against you, but that's it" (CZ12). In this sense, an interviewee, himself a playwright active in the opposition, told the story of a Chartist comrade who had been sued for giving fifty illegal publications (samizdat) to a friend of his, to take them abroad:

During the process he asked the judge: "I am a worker. I am not educated and I don't know what samizdat is." He really worked as a blue-collar worker but he had graduated in history from the faculty of arts. "Explain to me what samizdat is so I know what I have done." It is really a funny story. The judge told him: "Yes, the prosecutor should explain it." It turned out that the prosecutor didn't know what samizdat was. Later it turned out that the judge didn't know either. "I adjourn the process until we find out what samizdat is, so we could explain it to the defendant." The process never resumed. Ordinary people found out that the regime's dog didn't bite anymore, that it only grasped one arm with its toothless jaws. (CZ12)

Indeed, personal stories of interactions with the repressive apparatuses are also mentioned as clues of a perceived weakening of repressive willingness or even capacity. So, for instance, a playwright and activist vividly recalled an anomalous interrogation by the police:

As soon as I entered the cell, a policeman came to me and told me: "You are called for questioning." I said: "I was already questioned in Brno ...," and he said: "Look, I was told to bring you." "Ok, I'll go, no problem," I said, and we left. When we got to the office the police captain asked me two questions: "First of all, do you want a cup of tea?" I said I didn't want any. He said: "I have a really good one. I have Darjeeling"; I said: "Ok then. If you have Darjeeling, I will have a cup of tea." Then he asked: "Second question. If the regime changed what would happen to us? Would you hang us on the lamppost?" It was 28 October 1988 and this was the first questioning that was done in such a way. In that moment I realized that the regime ... was on its last legs. ... I said to the policeman: "Look, we strive for respect for human rights and even you have these rights." He said: "Look, you can trust it but I don't." This was our dialogue. (CZ12)

In addition, the belief was widespread that police would then take cues from the number of participants at a protest, and react accordingly. In the assessment of the future head of the Czech government, "When policemen estimated that there were 100,000 people in the streets they gave it up. It was not technically possible. They knew it was over" (CZ13).

UNPREDICTABLE TIMES

> In that transition situation, it was all very fragile: we didn't know yet if the old power holders would return; even after the fall of the wall, it was not yet clear if the Russians would stay in the barracks at all, and how Moscow would decide: it was all not yet certain that we had changed the situation. (GDR2)

Intense times are described as times of transition, in which crucial decisions have to be made quickly, in the heat of the moment. While strategic approaches assume at least constrained rationality, with relations based upon some information and expectation about others' behavior, in intense times decisions are based more on betting than on knowledge, as the identities, preferences, and interests of the involved actors shift and change. Predictability is radically reduced by constantly moving targets and lack of routines. Contingency acquires leverage.

Time is in fact accelerated because of the breaking down of previous institutions, rules, and norms, and the capacity of movement actors to occupy these spaces, changing them in the process. In a sort of hydraulic system, empty spaces are filled in by mobilized citizens. This was particularly evident in the GDR transition, presented by activists as "a situation in which a power vacuum existed." Indeed, in the fall of 1989, the assessment spread that, as a founder of Democracy Now put it,

> The SED was not accepted anymore as the leading force, and neither were the state cadres invested by it. The communities were suddenly without leadership. And from that a necessity emerged for the citizens to somehow make decisions themselves. On top of that, the euphoria of the new start, suddenly there was also an atmosphere in which ideas were listened to. Ideas were needed and the implementation of ideas. New ideas seemed possible because there was no longer anyone who said you have nothing to say here. (GDR2)

The weakening (up to the collapse) of the old regime is then filled, at the institutional level as well, by representatives of the opposition – designated by the old governors to provide the legitimacy and resources needed for completing the transfer of power. In the transitional period in the GDR, roundtables, at the national, regional, and local levels, also took over this task of filling the gap left by the moribund regime. Although the roundtables were conceived as "an instrument of transition with a specific objective, and that was also made clear from the beginning without the expectation of permanence" (GDR2), they prefigured a very participatory form of democracy, as there were "roundtables on various topics that different interest groups were invited to participate in, in order to develop new approaches, new structures" (GDR2). However, innovation emerged not only within the roundtables, in general, but also, specifically in the GDR, in the Volkskammer – as the head of the government, who was supposed to negotiate with the movement, threatened to withdraw if the dissidents did not join the government as ministers without portfolio.

The empty space was thus filled in by the citizens, in a euphoric atmosphere that, as this interview vividly suggests, quickly spread in the GDR – especially in the fall of 1989, as citizens perceived the chance to speak up and decide: "in this period the movement gained a great breadth, extending into the smaller towns and villages." Thus, a former spokesperson of the citizens organization Democracy Now recalled when he "was invited everywhere, in the different towns and villages," and met people who

until then had shaded away from the state power, and suddenly took their own matters into their own hands. They dismissed the mayor ... and then elected a new communal parliament and deliberated together what they wanted to change in their communal contexts. So [there was] a euphoric atmosphere, a very big upheaval, a grassroots democratic emergence. ... I got there as a representative of Democracy Now, but it was not like they wanted to hear from us how to continue: they decided by themselves. We did present our hypotheses and voiced our opinions, but everyone – almost everyone – was suddenly political, and participated in action, and in thinking, and nobody wanted that to end, that again some avant-garde strivings for power ... and that was a great atmosphere ... it did have a little bit of anarchy, because there were no hierarchies anymore and no authorities anymore, because really there was only the responsibility of the individual citizen and the convincing power of his words, and the organizational talent.

As expectations of others' behavior have weak foundations, organizers must bet on positive results. So, in the fall of 1989 in Berlin, an oppositional pastor recalled, decisions were made in the heat of the moment:

we thought this Chinese solution, that's what they saved for us here as well. Thus came the 9th of October with horrible fear, ... but the more serious it got, and basically you couldn't do anything, the calmer I got. ... the week before, we asked all churches in the inner city to hold peace prayers at the same time, so that as many people as possible can have the protection of the church and hear the message of Jesus of nonviolence. And we got ... an inconceivable crowd of people, who all stood between the churches ... everywhere somehow. And when we wanted to get out, the square filled with people holding candles in their hands, you have to use both hands otherwise it's blown out, so you cannot hold a club or a rock in your hand: so (with the candle) it was visible, visually they want to remain nonviolent. I said, a little helpless, "folks, step aside a bit. There are more than two thousand who want to get out of the church and we want to be together with you." Then it took another half hour. The troops waited until we were out, and then the troops set in motion, and everywhere people came streaming in. From Augustusplatz, which then was still called Karl-Marx-Platz, on the station, on the four lane road which around the so-called Leipzig Ring leads around the city center. . . . Nothing happened: the people, between fear and hope, proceeded meter by meter on the road . . . a miracle of biblical dimensions: we never succeeded with a revolution, that was the first and immediately without shedding blood. The greatest thing you can imagine. (GDR7)

Intense times involve moments in which expectations are based on weak clues and bets are made about the reaction of the opponents, as was the case in Leipzig in the key moment of the protests. Thus, this account of a critical juncture in the development of the eventful democratization in the GDR, in one of the Monday demonstrations in Leipzig, shows the protestors' attempts to strategize – even trying to constrain the dynamics of protest through its own choreography – but at the same time their desperate search for clues about what other actors will do.

In these times, no clear assumptions can be made about the behavior of other relevant actors, while at the same time decisions are quickly needed. This was, again, particularly clear in the case of the GDR, where the consolidation of a democratic state was perceived as particularly urgent, given the vagaries of the geopolitical context – with the perception that "one had to swiftly realize the international law aspect of the German reunification because nobody knew how long Gorbachev could stay in power, and the consent of Margaret Thatcher and François Mitterrand was also a bit fragile" (GDR2). Uncertainty is also remembered as pushing toward quick adjustments under stress, thinking about but not daring to predict potential moves by influential actors.

A similar lack of predictability in the most intense, if short, time of the upheavals was noted in Czechoslovakia. The acceleration of time in fact results in a change in the atmosphere, with a simultaneous need for decision making in situations of uncertainty. As observed by one of the influential activists who led the mobilization in 1989, "suddenly *one had to react very quickly*. One came home at 3 A.M., and at 6 A.M. one got up. We made plans just for one day, at maximum for a week. *We didn't know anything and everything had to be tested.* . . . We dealt with it ad hoc and with some intuition" (CZ6, emphasis added). Basic knowledge was also missing, as summarized by a future minister of the first Czechoslovak government after transition:

On Monday and Tuesday I had no idea who Havel was. On Wednesday I met Pavel Pecháček, and on Thursday I met Havel for the first time. On Friday . . . I met Monika Pajerová, Klíma, and other students for the first time. . . . On Sunday I was offered to be the minister. It was about hours. It went really quickly. And in this situation, trying to think if you are doing well or not ... it is really fast. (CZ11)

While these times were intense, activists also believed they could not persist. As one lamented, "That was unfortunately a time that did not last ... was abruptly finished with the fall of the Wall" (GDR2); another concurred, "every revolution ends at a certain point. You cannot be the revolutionary forever" (CZ11).

CONTINGENT TIMES

They couldn't believe that we would be able to master the situation in the way we did. I don't want to say that it was because we were so capable. It was only a coincidence. (CZ10)

Normal times are said to be structured: context plays a (smaller or larger, according to the different approaches) role in determining the course of the events. The *longue durée* determines to a large extent short-term behaviors, established routines constrain choices, and existing institutions structure events. These limitations on contingency, however, are drastically weakened in intense times – times in which some contingent encounters could make a difference in the development of the process. Through a series of micro decisions, with (at the time) uncertain effects, particular individuals or small groups can acquire unexpected influence. The narratives of our interviewees point indeed at this open-ended character of eventful democratization, in which contingent happenings can make a significant difference.

An illustration of the role of contingent developments as products of actions by small groups (or even individuals) emerges from the activities of Bridge in Czechoslovakia – a group of "some musicians and a lyricist" formed by a very small network of activists, with the aim of constructing a bridge between the dissidents and potential moderates in the regime. Contingency in this process of negotiations, which ended up supporting the peaceful evolution of the transition, is again and again stressed in the account of the events given by a member of the group.

First, protest action is seen as opening a breach in the government, with a cleavage often emerging between party leadership and institutional leadership, and communist prime minister Ladislav Adamec opening spaces for mediation. The narrative then addresses the dynamics of internal conflict within the regime party, within the institutions and between the two – particularly between the regime moderates (led by Adamec) and the radicals (led by the minister of defense, who was suspected of planning to send the army to suppress the mobilization). In this struggle, the presence of informal negotiations between Adamec and Civil Forum gave the former more leverage, as members of the group "were at the government every day at 8 A.M., with Krejčí or with Adamec himself. We were preparing the meeting." In this mobile context, Bridge tried to "keep under check" the leadership of the communist party.

During intense protests, negotiations also developed with the repressive bodies of the regime. Here as well, the accounts stressed the role of contingency in the interactions between the opposition and the army, in particular the West–military garrison, which "had already set out for Prague to suppress the revolution, but they turned back" (ibid.). An important moment occurred as Civil Forum and Bridge members went to meet the general in command of that garrison, who was "afraid of being hanged on the lamppost. He started to talk about it very openly." So, the conversation is recalled:

I told him: "General, we are here to tell you not to go with the army to massacre the revolution." And he said: "To massacre the revolution?" It's something they couldn't accept – that someone would massacre people. But, because I talked to him so openly, he replied in the same way. Instead of telling me that he would never massacre people or that he would only come to secure the order so the dissidents didn't massacre people, he said: "Ok, but I have my orders ..." I told him: "Don't follow the orders, defy them or you are going to have blood on your hands. You know it from history. The revolution has been in process and nobody can stop it. You can only make it bloody. That is all you can do." He got very scared. He started to talk about himself in the third person, and, said that he was not going to make it bloody ... "but I am under the command of the general military headquarters. I am not the commander-in-chief." I told him: "Ok, we will talk to general military headquarters, but promise me you won't follow the order if it appears and you won't act by yourself." He couldn't promise it exactly the way I told him but it was evident that he was in favour of our plan. Then he informed commander-in-chief Vacek. ... Later on, Havel had a meeting with the army and Vacek. He came with some commanders and we definitively made an agreement there. (CZ10)

Promising "not to hang him on the lamppost, especially not the army officers," the compromise was reached (CZ10).

Negotiations also developed with the Soviet Union. Again, in the account of the leader of Bridge, contingent events played an important role. So, his group wrote a letter to Gorbachev, stating that they wanted to start negotiations about the departure of the Soviet army:

We took the letter to the Soviet embassy where some executive called Filipov accepted it. We even had some problems getting to the embassy, because there was a demonstration. . . . When we arrived at the embassy we explained to them what was going on. . . . Filipov accepted it, and three days later we obtained the answer. Gorbachev wrote that the negotiations had to be started. We had enormous influence after that time. . . . They also told us that the Soviet army would not intervene anyhow, they guaranteed it. (CZ10)

Again, in the following account of an important moment of the Velvet Revolution, we see how protest paved the way for negotiation, through unexpected moves with occasional interactions of even an informal character. This is how the encounter with Adamec, which ended up with a sort of appointment of Havel to presidency of Czechoslovakia, is narrated. Notwithstanding the reciprocal fear of the stigmatization that negotiations could raise, they met:

I came to him and he asked: "What would you like to drink?" I answered: "I drink mineral water, only," and he said: "Let's have some drink." This was not usual: it works like this in capitalism; I didn't even know he had any drinks there. "If you have any vodka or whatever you have," I told him. He poured me a glass and sat opposite to me. I knew it was going to be very important. It must have been something big, I thought. I was used to the meetings we had had and I knew the routine: this had a different character. I realized it immediately. "Have you already thought about who would replace current president Husák?" I was really surprised because we hadn't ever talked about it. Husák was still president and his position hadn't been questioned yet, so I said to myself that I had a unique opportunity to run a revolutionary bluff – "I will do it. Fuck it. I am a rocker." . . . Well, I told him: "Mr. Prime Minister, Václav Havel is the only choice for us." It just came to my mind in that moment. I thought they wanted Dubček as president, and they really did. Everybody talked about Dubček and I said Václav Havel, only him. Now guess what his reaction was. . . . He said: "That's a load off my mind." I didn't understand it at first, but then I found out why he said that. And he said: "Right, I thought the same." Fuck. I really don't understand why I thought it. . . . He calmed down when he learnt it was not going to be Dubček. There was one simple reason. He was sure that nominating Havel was total stupidity. . . . So there was only one person remaining – him. . . . But then he said: "What if Havel isn't approved?" I asked: "Why shouldn't he be approved? We won't ask anyone in Moscow." He replied: "I don't suppose you are in contact with Moscow. But what if the development of the situation doesn't progress the way you want?" I said: "It doesn't matter." He continued: ". . . I thought about it and you know we have made such progress so if it was necessary, I could be the president." He simply asked for it. Then he said: "This is my last chance." (CZ10)

In this account, it was this move, in an informal bilateral conversation, that accelerated the process of transition. In a narrative that indeed stresses contingency and the open-ended process, this chance event then had significant consequences, as it resulted in the appointment of Havel as president of the new republic. The narrative of the same interviewee stressed, in fact, the unplanned (and to a certain extent unexpected) development of the events:

I was returning from the meeting and said to myself: "Fuck. If I tell anyone at Civic Forum, they will kill me. Who am I to decide who the next president will be?" ... I said to myself: "I am screwed. I have to tell them." I knew I had gone too far. I got there, raised my hand, and started to inform them about the situation. Jičínský got very angry ... "You talk with Adamec about things we haven't discussed here." Vašek (Havel) was sitting there. There were about 30 or 40 of us. "And you even don't know if Vašek wants to be the president and moreover we haven't discussed it" ... we voted and there were only four people who voted for Havel. ... So we lost it in the first round. But then something unbelievable happened. I met a reporter from ČTK (Czech News Agency) on Wenceslas square. ČTK had already been on our side. He told me: "I heard something interesting in Moscow yesterday, when Gorbachev had a meeting with some heads of the former eastern bloc. Adamec was there and he started to talk about the presidency and about that he would have liked to be a president. Gorbachev brushed it away, totally." I told the others at Civic Forum immediately. ... It was a coincidence that I met the guy from ČTK. Then we voted in the second round and Havel was ahead. (CZ10)

Contingency is often cited to explain the development of the events. This was the case, for instance, with the rumor that a student had been killed by police:

It was an unbelievable power of history. I'm not sure if all of them knew it but the crowd was somehow aware of it. Then an absolutely coincidental circumstance occurred. ... I am speaking about the death of the student. It was simply a coincidence. He really got a painful blow on his elbow. Ok, so there was a victim: "The Gestapo is murdering our students again." If there wasn't this coincidence, I think Wenceslas square wouldn't have been full of people on the next Monday. But it was full, and on Tuesday it was even organized. Simply, there had to be a victim. That's what gets Czechs to the streets. It was a mistake: there was no victim. Anyway, it didn't matter – it had the effect. After that time it was unstoppable. (CZ13)

LACK OF INTENSE TIME

If time intensification is a common memory in the cases of eventful democratization, this does not happen to the same extent in the cases of participated pacts.

In Poland, the times of the roundtables are perceived as quite dull: participation was remembered as intense in 1980, but *not* in 1989. In the memory of the activists, it is the years 1980–1981 that are recalled as characterized by the euphoria and sense of open opportunities that the

GDR and Czech activists mentioned for 1989. In Poland, an influential dissident observed,

1980, it was the spring of the Nations ... for only once in my life I saw those people, which were not crowds, but some sort of collectivity ... you could feel some kind of upcoming beliefs and identity in the crowds. And you could walk nicely through these crowds. I remember in Gdańsk, ... I felt safe in the crowd, whereas normally I am afraid when I am in a crowd. And it wasn't like that anymore ... in Gdańsk that atmosphere was unbelievable, everybody there was a human being, the subject. And that was the time, when a lot of bridges were crossed between classes, between groups of society, between workers and intellectuals, students and hippies, they were friends with the workers suddenly. (PL13)

If 1980–1981 were exciting times, Polish interviewees tend to agree that, instead, "1989 was a poor year." In contrast to the positive energy of the early 1980s, in the late 1980s they identify a struggle for power within Solidarity, which had become "a power movement"; "a cemented organization: the social support for it was marginal" (PL4). As recalled by a former activist of Solidarity since the foundation of the group, "The peak was the years 1980 and 1981 until the martial law, and the martial law broke this dynamics through repression and chicanes, and it led to demobilization. We, the people of Solidarity, are saying now that Solidarity at that moment was not broken, that it has survived, ... but it's not exactly true ..." (PL7). In fact, another organizer of Solidarity in the Silesian region noted that in the beginning,

Solidarity was not a political organization, it was a place for everybody to come [to join in], regardless of their past, with the thoughts of doing something positive for their environment, for their country. In 1989 there was no such a way of thinking ... every war destroys and scars the society: the martial law was such a war, which stripped the society of sixteen months of freedom. (PL3)

The martial law is in fact considered as responsible for the quick decline in the euphoria of the early 1980s, and the beginning of a time devoted only to survival. Repression, moreover, discouraged networking or bridging of different generations as, during the authoritarian regime, a fairly strong youth counterculture had interacted little with the mainstream organizations of the opposition. In fact,

from the mid-1980s, with the growing popularity of subcultural-based movements (such as punk or concepts of deep ecology) and the lack of interest in them from the dissidents, a "third cycle" was created, consisting mostly of zines, brochures and pamphlets, but attracting lots of attention from young people. ... This split between the increasingly professionalized dissidents and the creative youth grew stronger, the more the Solidarność movement leant towards liberal or neoliberal positions. (Piotrowski 2009)

Thus, the younger generation instead participated in the events of Orange Alternative groups, or "Free the Elephant," with the growth of an "alternative cultural scene with hundreds of magazines ... you had street happenings and so on" (PL4). As a young activist suggested, while transformations in Solidarity during the martial law and the increasing influence of the church made it less attractive to young people, in the second half of the 1980s,

it's also the time when you have the new mobilization, on one hand it's on the side of the young workers because the new workers are coming that hadn't experienced Solidarność and they are entering the production age, ... there is a new wave of mobilization emerging and there are new movements coming from the youth, be it students or more generally the kind of youth movement, but also high school students. (PL7)

The Freedom and Peace movement and the Orange Alternative provided a highly attractive model for all youth subcultures (Gliński 1994), but neither coordinated much with Solidarity.

In Hungary, the pace and intensity of the 1989 mobilization was unexpected. In the account of an oppositional unionist,

The mobilization starts with the dam on the Danube question and peaks at the reburial of Imre Nagy in June of 1989, and this mobilization shows a very great power ... this shows the one-party state that, in a confrontation, they could only lose. The opposition wins with this mobilization and this is really what leads to the transition. This mobilization practically ends on June 16, 1989. From then on there are no more such mobilizations. (HU7)

Hungarian activists remember many and large demonstrations in 1989, with a quickly accelerating pace. Against an image "that Hungarian society was largely passive and the transition was conducted by elites," 1989 was remembered as an intense time,

with participation, activism, joy, and parties. ... I practically didn't sleep at all. I just didn't. So ... we made babies ... all of that ... we got married ... the only thing we didn't have the time for was sleep. ... it was a feverish revolutionary time ... it was amazing, wonderful ... and also frustrating and awful, but wonderful nonetheless. (HU5)

As a former Fidesz activist pointed out, however, protests were limited: "when there was a need for demonstrations, people were ready to overcome their fears, take the streets, and say aye to democracy. Beyond that, however, it is true that there wasn't a lot of noise or permanent mobilization ... it wasn't like in the GDR" (HU9).

Moreover, it was often remarked that the excitement did not last long: the intense time disappeared quickly as, in the words of a former activist of liberal SZDSZ, "all this stopped at once, as my friends turned into bureaucrats. ... Revolutions rarely decompose this quickly. We only needed a few months for that" (HU5).

CONCLUDING REMARKS

In a macro perspective, scholars have often stressed contextual dimensions as structuring, at least, attitudes and behaviors – either political, economic, or cultural institutions are seen as long lasting constraints. While these descriptions can be considered as more or less fitting for normal times, in periods of transition the power of structures seems instead to decline. Indeed, change is produced exactly because structuring conditions weaken. As mentioned, these times have been appropriately defined as underdetermined, in contexts in which structural or behavioral parameters are too weak to influence the outcome (O'Donnell and Schmitter 1986, 363; see also Di Palma 1990).

In a micro perspective, the individual choices that drive mobilization for democracy have been explained through threshold and signaling models. As the number of those who dare to manifest increases, the risks of collective action are reduced and the expected advantages grow. Indeed, not only are large demonstrations more difficult to repress than small ones, but the costs of potential social stigmatization shrink as, vice versa, there is a positive expectation linked with the affective support for – as well as the reputation from – participation in the opposition. In Kuran's (1991) terms, as private preferences become public, this signals the weakness of the regime and therefore also the potential opportunities for change. As Biggs (2003, 218) observed, waves of contention are accompanied by "dramatic changes in expectations. People are taken by surprise. Optimism escalates with participation: what was unthinkable now seems inevitable." Endogenous to these waves of intense contestation are positive feedbacks, so that "an increase at time t leads to an increase at time $t +1$, and so on. In other words, protest incites further protest; an influx of new members encourages others to join" (ibid., 220). This intensification of time and relations has been linked to interdependence – as everyone's destiny is linked to that of the others – and inspiration – as the collective action of one group inspires other groups to act (ibid.).

In Michael Biggs' synthesis, interdependence works as an endogenous mechanism producing positive feedback that changes individuals' perspectives. Times appear ripe, as the more people participate in protest, the higher the hopes of success as well as the sense of moral obligation, and the smaller the fear of retaliation by the regime (Biggs 2003, 225). As for inspiration, the information about collective action pushes others to consider the possibility of mobilizing themselves, all the more so if that action has been successful (ibid.). Mobilization thus activates information cascades, as the actions of others are used in the search for signals to guide one's own behavior.

In a meso perspective, I have focused on some specific changes in the way groups interact, referring to mechanisms of time intensification that then gave way to time normalization. Transitions, especially when driven from below, are typically described as surprise moments, characterized by an intensification in the perception of time. Protests cluster in these moments, pushed by some specific mechanisms. Opportunities are also expanded, as the expectation of changes actually triggers changes by transforming actors' perspectives – preferences, but also identities. If a rational choice approach assumes, in fact, that the number of people participating in protest is a signal that pushes citizens already endowed with some interests to mobilize, the processes I described are much more radical, as previously existing preferences are transformed in action, previously established actors no longer exist, and previously accepted (or even internalized) routines are no longer convincing. A power vacuum, created by the misalignment in the regime-supporting coalition but also to a certain extent by the dissolution of old elites, is then filled by the activation of new groups.

As calculations cannot be based on routine, and predictions are all the more shaky, in intensified time, contingency is cited as prompting new visions and opening possibilities that then develop in action. While calculations require fixed identities on the basis of which to assess long-term benefits (Pizzorno 1993) and rooted expectations about the behaviors of others, the very speed of change challenges these conditions. In addition, the intensity of the events reduces the availability of the time that would be necessary to collect information, to reflect, and to deliberate. Decisions are then based on betting, moved by dominant sentiments. Rather than being routine oriented, they tend to praise creativity and innovation.

Intensification of time does not last, however, as time normalization is expected and even desired. The perception of times of change as exceptional times then produces the image of a break, from which reconsolidation should follow. As Michael Biggs (2003, 228) noted,

Positive feedback cannot continue indefinitely, of course. At some point, the growth of collective mobilization and protest must be reversed. Although reversal is beyond the scope of this article, we can outline its causes. Almost by definition, mobilization and protest are inherently short-lived for any one group. Commitment cannot be maintained indefinitely at fever pitch: it dissipates unless channeled into protest. Similarly, protest cannot continue indefinitely: it eventually ends in decisive victory or defeat. There are also two more substantive causes of reversal. Firstly, an upsurge of collective action is driven by rising expectations of success. Confidence, however, is a double-edged sword, for overconfidence undermines the chances of success. A radicalization of demands tends to polarize the protagonists: moderates want to secure a minimum, while radicals want to push for more. Secondly, opponents eventually react. There is always a lag between mobilization and countermobilization. When opponents are taken by surprise, they need time to coordinate their resistance; they may also decide to delay a counterattack for strategic reasons. Nevertheless, at some point the real extent of their resistance becomes clear, which leads the protagonists drastically to lower their expectations of success.

Also in our cases of eventful democratization, energetic times were then overcome by routine. Private life won over public life. As we will see in the following chapters, however, intense times leave their legacy when times normalize.

6

Civil Society Organizations

Decline or Growth?

In 1988–89 everyone is preoccupied with what form to find for politics. What is the organizational form in which one has to be active? This is like, in biology, the development of the fetus … after conception, the zygotes in different species can be mixed up, you don't know what is what. A geneticist of course knows, but you can't know simply by looking at it. Just like this, in 1989, no one knew who was who and what: the political forms weren't clear. Everyone called itself a civil organization; everything was called a civil organization, or an "alternative." That was the word. … there was a booklet that listed all the "alternatives": the first was published in 1988 and the next in 1989, and then they stopped because there were many hundreds. So, FIDETZ was alternative, or the Network of Free Initiatives, or the Hungarian Democratic Forum (MDF); these were all alternatives. They didn't know how to define what it was and then a fight began … there weren't enough political definitions. It was a big internal fight in all of the organizations on how they should be defining themselves. There were some who were very quick to transform themselves from an alternative organization to a political one. And this was the hardest. Because, on the one hand these organizations had an identity as an alternative to the one-party state, but on the other hand they had a strong need to identify themselves as the only alternative. And for an organization to get to the point to realize that they're one of the alternatives and not the alternative was very hard. … The other problem was that in the first phase of mobilization every organization had the identity of a social movement. They all said that there was practically no hierarchy. They identify themselves against the government, so they all have the same values. There are no leaders, … there are all kinds of spokespeople. … To change from this to having an organizational hierarchy, a bureaucracy, that there are leaders. … Then, slowly these organizations split and either turn into political parties, or remain in their movement-like form; some become NGOs, like environmental NGOs. … Simultaneously, the transition processes are taking place, and gradually the

> arena for party politics is established, with former civil society actors
> technically becoming parties and trying to find their roles in this quite
> loaded arena of party politics. (HU7)

As this citation from a Hungarian oppositional unionist indicates, transition represents (to various extents) a success for the civil society organizations that mobilized against the authoritarian regime; however, it also presents (often deadly) challenges to them. While civil society organizations do not disappear after transition, much research on civil society and democratic consolidation stresses the specific forms nongovernmental organizations take: externally funded by donors, mainly top-down, with little connection to rank and file. This seems puzzling given the importance assigned, during transition, to civil society groups as spaces of participation and deliberation. As we will see in this chapter, in the East (as, by the way, in the West), civil society holds a much contested meaning as well as diverse expressions. While the image of civil society spread from above depicts it as depoliticized and service-oriented, social movement organizational formats do survive, with mechanisms of legalization and legitimation of forms of citizens' participation – although with cross-issue as well as cross-country differences that are at least in part related to the different paths of transition.

In what follows, I will first develop some reflections on how paths of transition might affect the development of civil society (and how civil rights are linked to them), continuing with an analysis of specific visions of civic society after transition in the Central Eastern Europe (CEE) region. I will then use the empirical data I have collected to show some cross-country as well as cross-movement type differences. In general, I will stress that civil society did survive after transition, often building upon resources constructed during the struggle against the authoritarian regime. Post-transition, civil society underwent a strong internal differentiation between the NGO type of association and social movement types. In addition, the characteristics of the new regimes affected the resources and opportunities available, at the legal as well as the cultural levels, for different groups mobilized on different issues.

NGO-IZATION OR SOCIAL MOVEMENT SOCIETIES? CIVIL SOCIETY AFTER TRANSITION

In the social sciences, accounts vary on the role of civil society as either a cause or a consequence of democratization. In CEE, in more optimistic views, "rather than re-emerging after the fall of communism, civil society ... was itself responsible for helping to bring down the rotten edifices of communism" (Mentzel 2012, 625). However, while some see a general "rebirth of civil society" after transition (e.g., Stark and Bruszt 1998, 16–17), others note "the fragility of these anemic, almost still-born societies trying to grow in the civically impoverished postcommunist landscape" (Mentzel 2012, 625). In previous waves of democratization, too, the creation of a "civic culture" made up of a rich associational life has been considered as a most difficult task.

In fact, part of the reason for the pessimistic account of the status of civil society after transition to democracy in many regions of the world could be related to two parallel disappointments, linked to very different definitions of civil society. For activists of the movements for democratization, who had put great emphasis on civil society as the expression of a community of destiny, what emerges after transition is clearly disappointing. Rather than the self-management of the society, they see a quite bureaucratic and professionalized associational world that is rarely capable of earning the trust and commitment of the citizens. Democracy promotion then seems, at best, oriented to tame social movements; at worst, to defeat them through the channeling of energies toward single-issue, apolitical, Westernized forms of participation. The second type of disappointment is, usually, on the part of those scholars who operationalize civil society in terms of specific types of associations, more or less widespread in the West, and who see them as the main carriers of civicness.

These developments might vary with the characteristics of the transition path, with eventful democratization (with respect for civil society) contrasted against participated pacts (with demobilization of the civil society). In particular, I expect eventful paths of democratization to be reflected in more inclusive outputs and outcomes with regard to civil society in consolidation time – and therefore the civic qualities of democracy.

Different Paths, Different Qualities? An Excursus on the Iberian Peninsula

This type of link has been proved in the Iberian Peninsula, with different achievements on civil rights issues between the cases of Portugal (eventful democratization) and Spain (participated pact). These differences have been related to three main mechanisms: first, the masses as key actors brought about legal recognition and institutional embeddedness of civil society; second, more egalitarian policies increased the available resources and capacities for collective action; and third, political culture welcomed principles of egalitarian participation and social change through collective action (Fernandes 2013).

In Portugal, the Carnation Revolution brought about a deep reconfiguration of political hierarchy and cultural framework, with, at least in the beginning, bottom-up purges in ministries and universities. Later on, as well, practices to address protest in the street and interactions in institutions remained more inclusive in Portugal than in Spain, with consequences for the capacity of those countries to achieve political equality (Fishman 2013; see also Fishman 2011). This continued well into the next four decades, as "Portuguese elites have celebrated the voices of discord in public statements, commemorative displays and in actual practice: in certain crucial instances parties across the political spectrum have welcomed protestors into conversation" (Fishman 2013, 12), while Spanish elites expressed skepticism and fear of protest. Not by chance, while Portuguese citizens protest in front of parliament and sometimes inside it, Spanish protestors are not admitted before the Congreso de los Diputados. Transition in fact represented a historical turning point with important institutional effects, as "The cross-case consequences of these divergent democratization paths are manifest in formal institutions – for example, in the extraordinarily broad inclusion of social rights in the Portuguese Constitution – and informal social practices that govern routine action in civil society" (Fishman and Lizardo 2013, 216).

Historical pathways to democracy had effects on civil society and civil rights development. In Portugal, in fact, the revolution generated positive consensus on the ideals of equality and participatory democracy, making civil society organizations as well as parties more robust and influential. As Fishman (2011, 237) observed,

Two crucial features of Portugal's postrevolutionary democratic practice are the openness of the communication media to the voices of relatively powerless protesters and the relative permeability of institutional power holders to their message and tactics. The voices and varied tactics of demonstrators are broadly accepted as normal components of politics, which merit attention. ... The Portuguese revolution ... generated the basis for a broad and socially inclusive national conversation on politics, one that is relatively free from hierarchical barriers to meaningful entry.

This inclusive process was facilitated by very tolerant legislation for associations, which required no granting of license or control, as was instead the case in Spain. Moreover, procedures were established for parliament to consult with associations and access institutions from below (for instance, petitions need only 1,000 signatures to be discussed in parliament). There was also a recognition of neighborhood associations' role in assessing budgetary priorities and the implementation of policies on housing, water, transport, sewage, welfare, medical care, and childcare support. The results were a large agrarian reform as well as the declaration of housing as a constitutionally protected right and the expansion and democratization of the health system through participation of workers and citizens in its management. Policy partnership also developed with unions, with national bodies and equal representation of labor and business. Membership density in unions remained much higher than in Spain, at about 30 percent. The strength of the government is related to the large role of the public sector. Building upon the corporatist tradition, democratic Portugal also constructed formal institutions that were pivotal in establishing agreements such as those on modernization of the economy in 1987 and 1988, as well as various social pacts in the 1990s.

In Spain, in contrast, the Moncloa pact brought about a higher dominance of the executive, with demobilization of the civil society. The political elite spread a culture of depoliticization and deference to authority, and many old regime restrictions on civil society remained in place, including the need for a declaration of public utility, discretionarily issued. Few associations achieved public status, and rather clientelistic relations developed with those in power. In terms of interest representation, associations tend to have weaker channels of access to policymakers and interactions with governments tend to be limited. Unionization is discouraged, and it is easier to dismiss workers. Even if some quasi-corporate economic bargaining developed when the socialists were in power, unions have low membership, much lower than in the other southern European states, with around 10–15 percent of unionized workers during the 1980s. In addition, unions are moderate collective bargaining organizations rather than transmission belts for political ideas (ibid., 224; also Perez Diaz 1996; Fishman 1990).

According to the data collected by Tiago Fernandes (2013) on civil society in Portugal and Spain, the revolution in Portugal had in fact a long-lasting positive impact on the self-organizing capacity of workers and the middle classes between the 1960s and the 2000s. As a result, we find higher union density in Portugal than in Spain (in 1990, 32 percent of the active population in the former against only 18 percent in the latter). Similarly, sports associations involved 50 percent of the population in

Portugal but only 10 percent in Spain in 1984; cultural organizations, 24 percent against 8 percent in the mid-1980s; professional organizations, 10 percent against 5 percent in the same period; and religious groups, 5.7 percent against 3 percent. In a similar direction, Portugal has higher levels of party identification than Spain.

In their analysis of 61,000 associations in Portugal, Rui Branco and Tiago Fernandes (2013) noted not only an enormous increase in numbers but also increasing pluralism in terms of the issues addressed. There is also a particularly large number of welfare organizations that provide social services in an egalitarian welfare state for the health system, and a Bismarkian one (based on occupation) for social security. Portugal also saw a continuous growth of economic associations; civic and political movements; environmental, educational, scientific, migrant, social welfare, recreational, and youth associations; and cooperatives (ibid.).

The broad civic culture also differs between the two countries, as the Portuguese revolution overturned hierarchies in numerous social institutions and brought about a nonhierarchical educational structure. The presence of more culturally omnivorous patterns of consumption among the youth in Portugal than in Spain has been linked to multicultural tolerance as well as an antiauthoritarian esthetic, as the Portuguese revolution "self-consciously took an expansively cultural turn, attempting to activate new sensibilities and capacities while also creating new sources of identity and meaning" (Fishman and Lizardo 2013, 224). In Portugal, indeed, a salient inversion of hierarchy emerged first in the military, then moving to other institutions, eventually transforming gender relations – while in Spain, a compromise on education allocated public funds to private Catholic schools.[1]

As we will see, parallel differences are evident between cases of eventful democratization and participated pacts in the CEE area as well. Distinctions emerged in the quality of legislation and policies on civil society, as well as

---

[1] In Portugal, democratic changes also involved decision-making structures and educational philosophies in the society. As the army launched a cultural dynamization campaign, a positive attitude developed toward bringing the school out into the streets and the streets into the school, through the spreading of music, dance, poetry, and theater. Not by chance, the budget for primary school cultural education is twice as much as in Spain, and the investments in education are higher in general. There is also a strong emphasis on extracurricular activities, and the teachers' self-conception is less hierarchical than in Spain, where teachers lament restraints on creativity imposed by school directors and a canonical approach to cultural education. Instead, in Portugal, inclusive conceptions allow for the incorporation of different voices within anti- or post-canonical visions, centered on student-centered capacity building (Fishman and Lizardo 2013).

the presence and strength of civil society organizations in terms of numbers, members, influence, and trust.

A Weak Civil Society in Eastern Europe?

Social science literature on contentious politics in Western Europe has often talked of a social movement society, with protest as a widespread form of participation and a strong civil society. Research on civil society in CEE tends, however, to stress primarily its general weakness. Not only are membership rates, material resources, and capacity of influence lower than in the West, but in addition, researchers often concluded that civil society tends to be weak, hierarchical, and depoliticized (Korolczuk 2013).

Explanations for this weakness point, first of all, at the experience with "real socialism," which is supposed to bring about a "civilisational incompetence" in terms of rules, norms, habits, and values (Sztompka 1993). While Stalinism imposed a negation of civil society, post-totalitarian regimes did not welcome autonomous organizations either (Bernhard 1996). As the public space was controlled by the regime, this stance pushed toward a retreat into the private sphere, with low interpersonal trust and atomization of personal relations (Kaldor and Vejvoda 1999). Additionally, it was observed that the state, under the legacy of real socialism, kept its monopoly in the provision of services, especially in the core welfare state areas of social services, health, and education, thus reducing the space for the development of a third sector. While in Western countries about half of the third sector is, in various ways, financed by the state, this is the case for only about one-third in the East (Gabor 2013).

Another explanation for the weakness of civil society is related to the social consequences of the economic transformation, as the economic crisis left little space for post-materialist concerns. In fact,

With the introduction of economic reform (i.e., abolition of the branch-ministerial system of economic organization, imposition of hard budget constraints, monetary stabilization, property reform), whether quickly or incrementally, the vast economic structure built up by decades of communist rule faced the challenge of adapting itself to a radically new economic environment. ... Such changes not only provoked recession, inflation, and unemployment, but also brought about massive changes in the structure of the economy. (Bernhard 1996, 316)

In order to assess the weakness or strength of civil society, however, we have to look at the diverse meanings attributed to civil society by the democratic opposition during transition and, later on, within the domestically and internationally promoted policies. In fact, in the mobilization for democracy, civic society was proposed as essential for self-government. For the opposition to the authoritarian regime, civil society was "a normative concept which held up the ideal of societal space, autonomous from the state, wherein self-management and democracy could be worked out. That is, the idea of civil society was political and prescriptive" (Baker 1999, 2). Since the 1990s, a top-down conception of civil society, promoted by various institutions, tended instead to refer mainly to the interest groups and NGOs that were expected to

act as a constraint and check on state power, assume some of the functions of the overstretched state, and generally help consolidate democratic practice. Though the implicit assumption was that creating such a tier would enable greater participation and representation, in practice the focus quickly shifted to increasing professionalism amongst activists and turning them into partners in the policy process. (Fagan 2005, 529)

After transition, the idea of civil society becomes external to democracy, conceived as liberal democracy. The model of civil society as community and solidarity now forgotten, it is assigned a subsidiary function, being defined as "relatively insignificant or apolitical beyond its role in mediating between society and the state" (Baker 1999, 22). While in a "republican view" civil society as active citizenship is an end in itself, "equating democracy with the negative liberty which is supported by free market capitalism means that civil society and the market ... are often discussed as if they were coterminous, or at least mutually reinforcing" (ibid.).

International Donors and the Distortion of Civil Society

This minimalistic view of civil society was embraced, with much emphasis, by international donors, especially through programs of democracy promotion, which have supported institutionalized and centralized NGOs, with limited capacity to mobilize volunteers. As dependency on Western donors and international mother-organizations reduces autonomy in the choice of issues, international organizations are perceived at best as benevolent colonizers (Anheier and Seibel 1998).

First of all, international donors have influenced the development of civil society organizations toward bureaucratization, elitism, and depoliticization, with limited institutional recognition. American intervention for democracy promotion in the area is seen as based upon the assumption the "civil society is primarily embodied in NGOs," as "bureaucratically suitable vehicles for donors' funds" which "looked attractive as both partners and recipients, because they cost far less than traditional government-oriented development" (Aksartova 2006, 20). Similarly, later on, EU requirements for funding did influence the organizational structure of many groups, through the preference for hierarchical, formal structures, resulting in institutionalization of nongovernmental actors, professionalization, and specialization (Hicks 2004). Along with the tendency toward bureaucratization came a narrowing of issues and the spread of nonpolitical framing, as well as a move away from broad social issues and toward single issues instead (Fabian 2006). A push toward depoliticization has been noted, along with goal moderation (VanDeveer and Carmin 2004; Císar and Vrablíkova 2010). Patron–client relations developed between international donors and recipients (Henderson 2002), and competing for funds creates high internal fragmentation, as the presence of foreign donors stimulates the creation of new organizations. The price paid was some isolation from a potential constituency, which in turn increased the dependency on foreign donors.

In what follows, we will assess the extent to which this picture applies and can be generalized to all analyzed Eastern European countries, as well as to different social movements.

PATHS OF DEMOCRATIZATION AND THE INSTITUTIONS OF CIVIC SOCIETY

Democratization brings about civil and political freedom, with a tendency toward legalization and legitimation of civil society organizations. The degree and forms of these vary, however, and, also in the CEE, they are influenced by the path of transition – especially the degree of involvement of social movements in it. In particular, as far as the associational life is concerned, governmental policies act through the legal definition of requirements for founding and funding as well as granting access to policymaking. According to Ekiert and Foa (2011, 21), "legal and institutional changes regarding registration procedures, financing and taxation mechanisms, restrictions of activities, subsidies, etc., have pushed civil society development into diverging trajectories across the region." This is very visible if we compare Czechoslovakia, as a case of eventful democratization, with Poland, as a case of a participated pact.

Czechoslovakia developed an inclusive system of rules toward civil society associations. The Act on Citizens' Associations, enacted in 1990 (Law No. 83/1990), provided for an inclusive framework for the establishment of nonprofit associations, imposing no restriction on their functioning. Immediately after transition, especially between 1990 and 1992, voluntary associations were involved in policymaking. In 1992, a Foundation Investment Fund was created, funded with 1 percent of all shares in the "voucher privatization," with about 90 million euros allocated to finance civil society organizations. The Council of Foundation, made up of members of nonprofit organizations, was established as an advisory board and a space for dialogue between the civil society associations and the government.

Following the transition, activists of independent environmental organizations received much support. After the first government was elected in June 1990, led by former dissident Petr Pithart, "several movement leaders became ministers, representatives in parliament, party activists, and agency officials. In the early stages of the new democracy, efforts were also made to foster communication and interaction between NGOs and government agencies" (Carmin and Hicks 2002, 314). Moreover, as many members of the public administration had previously been involved in associational life, "this allowed for building several ad hoc personal coalitions with politicians and civil servants at the central level, and consequently, leaders of the nonprofit organisations enjoyed influence over the decisions of public administrators and could shape the directions of public policy" (ibid.). The result was a generous amount of resources distributed at the national level, with some institutions functioning as arenas for dialogue between the state and civil society. Indeed, the legacy of financial support during the socialist regime combined with the support by the first government after transition.

While these good relations were discontinued during Václav Klaus' government, since 1992, they were however reestablished after his defeat. In 1998, the government led by the social democratic party created the Governmental Council for Non-state, Nonprofit Organisations; more than half of it comprised of representatives from nonprofit organizations. This council was conceived as an arena for dialogue on nonprofit related matters. This inclusionary choice was resilient, as

nonprofits in Czech Republic found themselves in a particularly fortunate situation during the crucial pre-accession period between 2000 and 2004. Relatively rich and well-managed pre-accession funds provided them with an opportunity to gain valuable skills of project writing and implementation. Through inclusion in the developmental governance they made their contacts with public administration, as well as developing a general understanding of the bureaucratic logic of operations. (Gabor 2013, 142)

This support had long-lasting consequences, as Czech associations obtained the largest share of EU pre-accession funds devoted to nonprofit organizations.

Foreign help is perceived, however, as potentially affecting civil society independence. As a former activist observed, international donors "helped us in the beginning, especially they helped Civic Forum. They provided us with computers, communication technology etc. We felt that the material help would be better than their advice because they were little bit strange – from a different world" (CZ9). More suspicions emerged, in fact, when material help was coupled with attempts at influencing civil society. Thus, as the National Democratic Institute arrived to organize seminars about building civil society and independent media, "only few people were interested. Everybody here thought: 'What do the Americans want to tell us? We know what to do, we even know better than they, because we made the revolution'" (CZ1). The impression is in fact that the most important lessons were not offered. As this Czech former student activist observes,

On the one hand, they brought money; on the other hand, they brought a lot of strategic thinking, training, and attention towards some themes. But they didn't have any experience with the process we experienced. So the important message – "Focus on control, exert pressure on the new elites" – has not been told to us, or we haven't heard it. . . . When young people in Libya, Egypt, and Burma ask me, in countries where I go and try to pass on our experience and mainly our mistakes, what the most important thing is, I gradually came to the conclusion that the most important thing is not to fall asleep and let the new elites do what they want. And I tell them that is the biggest mistake we have made. (CZ4)

Thus, another student activist concurred that suggestions by donors often looked naive:

the ideas they brought were not feasible here. They kept repeating: "You have to have youth organizations, women's organizations, and trade unions and nearly even football organizations." . . . Yes, the West tried to help but . . . they thought they knew everything best and that we had just left treetops, that we didn't know the structures of the society and the way they worked. . . . But their advice didn't work, they were unrealizable. (CZ7)

Additionally, help was discontinuous. As a leader of Charta 77 observed, "Well they helped certainly. . . . But after some time they said:

'We are sorry. You have learnt something but look at the Ukrainians. We have to go and help there now.' It was a shock for lot of people. It often meant that some organizations ceased to exist because they were too dependent on them" (CZ13).

The situation was only partially similar in the other case of eventful democratization as, after *German* reunification, civil society organizations also received support; but this was mainly embedded within the West German vision of subsidiarity. Given the dynamics of consolidation, the third sector in East Germany is in fact sometimes seen as an expression of the civil society, democratic and participatory, but, at other times, as "largely an extension of West German organisations that, in the process of 'peaceful colonisation,' created 'organisational shells' without a corresponding 'embeddedness' in local society" (Anheier, Priller, and Zimmer 2000, 1).

Vice versa, *Poland*, with its participated pact, offered far less institutional and material resources to civil society organizations than did the Czech Republic or even Germany. Even though nonprofit activity was legalized, institutional arrangements were criticized for "lack of clear definitions, restrictive interpretations of the law by the courts, time consuming registration processes for foundations and unclear tax regulations and restrictions regarding economic activities" (Gabor 2013, 148). There was, indeed, some mutual hostility between the nonprofit sector and the government, with ambivalent and discontinuous openings of policymaking to representatives of the civil society. A lack of long-term strategies for the development of the nonprofit sector has been linked to a lack of political will: "Negative attitudes were manifested by attempts to control the sector (in the years 1992–1997), not involving them in the preparation and implementation of major social reforms (1997–2001) and by highly instrumental treatment of the sector in the years 2005–2007" (ibid.). So, "the role of nonprofit organisations in local politics was predominantly based on ad hoc decisions and personal ties. There was no legal framework regulating the involvement of nonprofit organisations in local planning or distribution of funds" (ibid.). The 2003 law allowing citizens to support NGOs of their choice with 1 percent of their taxes was criticized for its selective effects, further advantaging already rich NGOs and disadvantaging groups active on controversial issues (Korolczuk 2013). Civil society organizations in Poland thus remained structurally too weak to exploit new EU support for inclusion in policymaking (Gasior-Niemiec 2010). There was also low trust in public opinion. In parallel, civil society organizations mistrusted the state. In sum, the Polish system of provision of public funding for nonprofit organisations is characterized by scarcity of resources, ambiguous regulations, and deep decentralisation. Those features were mainly a consequence of the inconsistent and unsystematic action on the part of the Polish government, which failed to define and acknowledge a role for nonprofit organisations in the system of financing and delivery of public services. (Gabor 2013, 176)

In this context, international donors are suspected of having distorted civil society development even before the transition. In the words of a Polish former activist,

In my region we had our own money but we were kind of the exception in Poland because we were independent from the Vatican or from Reagan and foreign trade unions; but that was a unique case, and keep in mind that ... through the National Endowment for Democracy, Solidarność receives a few million dollars. Hundreds and thousands of leaflets we have printed, books: this has radically changed social consciousness. .... But on the other side we are still within the frame of these very elitist and top-down processes, and the question is how strongly they were rooted into the social level. It is the same question with NGOs today because in my opinion the NGO sector is completely degenerated. ... The problem is that foreign funds are on one side a good thing, but on the other they are a very dangerous thing because someone else comes up with the program, and it is implemented here. And that is a problem of Polish NGOs, to what extent they are genuine and to what extent they are creating new social capital? And to what extent they are just a transmission belt that is servicing the funds? I am not only criticizing and I'm not against NGOs, but I have my concerns. (PL7)

Similarly, a former Solidarity organizer lamented that the "lot of money" that came from the American side meant that "Solidarność resembled many organizational forms that are present in Western countries" (PL2). Whatever the intention, these activities appeared moreover as biased by a lack of local knowledge. As a consequence, the opinion is widespread that

this promotion of democracy had really marginal influence ... none of these people, either the ones who were advocating democracy or the ones promoting the economy: they really had no idea about what communism was. And it was so easy for them to say things. It was as easy for them, when they were saying that 2+2 = 4, and in Poland 2+2 still could have been six or eight, and they had no idea why. (PL3)

In the other case of participated pact, *Hungary*, the dominance of party patronage is said to leave the country without a real civil society – as one of the promoters of the Foundation for the Poor explained, "NGOs got a huge push from the transition and the right to association ... and civil society organizations received some state support too, albeit very little. .... How much money they got depended on how loyal they were to the government in power" (HU12). In this narrative, given their relations with political parties, civil society loses autonomy and support. As a founder of the Independent Lawyers' Forum noted,

I can tell you about each and every one of them where they belong. Especially in this extremely polarized, divided society ... the greatest problem of post-transition Hungary is that it's basically a political war zone. And let me add that it was like that from the very first minute, and it only got worse ... civil society organizations ... might have survived formally, maybe, but they lost all significance. And civil society organizations became linked to parties. ... After the transition everything became entrenched in these extremely polarized political struggles. There are simply no civil society organizations without affiliation to this or that political party. (HU10)

At the same time, as legal guarantees facilitated the establishment of an NGO, a former Fidesz MP observed, "to a great extent civil society became apolitical ... it is hard to talk about mobilization in this case" (HU4).

Democracy promotion is considered, here as well, to have contributed to a depoliticization of the civil society, orienting it toward service provision. As this oppositional unionist recalled,

Soros was more direct: he gave money, and I guess you could say that the roundtable barely had a member who didn't get some support from the Soros Foundation. After 1989 everybody was in democracy promotion ... the Friedrich Ebert foundation, and then the British, the Dutch ... everyone had their own. ... And then came 1997–1998, and a gigantic dinosaur, the EU appears here, coming in with millions, and thinking in terms of a completely different civil society, which is primarily service-oriented, lobbying, in part like a watchdog. Certainly not movement-like ... that was their policy when they came into Central Eastern Europe, that they need lobbyist-type service NGOs. (HU7)

Different policies produced different civil society infrastructures. In East Germany, especially in 1989, there was an explosion of associations, although they remained small. By the mid-1990s, the third sector accounted for 4.9 percent of total employment in both parts of unified Germany. In addition, the associational density in East Germany was similar to that of the West (about 650 associations per 100,000 population), even if membership rates were lower in the East than in the West (Anheier, Priller, and Zimmer 2000). In East Germany, the extension to the new federal states of the legal and institutional system of the Federal Republic implied the spread of the principle of subsidiarity, with about 70 percent of the third sector financed by the state (ibid.). This was particularly advantageous for the already strong associations of the

West, which had "successfully expanded their market as suppliers of health and social services into the new *Länder*. The population of the new *Länder*, they suggest, does not regard these institutions as independent non-profit organizations, but as public or quasi-public institutions" (ibid., 6). Moreover, nonprofit organizations there can rely on government support for the majority of their funds, as compared to a lower 40 percent of government funding in the Czech state and 26 percent in Hungary, with even lower levels in Poland (ibid.).

While the Czech experience approximates the German one, differences have also been noted within the cases of eventful democratization, as while in the former the reconstruction of civil society followed an indigenous development, in East Germany it adapted to a model imported from West Germany (Anheier, Priller, and Zimmer 2000; Mendelson and Glenn 2002). In terms of the spread of civil society organizations, Czechoslovakia follows the German case on most accounts, with a dramatic increase in the number of NGOs since 1989 – from about 2,000 registered civic associations in 1989 to more than 20,000 nonprofit organizations in 1992 and then 40,000 in the Czech Republic, of which about 8,000 were involved in the policymaking process. The nonprofit sector represented 2.7 percent of total employment, with 1.6 percent of the gross domestic product (Potucek 2000). The not-for-profit sector occupies, in fact, a workforce with the equivalent of 74,200 full-time paid workers, representing 1.7 percent of all nonagricultural workers, 3.4 percent of service employment, and 6 percent of public employees, with 10 percent of the Czech population that reports contributing their time to nonprofit organizations – that is, about the equivalent of 40,000 full-time employees, for a total of about 2.7 percent of employment (Fric, Goulli, Toepler, and Salamon 1999). The state financed 40 percent of the nonprofit revenue, given the resilience of the centralized system of state funds for voluntary groups inherited from "real socialism" (Fric et al. 1999).

Civil society appeared as weaker in the cases of participated pacts. In Hungary, civil society organizations emerged as smaller in terms of members and lacking influence, although after transition many new groups were founded (Smolar 1996). On the one hand, "a very rich organizational world unfolded then. By the mid-90s there were about 40,000 or 50,000 such organizations, most of which were service NGOs, clubs for disseminating information, or sometimes umbrella organizations grouping other organizations and coordinating their activities" (HU7). On the other hand, "it was just a fraction of these organizations that were involved in lobbying or were actually engaged in civil politics" (HU7).

In comparative terms, Poland presents the weakest profile, as the transition in Poland was based on a logic that contributes to the weakening of civil society: "with the beginning of negotiations political society takes center stage in the democratization process while civil society moves into the background" (Bernhard 1996, 313). Here as well, registered foundations increased with the change in regime, growing from 200 in 1989 to 5,000 in 1994, when there were 700 environmental groups, 30 women's organizations, 1,000 church-run local newspapers, and 54 minority organizations, with 361,000 members (Ekiert and Kubik 1999, 104). In the 2000s, only about 12 percent of Poles participated in NGOs, while membership in unions declined from 22 percent in 1990 to 12.5 percent in 1995 and 2.6 percent in 2003 (Gliński 2006, 273). Large differences were also noted between the few, ever-richer organizations and the large number of very poor ones, as only half of the about 64,500 associations and 10,100 foundations recorded in the National Court Register in 2008 had an income of more than 4,500 euros per year, with a trend of increasing differentiation, the top 5 percent getting up to 80 percent of the income of the whole sector (Korolczuk 2013). Fragmentation of the civic society emerges as specific to post-communism in Poland: in 1994, there were 29,580 associations with 53,000 full-time employees (Ekiert and Kubik 1999, 101).

As we will see in the remainder of this chapter, with regard to civil society organizations, NGO types and social movement types are present in all countries, with different balances and characteristics that in part reflect the dynamics of the transition. In addition, the conditions of civil society vary in different areas, with clear distinctions linked to specific social movements. In particular, while some movements gained a high profile (as was the case for the environmental movement), others (such as the labor movement) encountered more difficulty.

ENVIRONMENTAL MOVEMENTS IN CONSOLIDATING REGIMES

The environmental movement had been, in all countries, quite relevant in the transition phase, and also to a certain extent during consolidation. Especially in the late 1980s, various protests developed on environmental issues, as new environmental organizations formed. After the regime change, however, even if international aid gave "Environmental organisations ... new opportunities to participate in international conferences and to build far-reaching networks," it channeled them toward "patterns of action and organisation that closely mimicked those found in the West" (Carmin and VanDeveer 2004, 7). While the number of environmental groups increased, protests remained rare (Botcheva 1996). The development was, however, different by country and in different periods.

In the *Czech Republic*, there was high-capacity political activism. Before the transition, the environmentalists were often perceived as a "most visible expression of an immanent civil society," as

the movement seemed to encapsulate the heady ideals and aspirations of the new civil society: a submerged network of politically engaged activists, highly eclectic and radical in terms of ideas and strategies. By bringing together scientists, students and citizens as well as hardened activists, the embryonic environmental movement seemed to reflect a new type of post-communist politics in which movements and civic activism would exercise agency within a vibrant and deliberative public sphere. For both the academic research community and foreign commentators, the environmental movement acted as metaphor for the new politics in the early 1990s. (Fagan 2005, 534)

However, this situation changed with the transition, with a perceived need to adapt to transformed circumstances. The main organizations of the opposition to the authoritarian regime seemed, in fact, unfit for democratic politics, as it had developed after transition. As was observed for Charta 77 by one of its first supporters, it

was at a loss after the year 1989. They solved it the best way they could: "Look, we were interested in human rights and human rights have become part of the Constitution so what else do you want? Official authorities have been established to check if the Constitution is respected. We can help them, of course. Anyway Charta ends." Well, there were some Chartists who said: "It is not true, the law is violated." These were the radical movements, but it didn't last long. I really think that the fight for human and political rights finished when these rights became part of the constitutional system. (CZ12)

As for environmental organizations, although after 1989 they were capable of exerting some policy influence through participation in the Green Parliament and personal relations with officials, adjusting to changed political circumstances was not easy. In fact,

Environmental protest had emerged as illegal or semi-legal clandestine opposition movements under authoritarian rule, enmeshed within a submerged and highly politicised "parallel *polis*" ... after 1989, the environmental NGOs were required to enter the formal political sphere and co-operate and negotiate with the new democratic regime. They were being invited to sit round a table and help draw up a concrete policy framework; they needed to deal in facts and realistic strategies in order to help ameliorate the ecological degradation of the preceding decades. (Fagin 2000)

At the same time, however, it was noted that "the nascent NGOs lacked internal structures, cohesive ideological platforms on domestic issues, and appeared to shun the formal political policy process in favor of remaining enmeshed within a nascent civil society" (Fagin 2000, 143).

From the point of view of numbers, the mid-1990s environmental movement included some hundred groups, with only about 20,000 members in total. Most groups were small in terms of membership (less than twenty-five members) and budgets, with only about a half-dozen national groups (Davis 2004). A weak capacity to get support from below was noted, as

with a few exceptions, the core professional environmental NGOs that dominate policy arenas, comment on policy drafts and articulate the dominant environmental discourse in the media and within the political sphere have failed to root themselves within society at large. Their campaigns continue to reflect the interests of their donors rather than indigenous communities, and are not effectively channeling grass-roots societal interests to the political arena, nor mobilizing popular opinion around their campaign agendas. (Fagan 2005, 529)

Some have also lamented that the limited size of environmental supporters reduces their political influence, as "they are not seen by politicians as representing any sort of notable constituency or voting bloc and this, of course, limits the political pressure they can bring to bear" (ibid.). The international support often oriented environmental NGOs to fundraising rather than fee-paying membership (Fagin 2000), with continued dependency (Fagan 2005). Lacking funds from members, some groups have to rely upon donors, with a related stigmatization as nonautonomous and uncertainties about survival (Davis 2004).

If this picture applies to some of the environmental groups, alternative ones did also flower, however. While some larger organizations, mainly based in Prague, have adopted a modernization agenda (Carmin and VanDeveer 2004) and international donors channeled organizations toward professionalization, this evolution did not always imply depoliticization, deradicalization, or co-optation (Císař 2010). Most of the about 800 groups existing in 1990 consisted of students who had been sensitized to environmental issues during the protests for democracy (Fagin 2000). Grassroots groups also developed in the 2000s with a growth in community-based organizations mobilizing on local problems – such as, for example, the construction of a ring road around Prague in the late 1990s or other road building with related destruction of green space. From 1998 to the early 2000s, the number of these types of organizations increased from about 20 to 250. As for their structure and strategies,

Though there is substantial variation between the organizations in terms of their campaign strategies, issues, support base and size, they tend to be volunteer based and typically involve a core of between 10 and 20 part-time local activists plus an outer core of up to 50 supporters and volunteers. Though most organizations obtain small amounts of revenue from donations and membership fees and appear adept at mobilizing volunteers from within the community as well as other resources, they have not professionalized their operations and appear to have gained little access to the skills and know-how acquired by the larger NGOs. (Fagan 2005, 536)

While pragmatic, the majority of the groups exhibited a "particularly strong anti-organizational ... and anti-hierarchical tendency" (Davis 2004; see also Jancar-Webster 1998), combining "conventional lobbying with mild non-violent direct action towards the local municipality" (Fagan 2005, 536).

Environmentalists also seemed quite effective in terms of policy outcomes, thanks especially to a network of contacts within the public administration, even if the degree of institutional support varied. After transition, in a first phase,

a brief environmental "golden age" commenced under the leadership of the Civic Forum, comprised mostly of the very dissidents and intellectuals responsible for the Revolution. Prominent environmental activists were named to posts in the Environmental Ministry and a host of new environmental regulations and initiatives were passed by parliament. Also hundreds of environmental groups began to form across the nation and, perhaps most significantly, 83 percent of the public in a 1990 poll ranking issues, considered environmental protection as their greatest priority. (Davis 2004, 377–8)

The perception in the beginning of democratization was therefore that there was no need for protest – as an activist lamented, "In 1990, we did nothing against the construction of the nuclear power plant at Temelin. We thought: There is a new government, the government of our heart, democratic, and they will certainly close Temelin" (in Sarre and Jehlijka 2007, 354).

These privileged institutional relations were abruptly interrupted during the conservative government of Václav Klaus, since 1992. As "the euphoria of the Velvet Revolution wore off amid recession, and the difficulties of the enormous and painful economic transition became apparent, public confidence turned to fear and caution" (Davis 2004, 378). The electoral victory of the Civic Democratic Party under Klaus' leadership represented a move toward support for the values of free market and privatization, with a downsizing of the Ministry of Environment and a drop in environment-friendly policies. What is more, in 1995, the four main environmental organizations, including Greenpeace, were included in the list of subversive organizations of the Ministry of Interior. In fact, Klaus was said to have led "a personal crusade against anything with the slightest tinge of green" (Beckmann 1999, 3), considering environmental regulations a hindrance to economic development. So, as concerns for job security and economic decline grew, "environmental groups found themselves increasingly fragmented, marginalized, and unable to connect with the mass public. Public concern over environmental issues seemed to vanish overnight along with many of the groups that formed immediately after 1989" (Davis 2004, 378).

This changed once again, however, after Klaus lost the elections. Since 1998, environmentalists have gained back influence with the advent of the social-democratic minority government, which encouraged informal as well as formal links. At the end of the 1990s, environmental groups seemed in fact to enjoy a good capacity to access the policy process, with some institutionalization of large NGOs (Fagin 2000). The environmental sector therefore seemed able "to combine lobbying with carefully orchestrated direct action, reflecting the campaign strategies currently being pursued by environmental campaigners across Europe" (Fagin 2000, 152). They also enjoyed support in public opinion – in 1996, 87 percent of the population considered them as useful and important – as well as an increase in fund-raising capacity (Fagin 2000).

Environmentalism was less supported in *Germany*, the other case of eventful democratization, debouched in reunification. In general, between 1989 and 1994, environmentalism kept a low profile in both parts of the country, reemerging thereafter with increased capacity to mobilize. Especially problematic for environmental NGOs in the former German Democratic Republic (GDR) was the fact that

many official responses to postsocialism have been inspired more by Western frameworks than by the wishes and concerns of local populations. ... Adopting Western-style methods and solutions to postsocialist problems and defining these problems in terms of the West resulted only in compounding the already serious challenges of postsocialism by failing to acknowledge the diversity and specificity of different postsocialist societies. (Herrschel and Forsyth 2001, 573)

The dominant economic neoliberalism of the time affected environmental reforms. However, environmental conflicts later reemerged, showing the capacity for mobilization of local groups fighting pollution as well as adapting to the corporatist path of interest group representation dominant in West Germany (Rucht 1995). Many groups grew, indeed, in tensions between acceptance of state support and defense of autonomy (Rucht, Blattert, and Rink 1997).

Environmental groups appeared as even more divided in the two cases of participated pacts. In *Hungary*, environmental campaigns had been particularly relevant in the late 1980s, with many environmental groups founded in the early 1990s. Our interviewees confirm that if 1989 "marked civil society's triumph over politics, and the beginning of liberalization for civil society" (HU7), the movement against the construction of the dam on the Danube played a most important role, with a large base of supporters and a huge number of small organizations (ibid.). After 1989, this experience fueled what was considered as "probably the most successful civil society sector ... there are about 5000 to 6000 such green NGOs in the country, with an ideological core that grew out of the Danube movement" (ibid.). In the mid-1990s, these groups

diversified tremendously, with groups on local, regional, and national levels working on such themes as traffic, air quality, advertising and consumer education, toxic waste management, and river ecosystems. Since the late 1980s, scores of community actions have demanded greater public participation in political decisions that affect local environments, and members of environmental groups have successfully run for local offices. Environmental groups from outside the capital city have gained greater prominence, bringing a distinctive perspective to the movement. (Harper 1999, 99)

Some of these groupings kept a social movement profile, as many organizations mobilizing in anticorporate campaigns are small groups, with grassroots structures (Harper 1999). Environmentalists in Hungary were also said to have been capable of adapting to democracy, as "It was felt that a well-organized movement, which had won a considerable reputation either in the neighbourhood or nationally, could and should take up the wider role of representing people with environmental problems and should continue to exist on this basis" (Pickvance 1997, 43). From the original protest movement NGOs emerged, engaging at the same time in lobbying activities, service provision, public education, and protest activism, so that, as an oppositional unionist assessed, "this movement is probably the most successful survivor of the transition" (HU7). Green groups are said to have established

a complex system, in which they operate as NGOs, lobbyists, they mobilize, participate in transnational affairs, address global issues ... the same organization and actor can organize a protest action against a local supermarket and participate in drafting World Bank regulation at the same time ... as in the organization of the European Social Forum, and conducting workshops at Sziget festival where they teach people how to be environmentally conscious. (HU7)

Environmental campaigns have also been fairly successful on specific claims, also earning a general reputation for themselves and their cause (Pickvance 1997), developing a capacity to interact with institutions (Petrova and Tarrow 2007).

What is more, an emphasis on local self-government is rooted in the vision of several environmentalist movement organizations, which counterpose it to the greedy, top-down intervention of multinational corporations. In particular, "When environmentalists express disgust at corporate 'gifts' and 'goodwill marketing,' they typically draw comparisons between advertising and state socialist propaganda. After years of fighting for greater public access to information and freedom of the press during the 1980s, environmentalists see advertising itself as a threat to democratic culture" (Harper 1999, 108). They thus link environmental concerns with a critique of capitalist developments, the commercialization of the public landscape, mass marketing, and advertising, promoting instead democratic developments also in the sphere of consumption (Harper 1999). Nevertheless, in the assessment of a Fidesz founder, "Because of the transition many interest groups, professional organizations, and clubs were formed, but the kind of vocal civil society, which would be an active participant of politics, a characteristic of the 1980s, that could only be revived by Fidesz in 2010" (HU8).

In *Poland*, with much less institutional support than in the Czech Republic or Germany, environmental organizations remained quite small and divided. In 1989 there were more than one hundred groups, and more than a dozen foundations, with "a pluralism that brought together various segments of society: young people, religious groups, technical specialists, professionals, local associations, etc. Individual groups differ in their degree of institutionalization, demands, legal status, involvement in societal conflicts, the geographic and social range of their activity, involvement in politics, and their search for alternative cultural models" (Gliński 1994, 148). After 1989, changes emerged in the organizational structures and action strategies of the groups, with some organizational professionalization and pragmatism:

More and more, protest actions were supplemented or even replaced by constructive and positive action. Informational networks were set up and non-governmental experts engaged. Movement activists trained themselves to conduct environmental campaigns and programs, to administer non-governmental organizations, and to become familiar with legal codes. They learned how to work with state agencies and the mass media and to raise money for ecological activity. (Gliński 1994, 147)

Youth groups tended to develop, however, quite apart from the more traditional groups, with some radical framing, drawing on counterculture traditions that challenge consumerism in "their quest for alternative values, their distance from the political system, and their gentle, if often ironic, form of communicating with the surrounding world" (Gliński 1994, 146). These groups have developed expressive strategies to address everyday life: "They orient themselves toward the present, searching for new forms of cultural transmission. Their substantive content, practical goals, and programs are dominated by forms of activity pursued as valuable in itself." In most cases there was a refusal of institutional politics in the name of a decentralized and participatory democracy – with groups promoting "direct democracy (local self-government based on relative material and cultural self-sufficiency – participants in the movement speak less of democracy and more about demo-creation, i.e. the creation of human communities from below), and . . .[supporting] consensus over the majority principle ('the majority does not have the right to impose its will on the minority')" (Gliński 1994, 147).

Youth counterculture, which had played a relevant, even if rarely recognized, role in the opposition to the authoritarian regime, continued to mobilize later on. Youth protesters were especially sensitive to environmental issues, with organizations that refused to take part in the emerging political institutions. Activists from the "generation of 1988" included "the young workers who initiated the two powerful industrial strike waves of that year and student activists fighting for the legalization of the Independent Student Union. This generation was marked by the radicalism of their demands (unprecedented for a social movement operating under the conditions of real-existing socialism), and their innovative psychosocial energy in pushing for social change" (Gliński 1994, 145). A search for autonomy also followed the marginalization of youth and youth counterculture by the elite of Solidarity, with a reciprocal hostility and lack of dialogue, or even police repression (ibid.). Indeed, at the 1991 parliamentary elections, only 30 percent of young people went to vote (ibid.).

On more conflictual issues, cross-national horizontal links contributed to strengthen the civil rights campaigns. As a Polish activist of the new generation recalls,

What was very interesting was … the very horizontally organized help by other organizations. It was very interesting for us from Freedom and Peace and the anarchists and also the environmentalists: we met a lot of people from the West who came in usually, well, as friends. … They talked about their activities, we hosted them in our places, but they also helped us to go abroad and it was a very strong exchange. Kind of an ideological and organizational one and also among friends within the anarchist, pacifist, feminist, and environmental movements. That was a very independent exchange just between the organizations. It wasn't supported by any bigger bodies or networks, and we learned a lot about activism from them. When we received an American anarchist journal that was properly printed, and you could read in these magazines about some actions we organized in Poland – we were bursting with pride. … We had the feeling that we were part of a bigger thing, even during the regime, that we belonged to a worldwide movement just like that, and not that we were some isolated people in the peripheries of the world. (PL4)

Young people also participated in some large protest campaigns, such as the (successful) one against the construction of a nuclear power plant and another against the construction of a dam at Czorsztyn (Gliński 1994).

WOMEN'S MOVEMENT

The reunification with the old federal republic was the last thing I wished for. Among those for whom the gender issue played a big role this is pretty much consensus, because from our perspective there was a rather old-fashioned state at the time or the conditions were old-fashioned, especially the view of women. [The phrases I heard] in connection with the discussion of abortion, they would have been unthinkable in the GDR. … Also the interaction of men with women, very concretely, I hadn't experienced that before in the GDR. For example, I flew to West Germany to an event with a party friend … we were welcomed by a young colleague, and from then on he talked to him past me: I didn't exist, I had not experienced that before. … Catastrophe, simply a great catastrophe; I don't see a perspective here; it is not my country. (GDR1)

If environmentalists seemed to have adapted well to the transformed contexts, even obtaining some success, women's activists (as this German one) tended instead to perceive themselves as on the losing side of consolidating democracy. In general, in fact, gender rights score badly in the new democracies, even worse if compared to the situation in the "real socialist" states on many of the claims put forward by Western feminists in terms of equal educational opportunities, equal pay, childcare facilities, maternity and parental leave (Einhorn 1991). Women have had only a low presence in parliament: about 10 percent of deputies in the first democratically elected parliaments of CEE, compared with around 33 percent in the old state-socialist parliamentary structures (ibid.). This was particularly problematic given high levels of women's unemployment, the reduction of childcare facilities, and limitations on women's reproductive rights (ibid.). At the same time, unemployment helped to spread an ideology supporting the woman's primary role in the family. This also represented a move backward, as

Despite the problems of the dual burden, compounded by discrimination in the labour market, it should not be forgotten that women in many East Central European countries were not forced to choose between a career and children. Rather, generous maternity-leave provisions and the availability of childcare facilities gave them a degree of choice about whether and when to have children, whether and when to return to their jobs – which had to be kept open for them – after giving birth. (Einhorn 1991, 21)

The deterioration of conditions for women is in fact lamented by several of our interviewees, as the situation on gender equality (in cultural and material terms) was perceived as more advanced in the socialist regime than in the new one. For German women's rights activists, reunification meant in particular "frustration but also … an exhaustion" when abortion rights were restricted – as "now it was again about abortion, which is something that we had twenty, thirty years behind us. And then without hope for success – because that is also, I believe, an important factor in [civic] engagement that there is a trace of hope, that you can prevail with it" (GDR1). More in general, interviewees point at the fact that women in the East did not have "such a marginalized role, like in the West. In work life they were fully integrated; they had an employment rate of more than 90 percent that has quite different ramifications for gender relations if women and men … met on equal footing rather than one comes home in a male dominated world and finds one's housewife there, that's different conditions" (GDR1).

The women's movement found it difficult to develop an original discourse that could avoid the risks of being assimilated, either with the women's rights framing of the former regimes or with a Western feminism that was considered as often of little resonance in the East. There were in fact negative views of "bourgeois feminism" spread under the old regime, as well as the risk of identifying feminism with the stigmatized policies of real socialism (Ferber and Raabe 2003). Western feminists were often seen as imperialistic. In particular, in the former GDR, women's groups had developed in tension with those in the West, with conflicts addressing the very conception of a feminist identity (Ferree 1995). While in the East women had criticized a public patriarchy that "supplanted the individual male head and thus embodied principles of public patriarchy," in the West, in contrast, private patriarchy had been supported by state policies within the social market economy. So,

In West Germany, there was a conceptual package invoked by the phrase "wife-mother": these two roles were inseparably bundled together. ... For East Germans, the conventional woman was not at the disposal of an individual man but instrumentalized by the state as patriarch. The image of woman was thus the "worker-mother" who contributed both reproductive and productive labor to a collectively male-defined state. (Ferree 1995, 15)

Western feminism is also criticized among our interviewees, specifically its conception of a "women's republic without men," "this rigidity of separating from men," while in the East the groups aimed at "coequal relations between women and men as ultimate objective" (GDR1). Disagreement was expressed with the Western feminist critique of the welfare state, and, especially, the pretention of spreading good advice, as "good advice is always tricky especially if one comes from a different background and knows things differently or perceives them differently or has experienced them differently than what is important in the world she is coming from" (GDR1). A risk of co-optation was particularly felt by women's groups that, especially in the GDR, found themselves diminished by their Western counterparts. As a feminist from the former GDR recalled,

We sat also with two women at the roundtable and established ourselves ... as a political force. ... On the West German side there was the women's council [Frauenrat]. In our naïveté we expected the women's council to at least get in touch, or somehow maybe we'd consult each other on how to somehow do things together or what possibilities for cooperation there are and so on. Nothing like it: the women's council simply established branches in the East by virtue of its financial possibilities. What could we do? ... I mean, we didn't have the money ... I can remember the outrage also about this ignorance. But that was the general experience anyway. From the West German perspective it was only about taking over the GDR; it was not about seeing what can be shaped together, where you can build on experiences ... it was only about completely delegitimizing the GDR ... nothing had to remain ... the East had to go away. (GDR1)

Here as well, however, some cross-country diversification of civil society organizations was noted. Although women had been present in the opposition to the authoritarian regime, their degree of organization varied by country, from a relatively substantial participation in the GDR to a more limited role in Poland – with the other two countries somewhere in between. In East Germany, an Independent Women's Association had been created, and "almost every local council was persuaded to let women's groups take over former Stasi buildings with a view to establishing women's centres, some of them doubling up as women's refuges ... and providing crèches, cafes, counselling for unemployed women and a wide variety of courses" (Einhorn 1991, 27). However, this did not last into the reunification period, when "funding for the posts of spokesperson for women as well as women's refuges, women's centres, and retraining courses for women, are threatened" (ibid.). As one of our interviewees observed, even if some of the old groups are "still around today ... women's groups, women's cafes, and women's infrastructure," they are considered as rather apolitical and local in scope: "nothing with a claim to societal influence. I don't want to diminish that, not at all, but it is a different level so practically local" (GDR1).

Women's mobilization was less present in Poland, where Solidarity had never paid particular attention to women's rights. As all movements in Poland are said to contain some "seeds of Solidarity" (Meardi 2005), there is a belief that, even on women's issues, "if considered globally as a social movement, Solidarity created nonetheless also an indispensable ground for the emergence of feminist identity: it raised society's subjectivity, making the individuals aware of the right to define themselves in individual categories, as well as of freely constructing collective identities" (Malinowska 2001, 27). In fact, "the strategy of 'sowing Solidarity seeds' – both by drawing on Solidarity legacy and engaging in coalitional politics should be seen as positive, as it has enabled the organizers and movement participants to mobilize on the basis of subjectivity" (Gruszczynska 2009, 325). However, female activists, even internal to Solidarity, often denounced a macho attitude within the organization, with men "sitting for long hours in cigarette smoked rooms" and women going "back home to take care of the children and cook dinners for the families" – so much so that at the first internal elections in Solidarity in September 1981,

it was such a masculine group that only men got elected. Solidarność quickly became a male dominated group, I don't think that Solidarność changed anything regarding gender relations. It was a backwards and reactionary movement. ... Catholicism is the only religion, and the only value of the woman was to sit at home and take care of the kids when the men are taking care of the revolution. (PL11)

Specific to Poland is in fact the dissatisfaction about the increasing influence of the church on the state, on the part of the secular activists who had participated in the mobilization for democracy. An actress who was very active in the opposition thus remembered: "we didn't appreciate to a large extent how the Church has taken over the state, we also didn't realize to what extent the state was taken over by Balcerowicz and his neoliberal reforms. We were not able to assess it, to judge and to distance from it" (PL6).

A polarization evolved on claims for gender rights, in particular on gay rights, as LGBT (lesbian, gay, bisexual, and transgender) activists found a very hostile climate:

in the postaccession landscape, sexual minorities have found themselves in the position of a living symbol, as an embodiment of ideological tensions in Polish politics and society. Through public activist events, the figure of the homosexual (even though real lesbian and gay individuals may continue to live in the closet) has moved from the margin of collective consciousness to the centre of an increasingly polarized public debate. (Gruszczynska 2009, 326)

Escalation started in 2005, as the local government in Warsaw prohibited the gay pride and various groups mobilized transnationally in solidarity with the Polish activists (Holzhacker 2012). Mobilization (via polarization) grew from 2005 to 2007, when gay movement leaders were targeted by the populist right-wing governments (O'Dwyer 2012). LGBT activism then began to make use of transnational resources such as social spaces and organizational capacity (Ayoub 2013). In fact, repression in the mid-2000s brought about waves of solidarity, which changed LGBT groups in the East as well as in the West. Effects of the transnational relations were also felt in the West, where older activists were influenced by the much younger ones in Poland, who initially resented some paternalism by the (older) Western activists – "like this perspective as an expert, like 'we have already the LGBT movement 30 years and we know what is the right way" (in Binnie and Klesse 2013, 588). However, thanks to those transnational protest campaigns, the LGBT movement emerged as stronger, having built organizational resources as well as a capacity to influence public opinion and decision makers (O'Dwyer 2012, 238).

UNIONS

Traditional trade unions started to organize only when, according to any economics or sociology textbook, it was the wrong time for their formation: during the greatest recession, when unemployment was extremely high and it had just increased from zero to about 20 percent. About 25 percent of people had exited the labor market in a heartbeat, and let me just say that in these circumstances it's no joyride to organize labor unions. ... the sheer fact that by the mid-90s about 7 percent of the employed workforce in Hungary was organized, and there were blue-collar workers among them, was an accomplishment by itself, not to mention surviving the transition. I have to add that trade unions didn't really have a solid ideology for mobilization, since in a context where the system was just being trans- formed from a planned economy into capitalism, of course everybody was pro-capitalist. So it was really hard ... trade unions had to be supportive of the transition, while trying to impose checks ... this is a hard sell in a situation where hundreds of thousands of people are losing their jobs. "Uphill struggle" is a very nice and fitting expression in English. (HU7)

In contrast to the more successful example of the environmental groups, and to the mixed experiences of the women's groups, the unions' path into democratic consolidation is considered – as this oppositional unionist said – "uphill." In the CEE area, unions weakened, indeed, but with qualifications. In general, low membership was combined with low con- tract coverage, along with limited institutional recognition. Here as well, the explanations for this weakness have been located in the legacy of the past regime, in which "the unions were typically allies of management, encouraging increased production, and often operated as social welfare agencies, dispensing benefits to members, who often viewed such benefits as the single advantage of union membership" (Crowley 2004, 420). An alternative explanation linked however this situation of structural weakness to privatization and related unemployment, as well as the decline of occupation in the industrial sector and the growth of precarious labor in the private sector (Osa 1998).

In general, union membership rates dropped from the very high level of almost compulsory unionization in socialist regimes to one that was however, in 1995, still higher than in the West – with an average union density of 38 percent in West European countries versus 49 percent in Eastern Europe (Crowley 2004). Where differences were more worth noting was in the rate of strikes, with an unweighted average strike rate of about 100 days not worked per 1,000 workers per year for West Europe, against only 25 percent in the East. In addition, the collective bargaining coverage rate was much lower in the East than in the West (44 percent versus 75 percent) (Crowley 2004). While union membership moreover declined drastically, and more in the East than in the West (between 39 percent of the labor force in East Germany and Hungary and 23 percent in Poland), trust in the unions was indeed very low: in

1998, as many as 53 percent of East Europeans did not trust them (Crowley 2004). Additionally, unions had a very low influence: "as continued downsizing, increased wage differentials, increasingly authoritarian management, and the almost complete absence of unions in the new private sector make clear, they have been unable to bring about an inclusive form of capitalism" (Crowley and Ost 2001, 4). There was, moreover, a special type of tripartite management of labor policy, which was variously defined as "paternalist," "fragile tripartism subordinate to neo-liberal dictates," a "political shell for a neo-liberal economic strategy" (Crowley 2004, 409), or an illusory corporativism, based on non-binding agreements (Ost 2000). As a result, "objectively and subjectively, workers took a beating. And ... labor's response has been almost universally minimal" (Crowley and Ost 2001, 2).

Here as well, however, internal differences across countries are worth noting, with higher levels of recognition in cases of eventful democratization and lower ones in cases of participated pacts. According to all statistics, unions were comparatively better off first of all in our main case of eventful democratization: *Czechoslovakia*. Even though unions were certainly inexperienced in dealing with capitalist economies, the Prague Spring provided them an experiment in democracy, with a workers' council elected in 1968 demanding self-management. As the general strike on November 27, 1989, gave unions legitimacy, oppositional unionists of the National Association of Strike Committees were able to take over the old unions from below already in the early months of 1990 (Pollert 2001). The future minister of labor thus recalled the mobilization in the factories, which he helped to organize:

It was successful. That is the achievement. We managed to mobilize people. ... I was surprised how well it functioned. They broadcasted that at 11 or 12 A.M.. The work would be stopped. At 12:15 A.M. the march started to form in Militia Square. ... We called Lokomotivka, Dukla ČKD, Trakce and steel foundry if they were prepared. Meanwhile we coordinated it so they could start and the others would join them on the way. Elektrotechnika were the first to come out, and then the others joined. It was huge, and I think this was a real success. (CZ11)

Relatively strong unions were later active in campaigns around the labor code (with 600,000 signatures collected in four days on a petition protesting a first draft of the code), but also heavily involved in drafting that code, with the help of the International Labour Organization. Thanks to the Act on Wages in 1991, an amended Labour Law, and the Act on Collective Bargaining in the same year, unions acquired strong organizational rights (Stark and Bruszt 1998, 184), including protection of the unions' rights to bargaining and strike, protection of workers against dismissals, and prohibition to hire during strikes (ibid., 185). The Council of Economic and Social Agreement provided the forum for negotiating these laws as well as the agreements on the low-wage/low-unemployment course that secured the lowest unemployment rate in Europe. Since 1991, the Czech unions have made full employment their central theme, also obtaining investments in active labor market policies and social protection. So "in the Czech Republic, we see a state that has recognized the network properties of liabilities and that participate in meso-level networks for renegotiation and recombination of assets" (ibid.).

In terms of recognition of social partners, there was an initial rise, as the Council of Economic and Social Agreement was formed at the federal and national levels. A compromise was thus achieved on low wages in exchange for low unemployment, with social policies oriented to compensate for the low salaries. Although binding in principle, in practice the council took only a consultatory role due to lack of governmental resources. However, it survived the hostile times when Václav Klaus led the government. With the reemergence of the labor conflicts, especially since 1995, the unions shifted from support for free market reform to the defense of workers' interests, especially after some initial success in defense of public employees (Pollert 1997). After years of tense relations under Klaus, the December 1997 change in governments again stimulated the development of civil society organizations and improved their access to the policymaking processes, with an important role in the administration still played by former members of Charta 77 and Civic Forum (Green 1999).

The situation was partially different in the *GDR*, where the regime-controlled union, the Free German Trade Union Federation (Freier Deutscher Gewerkschaftsbund), had been impervious to internal opposition. Initially strong in numbers, unions lost members to growing unemployment, notwithstanding offers of services by the union. Membership in unions tended to be passive, with (as in the West) increasing deinstitutionalization of worker relations, while it was particularly resented that leaders of unions were often Westerners. During the economic changes, managers and workers then tended to ally with mutual accommodation, while worker councillors tended to identify with their own factories. The German unitary union, the Confederation of German Trade Unions (Deutscher Gewerkschaftsbund, DGB), expanded to East Germany

through a takeover of the regime union, which "was to voluntarily dissolve itself and recommend its members to transfer their enrollment to the
appropriate branch union of the DGB" (Schnabel and Wagner 2003, 3).

While this strategy did produce an initial increase in members, it was
not able to develop loyalties (Schnabel and Wagner 2003). Although
membership remained low in the private sector and collective wage bargaining remained weak, there were some higher membership rates among
unions, although concentrated in the state sector (Padgett 2000). In general, "membership problems are often attributed to the widespread dein-
dustrialization and the huge employment losses in the transition process in
eastern Germany, but insufficient union activity at the workplace,
a disregard of the different history, socialisation and socioeconomic characteristics of the members in eastern Germany as well as membership
identification problems may also play a role" (Schnabel and Wagner
2003, 11).

The situation was even more difficult in *Poland* where, after 1989,
trade unions underwent two decades of declining membership as well as
a drop in influence, with overall trade union density falling from 38 percent in 1987 to 15 percent in 2010 (Gardawski, Mrozowicki, and
Czarzasty 2012). Mobilizing capacity was particularly low in feminized
industrial branches such as textiles or the food industry, with more
exposure to privatization and global competition, as well as in the retail
sector. In the 1990s, the lack of strong industry-level organizations, the
low prioritization of membership recruitment, the involvement in party
politics, and the renunciation of codetermination rights in the workplace
were elements also cited to explain union decline, which appeared as all
the more puzzling in the country of Solidarity (Krzywdzinski 2012).
In general,

> The privatization and restructuring of companies have led to a weakening of
> earlier union bastions. Moreover, the traditional union strongholds in heavy
> industry or the public sector influence the economy less and less, while new
> service and industry branches are gaining in importance in a field which is
> strongly dominated by foreign investors. Employers in Poland often have
> a hostile attitude toward unions. Particularly in small and middle-sized
> companies there dominates a paternalistic model which rejects trade unions.
> (Ibid., 67)

In particular, politicization of the main unions, especially in terms of
party proximity, "has led to a neglect of membership recruitment as well
as to a blockade of cooperation between unions, the dominance of union
organization at the workplace level and the lack of structures which can

organize new members and companies, the lack of resistance by the unions to the abandonment of co-determination rights in companies at the beginning of the 1990s" (ibid.). Additionally, Solidarity in power escaped from tripartite negotiation, notwithstanding the long tradition of negotiated pacts. Already in 1992, however, huge strike waves forced dialogue. These trends affected the Solidarity union (with its 1.7 million members), but also the post-communist All-Polish Trade Union Federation (with 4 million). Politicization and fragmentation were additional weaknesses. Formerly symbolically strong unionism had in fact very negative results, with a 30 percent decline in real salaries between 1989 and 1991, abolition of workers' self-management boards, up to 25 percent unemployment, the loss of secure jobs, and insecurity of new ones (Ost 2001). Some revitalization would be seen only later on, especially with the introduction of workers' councils (Krzywdzinski 2012). Women also led grassroots efforts in support of trade unions, and a wave of strikes and protests in 1992 and 1993 pushed Solidarity in the direction of more critical positions toward the market reforms – as "Upon realizing its possible eclipse either by the more radical workers' organizations or more conventional trade-unionism, the Solidarity leadership abandoned its tactical restraint; it became critical of government policies and more supportive of demonstrations" (Osa 1998, 32). However, a return to political action came with the electoral victory of the post-communist SLD Alliance of the Democratic Left in the 1993 parliamentary election, as well as the 1995 presidential elections (Krzywdzinski 2012). The post-communist government instituted a tripartite commission on socioeconomic issues in 1994, also kept by conservative governments, but weakened by divided unions.

In *Hungary*, as well, unions were on the losing side during consolidation. Throughout the authoritarian regime, as one of the organizers of the protest against the dam on the Danube recalled, "trade unions had been discredited, as they were regarded as transmission belts of the Communist party instead of an organization potentially providing protection for employees" (HU9). Later, the dominant neoliberal paradigm suggested that unions "are not needed, because they are a hindrance to free competition" (HU9). In fact, after transition, the situation remained unfavorable for unions since, as an interviewee from the Hungarian Helsinki Committee recalled,

the trade union after 1989 remained the official successor of the official state trade union, and while other communist satellite organizations were practically liquidated, no one dared to touch the trade unions ... in some sense the government's concept was that an overarching alliance of trade unions should be created, like in Austria or Germany, and not a variety of politically different trade unions. And so they were not supportive of Liga, the trade union spontaneously organizing bottom-up, but of the official MSZOSZ. (HU1)

Here as well, union significance actually declined in privately held companies, where they were most unwelcome. In addition, there was little and delayed mobilization on economic issues as, a Fidesz founder recalled, "there were no serious protests, or social protests against capitalism. In this sense, there was order in the country, there was no active class struggle going on ... much less than elsewhere" (HU6). Tripartite institutions, such as an interest reconciliation council, founded under the socialist regime and revived in 1990 were weakened. Repressive laws also played a role after transition. According to a leader of the SZDSZ,

Obviously, neither the state, nor capital has an interest in the establishment of a counterforce, and they didn't even need a lot of oppression to kill these movements. Clearly, legislation is very repressive in Hungary, especially labor law. Collective bargaining rights are minimal and decreasing. And the fact that political mobilization sucked everything else into itself created a situation in which legislation securing the autonomy and financial security of civil society was never even conceived. Whatever you have left from somewhere around the 1980s is in some corner under a lot of dust, without anyone noticing it, or using it, or referring to it. (HU5)

In sum, while the development of social movements was complex, with cross-country as well as cross-issue differences, civil society remained active in various forms, with trends resembling more and more those visible in other regions in Europe.

CONCLUDING REMARKS

Democracy is usually seen as providing for a most propitious environment for civil society. Civil rights grant the freedom to found and participate in various types of associations, incentives (material and others) are often given in order to support them, not-for-profit organizations are devolved to public services, and interest groups find paths of access to institutional decision making. These processes were clearly at work in our cases, with a steady increase in the number of formal and informal groupings.

Nevertheless, and in contrast with expectations, observers and activists converge in lamenting a weakness (and weakening) of civil society during consolidation. Due to either the legacy of authoritarian regimes or the difficulties of the economic transition, CEE countries have been noted to lag behind the West in terms of some indicators of civic life, such as the number of members of voluntary associations, people involved in voluntary activities, and influence of and support for civil society organizations. What is more, notwithstanding or because of support by external donors, the existing nongovernmental organizations have been described as top-down, bureaucratic, dependent from funders, detached from potential bases of support, focused on narrow issues, and either apolitical or too much linked to party interests.

In this chapter, however, we noted that this picture is incomplete, and thus also potentially misleading. First, the civil society did not disappear or institutionalize with homogeneous trends. Informal groups remained dominant, and often capable of bridging lobbying with protest, and the provision of services with information campaigns. Moreover, several groupings remained embedded within the conception of civil society as the self-organization of the citizens that had characterized the struggles for democracy, with support for horizontal forms of organizations. The conception of civil society as apolitical NGOs applies indeed only to part of those groups. Social movement types of activities and organizational strategies then survived, adapting themselves to the democratic transformations. This happened, we saw, in different forms and with different degrees of success in different areas, with environmental movements quite successful in exploiting the political openings and the labor unions instead tending to be on the losing side, with women's groups somewhere in between.

The legacy of the struggles for democracy explain, at least in part, cross-country variation, with eventful democratization reflected in broader institutional inclusiveness as well as larger membership, sympathies in public opinion, and institutional influences, and cases of participated pacts characterized instead by more exclusive institutions and smaller and more isolated civil society organizations. Recognition of civil society groups was particularly high in Czechoslovakia, where Civic Forum activists in power after transition set up institutions that reflected their confidence in self-organized citizens. Not only could environmental groups count on some sympathies in the public administration but unions – legitimated by their participation in the general strike that contributed to the fall of the regime, and supported by unionists in power in the very first years of democratic consolidation – emerged as much more solid and influential than in the other countries, with the partial exception of the former GDR. In East Germany, unification brought about the selective inclusion granted by the West German system of interaction between state and society, characterized by neocorporatism and subsidiarity. Instead, strong mistrust of civil society has been observed in Hungary as well as Poland, where notwithstanding the past strength of Solidarity as a social movement organization, participated pacts were based on demobilization and mistrust of citizens. The NGOs' development in both countries is indeed characterized by patronage relations with political parties.

This does not mean that only eventful democratizations were propitious to social movements. These indeed developed in all four countries, through mechanisms of legalization and legitimation, but with different characteristics, tending to be stronger and more influential but also more moderate in cases of eventful democratization, sometimes smaller but instead more radical in cases of participated pacts.

7

A Normalization of Politics?

Oppositional groups transformed into parties. The first were the social demo-crats, then New Forum came, then Demokratischer Aufbruch, then Democracy Now, then Initiative für Menschenrechte, then came the Green Party ... and very late, right at the end, the Vereinigte Linke and the Frauenpartei formed. ... That was partly a matter of vanities: because people who found themselves incredibly important weren't asked to participate in the founding initiative for New Forum, they founded Demokratischer Aufbruch. ... We stood then so to speak quite splintered, with seven opposi-tion parties ... very soon the Volkskammer [GDR national parliament] elec-tions came through the pressure of the demonstrations. The demonstrations continued and initially the Volkskammer elections were to take place much later, end of June, but through the pressure on the street who wanted the elections very fast, they were called on March 17. That was a short electoral campaign ... and then it was so to speak not a GDR electoral campaign anymore but it was a preliminary Bundestag [FRG federal parliament] elec-tions. Then the other parties in the Bundestag became nervous and then came the CDU by way of Rita Süßmuth, the president of the parliament. At the time, she first tried to convince the civil rights parties ... to create an electoral alliance with the CDU. We rejected that except for parts of Demokratischer Aufbruch ... contrary to all predictions the SPD barely got 24 percent or such. We civil rights parties were all below 5 percent ... and Allianz für Deutschland barely missed the absolute majority – they then had to do a large coalition with the SPD. ... And then it was headed for the swift reunifica-tion because as soon as the Volkskammer was formed and started working, the demonstrations still didn't stop but moved so to speak in front of the Volkskammer, which convened in the then Palast der Republic, and the people demanded the fast reunification without fuss or quibble, and they got it too, and then the task was to construct this unification process. (GDR5)

As this excerpt from an interview with a German pacifist and later mem-ber of the federal parliament indicates, founding elections – considered as the closing moments of the transition – are often perceived as a burden by activists of the movements for democratization, who find themselves abruptly marginalized. As we will see in what follows, however, despite the belief that the electoralization of politics is unfavorable to the opposition, activists do also participate in institutional politics.

As in other chapters focusing on democratic qualities, I shall start with a review of the social science literature evaluating the quality of political rights in the analyzed countries, continuing with assessments of the changes by former dissidents. Data and reflections will be presented on the general quality of political rights during consolidation in the Central Eastern European (CEE) countries, as well as the differences that seem to derive from different paths of transition, comparing participated pacts versus eventful democratization. Here as well, I will point at how, in eventful democratizations, mechanisms of legalization and legitimation of some rights were set in motion and improved democratic qualities.

POLITICAL RIGHTS AND CONSOLIDATION: AN INTRODUCTION

Civil rights are strictly connected to political ones, such as those related with citizens' participation in institutional politics. Research comparing democratic quality does not assign a higher value to one form of government or electoral system over others, rather singling out trade-offs between advantages and disadvantages in types of majoritarian versus consensual institutional systems. However, there is agreement that institutional checks and balances, protection of minorities, accountability of elected politicians, and opportunities for political participation are all important elements for high-quality democracy. The political process approach has stressed similar institutional qualities as fundamental for a healthy democratic life. Citizens' political culture, as well as their level of satisfaction, is also considered as an indicator of the functioning of democracy. CEE countries have been considered as deficient on several of these dimensions, especially when judged on Western standards. Nevertheless, as we will see in what follows, a more variegated picture emerges here as well.

Different Paths, Different Political Rights?

Political rights – free elections as well as control of the executive by the parliament – are the obvious outcomes of transition to democratic regimes. Indeed, the first free election is often considered as signaling the end of the transition period, giving way to consolidation. Besides free elections, however, constitutional politics acquires relevance in defining the qualities of the consolidated democratic regimes. In these founding moments, many of what social movement studies define as stable political opportunities are set, through the definition of the degrees of checks and balances, the functional distribution of power, the territorial assets, the presence of channels of direct democracy, and also the extent of the right to protest (della Porta 2013a).

As we will see in what follows, choices about the timing of the various democratic milestones – in particular free elections versus constitution making – have relevant consequences, and, here as well, the paths of transition affect democratic qualities in terms of political rights. Once again, research on the Iberian Peninsula showed that the quality of political rights differed, being higher in the case of eventful democratization (Portugal) than in the participated pact (Spain). As for institutional assets, Portugal has chosen a more pluralist and inclusive model than Spain (Fishman 2011). In Portugal, the head of state has powers of guarantee, while the constitution of 1982 gives more power to the prime minister, also recognizing an important representative role to the parliament (Morlino 1998, 55). Indeed, parties prefer to negotiate laws in parliament rather than imposing them via governmental initiative. The division of power between the executive and the legislative is more ambivalent in Spain, with a dominant executive and a less-developed role for the parliament, as "an overwhelming part of legislative output has governmental origins" (ibid., 68).

Although developing out of a military coup, Portugal was moreover more successful than Spain in establishing a civil power, clearly separated from the military. In Spain, instead, the military has often intervened on decisions by the representative institutions. There, "the establishment of civilian supremacy is characterized by initial ambiguity and later reactions to the decision of eliminating military prerogatives" (ibid., 74), with discontent and occasions of contestation as well as conspiracies by the military even increasing in the late 1970s and early 1980s. Although widespread in both countries, corruption has been more of an issue in Spain (where investigations also attested to governmental protection for anti-Eta armed militias) than in Portugal (ibid., 77–8).

As for political attitudes, between 1985 and 1992, those who declared to prefer democracy over other regimes increased from 70 percent to 78 percent in Spain and from 61 percent to 83 percent in Portugal. Identification with political parties declined in Spain from 47.5 percent in 1985 to 30.5 percent in 1989, while it remained stable at 49 percent in Portugal (ibid.). Party membership as a percentage of the electorate was in the 1980s above 0.04 percent in Portugal, while below 0.02 percent in Spain (Morlino 1998, 171), with the rate of membership in the Partido Socialista Obrero Español (the Socialist Workers' Party) at 2.7 percent in 1989, as compared to 4.2 percent for the Socialist Party in Portugal in 1990; 5 percent and 10.5 percent, respectively, for Partido Popular and Centro Democratico e Social. Dissatisfaction with democracy was also higher in Spain, growing throughout the first half of the 1990s from about 40 percent to over 70 percent in 1994 (ibid., 299) but oscillating between 30 percent and 50 percent in Portugal. Strikes and demonstrations were more frequent in Spain than in Portugal between the second half of the 1980s and second half of the 1990s. Parallel differences emerge also in our cross-national comparison.

Political Participation in CEE Countries

Various studies have addressed specific trends in political participation in Eastern Europe. While there is a general assumption that East Europeans participate less in politics than West Europeans, there are qualifications for this statement. First, electoral turnout in the East was initially only 7 percent below the average in the West, with a declining trend due mainly to the high participation in the founding elections. In general, voter turnout in the post-communist area has been characterized by a high electoral volatility, which accompanied economic instability (Pacek, Pop-Eleches, and Tucker 2009).

Research on trust has indicated the negative effects of the lack of social development throughout the 1990s, as perceptions of widespread corruption triggered mistrust (Kostadinova 2009). The New Democracies Barometer surveys, which measured trust in fifteen institutions in nine CEE countries, revealed high levels of skepticism, with particular dissatisfaction regarding current economic performance.[1] There is variance, however, with popular trust being influenced by the perceptions of freedom and fairness as well as by the evaluations of economic performance (Mishler and Rose 1997). Also in a long-term perspective, citizens remain critical of their institutions. In fact, in 2007,

---

[1] Only the army (mean: 4.4), the churches (4.1), and the president (4.0) reached positive values, with higher distrust in political parties (2.8), parliament (3.1), and trade unions (3.1) – although all scores are closer to the midpoint on the trust scale (4.0) than to the distrusted extreme (1.0).

On average, just 21 percent of the citizens in post-communist Europe trusted their assemblies, compared to 36 percent in the rest of the European Union. ... Even lower are the relative numbers of those who think of political parties as trustworthy. On the average, just 11 percent of the Eastern Europeans (compared to 18 percent in the rest of the European Union) trusted parties as representatives of people's interests in the spring of 2008. (Kostadinova 2009, 706)

Participation in protest, as expressed in opinion polls, is quite lower in the East than in the West, with an ever increasing gap. Forms of contentious participation in the Western European countries, like signing petitions, grew from 50 percent in 1990 to 56 percent in 1999; attendance at demonstrations rose from 22 percent to 27 percent in the same period. In Eastern Europe, instead, the levels of protest declined during the 1990s by up to 9 percent for demonstrations and 10 percent for the signing of petitions (Bernhagen and Marsh 2007).

Explanations for this gap between Eastern and Western Europe usually refer to the long-lasting legacy of authoritarianism, which kept trust levels low (Bernhard and Karakoc 2007), but also to the economic difficulties of the double transition, which focused attention on more urgent concerns and destroyed existing institutions. Other interpretations focus on social characteristics, such as the lack of a middle class, or on a "demodernization" process (for a review, see Anheier and Seibel 1998). High levels of mistrust and low levels of political participation have been related with economic conditions, as insecurity negatively affects citizens' democratic participation. Economic and social reforms produced dissatisfaction, in fact, as the perception of one's own change in social status (family's social status) and economic situation (family's wealth) during the years of transformation was often pessimistic, reflecting an appreciation of deterioration of one's own relative position, which also affected political attitudes. In general, in CEE,

attitudes about the economy have been mixed, but with some troubling negative indicators. Satisfaction with economic transformation held at about 30% from 1992 to early 1996, and overwhelming majorities thought that privatization had lacked controls, average citizens gained nothing, and owners had used bribes to obtain advantageous conditions. ... Following the 1996 elections, satisfaction with economic transformation began a slow slide to only 5%. (Green 1999, 222)

On both conventional and unconventional forms of political participation and political attitudes, however, there are cross-national differences, with more political commitment in eventfully democratized Czechoslovakia and East Germany than where democracy arrived through participated pacts, as in Poland and Hungary (Bernhagen and Marsh 2007). In fact, "Where civil society began earliest, developed furthest while communists still ruled, and exhibited the most extensive activity – namely, Poland and Hungary – voting participation is proportionately lower, public cynicism higher, and trust (or confidence) in the president, parliament, and political parties is far less than in the military or church" (Nelson 1996).

Cross-country differences have been noted in terms of electoral participation as well. Participation in elections appeared to be affected by paths of transition: First of all, rates of participation were higher in the founding elections in Czechoslovakia (with 90 percent) than in Hungary and Poland (with about 66 percent and 50 percent, respectively). Later on, they tended to decline after the founding elections but with still relevant differences (Kostadinova 2003), remaining higher in Czechoslovakia.

Different degrees of dissatisfaction with the working of democracy were reflected in different degrees of mistrust in political institutions. In 1995, in Hungary, as many as 63 percent perceived themselves as losers, only 12 percent as winners; in Poland, those who felt like losers amounted to about 55 percent of households (about 18 percent felt like winners). Somewhat differently, those who felt like losers were a (substantial) minority of 29 percent (against 39 percent who felt like winners) in East Germany and 36 percent (against 28 percent) in the Czech Republic (36/28) (Matějů 1996).[2] In all countries, "being a loser is a common significant predictor of a left-wing political orientation … even after controlling for other objective and subjective characteristics (class, unemployment, objective poverty, feeling of poverty, etc.)" (Matějů 1996, 10). Indeed, trust proved to be, in the East as in the West, endogenous to the political system, related to a satisfactory performance by the institutions. Empirical research has shown that the strongest predictor of trust is the extent to which people think the new regime treats citizens more or less fairly than the old one. Also relevant is whether respondents believe that the government is less corrupt now than in the communist past and that the new regime has increased freedom or created more space for personal political influence with strong effects on political trust (Mishler and Rose 2001).

In the CEE area, it was noted that where market transition was slower – especially in Czechoslovakia but also to a certain extent in the former

---

[2] Among those who felt like losers, farmers and ordinary nonmanual workers were overrepresented.

TABLE 7.1 *EIU Rankings (1–10, 10 Best) 2011*

	General ranking	Score	Electoral process	Civil liberties	Political participation	Political culture
Czech Republic	16	8.19	9.58	9.41	6.67	8.13
Poland	45	7.12	9.58	9.12	6.11	4.38
Hungary	49	7.04	9.58	8.24	4.44	6.88

German Democratic Republic (GDR), our cases of eventful democratization – citizens maintained a higher assessment of their ability to influence politics. In the 1990s, in the Czech Republic there was also high support for state responsibility (57 percent) and preference for secure over well-paid jobs (60 percent). In the evaluation of the political and social system, approval for the present situation reached 62 percent, against (a still high) 42 percent who approve of the past. Moving to economic issues, however, only 43 percent approved of the present, against 61 percent (less so in the Czech Republic) preferring the past regime (Padgett 2000, 106). Here as well, cross-national differences go in the expected direction – higher levels of participation are to be found in the richer Czech Republic, and more passivity in poorer Poland, confirming a negative relationship between political efficacy and economic development.

Additionally, as revealed by other pieces of research, protests before transition had an impact on the kind of institutional assets that were chosen thereafter, as countries that had seen more protest opted for parliamentary institutions and included more checks and balances (Bruszt, Campos, Fidrmuc, and Roland 2010). Comparing within the Visegrad states (Poland, Hungary, Czech Republic, and Slovakia), excluding the GDR for which no data as a separate entity from FRG are available, we can see that indeed, on indicators of democracy, the Czech Republic comes first in all of the rankings reported below (from Agh 2013). According to the EIU (Economist Intelligence Unit) ranking for 2011 (Table 7.1), the Czech Republic ranks 16th, as compared to 45th for Poland and 49th for Hungary, with better scores also on the electoral process and civil liberties as well as in political participation and political culture. A similar ranking emerges from the BTI SI (Bertelsmann Tranformation – Status Index) (Table 7.2) and NIT (Nation in Transit, Freedom House) scores (Table 7.3) on parallel dimensions for 2012.

TABLE 7.2 *BTI SI Scores (10 Best) 2012*

	Rule of law	Political and social integration	Political transformation
Czech Republic	9.5	9.3	9.65
Poland	9.3	8.8	9.20
Hungary	7.8	7.8	8.35

TABLE 7.3 *NIT Scores (10 Best) 2012*

	NIT democracy score (1 best)	Freedom in the world. Civil liberties (60 best)	Freedom in the world. Political rights (60 best)
Czech Republic	2.18	57	38
Poland	2.14	55	38
Hungary	2.86	52	36

What was different cross-country was also the specific semantics of the Left–Right cleavage. It has been observed that, under real socialism, a *bureau-cratic-authoritarian* communism in East Germany and Czechoslovakia facilitated a straightforward use of left–right in economic policy terms, while a *national-accommodative* communism in Hungary and Poland linked the left–right meaning more with sociocultural issues (Kitschelt, Mansfeldova, Markoswski, and Toka 1999; Bernhagen and Marsh 2007). Also in the new regimes nationalism was used, especially in Poland and Hungary, to distract attention from the disruptive economic reforms, which were sometimes supported by left-wing parties (Weiss 2003).

In part related to this were differences in the type of post-communist parties in the region. In general, as it has been observed, "While the founding elections of 1990 were by and large electoral disasters for ex-communist parties, the electoral returns of the second round of national elections in post-communist states (1992–1995) surprised many analysts: the renamed and 'reformed' communist parties staged a dramatic comeback in national and state elections across the former communist world" (Ziblatt 1998, 120). It has been noted, however, that "the ability of the communist parties to adapt to their changed circumstances is due in good part to organizational strength and leadership skills inherited from the communist past" (Waller 1995, 487–8). Later on, dissatisfaction with neoliberal policies found a way in party politics, where parties already present in the old regime often succeeded in channeling discontent with some adaptations. In fact, the success of a former communist party has been linked to perceptions of the difficulty of the economic transition (Ziblatt 1998). Representation of the losers on the Left in fact developed through different strategies, with different degrees of success. While in the former GDR, given a closed political opportunity structure, the Party of Democratic Socialism has chosen to represent Eastern interests but also opened to new social movements, in Hungary the Hungarian Socialist Party presented itself as pragmatic, representing workers but also pointing at experts (Ziblatt 1998).[3]

CONSTITUTIONAL DEBATES AND THE POLITICAL QUALITY OF DEMOCRACY

As civil and social rights are reflected in political ones, with higher rankings for the cases of eventful democratization than for those of participated pacts, the timing and forms of the constitutional process have a most important impact. In the perceptions of the activists we interviewed, the constitutions, their content, and also their processes of approval have consequences in terms of the legitimation of the new democracies.

The most successful case appears here to be *Czechoslovakia*, one of our cases of eventful democratization. The widespread impression about Czechoslovakia is that the first years of the new regime were important in order to set the basic institutions in place. As stated by a student activist who was later among the founders of the Christian Democratic party, the influence of former dissidents was crucial at this time:

We have democratic institutions here. With some exceptions, these institutions were built well. I also include the public administration. ... I think the Constitutional Court was well designed, so was the Senate. I think bicameral systems are very important for fragile democracies. When some scandal or political turn appears and the majority in one chamber changes, then the other

---

[3] Sequencing, pace, and timing are important in explaining these adaptive capacities. Extraordinary congresses of 1989–1990 were the moments in which elites performed their agency – "Party trajectories tended to be highly contingent at the outset, but became increasingly fixed, as they solidified quickly" (Grzymala-Busse 2002, 280). So, "elite decisions, and especially the elites' initial organizational strategies, determined the parties' ability to make responsive appeals, effectively disseminate them, and maintain parliamentary cohesion" (ibid., 283). The legacies of the past that mattered were those that were "clear, sustained, and transmitted through personal or institutional mechanisms" (ibid., 281).

one remains at least two thirds the same. Only few people realize how important it is. In other words, it means that it is not possible to change the constitution impetuously or under some pressure. ... We passed the so called Small Law on Political Parties. ... I think this regime is very tolerant of political parties. It supports even the small ones. (CZ13)

The primary importance of constitution making is highlighted also in a comparison of Czechoslovakia and Poland. As a Czech activist and later prime minister noted, the focus on constitution first, as well as the involvement of former dissidents in its writing, made for more inclusive institutions with higher levels of internal checks and balances:

Poles waited eight years for their big constitution; the small one was passed immediately. We designed our constitution while being pressed for time, but we managed it. ... I think we managed it well. It was not a coincidence. People from dissent and the "Grey Zone" designed it. We deserved a good quality constitution. It was not a coincidence. ... It was a contribution of dissent. (CZ13)

Naturally, the situation in the former *GDR* was dramatically affected by reunification-through-annexation, which worked as an additional condition, constraining the effects of the eventful democratization. Here, in fact, most of the dissidents did not feel that they had gained power, but, rather, that they had lost their battle. The debate on institution building is heavily focused on the failed attempt to write a constitution, considered as particularly frustrating by those who had hoped for a different type of unification. In fact, for the activists who had started the mobilization for democracy, the achievement of a new constitution was considered as a cornerstone in the establishment of a participatory democracy: "A new constitution was still perceived as important even as unification of both German states became more and more likely. At this point a new constitution was supposed to provide creative input for the negotiations concerning unification" (Rucht 1996, 42). After citizens' initiatives had worked within the roundtable toward drafting a new constitution, they however could not implement their project.

This breakdown in the constitutional process is strongly criticized by many former activists, who saw that a constitutional process would have been positive for both parts of the country:

All of that is written nicely in the roundtable constitution. In the area of environment we had new proposals, also for the constitution regarding peace politics (for instance, banning weapons trade, banning production of certain weapon systems, and such things); we proposed changes regarding data privacy and personal rights to access (files/records). And ... [on] further development of grassroots democratic elements, as a supplement to parliamentary democracy, referenda, for instance, also on a federal level and such (things were included). (GDR2)

In addition, the work of a pan-German initiative to provide a new constitution to the federation of German states failed. As one of the founders of Women for Peace recalled, the aim of this initiative had been "to set a broad constitutional debate in entire Germany in motion ... the new constitution which surely would have taken over quite a lot from the Basic Law, but also would have worked a few improvements from the roundtable constitution into it, this draft constitution had to be then eventually be approved by referendum" (GDR2). This constitutional process, and especially a broad debate around it in the west and the east, would have given East Germans "the feeling to have been asked, to have co-determined, that one would have given the East Germans the opportunity to take part in decision making about the constitution of the new German polity, that would have had at least psychologically an important and good effect" (GDR2).

There was therefore much frustration as, without previous discussion, on April 26, 1990, the parliament rejected the draft constitution, with a small majority of 179 against 167 (Rucht 1996).

The refusal to write a new constitution and the acceptance of the West German one is presented by several of our interviewees as proof of a sort of annexation, which delegitimized the transition process. As one of the founders of New Forum noted:

It would have taken the positive things of both to write a new constitution, which would also have been a step that would have brought the population in both parts on board ... in the direction of an equal unification of both parts. Now, it turned into a takeover. What later happened with the Treuhand and with the taking over of the significant property and land houses in the East by Western moneybags [*geldsäcke*] ... this feeling of being colonized, that could have been significantly reduced in that way. I found that to be a big political mistake. (GDR10)

This situation was considered as particularly negative, as "to be integrated into the federal republic, that was not the objective" (GDR10). As this activist argued, "I have great difficulties with the federal republic, today with the unified federal republic, because many things which we criticized fiercely at the time in the autumn about the GDR are today (almost) worse than at the time" (GDR10). If the constitutional project, with its emphasis on participation and human rights (GDR12), failed at the national level, however, "These attempts intensified from May 1990 onwards and later resulted in a new constitution for each Land. In contrast to the national level, some constitutional elements proposed by the citizen movements were adopted in the Länder, although they usually consisted of 'weaker' versions" (Rucht 1996, 43).

Institution building was even more exclusive in the cases of participated pacts. In *Poland*, the sequencing of the reform is criticized as having produced rather exclusive institutional opportunities for civil society. In particular, the speed at which first elections were held, before the legalization of Solidarity and other oppositional groups, was perceived as negative by those who had mobilized for democracy. In the word of a former leader of Solidarity in the Silesia region, "the situation was reversed: free elections were overlapping with the legalization of Solidarność, meaning that the trade union in working places could not reconstruct itself, didn't have the time, and that was one of the reasons why there was no serious political formation that came out of Solidarność" (PL7). This hastiness is also cited as responsible for the embracing by Solidarity of a compromise course at the political level and a neoliberal one at the social level:

Few months after the elections, in December it agreed without any deeper thought, to the Balcerowicz plan, which was against its electorate. The same one that did the revolution of 1980. … So it was a paradox that the democratization, meaning the creation of both political parties and reconstruction of the trade union, was accompanied by demobilization. Look at this, the whole year around the Round Table and also the elections none of the leaders of Solidarność, … they haven't called for social mobilization. It was similar to the case of Spain after Franco died. There was a pact … the Socialist party and trade unions went to the streets and it was put down there as well and the pact was about … waiving their rights, not prosecuting perpetrators from the old regime and not pushing their agenda regarding social issues and trade union issues. And this led to the self-destruction of the Spanish Communist Party. It was exactly what has happened to Solidarność. (PL7)

The institutions of democracy indeed emerged as more problematic in Poland. Here, the year 1989 is recalled for the (democratically ambivalent) "contract parliament," which, with low legitimation as based only in part on free vote, is held responsible for the introduction of heavy economic reforms, through the government led by former Solidarity activist Tadeus Mazowieski. According to one of our interviewees, fundamental changes were decided upon without sharing of information, let alone participation by the citizens:

The contract parliament should have been disassembled before such a revolutionary decision, as it was the plan of Balcerowicz that was voted by the contract parliament, between Christmas and New Year in 1989. I am a Member of Parliament and I know how much can be done between Christmas and New Year: nobody was capable of reading, to know what was going on in this plan. And this plan was the one that created today's reality in Poland. ... It was similar to the decision that was taken in 1948 on Stalinism, on forbidding private ownership and private businesses: it was such a structural breakthrough, and the thing that was voted by the parliament did not have the democratic mandate, it did not have the legitimacy to vote for such a plan. (PL7)

Here as well, constitutional politics is considered as crucial – and in this case, negative outcomes were attributed to the postponement of that process:

after the elections and after the introduction of Mazowiecki's cabinet, new elections should have been called and the Parliament should have voted and changed the Constitution. In Poland, this Parliament lasted for a year and a half, and the question is why? ... In Czechoslovakia the Communist Party was dismantled and thanks to that, the Social Democratic Party was built ... in Poland the old system was artificially kept alive for no reason. And ... it had catastrophic results for the decisions on social and economic issues. (PL7)

Similarly in *Hungary*, in the activists' narratives, the compromises of the pacted transition are said to have promoted a quite exclusive political attitude toward social movements and unconventional forms of participation. Once the new regime was established, according to a former promoter of the protest against the dam on the Danube,

All protests were in vain, so to speak, the government was completely insensitive to mass movements. The last moment when the government paid attention to a movement was during the previous regime, when Miklós Németh suspended the construction of the dam as a response to the mass demonstrations at the time. I can safely say that no one has taken any of the demands of social movements into consideration since. I am not exaggerating. (HU3)

In sum, constitutional politics emerged as also symbolically important, with important effects on the political quality of the new regimes, and the perceptions thereof.

ELECTORALIZATION OF POLITICS?

We were far from ready at the time when ... the chance materialized to take the groups out of the church and mold them into parties or other forms of organization. We would have needed at least three, four, if not even five years because that was actually the most difficult phase ... one would have needed more time ... in order to grow into that role at all. ... Now it all steered the search for meaning towards becoming a party, otherwise one could have disbanded ... I am actually fed up because it is not any more what I used to participate in, it became something completely different. ... They also had the administration, they had the experience. This was the main line of reasoning: They have the experience, they have the laws, they have the money. So, it was all already existing and actually you only have to submit to it. That was what revolted me so much: at the beginning it was really a bought up revolution and therefore it wasn't a revolution at all, but actually only an implosion. (GDR8)

In the CEE region, 1989 is a year of revolt, but also of the beginning of electoral politics, which, to a certain extent, is supposed to signal the victory of the oppositional groups. Yet, it tends to be perceived by many of them more as a curse than as an opportunity. The development of representative institutions is in fact seen – as by the quoted German interviewee – as, in several respects, detrimental to protest politics.

The social movement organizations that had mobilized against the regime proved in fact unfit for electoral politics. This was the case in Czechoslovakia with Charta 77 – which, one of its leaders stated, "lost its raison d'être after the revolution" – but also of Civic Forum, which, although it won the first election, saw its popularity briskly declining, with the progressive side badly losing the second election after the two-year term. This decline was indeed linked by former activists to its very nature, as "only special purpose movement with the goal to bring the country to the first free elections" (CZ6). Within this conception, participation in the first elections was considered as an exception, necessary given the accelerated time of the transition, but the aim of representing the whole nation as in contrast with the very logic of representative democracy. So,

Civic Forum stood for election, logically, because there was no time. There was only half a year, from December till June: they stood for the elections and won. Havel was one of those who pushed through only a two-year term, which is unusual. Normally the one who stands for the elections and is about to win it – and it was obvious that we were going to win it – wants to serve for four years, because you cannot do anything within two years. When we talked about it at that time, we anticipated it – that the unity could not last. That is why the first term was designed for only two years. (CZ6)

Civic Forum's conception of politics is indeed seen as unfit for electoral politics, as this implied a challenge to its own all-encompassing identity. As one of the members of Charta 77 noted,

Civic Forum stood in the election as a representative of the whole society. It was in the year 1990 when there were no classic political parties. ... The electoral term was for two years and Civic Forum started to lose the position of the representative of the whole society; it started to differentiate internally, stratify, and its role in this period weakened. ... Normal political parties emerged ... the fully-fledged representative role was taken over by political parties in the free elections. (CZ3)

Electoral politics is indeed perceived as bringing internal disagreements to the fore. In the words of a former student activist, "we wanted democracy ... only later we clashed about the content of democracy, how to deal with the past, whether to approve lustration law, if we should have restitutions, if we should privatize" (CZ7). The internal heterogeneity of Charta 77 thus made its survival as such impossible. Indeed, Charta 77 is presented by a dissident as "a group of people gathered together under pressure of the system. These people didn't have the same ideas, opinions, conceptions, and visions. They were very different and Charta was politically heterogeneous. Only the pressure held them united" (CZ8).

Activists also point at the differences between protest politics and party politics as an element that jeopardized their potential participation in the latter. As one of them pointed out, party politics requires different skills, as "there is a difference between signing petitions, occasional participation in some demonstrations and systematic work of legislators in times when political parties were being formed, when it was not just about a good idea but about if you manage to push your bill through the house. Somebody adapted to it more, some less" (CZ6).

In fact, some saw a weakness of Civic Forum in its refusal to be a party, instead remaining a "conglomerate of civic groups, protest initiatives." According to an interviewee from inside the organization, the electoral failure in 1992

was because CF resigned from being a political party with a real political programme which would gain public support. CF was satisfied with winning elections in 1990, and it vegetated somehow until Klaus realized that he could tunnel CF, create ODS from it. ... We did not know how to approach the public at all, in the 1992 elections we had 4.9 percent. ... In the election campaign in 1992, we tried to use arguments: "We are CF, we want civic freedom, individual development, fairness, solidarity, we do not want heady economic success. We want to be center-left." They knocked us down as leftist, which meant communists, and that the ideal is not any kind of fantasizing about social state, but personal success for everyone. That was what Klaus promised: "If you give me the vote, you'll have 20,000 Kč a month and you'll have not just one but two cars." (CZ1)

Beyond the specific developments within Civic Forum, electoral politics was mainly regarded with some skepticism, as a substitute for protest politics, as "Protests turned into meetings later. These meetings were organized with the election campaign" (CZ11), and as people joined political parties, "for a long period so they didn't go and protest" (CZ14). Additionally, party politics is perceived as a partial failure, as parties generally remained small. This low propensity to join parties also facilitated corruption. As a member of Civic Forum and later minister recalled:

The time brought completely new themes and demands that we hadn't had any idea about. For example, it showed that post-communist societies didn't tend to political party membership. Civic democrats had about 21,000 members during its boom. In Brno, ODS had about 1,200 members. If you were a businessman, and you needn't have been a billionaire, you could buy 700 votes. It means you paid 700 CZK membership fee for them: "Guys, come to the meeting and vote for me, ok?" It didn't literally happen like this, but this potential has been present. We had no idea about people's unwillingness to join political parties. They didn't want to join political parties; so political parties have been something like mini clubs. It is very dangerous. We really had no idea that this would happen. We all thought: "Well, we won't have one and half million members like the communist party has, but we can have 100,000–200,000 members." We were really surprised. (CZ12)

The impression was indeed that electoral politics defeated the ideals of a highly ethical vision of politics held during the struggle against the authoritarian regime, stimulating the lowest instincts. In fact, during the election campaign in 1992, the main parties are seen (for example, by this speaker of the University Strike Committee) as openly denying

all the ideals that revolution was based on. And it worked, because people were perhaps tired of that contemplation. They had enough of us, they did not want to listen to Havel, Dienstbier, Pithart, Pajerová, Mejstřík, Kocáb anymore, how they talked about individual freedom, individual development, environmental protection and that we are part of a bigger community and that we should have learnt languages and that we should have apologized to Sudeten Germans. Normal Czech men after two years of this exalted moralizing wanted to have something sure. Klaus promised it and that's it. (CZ1)

The perception nevertheless remained of a positive legacy of Charta 77 and the Civic Forum – as "It was Charta with everything that was connected to it and because of its significance. Everything else is based on Charta" (CZ7). There is in fact the widespread belief that the civil society had kept its ownership of change, that it had been successful:

People decided to do that, and they joined. That means that the society has some ownership of the change, and the change didn't happen at the high levels, but it was a change that was actively supported by the majority of citizens. It also helped us in the 1990s, during the economic transition and other transition as well. . . . the transition was quite successful in long-term time horizon. . . . It had generated the energy and joy, the zest to manage it. It helped the Czech Republic. (CZ4)

In Germany, electoral politics was considered as even more hostile to the movement as, in the activists' memories, electoral defeat resulted from the fact that elections arrived too early, before the activists could acquire the necessary expertise. As a former German activist lamented, "The first bummer came with the elections, where the Bündnis 90-die Grüne got 2.9 percent; I didn't expect anything different but some were very disappointed. We were also dreamers to a large extent. . . . There were no experts; most weren't even allowed to study" (GDR2). Electoralization was thus perceived as leading to the marginalization of the former opposition, given the activists' lack of experience with institutional politics: "most from the citizens' rights groups had no political experience whatsoever: didn't have experience with governmental practice, with administrative practice – that is, we were too dependent on help from the outside by independent people but also from the other parties" (GDR9).

Here as well, the fact that politics is permeated by elections is perceived as jeopardizing protest. So, former members of the opposition lamented the large number of elections in 1990 as they took time away from other activities, and especially because (under the pressure of the main parties) they were organized too early for the citizens' groups to prepare adequately:

It was about elections, elections, elections. It was the Volkskammer elections in March. It was imperative to prepare for them, and we had little time. The party congress was in February in Halle, and the elections were in mid-March. As advocated by Demokratischer Aufbruch, the CDU and DSU . . . and the SPD also wanted the early election date because they realized, well then they ran a bit better chance. All other groups from the opposition actually didn't want it: we were out of our depth, we had practically not even four weeks' time to plan the election campaign out of thin air after the party congress in Halle, to organize the campaign and to nominate candidates and perhaps even to talk to other opposition groups if we want to do something together . . . there were elections again in the new federal states in autumn 1990, and in December 1990 there were the first pan-German elections, when the Western Greens were kicked out of the federal parliament. So it was permanently overstrained, *elections, elections, elections*: building up structures, preparing and conducting campaigns. There was little time to do significant programmatic work. (GDR3, emphasis added)

Party politics is also perceived as too specialized, and thus resonating little with the broader visions developed in the opposition. A narrow focus was considered as characterizing Western politics – even as far as the German Greens were concerned: "Today it's different, but at that time it was like that: those within the greens who really saw also human rights, who [saw] the development of democracy, who [saw] a democratic economy as an aim, were in the minority, while those were our central issues" (GDR9).

Not only those Eastern parties that were sponsored by their Western counterparts but also the old regime parties were considered as enjoying far more resources to invest in the electoral competition than did the human rights groups that had opposed the regime. In Germany, SED

had the advantage that they basically could retain all the structures they had. They could basically keep the money, put it aside; they retained their membership to a large extent and had a much stronger starting position with that, already before the Volkskammer elections and then mainly in reunified Germany, than we did, coming from the citizens' movements. They had a perfectly functioning infrastructure, they had very, very, very expensive and very, very performative party soldiers, which of course we didn't want to have ... that was really a tactical advantage. (GDR9)

The electoralization of politics and internal divisions in the former opposition were even quicker to develop in cases of participated pacts, in which no strong linkage had developed during mobilization against the regime and, instead, full-fledged power struggles had had time to grow.

In *Hungary*, in the spring of 1988, Network, Fidesz, and the Hungarian Democratic Forum (MDF) had been formed, with membership growing fast, as "This mobilization was so dynamic that every week thousands of people would join" (HU4). However, this rapid growth was perceived, for example by this former MP for Fidesz in the early 1990s, as having brought about an organizational bureaucratization:

By 1989 these organizations had lived through a few substantial transformations, in each case in the direction of professionalization – the Network became an alliance; MDF's forum also turned into an alliance; Fidesz defined itself as an organization to start with which later turned into a party, and all these organizations turned into parties anyway. ... The greatest mobilizing influence, when you would start to be politically active from scratch, would be during 1988, ... 1989 was for the most part about how these organizations could channel their interests towards the government. ... Up until 1990,... civil activism stayed on, with great street protests, and rallies, and this peaked in the summer of 1989 with Imre Nagy's reburial. ... From the moment the new parliament was formed in 1990 things changed to a great extent, a significant proportion of activists turned to professional politics and a lot changed, including the civil society. Those civil activists who used to be engaged in politics became politicians, and those who didn't, they distanced themselves from politics. (HU4)

Electoral politics is thus located at the core of demobilization. In the narrative of a Hungarian former activist of the liberal SZDSZ, demobilization began

naturally, when democracy set in. . . . SZDSZ, which had an important role in the transition, the party to which I also belonged along with all of the former dissident movement, . . . also underwent some important changes. It first became the Network of Free Initiatives, which grouped all kinds of different civil society organizations without any sort of hierarchy, and then turned into a classical bourgeois party with a rather strong leadership, as a party like this has to be in order to achieve good results at the elections . . . blah blah blah. So this is a story of success and defeat at the same time, because doubtlessly, this civil society managed to defeat the enemy, I mean the party state and Communist dictatorship. . . . At the same time, it ceased to exist with this victory. (HU5)

Similarly, another of the oppositional parties, Fidesz, changed organizationally as well as strategically. As a Fidesz founder recalled,

Fidesz was a quasi-democratic community; for a long while they didn't even have a leader . . . the sessions of the most important executive organ, the board, were open to the public: anyone who wanted to go, could go. Only when Fidesz was elected to the parliament did it became part of the agenda that not everyone could sit in at the sessions of the parliamentary faction, because you can't just enter the Parliament. . . . This is when professionalization began, bit by bit. More and more, politics was made via the elected organs. (HU6)

As Fidesz turned into a party, however, it performed badly at the 1994 elections, then radically changing its aims as, another Fidesz founder observed, "It went from being a liberal party to being . . . a centrist formation with a touch of radical right. So clearly it survived itself pretty well, but it changed everything from head to toe: its ideology, everything. There's not a trace of the notions of 1988/1989 Fidesz left in it" (HU8).

This outcome is considered as all the more aggrieving in a situation in which political parties remain very elitist. If, especially in participated pacts, party politics is then seen, for instance by a former leader of the MDF parliamentary faction in the early 1990s, as "the only way out" – as "Politics will be done by the parties, this is obvious" (HU10) – the widespread impression is that this cannot but divide the opposition. So, a Fidesz member agreed, "in 1989, movements turned into parties" (HU9). Here as well, as one of the promoters of the protests against the dam on the Danube observed, parties remained tiny, as "the membership of all the parties combined doesn't reach 100,000. I mean this politicized elite is completely detached from the society . . . since there is no other mass organization apart from them, this suggests that Hungarian society is in a completely disorganized state" (HU3).

Similarly, in *Poland*, activists pointed at a difficult adaptation of Solidarity during and after transition. Evolving from being the main dissident organization into being a political party, Solidarity changed its organizational structures and ideology. As a Solidarity activist and later minister recalled, the organization was already internally divided in 1989: "Practically in Poland there was one mass organization, it was Solidarność, but you have to remember that it was after the Carnival of Solidarność: it was tormented, it was functioning in a very fractured way." Initially, the need to oppose a threatening regime helped in keeping differences at bay:

All the groups worked exclusively with Solidarność; in 1980 and 1981 it gathered almost every opponent of the government, of the authorities. In large part because of that pressure of the authorities, it was possible to overcome the political differences between these particular groups. I remember these differences, but they weren't expressed because it made no sense. What was more important was still to get rid of the authorities and not whether one group was more right-wing oriented and another one was more left-wing oriented. (PL2)

However, diversity later brought about splits: if before, "the enemy was one and common: the general Jaruzelski and party leaders from Moscow, and there was one ally that was the church and Ronald Reagan of course [laughs]" (PL8), with time, many internal cleavages exploded, with an increasing marginalization of the left-wing component.

Summarizing, electoral politics was perceived by those very activists who had struggled (also) for free elections as hampering rather than enhancing their own chances. Institutional politics was seen initially as a positive challenge in Czechoslovakia, but as rather frustrating in the GDR, with more of an adaptation in the cases of participated pacts.

CO-OPTATION INTO INSTITUTIONAL POLITICS?

It is about how one becomes a minister. It was very simple again. Just imagine you are at home. It was some evening after the huge demonstrations on Wenceslas square. It was Sunday and suddenly the telephone rang. It was around 8pm. I picked up the phone and I heard: "Look, we are at Laterna Magika, and we nominated you for a ministry. You have two hours to decide if you take it or not. We will call you back." Then, they hung up the phone. I looked at my first wife and told her: "I was nominated as a minister"; she said: "Minister of what?" I told her, I wasn't told either. Few minutes later the telephone rang again. I picked it up: "I'm sorry, I didn't tell you, Minister of Labour and Social Affairs. Call you back in two hours. Goodbye." Imagine the situation now. I didn't know where the ministry was located. I didn't know what it was about. I didn't know anything about labour and social affairs. So, I looked at old newspapers to see if there was any mention of that ministry. Later I found the ministry in the telephone yellow pages and learnt that it was located on Palackého square. When two hours had passed, the telephone rang: "What is your decision?" and I said: "I'll take it," and they told me: "Ok, come tomorrow morning." ... So this was how I learnt I was going to be a minister. ... It was very easy to become a minister, nothing difficult. ... I thought, of course, that it was decided in a hurry and that later a new government would be nominated. So I kept my locker in ČKD and didn't return anything. I thought I would be back soon. ... Next day I was appointed minister. It was Friday. About two months later I visited ČKD. It was an unbelievable change. I don't know if you have ever experienced that – the environment you consider as your home. I worked there for 32 years. I knew all the people there. Well and now I went for a visit there. Of course arriving in a 613 (a type of car that was used by government officials) was stupid. I always wore corduroys and a jacket when I went to ČKD. I brought a bottle of rum for my friends of course. But I had the feeling that I was a stranger there. It was very uncomfortable. Everybody stared at me the way they would stare at someone who didn't belong there. If one wasn't with them he wasn't one of them. It was very bad feeling for me, and I went there less and less until I stopped going. I didn't understand them anymore because I had to think in a different way. (CZ11)

As recalled by this activist who had organized the workers' participation in the Velvet Revolution and then became minister of labour in the first government after transition, in Czechoslovakia many of those who had led the protest acquired top positions. As he noted, this often meant losing their original rooting in the movement and adapting to new circumstances.

If electoral politics was perceived as often hostile to movement politics, narratives also report many examples of the influence of movements upon institutional politics. This generally takes the form of transfer of personnel. Along this line, the literature on consolidation has cited co-optation as an explanation for declining protest after transition is completed. In Eastern Europe, it was noted, "After their massive venture into parliamentary politics, most leading dissidents are now found in politics, media and research" (Flam 2001, 2). Once again, however, this long march into institutions happened differently in the various analyzed cases, with diversities also linked to the path of transition.

Co-optation seemed particularly widespread in one of the cases of eventful democratization: *Czechoslovakia*. As interviewees tended to agree, "almost all Charta members filled administrative or constitutional positions of power, e.g. parliament, government, the Czech National

Council, the Federal Assembly, mayors etc. ... Almost everyone was somewhere" (CZ9). Co-optation in institutional politics began with the participation of the opposition in the Federal Assembly. Explaining the decline of the movement after transition, Ivan Havel recalled:

The most important politicians of Civic Forum were leaving for official posts, to the government. My brother became the president. A group of people went with him to organize his life as the president ... another became the mayor of Prague. And another became the director of radio. Another became the director of TV. You see all the important positions were sucking people from Civic Forum. So, just a few people remained. And a lot of volunteers wanted to do something, but it was not easy to organize. (Long 1996, 31)

This impression was widely shared by our interviewees. A former activist, for instance, recalls,

It was one and half months since the beginning of the revolution when I, with seventeen others ... were parachuted into the Federal Assembly. It was fun because we came there and all the communists were sitting there. It was unbelievable ... [they] didn't have any other chance and possibility than to elect us to the Federal Assembly. They elected us unanimously. We didn't become MPs out of the people's will, but out of the will of the worst creatures which were at the Federal Assembly. It was fun. It was like if Nazis had elected seventeen Jews. So I looked at the faces of those creatures and I had to laugh at them. ... We became MPs to elect Havel president unanimously the next day. When I speak about it now it seems to me like a fairy tale. I can't believe it was all true. (CZ10)

With Havel, in fact, many members of the movement entered institutional politics. As an activist recounts, "I have a photos of some door in Špalíček. There was a list of 37 names on the door. It was an emergency committee: 36 out of those 37 entered politics" (CZ5). Yet another presents himself as "the only one who didn't ... I was not interested. I thought that if communists didn't own monopoly and free elections were approved, then it was a question for politicians" (CZ5). It is a common memory that "At the end of 1989 most or at least many of the most important members of Charta were in executive positions. So people had the feeling that their effort to change the society and human rights – Charta's goals – would be implemented from a position of power" (CZ9). Yet another talked of what he described as an "infiltration of the establishment," including the mass media, as "lots of us ... started working at the Ministry of Foreign Affairs, Ježek went to Rozhlas (Czech Radio). Yes, we infiltrated the establishment" (CZ1).

The effects of entering into institutions are considered as very relevant in terms of keeping a sort of control on the development of the revolution, as "People joined various structures, activities and governmental offices ... trustworthy people appeared in various offices. ... So people said: 'Let's see what this new representation can do' " (CZ8). A former activist, who then became a minister, recalls that, with many of them who had entered government,

Havel's ethos had been present there. It really was. I saw it within the Ministry of Social Affairs. They really tried genuinely to help people in need and they referred to Havel. ... There were really nice and very good people there and they were permeated by Havel's ideas. They weren't interested only in money and well paid jobs. They really cared and they didn't want to give it up. There are also lots of altruists in NGOs. (CZ10)

Indeed, the formation of the new government happened in a euphoric climate:

When the new government was appointed, it was a real euphoria. It was at the end of the year 1989, somewhere between mid-December and mid-January. Everything had been archived. Barbed wires on the borders were cut. ... It was done. And then we had to learn, I mean how it works in the world. Everybody was interested in us. You cannot imagine how crowded Havel's press conferences were. There were TV reporters from all over the world. ... It was unbelievable. We had everything, I mean we controlled everything. We even controlled the Ministry of the Interior. (CZ11)

The entrance of former dissidents into institutional politics also happened in the other case of eventful democratization. Even in *Germany*, in fact, notwithstanding the feelings of marginalization by the GDR activists, some interviewees stressed a massive presence of movement activists in parliaments and governments – although more at the local and regional than at the national level. As an activist recalled,

We were three thousand civil rights activists in the GDR, and actually almost every one of those three thousand took on a political office or mandate. ... We had twenty-four members in the federal parliaments who stayed in there for different amounts of time; ... I don't know how many: about one hundred members of state parliaments in the different state parliaments, or perhaps not one hundred but we had very many in all state parliaments, parliamentary parties. We were represented in each communal parliament. ... I don't know of a comparable group with this density of mandates. We provided several ministers, several state secretaries, in the meantime a federal president. So, you could say we are the most successful political group ever ... that wasn't noticed because we were in different parties and because the negative propaganda always said that the civil rights activists were pushed to the margins. (GDR5)

Especially if looking at the local level, the impression was indeed that

almost all of those who were active in 1988–89 in citizens' rights groups, they also remained active. There was quite a large number on the communal and county levels, who took on responsibility in the most diverse respects, who went into administration, who took over schools as principals, who built up children's projects, so in very many forms of immediate democratic participation; they worked as members of parliaments, as county commissioner, as county councilor, and so on and so forth. That was a very decisive potential too, where change really became possible. (GDR8)

Another activist suggested that "one in ten remained politically active, so in the city parliament, they became city councillors or mayor or member of the county parliament or something like that, most of them on a communal level and some few also in the federal parliament" (GDR2). Another concurred, "There were many mayors that were supplied by New Forum, many people in the county parliaments, federated state parliaments" (GDR10); "some went into the federal parliament, others into the county parliaments, yet others into communal administrations or into citizens' initiatives" (GDR2).

Notwithstanding the frustrations mentioned earlier about the taking over of the revolution by the *Wessis*, it seems that, here as well, some ownership of the revolution was kept alive as "the work in the communities, in the cities, on a local level was quite massively influenced by the citizens' movement that was very many people who took on responsibility coming out of the citizens' movement" (GDR9).

Co-optation in institutional politics also happened in the two cases of participated pacts, but mobilization had been weaker and demobilization faster here; the ownership of the changes seemed more firmly in the hands of (party) elites.

In *Hungary*, activists pointed at the number of former dissidents in the parliament – one of them, who had led the Foundation for the Poor, noted, "I for one felt that freedom had come, that we were the state . . . when you have fifteen buddies in parliament . . ." (HU12). There was a widespread perception that party politics found less resistance, to the point of dominating civil society. To use the words of an interviewee,

The intellectual elite was sucked into politics. Those intellectuals involved in mobilization in the 1980s and then all of a sudden, became legislators . . . they were drafting the constitution and a public institutional framework at the roundtable, and ended up in professional politics. Some intellectuals felt uncomfortable in this role and slowly pulled out from politics. Some stayed in parliament, some never even entered politics, and retreated to movement mobilization. (HU12)

The shared assessment by interviewees, however, is that this co-optation tended to have negative outcomes, as

parties started to dominate civil society entirely: the borderline between the two was blurred. ... For awhile, well for 15 years, NGOs also had a seat in the executive committees of public media outlets ... but really, NGOs were divided along the exact same lines and always voted according to their party affiliations. When there were elections for the president of the public television or radio, NGOs always voted in line with their parties. (HU11)

NGOs were in fact perceived as subject to parties, as "both the Socialists and Fidesz put a lot of effort into coopting, buying, and stealing civil society organizations, as well as forcing them into cooperation ... They established a lot of NGOs, which were really covert political organizations" (HU8). Party alignment of NGOs is in fact said to contribute to splits, as "in this largely polarized Hungarian society, political discourse relates everything to parties. ... The power of political parties has probably become even stronger: it encompasses all areas of our life" (HU11). Disappointment therefore emerges with the fact that

civil society was basically abused. Parties colonized it bit by bit, occupied civil society ... And because of the unresolved issue of party finances, NGOs played a role in putting away party funds, and pushed real civil society out of policymaking. Democracy was slowly reduced to being a multiparty system. Normally democracy is more than a multiparty system, it's not just about parties but also about citizens. (HU9)

In *Poland*, a similar transfer from movements toward parties was said to have weakened the movements, also cutting potential channels for future collaboration. As in Hungary, divisions and party dominance were stigmatized. After 1989, the movement indeed split – as a leader of Solidarity in the Silesia region recalled – between "the ones that are entering the world of new possibilities that were created by the institutional change of the Round Table" and "those who are criticizing old days from perspectives that are radically democratic, that criticize the top down institutionalization of democratic reforms from the perspective of radical democracy, meaning that the self-governance was betrayed as well as the workers, and the ones that are criticizing all of this from the perspective of populism" (PL7). In this process, the groups that represented the left wing of Solidarność were losing influence – as an activist recalled, "We left the stage and we became totally marginalized and we stopped having any influence on the reality" (PL7). The emergence of divisions also contributed to the electoral defeat, and then the disappearance, of some of the organizations that had led the opposition during the transition. This was the case for Freedom and Peace, which quickly dissolved because "in the times when you could openly organize or follow your beliefs concerning society and politics, the internal differences within the movement were so intense that you couldn't keep the whole organization together anymore" (PL4).

However, divisions are also considered as a sign of normalization. As a Polish former Solidarity supporter argued, normal politics as a search for power emerges from the Solidarity movement's ashes:

> Of course it was bad, but I think there was no other way to follow. I think the idea of "let's all love each other," which we had in 1981 and for the whole time of the martial law, came out of the only unifying element, which was a common enemy.... Later it came to politics, and all this changed in 1989.... Solidarność was not a trade union but it was more of a social movement in 1981.... Solidarność had ten million members and these came from a thousand perspectives and it was a phenomenal movement, if you look at it from today's perspective. The martial law has strengthened Solidarność, but when these limitations were removed then Solidarność began to divide. Especially, the new structures of power emerged and there was this natural competition about who is supposed to be in power, and many people wanted to be in power. Solidarność was created by people who were ambitious leaders, not by holy people that only went to church to pray. ... Lech Wałęsa is a good example of this because he wanted to become the president, so he created the war on the top, as a result of which he became the president. (PL8)

In sum, notwithstanding widespread pessimistic views on institutional politics, cases of eventful democratization have shown some capacity to penetrate institutions, bringing into electoral and non-electoral politics the skills and values that had been forged during the struggle for democracy. This was less the case in participated pacts.

CONCLUDING REMARKS

Elections and electorally accountable institutions are an outcome of successful mobilization for democracy. However, to a certain extent paradoxically, activists in the movements for democracy often resent institutional politics as being far from their expectations and/or standards about democratic politics. The very organization of elections, with privilege given to parties over citizens' initiatives, is indeed often perceived as a bitter defeat, a disempowering of the civil society.

Disaffection does not involve only activists. Research on political rights in the CEE converged in describing many elements that reduced the quality of political institutions. After the founding elections, electoral participation dramatically declined; while parties not only leapfrogged the phase of mass organizations remaining extremely small, they also had very low levels of support. High electoral volatility is then reflected in governmental instability, with some power of patronage but little capacity to consolidate party (and political) loyalties. What is more, a semantic challenge to the very notion of the political Left comes from its frequent support for austerity plans and the free market, which is then reflected in the emergence of populist and nationalist tendencies.

All of this is perceived by former activists with increasing frustration, as the attempts to build more participatory and deliberative institutions also failed. The difficulties of adapting to a new and unknown situation, but also the strong pressures by powerful actors inside and outside the country, are stigmatized as taking away the ownership of the changes from the civil society. So, institutional politics tend to be described with skepticism, as endorsing a different vision of democracy and requiring different skills from the ones promoted by social movements. Against the high moral standards of the former dissidents, institutions and parties appear as corrupted and corrupting. Nevertheless, institutional politics also seems to offer opportunities to activists through legalization and legitimation as transitions open the possibility to participate in parliaments and governments, competing there for a sort of ownership of the revolutions.

Here as well, however, there are cross-national differences, with a larger capacity to influence institutions from below in cases of eventful democratization than in cases of participated pacts – visible first of all in the very constitutional policies and then also in electoral politics, as well as in the capacity of entering the institutions. Not only do statistics usually reflect these differences, with higher ratings on many political qualities for the former than for the latter, but the activists' narratives also point at greater empowerment in cases of eventful democratization. This is particularly the case in Czechoslovakia, where the first years of consolidation were characterized by a strong imprinting of Civic Forum activists, who massively entered leading elected institutions but also, and with long-lasting effects, the public administrations. Decisions made in these years proved influential later on as well, even when Civic Forum dissolved after electoral failures. Even in the former GDR, however, where activists were particularly frustrated by the annexation to the

West and the refusal of any constitutional attempts, the federal states as well as the local governments provided channels of access to former activists. As for the cases of participated pacts, even when former activists entered institutions, this happened through a demoting of civil society organizations.

8

Socioeconomic Rights and Transition Paths

> If ... structures are predetermined, as they are already long established elsewhere, then they need to think little themselves ... it has more negative effects on the processes of democratization ... it is always better if you have to work something up. (GDR6)

In the German case, as in others, the speed of the change, the lack of specific skills in economics among oppositional activists, and the pressing influence of the West, with a ready model for economic reforms, are perceived as causes for the failure to develop a socially sensitive alternative. This previously existing model, as the activist cited above observed, reduced the need to think about and devise specific solutions to specific problems.

Social science literature has identified in the double nature of the transition – political and economic – some serious challenges for democratic quality. In this chapter, I will discuss how protests before transition affected the institutional assets adopted during the regime's installation and consolidation, through mechanisms of legalization and legitimation. As we will see, neoliberal reforms are perceived by former activists in the struggle for democracy as conflicting with the movement's demands for bridging democracy with social justice. In interviews with former participants, the immorality of capitalism is strongly stigmatized in theory and suffered in practice. Here as well, we will single out differences across transitional paths, but also within each of them, as Czechoslovakia developed more social security–oriented policies and Poland instead advanced more on the neoliberal model, with the other two cases somewhere in between.

Double Transition: The State and the Market
in Central Eastern Europe

Political economy studies converge in defining the consolidation phase in Central Eastern Europe (CEE) as an experiment in the exportation of neoliberalism to socioeconomic systems that had been characterized by state control of the economy. The transition came about in a moment of hegemony of neoliberal ideology, with its emphasis on privatization and deregulation. In Polanyi's (1957) terms, a second "great transformation" was indeed promoted by international actors pushing for free market over social protection. This global trend had obvious effects in the region I analyzed – as neoliberal models were promoted strongly by influential actors from the West.

Scholars have characterized the challenges of democratization processes in the Soviet Union and the satellite states in the overlapping of various types of transformation. Claus Offe has identified three simultaneous challenges for 1989. One is "the territorial issue, that is, the determination of the borders for a state and a population, and the consolidation of these borders within the framework of a European order of states" (Offe 1996, 35). That question – fueled by the USSR's territorial policies – was particularly relevant in the former Soviet Union and former Yugoslavia, but less so in CEE, where two other levels of transformation instead overlapped, defined by Offe (1996, 35) as:

The issue of democracy, that is, the dissolution of the monopoly claims of a party and its replacement by a constitutionally tamed exercise of authority and party competition in the context of guarantees of basic human and civil rights (glasnost);

The issue of economic and property order and the orderly political management of pressing production and distribution problems (perestroika).

Especially problematic was the speed of the process, as the types of evolution that had developed over centuries in Western Europe had to be mastered simultaneously in the transitions in the CEE region. In fact, Offe observed, two main elements of economic reform – price and property reforms – can come in tension with democracy. As he noted, "while freedom and property are conciliable, they are not conciliable with democracy if the consequences to be expected are very negative" (Offe 1996, 44). Thus, privatization might succeed in leading to marketization and prosperity, or it might obstruct democracy "through powerful interferences originating from domestic or international owners of capital" (Offe 1996, 45). Leaving aside the nationalist challenge for the moment, a characteristic of the transitions in CEE was therefore the double nature of the transformation: not only from one political regime to another but also from a socialist economy to a capitalist one. Political economists have addressed the characteristics of this double transition, singling out similarities but also infra-area differences.

Looking in particular at the German case, Claus Offe noted some more general problems in the social quality of democracy. On the whole, while there was no real economic breakdown before the transition, economic integration during consolidation failed to reach its aim. In fact, "the collapse of GDR was not caused by acute and dramatic disturbances emerging from within the system of economic organization and its mode of operation – despite some of its obvious deficiencies vis-à-vis West European welfare states and their economies. The critical defect of the system was not an economic, but a moral flaw" (Offe 1996, 19). Further, Offe stressed the delegitimating effects of the economic decline that followed transition: "The result of sometimes near-catastrophic conditions in areas such as communication, transportation, energy supply, real estate, health care and education facilities was that chances for the recovery of the economy, in the new market of open and unrestricted competition, declined instead of improving during the second half of 1990, and with them went the chance for autonomous economic recovery" (Offe 1996, 17).

Comparing the two periods of transition to democracy in Germany, Offe noted in fact the greater challenges presented in 1989 versus the post–World War II period. While the "hardware" was a main concern in 1945, as war had destroyed many material and human resources, the "software" of the transition, in terms of cultural resources, was quite straightforward. Vice versa, in 1989, while there was no major challenge from the point of view of "hardware," major problems emerged from the weak "software" available to address the transition. In the post–World War II Federal Republic of Germany,

the more intangible preconditions of economic reconstruction, such as human resources, the spirit of mobility, efficiency and technical modernization, as well as the basic institutional set-up of a private, capitalist economy, were all in place at the beginning of the West-German reconstruction, as were political elites from the previous regime, the Weimar republic. What was also in place was an extremely stimulated and encouraged "sense of direction," a widely shared notion of the values and goals that the new regime must pursue with high priority, namely a "social" market economy and a liberal democracy within the institutional framework of strong federalism. This convergent orientation of all major political forces was as much inspired by Anglo-Saxon models of liberal democracy as it was inherited from the welfare state project of Weimar, which together amounted to a widely shared ideological mix of "restoration" and "new beginning." All of these cultural, personal, institutional and ideological software resources stood ready for immediate use. Given the circumstances and conditions, the post-1945 transition was in fact easier to accomplish than the one after 1989. (Ibid.)

The situation reversed in 1989, with smaller challenges in terms of "hardware" and more significant ones regarding the availability of a sound "software" in terms of strategies for political and economic development. In fact, in East Germany:

The "hardware" – the stock of machinery, buildings and infrastructure – may be outdated and rotten, but it has not suffered from anything like large scale destruction that had taken place in the 1945 case. Up to its end the GDR was an economic system that was able to feed, house and employ its citizens at a level of prosperity unequalled by any of the other state socialist countries. But here the bottleneck variables appeared to ebb elite, institutional and cultural factors. The intangible, or "software," resources – mentalities, routines, habits, modes of coping, cognitive frames and expectations, familiarity with institutional patterns – that turn out to be of a surprising strategic significance as determinants of a sustained and successful process of reconstruction seem to be missing. (Offe 1996, 186–7)

Consequently, there was in 1989, when compared with 1945, a more ambiguous rejection of the old regime and no clear instructions on what to do (ibid.). This ended up producing less than satisfactory achievements in terms of social rights.

Going in depth in the analysis of capitalist diversity in Eastern Europe's periphery, Dorothee Bohle and Béla Greskovits (2013) noted that the double transitions to democracy and free market took a peculiar character in the Visegrad countries (including Poland, Hungary, Czech Republic, and Slovakia), following a model of embedded neoliberalism.[1] Using Polanyi's work as a point of reference, they built a typology that crossed free market and social protection as two distinct dimensions. Criticizing the simplistic distinction between liberal market economy and coordinated market economy, they defined embedded neoliberalism as combining a free market with compensations for transformation costs, ranging from sheltering domestic and transnational firms through tariffs, subsidies, and special regulations to social welfare policies (ibid., 29).

---

[1] In contrast, neoliberal regimes in the Baltic had been driven by private Keynesianism, with low credit rates and massive investment in construction and real estate. More social protection characterized Slovenia (ibid.).

In all four countries, democracy accompanied a deep transformation of a welfare state that had developed with socialism, including a generous system of social protection (in terms of pension, sickness, and disability benefits) as well as family policies, full employment, public health, free education, and price controls. In general, governments were quite successful at macroeconomic stabilization, but at the cost of draconic austerity programs. Moreover, a tradition of neocorporatist agreements was shaken by accession, bringing about a downward trend in terms of participatory and industrial democracy. As simultaneous transformations affected various groups, with internal competition and pressures, the Visegrad countries did still offer however social protection, with some resilience from previous regimes. The free market brought about dramatic changes in everyday life, with sharp increases in infant mortality, addiction, and crime.

The socioeconomic weaknesses reemerged during democratic consolidation and afterward. While economic recession had characterized the final stage of "real socialism," post-transition reconstruction of the market brought about some economic improvements only between the late 1990s and mid-2000s, while with EU enlargement, "the fragility of capitalist democracy returned with a vengeance" (ibid., 5). Social inequalities grew, as internal national competition developed for attracting international investments through services and low corporate taxes. Pressure for accession to the European Union, as a way to avoid speculative attacks on national currency, imposed a fiscal consolidation that thwarted welfare spending, with austerity measures imposed even by left-wing governments, which then lost support and legitimacy.

As Offe had observed, the "software" of the transition was indeed a challenge. Reform choices were constrained by the past, but also subject to political agency, with a central role played by political and technocratic elites. While initially lacking clear ideas on what to do, governments floated various concepts as possible alternatives – including self-management, laissez-faire capitalism, or Scandinavian social democracy – neoliberal think tanks played an important role in pushing for free market solutions (Bohle and Neunhoeffer 2009). Additionally, international financial institutions – such as the World Bank and the International Monetary Fund, and then (especially from the second half of 1990s) the European Union – pushed toward further (neo)liberalization (ibid., 87), while transnational corporations and foreign banks also played a major role, finding the Visegrad countries particularly attractive for experimenting with free market solutions. So, during the 1990s, neoliberalism dominated the development of the postsocialist capitalist economy (Bohle and Greskovits 2013). Lacking a capitalist class and even a bourgeoisie, the support for neoliberal economic reform initially was based on value orientations rather than material interests (Bernhard 1996). Therefore,

> The pro-reform side of this cleavage continues to be based in large measure on value orientations because of the lag in the emergence of material interests tied to the market.... The anti-reform side of this cleavage remains partially embedded in old etatist struggles over shares of state resources while increasingly adopting the popular protest strategies used by actors in the democratic struggle of interests. (Bernhard 1996, 326)

Trust in and perceived legitimacy of new democratic institutions suffered from the low quality of social rights. The repeated economic crises and permanent difficulties brought about waves of protest, as well as a radicalization of some moderate parties and the emergence of radical ones, with the spreading of nationalistic appeals. The crisis of the late 2000s produced further decline in satisfaction with and trust in democratic institutions: As party loyalty weakened and public opinion became increasingly fragmented and critical, political and economic instability ensued. In fact, after a short honeymoon between technocrats and citizens, the appeal of neoliberalism was shaken as Polanyi-like countermovements called for more social protection and politicians started to appeal to the nation. As the free market brought about dislocation and transformation of hierarchies, with disintegration of social ties, appeals to national identity proliferated (Bohle and Greskovits 2013). Pressures from below also helped to mitigate the implementation of neoliberal plans. Welfarist social contracts then emerged from a combination of neoliberalism and generous welfare, building on existing legacies (Bohle and Greskovits 2013). Influenced by a paternalistic welfare tradition with little participation, the system developed on the recognition of previous skills and rights, with widespread perceptions that entitlements (such as pensions) could not easily be taken away (ibid.).

VARIETIES OF CAPITALISM FOR VARIETIES OF TRANSITION PATHS?

While this description of the various dimensions of the transition fit well for all cases under scrutiny here, we can nevertheless observe differences in the ways in which both political and socioeconomic rights were addressed. Looking at the different transitional paths, we can assume that they influenced indeed the democratic qualities of the ensuing states. In particular, we might expect eventful democratization to bring about more propitious conditions for social protection, especially when those who participate in government after transition had promoted values of social justice. As I argued in Chapter 1, the assumption is that these first years work as critical junctures, bringing about long-lasting paths. Indeed, this assumption seems supported by research, linking paths of transition to democratic quality in the Iberian Peninsula, with Portugal representing a case of eventful democratization, and Spain instead a case of partici-pated pact. As Fishman (2011) noted, the road to democracy in Portugal deeply transformed social structures. In fact, "cultural processes at play during democratization and conditioned by the social and political para-meters of the regime change help to determine which actors are seen as legitimate claimants on the attention of political office holders and the broader public, not only in the context of regime change but also after-wards" (Fishman 2013, 18). When looking at social rights, in comparison with Spain, Portugal started after transition from a position of higher inequalities and lower access to education, as well as poorer economic conditions. However, the 1976 Portuguese constitution and legislation enacted in the following years reduced these inequalities, creating a very large public sector – with the nationalization of 244 firms and state monopolies in important areas such as banking, insurance, petrochemical industries, and other basic and infrastructural industries as well as com-munication. A large number of cooperatives were funded after the agrar-ian reform, while the Portuguese constitution declared housing and healthcare a right for all citizens and its provision a state responsibility; employment policies were similarly inclusive.[2]

---

[2] By the end of the 1970s, social security coverage was almost universal in Portugal (Garcia and Karakatsanis 2006, 126), and in 1981, a National Pension Service was created (ibid., 129). Moreover, the revolution quickly multiplied, by a factor of four, social security transfers as percentage of GDP (from around 2 percent to around 8 percent), with effects immediately visible in 1975–1976 (Castles 2006, 52). In cross-country Iberian compar-ison, while unemployment increased in Spain from 11.5 percent to 19.5 percent between 1981 and 1988 and up to 22.9 percent in 1995, it declined from 8 percent to 5.8 percent and then to 7.2 percent in Portugal in the same period. In 1999, unemployment in Spain was 11.2 percent for males, 22.9 percent for females, 21.7 percent for male youth (under twenty-five years old), and 38.3 percent for female youth – as compared to, respectively, 4 percent, 6.2 percent, 7.5 percent, and 11.1 percent in Portugal. Female participation in the labor force was 59.1 percent in Portugal in 1989 and 66.8 percent in 1999, against 40 percent and 49 percent in Spain (EU15 average is 54.2 percent and 59.2 percent) (Garcia and Karakatsanis 2006, 113).

To the extent that dynamics in CEE resonate with those in the Iberian Peninsula, we might expect that eventful democratization brought about more concerns with social protection than participated pacts. Within some common trends, differences were in fact noted as the two cases of participated pacts, Poland and Hungary, went further in the direction of free market reform, as bureaucrats also perceived the possibility to benefit from change, having already developed contacts with the West. The situation was different in Czechoslovakia, with no burden of excessive debt, where even right-wing Klaus supported opening the market but opposed foreign dominance. Here, privatization through vouchers, financed by state banks, prolonged state ownership until recession in 1996–1997. As for privatization paths, as Stark and Bruzst (1998) noted, there were, rather than one transition, multiple transformations across and within each country. With over 85 percent of productive assets as state property, types of privatization could be distinguished in terms of valuation of assets (administrative versus market-made), the actors targeted to acquire assets (targeting citizens of corporations), and resources (monetary versus positional).

In both cases of participated pacts, privatization was based on positional resources. In *Poland*, beginning still in Jaruzelski's time, privatization was influenced by the Liberal Congress, where businessmen and intellectuals met. As the search for international investments initially failed, a mass privatization program brought about the promise to Workers' Councils to give factory employees 10 percent of the related shares, while an additional share of vouchers was issued to every citizen. However, as these shares were exchanged in an asset manager, which then decided on investments, the result was "to give aggressive property management to foreign companies, within the constraints of a politicized citizenry" (ibid., 96). While especially the alliance of post-communist and peasant parties in power tried to build national capitalism, revitalizing the links with *nomenklatura* business circles and with subsidized restructuring for hybrid forms of industry, the development of privatization was toward direct sales to foreign capital.

In *Hungary*, a decentralized – case by case, firm by firm – privatization developed, while governments looked for foreign finances. The country combined bargained evaluation of assets, corporate ownership, and positional resources, as the State Property Agency sold the right to lead and manage privatization. The economic crisis was then more acute in Hungary, with Fidesz moving to the radical side of the right, and in

Poland, where the post-accession crisis was reflected in the defeat of the post-communists in government.

The situation differed in the cases of eventful democratization. In particular, the *Czech Republic* remained more committed to welfare than its neighboring countries did (ibid., 158). In the formative period, important portfolios were in fact in the hands of the social democratic wing of Civic Forum. Even as right-wing Václav Klaus won the election, "the fundamentals of the policy path that had been set in place during 1991 remained in place" (ibid., 180). Privatization was based on a distribution to each citizen of vouchers equal to 1,000 investment points. After initial enthusiasm, a neo-statist tendency reemerged in 1993, with growing disillusionment – as "production had plummeted, unemployment had soared, and tax evasion and corruption were pervasive" (Stark and Bruszt 1998, 119). In government, Klaus called for rapid and massive price and foreign trade liberalization; but these proclamations were not always implemented (ibid.). Recognizing that bankruptcy before privatization would have been dangerous economically, and also "undermine broader support for his broader reforms" (ibid., 156), in his "The Commandments Revised," Klaus instead praised gradualism and improvement of corporate governance as more important than privatization. In fact, he even waived the requirement of a citizen token in order to use vouchers, thus gaining support for his privatization program. The executive authority emerged, in fact, as "constitutionally, institutionally, and conjuncturally more constrained" (ibid., 179). Even after the separation of Czechs and Slovakians in 1993, no dramatic departure from the course was made: "on the social front, job creation subsidies were not dismantled and, instead of price liberalization, Czech residents continued to enjoy liberal subsidies for housing and public utilities" (ibid., 182). Czechoslovakia, first, and later the two successor states have in fact been more committed to maintaining a social security system, investing a larger share of GDP for these purposes than do the other CEE countries: "Consequently such programs as subsidies for food, energy and housing have helped boost the poor's share of income. ... Because these programs have included extensive provisions for families, such as maternity allowances, child benefits, and subsidies for transportation, they have also made it much easier for women to combine full-time jobs with homemaking" (Ferber and Raabe 2003, 418). Women's rights, particularly on maternity leave, remained quite generous, with the labor legislation passed in 1991 including anti-discrimination clauses (Ferber and Raabe 2003).

In general, in the Czech Republic, a well-consolidated party system decreased fragmentation favoring a bipolar party competition, focused on socioeconomic issues, and represented interests. As Klaus had no large majority, parliament remained a deliberative body that moderated free market orientations. The strength of parliament prevented radical neoliberal reforms, while a participatory conception of party organizations reduced electoral volatility (Biezen 2003). In fact, an inclusive legitimation and a stable party system produced a communitarian pattern of consolidation (Morlino 2012, 139).

In *Germany*, the steering of privatization was assigned to a specially created agency, the Treuhandanstalt, which focused initially on the one and only task of privatization, imagining that the invisible hand of the market would then create jobs. As the Treuhandanstalt favored corporate actors using monetary funds, this allowed West Germans to take over the market of Eastern firms and produced massive migration, with serious impoverishment in terms of human capital. In the former German Democratic Republic (GDR) states, "During the months following German unification in October 1990, East Germans witnessed a process that we can describe without hyperbole as colonization" (Stark and Bruszt 1998, 175), with the chancellor as unconstrained decision maker. Centralized structures then initially developed a free market–oriented program. As "unmitigated exposure to competition triggered not an economic miracle but an economic nightmare," the course changed, however, becoming more sensitive to the need to preserve assets, as decisions moved toward more deliberative forums that also involved the regional governments. In fact, the German privatization assumed a more moderate course as it became clear that "because the sources of the problems were more transparent and the political promises more grandiose, in Germany economic crisis carried the danger of political crisis" (ibid., 176). This risk was demonstrated not only by the assassination of the chief executive of the Treuhandanstalt by the Red Army Faction (RAF) but also by strike waves, occupations of factories, and protests in front of the state parliaments, with mobilization by the still-populous unions and alliances by federal states' politicians.

Different policies are reflected in different outcomes. As was the case for Portugal in the Iberian Peninsula, Czechoslovakia (and then the Czech Republic) as a case of eventful democratization in the CEE region is also characterized by better performances in terms of GDP, employment, human development, life expectancy, schooling, quality of life, and sustainability (Table 8.1). Specifically, Czechs saw a higher percentage of

TABLE 8.1 *Indicators of Performances on Quality-of-Life Indicators*

	Eurostat, GDP per capita 2011 (EU27=100)	Eurostat employment rate age group 15–64	Human development index. Ranking in 2011	Human development score in 2011	Life expectancy at birth	Means of schooling	GINI per capita in US $ terms	European quality of life Euro Barometer 2012	Environmental sustainability. Ecological footprint (10 best)
Czech Republic	80	70.9	27	0.865	77.7	12.3	21.405	21	5.3
Poland	65	64.8	39	0.813	76.1	10.0	17.451	15	3.9
Hungary	66	60.7	38	0.816	74.4	11.1	16.581	26	4.2

families with adequate income from regular jobs – 58 percent, as compared to 34 percent in Poland and 49 percent in Hungary. In general,
unemployment remained lower, and social protection higher in the Czech
Republic. There,

> the unemployment rate was extraordinarily low throughout most of the 1990s,
> and the CR was slower to dismantle the social safety net than other countries. . . .
> It has been widely noted that the Czechs, who eagerly embraced the return to
> democracy, have been far less eager to accept a move toward a pure private
> enterprise system and give up the social programs they were used to . . . most
> Czechs would like to combine the prosperity of the "West" with the security of the
> "East." Thus, poverty alleviation is still considered to be the state's responsibility,
> and many Czechs, particularly women, consider the "third way" preferable to
> either state socialism or an unrestricted market system. (Ferber and Raabe 2003,
> 409)

Concluding, as Gabor summarized,

> The Czech Republic is broadly regarded as the country with the most effective
> system of social protection among all East-Central European countries,
> characterized by centralized policy-making and generous redistribution towards
> vulnerable groups. . . . This is a consequence of adopting a social liberal, or social-
> market approach to the radical economic reforms during the regime change.
> Unlike in Poland, where pure neo-liberal recipes promoted by World Bank or
> WTO were put in practice, in the Czech Republic they were to large extent filtered
> by the social-democratic values advocated by Václav Havel and strongest social-
> democratic party in the region. . . . Furthermore, in the Czech Republic there was
> less pressure for radical economic reforms since the country was in better
> economic condition than Poland, or Hungary, i.e. external debt was relatively
> modest, and there was no threat of hyperinflation. (2013, 118)

In sum, explanations of differences in the quality of social rights are to
be located in the dynamics of transitions, as the foundation for economic
policy was marked by the first years of consolidation (Stark and Bruszt
1998, 179). As we will see, these transformations affected activists' expectations and assessments of their achievements.

EXPECTATIONS ABOUT SOCIAL CHANGE

> The martyrs of 1956 were all communists, with no exceptions. Within these
> by then enlarged circles, there was neither any ambition for restoration of
> the original pre-1945 regime, nor any reformist ambitions to resurrect the
> official ideologies of the regime. . . . In the meantime, . . . from being
> a divisive and dangerous issue, 1956 turned into an issue that unified the
> popular opposition, as a movement (of course this is a myth) in which
> everybody participated who wasn't a Stalinist or an overt supporter of the

Soviet occupation. This was of course a complete optical illusion, since none of us knows what would have come out of 1956 after November 4th, since the Russians came and put an end to everything. What is sure is that none of the prominent figures of 1956 wanted regime change in the sense of restoring capitalism. (HU5)

In Hungary, as in the rest of the CEE states, those who had started the mobilization against the regime were mainly not supporters of the free market. The socioeconomic effects of the transition in terms of increasing social inequalities were indeed stigmatized by our interviewees as failures in all four countries, although with varying emphasis according to the socioeconomic qualities of ensuing democracies as well as the characteristics of the previous opposition.

Concerns for social justice are rooted in the continuity of the opposition of the late 1980s with those of previous moments in history when critiques of "real socialism" came in fact from the Left. First of all, in all four countries, the opposition to "real socialism" grew from within socialist visions, and these visions maintained their relevance during the mobilization for democracy. In *Czechoslovakia*, the Velvet Revolution brought some of the activists of the Prague Spring into power, so that "policymaking drew on this distinctive 'social democratic' legacy," bringing about some peculiar characteristics of welfare state, such as "stronger egalitarianism of the pension system, early abolition of privileged occupational categories, and overall greater concerns with preventing unemployment rather than compensating for job loss" (Bohle and Greskovits 2013, 153). Our interviewees tended to agree that "lots of people had the idea of the 1960s. It means socialism with a human face" (CZ9). These memories, and their effects on the search for a "third way," are so recalled by a student activist:

We imagined that we would not do it normally, like they did it in Germany or France, but rather that we would take our own third way, which would be more human and humanistic, and that it would not be wild capitalism. I think, because we grew up reading *My, Reportéři, Literární noviny* and other journals from the 1960s that were hidden in the cottages, we were mentally in the year 1968 ... we wanted a socially fair society that would not be only about money. (CZ1)

Given expectations of social justice, a founder of the Committee for the Defence of the Unjustly Persecuted and then of Charta 77 noted,

The big failure was the economic transformation. ... November 1989 raised enormous hope in people. They had the feeling that they didn't have to do anything and that heaven on earth would come true without them. They eased up in vigilance when economic transition was running and the results of the economic transition were not very stimulating for the morals of the nation. ... The moral impact of the transition was devastating for the people. (CZ3)

Similarly in the *GDR*, the idea of a democratic socialism was deep-rooted. There were in fact ideas to reorganize the economy through democratic decision making and collective ownership, as "Still believing in the ideas of democratic socialism, most representatives of the citizen movements initially sought to democratize decision-making in firms by establishing Verwaltungsräte (administrative councils) composed of representatives of workers and management, and experts" (Rucht 1996, 43). The opposition strongly nurtured ideas of solidarity and social protection, with an emphasis on extensive social rights. As Rucht recalled,

At the center of these efforts was the formulation of a Sozialcharta (social charter) which guaranteed work and housing, the "humanization" of labor, free education and health care, social welfare for underprivileged groups, and a certain share of state property for every citizen. The Volkskammer accepted the Sozialcharta with some modifications, but the proposal was not implemented due to a lack of resources and the anticipation of unification. (Rucht 1996, 43)

Among the original group of protestors, many were in fact aiming at a reform of the regime, as "Their dream was the creation of a new order that would expand elementary democratic rights (as they were secured in West Germany) as well as incorporate some elements of the former GDR – such as extensive social rights and some state ownership of property" (Rucht 1996, 43).

Also in the shared memory of the activists, the fight for freedom was accompanied by a fight for solidarity. In the interviews, the ideals of the movement are often – bitterly – contrasted with the results of the transition. In particular, the consumerism of the new society is stigmatized. As a feminist recalled, claims for economic policies played a most important role: "it was about decent work times, it was about rescinding the remaining residue of income inequality of different women, which is much worse today than it ever was in the GDR" (GDR1). In fact, as a future member of the federal parliament for Bundis 90/die Gruene concurred, "the idea was 'we change this GDR society, we create, like Democracy Now said, *a solidarity society, something beyond capitalism and socialism. Not a third way but something that does encompass the experience of the GDR*'" (GDR9, emphasis added). In general, "economic democracy was a big issue in the documents, ... that personnel have a right to have a say, the what and how and where it is" (GDR1). This vision was indeed linked to a strong criticism of capitalism, perceived as greedy and individualistic. Capitalism was rather contrasted to true democracy as, an activist argued, "democracy does not fit with capitalism because capitalism is always also an allocation of power on the one hand and of powerlessness on the other hand. ... Democracy presupposes an equal status and equal value of the actor" (GDR1).

In *Poland*, in parallel, the legacy of the first period of Solidarity was presented as mainly oriented to the development of a sort of self-governing republic, defending workers' rights. In the 1980s, "Solidarity emerged as a powerful re-creator of noncommunist national traditions and values and as an exponent of a powerful vision of reform and political change based on the self-organization of a democratic society against the post-totalitarian state" (Ekiert and Kubik 1999, 41). As a former organizer of Solidarity in the underground time explained in detail,

Solidarność of 1980 was especially about the building of a self-governing republic. This program is not mentioned by the union today, and nobody wants to take credit for it, but this is the only program that Solidarność has actually formulated in its classic time of activity. If you read this program that was adopted by the general assembly of Solidarność, it is a revolutionary program in the sense that this program is defining a new system: we have to deal with the combination of plan and free-market. It is revolutionary because it answered every real question, that we do not want to be a country of really existing socialism, or an authoritarian one, which was connected to the Stalinist regime, but we also do not want to be a capitalist state either. ... That was a very original creation ... today it can be situated amongst some anarchist or syndicalist utopias, ... but it could also function in that kind of leftist Christian democratic form. ... So that was a very emancipatory and universal program and at the same time it was well connected to the Polish tradition. ... And for this program what was most important was the self-governing body and not the privately owned workplace. (PL7)

As a Solidarity activist since the early 1980s and later minister concurred, "the claims that appeared during August 1980, most of them referred to the economic sphere and were quite egalitarian, also on social aspects. And here the transformation of 1989 was disappointing for some of the people, and these claims were not met" (PL14). In fact, Solidarity itself is presented as an egalitarian movement that, however, betrayed its origins.

These ideas, although nurtured at the beginning of the 1980s, were in fact marginalized at the end of the decade. Even if a self-governing movement survived in the factories during the martial law, according to one of our interviewees with long experience inside Solidarity, the ideal of a self-governing working place was destroyed in a completely thoughtless way, which I call, after Hannah Arendt, the lost treasure of revolution, meaning that the Solidarność wasn't ever capable of returning to its original program and its original thoughts after 1989. That was completely and absolutely lost, and today almost nobody knows about this program and these ideas ... self-governing bodies were functioning in the real way, but they were destroyed in the moment when the Balcerowicz plan was founded, mainly because of what was the biggest failure of Jacek Kuroń after the Round Table, that the Law on factories wasn't passed. ... If it had been voted through, maybe something could have been saved out of this social potential that was in Solidarność. (PL7)

In the late 1980s, the debate on socioeconomic issues was thus removed from the public sphere. As an activist from the youth movement noted,

we were not talking about rejection of capitalism and neoliberalism: it was an alien topic for us ... for the average young person, even engaged in the opposition, it was associated with full shelves in the shops and not with high unemployment and evil rules on free-market, not to mention the turbo version of capitalism today, the corporate way of capitalism that has nothing to do with original liberalism and capitalism. (PL4)

As a dissident actress lamented, some who had participated in the mobilization for democracy were dissatisfied with the increasing influence of neoliberalism – "we didn't realize to what extent the state was taken over by a set of Balcerowicz and his neoliberal reforms. ... We were not able to assess it, to judge it, and to distance ourselves from it" (PL6).

In *Hungary*, as well, the democratic opposition, inspired by Lukacs and the new Left, was formed mostly by heretics within the communist party. As a former leader of the SZDSZ pointed out,

it was in essence a leftist movement, coming from among leftist intellectuals. ... Most of the time this is what it was about. There were also the avant-garde artists who gradually ended up publicly opposing the regime ... but really, this was an interior affair of the Left outside the party ... this phase of heresy against official Marxism ... also happened to be very dangerous considering that it undermined the system's legitimacy to the greatest possible extent. These notions criticized the system relying on its very own premises, revising its pretenses such as Socialism, humane society, the pursuit of emancipation and the elimination of alienation, essentially pulling out the carpet from underneath the official ideologies. (HU5)

Here as well, a combination of private property and social protection was imagined. In the words of a founder of the Hungarian Helsinki Committee and then member of parliament for SZDSZ,

We all thought, and this was in the Social Contract, that the regime should have some sort of compromise with society. . . . And this concept of a compromise, the ideas of a market economy and competition were of course present . . . it was rooted in the fact that those who played such an influential role in the democratic opposition were thinking in terms of some kind of ideal socialism. And so the idea of having factory owners that would rule the workers did not suit their ideas of an ideal system. (HU1)

The legacy of 1956 was strongly felt in the development of ideas about democracy, and also about its social dimension. However, this legacy was taken also in Hungary as a justification for forming a roundtable in the name of the nation. In fact, this is how an interviewee from Fidesz remembered those events of 1956 and assessed their effects on 1989, through his memory of his father taking him to the "revolution" in a sidecar:

I was there when the Stalin statue was toppled; from there we went to the Radio headquarters; we parked on Guttenberg square. I was sitting, waiting for him in the sidecar, while my father entered Bródy Sándor utca . . . and I was sitting there when I heard the first round of bullets . . . everybody was leaving the place running . . . my father arrived as well. He was trying to kick the Pannonia bike . . . and it just wouldn't start. I was shitting my pants. . . . I'm sure this also played a role that I lived through all of this . . . and from then on the revolution of 1956 remained a wonderful event to me, an event of global historical proportions . . . when Hungary was among the world's leading nations. My way of thinking was fundamentally characterized by nationalist sentiments, and I regarded 1956 as a nationalist revolution, when the nation mobilized . . . showed that the Hungarian nation is capable of stepping up together for a noble goal, this example played an important role when the transition began . . . this is what gave us an impetus to impose the formation of the national roundtable . . . it demonstrated the power of the unity of the dissident organizations. (HU9)

Here as in Poland, the economic reform was not discussed during the transition: Focused on unity against the common enemy, the mobilization for democracy had in fact tended to postpone the debate on economic issues. Fear of conflict made issues such as the social dimension of the transition taboo. So, while "there was some sort of middle-of-the-road attitude present" (HU1), capitalism was not discussed:

It was like, you would never talk about sex in noble company in Victorian England. It was the same with capitalism; no one even used the term. It was maybe the Fidesz guys who first said it: we want capitalism, and that's all there is to it. In 1988–89 you had everything, ranging from ideas of a socialist mixed economy to a "Hungary of gardens," third way, you name it – corporatist system and what not. MDF was probably the most colorful in this sense, because you already had people thinking in terms of a market economy by 1988–89, although only on the periphery, and then mostly thinking in terms of a state capitalist system. On the other extreme, you had the populist writers, who were all about a Hungary of gardens. The kind of petit bourgeois capitalism, where everybody can prosper. (HU7)

The focus was therefore on the political transition, while economic and social issues were left for later. The same oppositional unionist thus summarized the situation:

We had like 6,000 people who were into politics at the time, and they started talking about free elections, no compromise. In this situation it was hard to talk about what kind of socio-economic system you envisioned, it was more about the main ideological basis, that as long as there is no legitimate source of power in Hungary, you cannot talk about any of this, since it can only be decided on a legitimate basis. ... That's why they called themselves alternatives, saying that "we have alternatives to propose, but as long as there are no rules of the game and no institutional framework that would provide an arena where these alternatives can be contested, there's no point in discussing the socio-economic system." And so when the Communists started to push this at the roundtable negotiations, that we should discuss socio-economic issues, the roundtable quickly refused, saying that there's nothing to talk about but a legitimate democracy. Until we have that, you can't impose anything on society. By the way when the negotiations started at the Opposition Roundtable, six economic expert committees were formed, to agree on economic alternatives. I was representing the independent trade unions, and I was leading the economic negotiations ... and our main mandate was to prevent any and all agreement. I was in charge of a negotiating committee whose only task was not to enter negotiations on anything. (HU7)

Important decisions about the capitalist economy therefore remained not spelled out, with a resulting gap between the promoted ideals and the implemented policies – as, in the words of a leader of the SZDSZ, "At that moment the struggles for supremacy in the party system and the parliamentary system set in, only one aspect became dominant, namely, the market. ... Social self-defense, autonomy, along with the representation of anti-hierarchic aspirations have been practically converged to zero ... trade unions are insignificant and servile bureaucratic organizations" (HU5).

In sum, socioeconomic issues were often little thematized; but when they were, different versions of a "third way" between capitalism and "real" socialism were put forward, if not elaborated in detail.

MOBILIZATION, DEMOBILIZATION, AND SOCIAL RIGHTS

The mechanisms through which social rights were more or less emphasized, and respected, after transition are to be singled out in the dynamics of the transition itself, in particular the mobilization versus demobilization of civil society.

In our interviewees' perceptions, different achievements in terms of social rights have also been linked to the dynamics of the transition. In Czechoslovakia, the influence of Civic Forum was fundamental in the first years of transition. So, one of its founders stressed the importance of the circle built around Havel in impressing a socially aware direction to the economic reform:

As Havel became president we decided to restore the so called tradition of *Pátečníci* (Fridays) which was brought by Masaryk. Every meeting lasted for five hours; I always invited various experts on a number of themes we discussed as well as the old members of Charta. When we were discussing the health care system, there were experts on health care systems and some Charta members; when we talked about the education system or Czech-German relations, then experts on these themes participated. We discussed every theme and some even twice. Within these discussions I managed to keep Havel within the intellectual circle that used to influence him. I wanted these people to stay in touch with Havel, Pithart and others. I counted: it was 1,000 people, ... and they were all giving perfect reflections on current social affairs to Havel. This was how Charta influenced local development. This community was very fine, very friendly, and lots of wisdom because all of them were intellectuals. We recorded all the meetings, and now they are being transcribed by people from my foundation. ... It is around fifty debates and it is thirteen or fourteen books. (CZ10)

In Poland, in contrast, the top-down dynamics of the transition are seen as having reduced the capacity of those in government to listen to the demands coming from the civil society. This is spelled out very clearly in the memory of a former member of the opposition from underground Solidarity, which contrasts the Polish case with the Czechoslovakian one. In his view, "Paradoxically, the Polish transformation was based on the agreement of the elites, and it was a classic example of an agreement of the elites from the top ... unfortunately"; and "this agreement of the elites was not accompanied by a major mobilization in this sense of strikes, protests, street demonstrations, but also not accompanied by grassroots activities" (PL7). This situation allowed some radical neoliberal reforms, as

Of course we had to enter the global market, we had to build capitalism and privatize things but we could still have had the Czech model ... costs into the Czech Republic are totally different, meaning the costs that were paid by the society. And we, as the Polish society, we paid the tremendous costs ... there was tremendous humiliation ... the source of this weakness of these institutions and the liberal democracy in Poland lies there, in this transformation that came out from the agreement of the elites, which was not accompanied by mobilization. And nobody wanted mobilization at that time, because they were afraid of strikes and popular protests. (PL7)

As he self-critically admitted, in fact, during 1989 the activity on the side of Solidarity

was based on demobilization. We feared this grassroots mobilization of the society mainly because we had the fear that it would lead to the destruction of this route, this scenario, this achievement, of some sort of democratization, right? ... The beginning of this democratic transformation is connected with some sort of demobilization. Of course, transition was accompanied by a reconstruction of trade unions, of political parties, but it was a very top-down process and a very cautious one. (PL7)

Polish consolidation is thus seen as based on the defeat of the workers, which happened during transition – as David Ost noted, "rarely has a social group fallen so fast from such dizzying heights. From their glory days as the heroes of 1980, the undisputed vanguard of nonviolent revolution that meant all things to all people, Polish workers found their social prestige steadily devalued throughout the 1980s" (Ost 2005, 37). So, working class activism started to be seen as a main danger for democracy, and the "new Solidarity did not approve of workers taking matters into their own hands" (ibid., 45). With the choice for a market economy, workers moreover disappeared as potential supporters. With no representative of the workers in the roundtable, unions were weakened in order to implement radical marketization. In fact, Solidarity did not trust workers' anger: "Having changed its view about the relationship of labor to democracy and having changed its view of democracy from one entailing broad political participation to one emphasizing elite leadership and a capitalist economy, the Solidarity leadership focused much of its energy in 1989 on making sure workers did not get mobilized as workers" (ibid., 57).

The dynamic of market reforms thus had a relevant impact on the degree and forms of discontent that affected CEE countries.

MARKET ECONOMY AND DISILLUSIONMENT

That we ourselves can move relatively freely in the entire world is of course a positive point. The flipside is that I know a lot of people who would also like to travel, but who cannot travel because they don't have the money for it. This financial problem, which has become the decisive problem today in many respects, I almost find it even more serious than the political problem which is connected to a dictatorship. If a dictatorship tries to hammer political nonsense into you, you don't have to believe it, you can force people only to a limited extent ... so, to a large extent, I myself have the freedom to decide against it or to think differently. But if your financial supplies are cut off, you can't pay the rent, you can't travel, you have to go to the authorities and beg for money and such, then freedom is finished and also personal development, or it is simply an empty phrase ... so many people are put under incredible economic pressure, and my belief is that they suffer more from that than from the political repression under the dictatorship. In the GDR there was quite a lot of safety: you didn't make as much money as in the West, but the rents were cheap and you could be practically sure that you wouldn't be put out on the street. (GDR10)

The challenges of the double transition and especially the implementation of embedded neoliberalism as a guideline for economic reforms have often been cited for their negative effects on the quality of democracy in consolidation, especially as far as social rights were concerned. The ways in which former dissidents perceived social injustice as characterizing the new system are well expressed in this extract from an interview with one of the founders of the New Forum in the GDR: The ethical appeal of the movement for democratization is in fact bitterly contrasted with the experiences within consumption societies, where freedom without justice is perceived as no real freedom. After the hopes with the breaking down of the regime and, in some cases, of the beginning of consolidation, a deep disappointment developed, in fact, especially on the economic costs of the double transition.

A general observation made about Eastern Europe is that, paradoxically, those who had most strongly supported regime changes were perceived – and perceived themselves – as losers in the process. In fact, given the decline in social protection and increase in social inequality, "Many of those who were initially against the reforms later succeeded in being among the winners, while the majority of those who initially supported the radical reform programmes soon found themselves among the losers (especially in economic terms)" (Matějů 1996). Privatization is in fact accused of having favored members of the old regime while badly damaging the rest of the population.

In the former GDR, given the existing expectations among the dissidents, the sense of disillusionment with their co-optation in the West was broadly resonant with experiences of the perceived brutality of capitalism in a unified Germany. For instance, the following account expresses deep frustration by an environmental activist. While Western professors had supported his oppositional action during the authoritarian regime, later on the university and research environments in the West seemed to him to be at least as unfree as the one in the GDR:

I built up contacts with a handful of professors in the West, who very generously over the course of many years sent information ... they practically mentored me and supported my studies from across the border. For that I am very grateful to them, and I thought, well that's just how professors are in the West ... and then the Wall fell, and we got to know each other better ... and today I know there is only a vanishing minority of people who are accessible in this field and think critically. The vast majority of the professors work, completely ruthlessly, in the service of the big industry and without hesitation write the untruth in reports and disseminate lies, simply blowing away people who have suffered harm to their health. ... And there are consequences for people who speak out against it, who criticize it – if a professor for instance does that ... you cannot lay him off, but you don't give him research monies for instance, or you can cut his assistants or such things. The university politics today is organized so that the research areas are practically forced to acquire the financial means for research, the so-called third-party funds: those who have money to finance research are the industry. That's reflected in the research: the only things researched are those that are of interest to the industry, and the industry must therefore be happy with the results of that research, otherwise it is not continued. ... Practically, there is no critical research at the universities anymore, and the professors who engage in disputes are simply starved out. (GDR10)

The perceived brutal social injustice of the capitalist system is stigma-tized also by many of the activists who found themselves in a reunified Germany. A former member of the Independent Women's Association explained her "exhaustion" with living in the West:

I cannot protect myself enough against all of what I find so horrible: it starts with homeless people or beggars or whatever on the one hand, and on the other hand people who don't know what to do with their money. So a system that produces something like that is dishonored: that can also not simply be changed with a few adjusting screws. That is immanent in the system: it is according to the rules that it has to be like this. ... And the worst thing was at Karstadt or some department stores ... really there were people sitting outside and begging, and inside ... I had a choice between thirty kinds of cheese. ... I find that quite horrible ... you see the difference so clearly, while people who grew up in the west experience this as completely normal. (GDR1)

In particular, dramatically rising unemployment is perceived as produc-ing at the same time demobilization and disappointment, as "people don't have work anymore, and we didn't know the issue of unemployment in the East: there was apparent full employment" (GDR6). Similar com-plaints address the failures of capitalism on issues such as militarism (with "the federal republic as the third largest weapons exporter in the world,"

GDR10) or the spying on the citizens (judged as worse than surveillance in the GDR).

Especially stigmatized from the point of view of its socioeconomic effects is the work of the Treuhand, the institution responsible for the privatization of East German enterprises. Developed from proposals at the roundtable, according to many interviewees, it quickly moved toward favoring Western capitalism and creating poverty in the East. In this detailed narration by a founder of the Green Party in the GDR, the appreciation of the economy in the East is biased by a lack of understanding of the ways in which the socialist economy worked:

At the Treuhand, there was the claim that the assets of the GDR companies should eventually benefit the former GDR. Then, the budget was checked, and one realized there was actually not much left: they were all heavily indebted. But they had to get heavily indebted, since they had to send all of their profits to the state bank of the GDR. But, suddenly, those debts were real debts and creditors emerged who had bought these debts, the private banks from the West, and ... the whole privatization went quite differently. One only saw the debts: who takes them over, who becomes a creditor, and these debts were initially no real debts at all. ... In the end many made a profit from it too. They were happy to buy the customer database, but took the East branches only as extensions, taking in subsidies and then closing them down at some point. (GDR3)

Colonization from the West on socioeconomic issues is also explained by the lack of expertise among former dissidents and by time constraints, as

fundamental training was simply lacking: you couldn't have that in the GDR, because the kind of economy taught in the GDR, that was no economy, that was Marxist nonsense. ... Only very few individuals really worked on economic problems ... that was not a central topic in the citizens' movement. Surely a mistake, but in order to really understand the functioning of a social market economy you needed theoretical skills, but also the practical experience in a functioning market economy, and none of us had that. (GDR9)

This is particularly problematic when the speed of change is so fast – "you cannot do that overnight, ... you would have needed more time" (GDR6) – and a ready-to-use model is offered from the West.

Dissatisfaction with the increasing social inequality and lack of economic growth is also noted in Czechoslovakia and, then, in the Czech Republic. Here as well, disruption in everyday life is the perceived consequence of economic transformation – as a dissident theater director noted, when privatization and restitutions started, people found out that they had to take responsibility for themselves. Then suddenly somebody lost his/her job because heavy industry was closing down and people could see that the economic structure was changing ... they had to take care of themselves. Well, there was no work, unemployment was rising and the situation of capitalism, a bit merciless. (CZ8)

This also had political repercussions as, while initially "people trusted politicians a lot," a former speaker of Charta 77 observed, "since half of the 1990s ... disillusion started to prevail and they realised that it won't be so easy. ... people had to psychologically reconcile with big social differences, because a new social class of very rich people emerged, irresponsible business activities showed up and became public as well, stealing of common property appeared" (CZ2). Again, while initially "there was euphoria and people believed that things would change, and this lasted quite a long time," here as well, with the passing of time, "people became worried about upcoming big social differences. And also it became apparent that among politicians and political parties there were rather people who wanted to enrich themselves instead of working for the public good, that there is wild privatization here" (CZ2). Rising expectations are cited as fueling first enthusiasm, but later disappointment. Euphoria was based on socioeconomic expectations that were not fulfilled – as "people ... assumed that in the near future their living standard would be at the same level as in Western Europe" (CZ2).

Also in Czechoslovakia, former activists lamented the lack of regulatory institutions that could have helped to steer the privatization process in a positive direction. Especially criticized is the weak institutional control on the economic reform that is seen as facilitating the spread of corruption, as, in the assessment of a student activist,

Klaus had pressed for quick liberalization and privatization before some regulatory mechanisms were set, I mean mechanisms that concern property, gaining of property, transparency, financing of political parties. And before these mechanisms were set, lots of the property had changed owners. I don't know the exact numbers, but quite a big number of them acted immorally. The idea that people would act morally by definition because we have more freedom is nonsense, of course. The fact that there were no regulatory mechanisms, when I think about it now, was absolutely crucial. It was a crucial problem, and a failure of Havel and the ones who proposed this point of view in opposition to the pragmatist who sees life through a prism of money and not through a prism of ethics. (CZ4)

Neoliberal reforms are indeed seen as responsible for a lack of concern with institutional controls. In the words of a founder of the Committee for the Unjustly Prosecuted, "We have a democracy, but neoliberal ideology has dominated brutally. I would say that it didn't enable lots of supervisory and monitoring elements to establish and function within the democratic system. It means that there were no institutions that were common in Western democracies. These institutions had been rejected for a long time: 'We won't regulate anything. That is what the previous regime did' " (CZ14).

Here as well, moreover, privatization is accused of having favored members of the old regime – as a leader of Civic Forum and the country's first government recalled: "Hungarian sociologists were the first ones to discover that old structures won in the first two rounds of privatization. Their theory was more or less validated in the Czech Republic. . . . Mainly people from foreign trade are the winners of the transformation. They had various connections and they knew languages" (CZ13).

However, dissatisfaction was less acute in Czechoslovakia, where the debate on economic reform was indeed influenced by the former opposition to the regime, now in power. As a former minister of labour recalled:

People were marching, clinking with keys and imagining the nicest pictures, which could have never become true. When the conception of the economy reform was coming into existence, Professor Tomeš said: "We have to come up with the conception of social reform, otherwise the economic reform won't work." Klaus didn't like it because he didn't need any social reform – social engineering, etc. I always told him: "Vašku, you know that if you exceed the limit of the social acceptability, your economic reform will be gone. The crowd will sweep you along." (CZ11)

A socially sensitive approach is also linked here to the general attitude in the population – in the assessment of a former prime minister, "This society is left-leaning. It is an egalitarian society" (CZ13). Even after Klaus took power, social policies continued – as the "Klaus government softened it so there was quite a low number of unemployed at the time when the transformation reached its peak. It was lower than in the West. This inspired Adam Michnik in his statement, 'There is right wing rhetoric but left wing practice politics.' The state was continuously sending money to the companies so they could pay wages" (CZ12).

Also in *Poland*, several interviewees pointed out the ethical inferiority of capitalism. Capitalism emerged then, in the words of an activist of the Orange Alternative, as worse than socialism on economic aspects: "during the crisis when banks were bailed out it turned out that, morally, it's far more disgusting than when the state factories were subsidized. At least that situation gave work to thousands of people" (PL9). Similarly, another

Solidarity activist mentioned frustration about the university system, as "While in the past, access was selective on political reasons, with the new system based on fees selection it was based on money. . . . Let's say I want to go to the university and study. And suddenly it turns out . . . that you have to pay for it. Until today it was free, but now you have to pay for it" (PL2). Demobilization is identified as a cause of those neoliberal changes. As a former dissident observed,

There was full awareness that it's going to hurt; it will produce numerous layoffs, the increase of unemployment. These people were looking for some supports in Solidarność, in the trade union. . . . but Solidarność has created a protective umbrella above the transition regardless of the fact that, in the first part of the process, they were very hurtful for the workers and employees. (PL1)

Those who had supported the change of the regime felt the socioeconomic outcomes of the transition in an especially negative way. As a former animator of the Citizens' Committee observed, "The frustration was shared by everyone . . . it was the result of workers' protests and this group has benefited from the transition in last place, and I think this was the most painful thing" (PL10). In sum, another Solidarity supporter noted, "it's some sort of tragedy for this movement, that the people who were mostly supporting it curiously were affected in the strongest way by the transition and the changes" (PL11).

Criticized for its lack of positive effects on the economy is, also in *Hungary*,

the dominant neoliberal ideology of the trickle-down effect . . . 'just you wait: yes, you're losing your jobs now, and you're going on the disability pension, but you'll end up doing well too, you just have to wait,' but in the end democracy will benefit everyone. So for a while people were buying into this, so they were patient . . . for quite a while, more than ten years. (HU9)

Here, as in Poland, neoliberal reforms became bipartisan policies, which were supported also by the center-left.

Summarizing, with differences in degree, former activists tended to be disappointed by the growing inequality and social insecurity that characterized, although with cross-country variance, the double transition in the CEE region.

CONCLUDING REMARKS

A main challenge for democratic consolidation in the CEE countries was the presence of an (at least double) transition: from authoritarian to democratic regimes and from state control of the market to capitalist economy. This happened in a period of hegemony of neoliberal visions, pushing toward what has been defined as "embedded neoliberalism" (Bohle and Greskovits 2013), characterized by a free market with some residual social protection. As Claus Offe (1996) noted, while in 1989 the "hardware" – in terms of economic resources – was not particularly problematic, a main difficulty was represented by a deceptive "software," lacking proper conceptions of how to pursue an economic transition. While not jeopardizing democracy, long-lasting trends of declining social security resulted in growing dissatisfaction among the citizens – as testified by opinion polls that signaled, already a few years after transition, a large component (sometimes majoritarian) of citizens who thought that, from the economic point of view, they were better off under "real socialism." Unemployment, poverty, privatization, and deregulation produced bitter disillusionment in the capitalist system and mistrust in democratic institutions.

This was all the more the case among the former dissidents who had conceived democracy as a system that could and should combine respect for freedom with social justice. The dramatic increase in social inequalities and high level of insecurity affected the everyday lives of many citizens, who found it hard to adapt to totally new circumstances. In fact, interviewees often remarked upon the immorality of luxurious consumption for the rich and misery for the poor, seeing in the worsening socioeconomic conditions their broken dreams of a more moral society. While some attributed frustration to excessive hope during the enthusiastic moments of the change, most activists pointed at very concrete experiences of injustice. With its roots in the previous waves of protest in Eastern European countries, which were mainly oriented to reform socialism rather than a move into capitalism, many dissidents were indeed disillusioned by their countries' entry into a neoliberal economy. Neoliberalism affected trust in the new regime, as it opposed deep-rooted values.

Movements for democracy in Eastern Europe have been accused of too easily having embraced Western capitalism. In a reactive fashion, leaders of the opposition were said to have supported ideologies fundamentally at odds with the regime's, while the idea of reformed communism survived only in the "exceptional" case of the GDR (thanks to large opportunities for exit). Jeff Goodwin thus summarized, "The reason for this absence of ideological innovation is undoubtedly quite simple: 'Bourgeois' liberalism and free market capitalism were appealing in Eastern Europe principally because – like Marxist-Leninism and the 'Society model' in the Third

World of the recent past – they seemed to represent the most visible alternative social order" (2001, 271). Our interviews tell us another – at least more complex – story. Especially, but not only, in eventful democratization, oppositional activists tended in reality to support a social vision of the market economy – a vision that was however difficult to assert in the years of rampant neoliberalism and in a region that neoliberalists had considered as a privileged area for their experiments with the free market.

While assessments of the socioeconomic developments during consolidation (including conditionalities for EU access and economic difficulties after access) were quite similar in the four countries, with continuous references to solidarity as a main value, conditions and perceptions varied between countries with different transition paths. In general, socioeconomic conditions remained better in countries that had experienced eventful democratization than in those that had undergone participated pacts. In the latter group, Hungary and, especially, Poland did in fact embrace the most radical changes in the direction of free market, with rapid increases in social inequalities. Top-down reforms followed neoliberal ideologies; these were imposed from the West and also penetrated across parties into the center left, which therefore lost their reference base. This was less the case in Czechoslovakia, where the first two years after transition saw Civic Forum's social-democratic ideas very influentially shaping institutions and policies toward more social protection, through mechanisms of legalization and legitimation. In the former GDR, activists stigmatized a colonization of their former country by the West, with quick and brutal privatization after unification. However, the emergence of protests and support by the political institutions of the "new federal states" were somehow successful in reintroducing elements of social protection over free market.

As in the Iberian Peninsula, in the CEE countries the participation of social movements in the transition maintained high pressure for social rights. This happened through the inclusion of former activists in the institutions, but also the pressure from below for more social distribution. As the GDR case indicated, however, the effects of the transition were filtered through the modes of installation. As powerful external actors steered the regime into a territorial change – through what many interviewees defined as annexation – the chances for those who had mobilized for democracy to affect the directions of the new regime declined, at least for a period.

9

The Protest Process in the Arab Spring

People took to the street again, and the killings of protestors started again, only this time by the Muslim Brotherhood. The police did not even want to attack and kill protesters, but then the Muslim Brotherhood sent their own people with weapons to kill protesters. The most famous incident of this is the Presidential Palace protests. Muslim Brotherhood gangs attacked people and even tortured them at the gates of the palace. Through that incident, people started to realize that President Mursi's legitimacy had failed. He was watching Egyptian people getting killed by his supporters without intervening. By then a lot of protests started against Mursi, and hatred against the Muslim Brotherhood was very widespread, and it is even now. A lot of the revolutionaries feel like the Muslim Brotherhood backstabbed them by making a deal with the military after the end of the revolution. Then there is another segment that hated them for their fascist ideology. They are not patriotic to Egypt but to their religion instead. This was something new for Egypt, and it is not acceptable because it divides the country. *(EGY3)*

Sit-ins continued, the demonstrations continued and the protests continued, because the governments that came after Ben Ali did not respond to our demands. Their principal goal was to stabilize the situation and to regain control. But the popular pressure was against what they were trying to do. Then came the government of Caid Essebsi, the end of the RCD and the ratification of the Constituent Assembly. But we were also thinking that with the realization of these two demands, it did not mean that all demands had been met. Because, until that time, there had been no effective and serious investigation into the killing of martyrs [during the revolution]. The corrupt [people within the state and society] were blocking an effective investigation. Was there a solution to the social and economic problems? A solution [to these problems] did not emerge [either]. Even if there was going to be an effective national dialogue, and a new government, etc. the same situation as we were living in before, the same situation remained in practice after the revolution. ... We tried to make [other] people [also] aware that the demands of the revolution had not been met yet. On the contrary ... we also denounced these people from the old regime that were returning to rule ... this was not according to the ideas of the revolution. *(TU11)*

During the Arab Spring, protest was a most visible catalyst for change. In 2011, Kasbah and Tahrir inspired contentious politics, not only in other countries in the Middle East and North Africa (MENA) region, but also in Europe and the United States, in a long wave of anti-austerity protests that continues today (della Porta 2015). Without explicit reference to them, the mobilizations for democracy in the Middle East and North Mediterranean countries addressed some similar challenges to those met by the protests against authoritarian (or, at best, hybrid) and neoliberal regimes in Latin America. The revolutions were failed cases, not only for those who claimed social justice but also in terms of civil and political rights: we can talk at best of some (soon reversed) liberalization in Egypt, with some moves toward democracy only in the Tunisian case.

In this chapter and the following one, I will address the revolts in Egypt and Tunisia as mobilizations for democracy, although with a strong emphasis on social justice. If in the Central Eastern European (CEE) countries there was attention to social issues, but no strong claims on them, dignity and social justice were central in the Arab Spring. Particularly in Egypt and Tunisia, a series of economic and social policies, requested by international financial organizations, had brought about misery (as poverty was decreasingly mitigated by social protection) as well as rampant corruption. As I will show in this and the next chapter, these differences have fundamental consequences for the characteristics of the mobilizations, even if some of their dynamics seem similar to those I identified in the CEE cases of eventful democratization.

In the present chapter, after looking into the evolution of protest, I shall single out a broadening gap between the conception of democracy promoted by the movement and the one proposed at the institutional level; a very high emotional intensity, with empowering effects followed by disillusionment; and a shifting perception of time. Here as well, at the cognitive level, protest cycles brought about a mechanism of *framing in action*, with visions of participatory and deliberative democracy, as well as of *framing consolidation*. At the emotional level, we will note, here as well, mechanisms of *emotional prefiguration* followed by *emotional adaptation*. Relations were, moreover, stimulated by mechanisms of *time intensification* and, then, of *time normalization*. As we will see in the following chapter, however, differences in power structure also had important effects on the perceived qualities of ensuing regimes, at least in their first years.

MOBILIZING FOR DEMOCRACY IN THE ARAB SPRING

Mobilization for democracy was extremely visible in the Arab Spring, accompanied by an image of a sudden rebellion, followed up by fast development into the ousting of the dictator (as in Tunisia and Egypt); bloody civil wars, followed either by the quick ousting of dictators (in Libya) or long-lasting fights (in Syria); and demobilization with (few) reforms (as in Morocco and Yemen). Even if outside the radar of mass media and international observers – which, after the short wave of attention to "the crowds," reversed to their more traditional focus, the elites – protests continued unabated, even increased, after regime change. This was in part because, given at least some liberalization, various social groups mobilized, emulating each other, on socioeconomic rights. More significantly, a competitive dynamic evolved among the various political groups that had opposed the dictators but which varied widely in terms of their political and social visions. In particular, a strong cleavage ree-merged between secular and religious-fundamentalist forces, competing for ownership of the changes. In this development, the history of past protests (as the rebellions were not that abrupt after all) played an important role, filtered through the dynamics of eventful protests in 2011. A comparison between Egypt and Tunisia shows similar dynamics in the growth of social protests (dynamics that were missing in CEE), although with different degrees of organization in the two countries. Also similar were the unitary efforts within the oppositional groups during the transition, and the renewed splits afterward – with a somewhat stronger tendency toward compromise in Tunisia than in Egypt.

Protesting for Democracy in Egypt

In Egypt, protests spread throughout the 2000s in various waves – including the pro-Palestine university mobilizations in 2000, protests against the US invasion of Iraq in 2003, the movements in Kefaya in 2004, the march of the judges for independence of the judiciary system in 2006, and workers' protests beginning in 2008. As El-Ghobashy (2011) noted,

The reality was that Egyptians had been practicing collective action for at least a decade, acquiring organizational experience in that very old form of politics: the street action. Egypt's streets had become parliaments, negotiating tables and battlegrounds rolled into one. To compel unresponsive officials to enact or revoke specific policies, citizens blockaded major roads with tree branches and burning tires; organized sit-ins in factory plants or outside ministry buildings; and blocked the motorcades of governors and ministers. Hundreds of protests have been registered at the workplace, in the neighborhood, as well as on human rights, inside and outside Egypt. (El-Ghobashy 2011)

Various mobilizations developed in fact during the 2000s, initially apart from each other, but later (especially in the second half of the decade) with some attempts at coordination. The human rights groups, so prominent in the CEE region, were accompanied here by organizations and groups addressing socioeconomic issues, as well as by various expressions of youth opposition to the regimes. State repression played a major role in the radicalization and politicization of these social conflicts. As Bayat (2013, 588) summarized, there was an evolution from organizational fragmentation to loose coordination:

Since the 1980s, activism had remained limited to traditional party politics, a tired method that lost much of its efficacy and appeal by the mid-2000s. Radical Islamists had resorted to Leninist-type underground organizations; student activism was forced to remain on campus; labourers, going beyond conventional organizations, launched wild-cat strikes; middle-class professionals resorted to NGO work; and all embraced street politics when permitted, for instance during demonstrations in support of the Palestinian cause. So, while the regimes were able to subdue "collective actors" or organized movements, they were unable to prevent "collective actions." ... Labour protests against the eroding traditional perks and security reached a new height in 2009 and 2010, and the young got involved in civic activism and voluntary work on a scale seen never before. When social media became available for them, the young began to connect, with some getting involved in mobilizing protest actions. ... These largely disparate voices and practices seemed to coalesce by the end of the 2000s to form the backbone of what came to be known as the Arab spring.

A first area of protest was labor conflicts. Between 1998 and 2009, over two million workers had mobilized in more than 3,300 factory occupations, strikes, demonstrations, or other collective actions. Between 2006 and 2009, labor unrest grew, especially in new economic sectors, with 140 labor actions counted in 2010, 829 in 2011, and 560 by mid-2012 (Adely 2012). A politicization of the workers' movement had in fact developed since 2006 as, an activist recalls, "more than 1.8 million of people were involved in strikes and that's not including their families and friends who thereby heard about it. The breaking of fear like that cannot be called insignificant, if you have 1.8 million who have somehow contended with authority in some way" (cit. in Warkotsch 2012). Developing democratic internal practices, activism within unions combined specific claims within a broader reference to Arab socialism or the Islamic notion of a moral economy (Beinin 2011, 183). Waves of protest against neoliberal turns in socioeconomic policies started on bread-and-butter issues and politicized during the 2000s (Beinin 2012). As Beinin (2011, 181) noted, "Egyptian workers have not received the message that class struggle is unfashionable." Dockers' mobilizations also played an important role, even achieving some success (Anderson 2013).[1] Also disruptive was the protest of garbage collectors in Cairo. Occupations and sit-ins were some of the workers' strategic contributions to the protest repertoire.

Another area of mobilization was around issues affecting citizens' everyday life, like housing (against the demolition of illegal buildings), increases in the price of essential goods, and the rights to drinking water and other basic services. On these claims, what Bayat defined as non-movements emerged, using forms of organization and action that were apt to reduce the costs for mobilization in the authoritarian regime, with some attempts at coordination in the 2000s (Bayat 2013). On these and other issues, a general resistance to the regime was also noted in the everyday behavior of Egyptian citizens. Rather than only private criticisms of those in power, frequent public complaints were noted. Again in Bayat's account,

From high prices and power cuts to police brutality and traffic jams – and incidentally, they mostly blamed, rightly or wrongly, the government for these misfortunes. Indeed, the practice of "public nagging" appears to be a salient feature of public culture in the Middle East, serving as a crucial element in the making of public opinion, or the "political street." This refers to the collective sentiments, shared feelings and public opinions of ordinary people in their day-to-day utterances and practices which are expressed broadly and casually in urban public spaces – in taxis, buses, shops, streets and sidewalks, or in mass demonstrations. (Bayat 2013, 588)

While the "Arab street" echoed the dissenting *voice* of the Arab public, ordinary practices of everyday life became relevant for political contention (Bayat 2013). Young people mobilized, as football "ultras" were also involved in collective actions that became increasingly politicized.

---

[1] This especially thanks to the specific, open spatiality of ports as "densely woven into transnational flows of trade, capital and also labour solidarity" (ibid.).

In the mid-2000s, workers' protests met human rights mobilization. In particular, in 2004, the Egyptian Movement for Change (Kefaya) organized collective action against Mubarak, in particular during the presidential referendum and parliamentary elections in 2005. Kefaya's mobilization later inspired groups such as Journalists for Change, Doctors for Change, Youth for Change, Artists for Change, and Workers for Change (Duboc 2011; Khosrokhavar 2012, 46). Claims for human rights were expressed mainly by left-wing activists, followed however by members of the Muslim Brotherhood (MB), who participated in the Egyptian Organization for Human Rights as frequent victims of state repression (Stork 2011, 93). In 2005, both left-wing and MB activists supported the mobilization of the judiciary, calling for its independence from the government.

In fact, even if protest events during the transition have been described as post-Islamist and the MB was reluctant to join the protest, religious networks (including the MB's youth organization) participated in the mobilization, as Muslims protested together with secular, nationalist and leftist citizens. Moreover, protestors referred to some religious rituals (such as praying in public), times (such as Fridays), and spaces (such as the mosques) (Bayat 2012).

In the years immediately preceding the upheaval, coordination increased: in the many protests carried out between 2004 and 2006, alliances were built (Khamis, Gold, and Vaughn 2012), even increasing cooperation between left-wingers and Islamists (including MB members) as well as supporters of former president Nasser (Abdelrahman 2011). The traditional antagonism between left-wing and religious groups had nevertheless left space for some cooperation at the grassroots already during the 1990s, with an intensification in the 2000s during the campaigns in support of the Palestinian Intifada. Notwithstanding historical cleavages within and between areas, there was also networking during waves of activism within the principle of cooperative differentiation, which meant working on the basis of consensus, avoiding divisive slogans, but also keeping independence. Even if small, protests represented important experiences of a cooperation that was then strengthened within the global justice movement, in particular through the work of the AntiGlobalisation Egyptian Group, with common conferences organized in Cairo under slogans such as "No to Capitalist Globalization and US hegemony," "No to the occupation of Iraq and Zionism in Palestine," and "No to authoritarianism in the Arab regions" (della Porta 2014a).

The protests then exploded in 2011, although with a long incubation period – "The revolution really started in 2005" (EGY3). The sudden intensification of participation is identified in the interviews, including a radicalization of aims. In the beginning, as a demonstration was called on the official days in honor of the police, "the intention was not to overthrow the regime per se" (EGY1). The mainstream narrative links the beginning of the successful, mainly peaceful, revolution to the demonstration against torture and police brutality called for by the Facebook group "We Are All Khaled Said" on January 25, the National Police Day. The call was immediately supported by members of various youth groups such as the 6th of April movement, the Coalition to Support El-Baradei, the youth wing of the Democratic Front party, and the Justice and Freedom movement. Protests then expanded rapidly. In the recollection of a member of the April 6 movement, protest spiraled with repression:

In the first days of the revolution we were able to mobilize thousands in the streets, as we addressed the needs of people ... people were eager to go in the streets. ... The 25th of January 2011 was the first day, we were in Midan Tahrir against the regime. There were from 10,000 to 20,000 people that day. Later on the 28th of January you found huge amounts of people in the streets to express their anger against the cops. After that day numbers increased again because the regime committed crimes against people, known as the camel massacres. These events played a big role in mobilizing people onto the streets again, after they saw peaceful protesters being killed. ... After the downfall of Mubarak, we made many million-people protests in the streets. (EGY2)

The Friday of Rage on January 28 represented a turning point, as the police attacked the protestors with heavy use of teargas; protestors responded with assaults to police headquarters as well as the headquarters of the regime party, the Nationalist Democratic Party (El-Chazli and Hassabo 2013, 203). Afterward, the camps in Tahrir Square, which lasted for eighteen days, attracted more and more people from different political and social backgrounds, including youth organizations, human rights groups, and emerging independent trade unions. Islamist groups, in particular the MB, only reluctantly participated in the protest. Initially present through its youth organization, MB tended to keep a low profile even after many young members joined the protest. Either because of fear of repression or mistrust for the secularist forces, MB members were in fact careful not to expose themselves (Ketchely forthcoming). The MB was not present in the various Million Marches that, beginning on February 1, were called on issues of justice for the martyrs of the revolution, prosecutions of those responsible for repression, and reforms of security services, as well as the end of military rule.

Labor protests became very visible throughout the uprisings, with three days of general strikes starting on February 8. Representatives of the four independent unions met in Tahrir and agreed to found the Egyptian Federation of Independent Trade Unions (Holmes 2012). When, on February 8, Mubarak ordered Egyptians to return to work, pushing the curfew back, workers went on strike: "Employees in both the public and private sector, including textile factories, newspapers, government agencies, sanitation companies, and petrol, mill, and transportation workers, all demanded economic concessions, as well as the ousting of Mubarak" (Holmes 2012, 406).

On their side, the "ultras" provided their skills in fighting with the police, which most other groups were missing. As one of them explained, "We fought for our rights in the stadium for four years. That prepared us for this day. We told our people that this was our litmus test. Failure was not an option" (cit. in Dorsey 2012, 413). During the occupation of Tahrir Square,

> the battle experience of the ultras was evident in the organization and social services that they helped to establish. Protestors were assigned tasks and wore masking tape on which they were identified by their role, such as medic or media contact. The ultras patrolled the perimeters of the square and controlled entry. They manned the front lines in clashes with security forces and pro-government supporters. Their faces were frequently covered so that the police, who had warned them by phone to stay away from Tahrir Square, would not recognize them. ... The ultras' battle order included designated rock hurlers, specialists in turning over and torching vehicles for defensive purposes, and a quartermaster crew delivering projectiles like clockwork on cardboard platters. (Dorsey 2012, 414)

Protests continued even after the ousting of the dictator, in 2011 and afterward, as a way to drive the transition process. After the transition, emulation of the successful groups but also competition about the ownership of the revolution produced a diffusion of protest. Interviewees agreed in fact that, in contrast to CEE, "There were definitely more protests after the transition" (EGY1).

First of all, the experience of the revolution had empowered different groups to mobilize for what they considered as their rights. This brought about emulative protests by various social groups. After Mubarak's fall, in fact, an unprecedented wave of union activities with daily demonstrations continued until early October, with large national strikes of teachers, doctors, and bus drivers, among others.

Union membership rose to two million, although jeopardized by threats of withdrawal of services by old unions (Mackell 2012). The Tahrir revolution in fact transformed the workers' movement, especially since the general strike advantaged the protestors, accelerating the fall of Mubarak (Warkotsch 2012). Workers did not only go on strike; they also articulated a political discourse.

After the ousting of the dictator, protests continued on specific, but broad, issues, with occasional victories that then fueled further mobilization in Million Marches on different issues. According to a women's rights supporter, success was important in bringing about emulation:

Throughout 2011 the regime was willing to submit to more demands just so people would leave the streets. During that time, we started to have protests for more specific demands. The next Million Man March was for social justice as a specific demand. And this idea of having specific marches resonated with people. ... We also had a lot of women's rights marches. ... Back then it happened gradually, more and more people would come to the streets for more and more causes. By now you have everyone protesting for everything, ... the barrier of fear was completely broken, and people now protest against everything. (EGY5)

Protests were used also, in a competitive way, to assess ownership of the revolution. Indeed, competition emerged – as this activist suggested – first of all between those who "wanted to continue until the entire regime fell. They wanted more comprehensive reform, and all elements from the regime removed," and those who, instead, wanted "to play procedural democracy, establish democratic institutions and gradually reform society along democratic lines" (EGY1). So, throughout 2011, there were protests,

many staged by secular groups who were not pleased with the road map towards the constitution agreed upon by the military. Some protests were also held by Islamists who were not happy with the decisions made by the Supreme Council of the Armed Forces (SCAF). When the SCAF issued decisions and decrees, which would have severely restricted the rights of incoming parliaments and presidents and enhanced military power, the Islamists organized the 1 Million Man March. Many liberals ultimately joined in these mobilizations. ... At some point in this mobilization the Islamists went home, while the Liberals stayed on to protest. It was then that episodes of violence against protestors by the military occurred. (EGY1)

From both sides, protests continued to be organized in 2012, especially in order to limit the power of the military.

In a complex fight among three camps – secularists, Islamists, and the military – protests revamped in several moments. Many large protests were staged by secularist and left-wing groups against the MB in power. Competitive protests developed, first, when the MB pushed for early elections, while the secularists asked for a constitution as a first necessary step. In particular, the constitutional process was characterized by strong protests, as secular movements mobilized against constitutional proposals that were perceived as moving far away from what the revolution had intended. So, on May 27, 2011, the Second Friday of Anger took place, with mass demonstrations calling for the realization of the objectives of the mobilization for democracy, whose main slogan was "The Constitution First." While several and various groups participated in the protests, the MB did not, "stating that there was now a need for the youth to focus on how to build the country, and that the sovereign will of the people that had been expressed in the March 19th constitutional referendum had to be respected" (Bernard-Maugiron 2011). In June, about forty political parties and social movement organizations launched the "Free Front for Peaceful Change" with the aim, among others, to address a petition to the SCAF, asking to write a constitution before holding the parliamentary elections and organize another march on this issue in July (Bernard-Maugiron 2011).

After the Maspiro massacre in October 2011, when the army killed twenty-eight demonstrators who were peacefully protesting against the demolition of a Coptic church, a mobilization on Mohamed Mahmoud Street on November 19 of the same year led to five days of fights between protestors and the police. These skirmishes – which left about forty protestors dead – marked the deepening of the cleavage between the MB, which had chosen to negotiate with the SCAF, and the secular forces, who wanted to push the military out of power. In the words of a student activist we interviewed,

We had thought we were all together. We knew there would be elections. But then the Muslim Brotherhood chose the elections at a time that was very early and good for them, and we chose the street. There was this feeling that we achieved nothing, so we are still going to be in the streets. ... And, from then on, it was very hard for us. ... We could barely take a break or even breathe. (EGY10)

In fact, after the Mohamed Mahmoud protests, further tensions developed during the cabinet protests in December, and the Port Said massacre on February 2, 2012.

After the presidential election brought to power the MB's candidate Mohamed Mursi, the outrage among secular activists was increased by a feeling of betrayal by the MB of pacts made at the election of Mursi, when even secularists supported him in the second round of the presidential elections against another candidate from the previous regime. As a human rights supporter recalled,

We have to remember that Mursi won the elections by only 51 percent. But he did not win because all of that 51 percent were Muslim Brotherhood supporters, but because we did not want his opponent from the former Mubarak regime to win. So the majority of people technically did not really want Mursi in power. It was easy for him to lose public support, and in the end he did. (EGY3)

In particular, MB's president Mursi and the MB were accused of brutally repressing the movement through their armed militia. In the recollection of a human rights activist, the conflict between the secularists and the Islamists escalated quickly: "After the Muslim Brotherhood took over the Presidency, protests initially calmed down. But then we realized that nothing was happening, and that the Muslim Brotherhood was trying to take over the country and create a fascist regime. They were putting their own people in the ministries, and trying to do what the Islamic revolution did in Iran" (EGY3).

A particularly significant event, with heavy consequences, was the protest against the constitutional draft in front of the presidential palace in December 2012, as the ensuing fights were considered by the secularist groups as a proof of the MB's willingness to use violence against them. As a human rights activist observed about the clashes,

Normally, if there are protests, it is police or army forces that are standing in front of the protesters. This was the first time it was not police but civilian supporters of the Muslim Brotherhood, and that was very hard for us. Even some people who were pro-Mursi, especially some of the youth of the Muslim Brotherhood, started to question what Mursi and the Muslim Brotherhood were doing, and what they are involving people in. (EGY10)

In the competitive dynamics of the protest, even the intelligence services are said to have played a role. This was the case, according to a MB supporter, of the infiltration of the Tamarod coalition, which was formed as a broad secularist front against the Islamists – in this vision, "Tamarod was quite made by the Egyptian regime. We can now see for example that Mahmoud Badr, one of Tamarod's founding members, is now a member of General Al-Sisi's Presidential campaign" (EGY4). But it was especially during the events between June 30 and July 3, 2013, that the military was accused of using mass mobilization in order to restrict democracy. According to a secularist interviewee,

[General] Al Sisi took the example of mobilizing people from the revolution. They used the same ways of activists to mobilize people by concentrating on the economic crisis, only this time *for* the regime. They had two approaches, concentrating on some things relevant to the people, and some things relevant to activists. For the people they focused more on the economic crisis. For activists they focused on the breaching of human rights under Mursi, and the breaching of his promises he made to activists. (EGY2)

More in general, protests were fueled by a widespread feeling of dissatisfaction with the missing achievements of the revolution. Contentious politics was therefore a way to reappropriate the revolution as, in the activists' perspective,

From Mubarak to Tantawi we saw the same regime with different people. But the socio-economic policies were the same, the bad behavior from the Interior Ministry was the same. I participated in lots of demonstrations like the one in Mohammed Mahmoud street in 2012, the Maspiro protests. Our only demand was the downfall of the military rule and a transition to civil rule. ... After the downfall of Mubarak, the left-over regime started a complete plan on how to regain power. The military coup that happened on 3rd of July was part of that. (EGY4)

In explaining the persistence of protests, a founder of the April 6 movement (among other interviewees) pointed out not only that "we had not achieved all of our goals" but also that there was increased militarization and repression, as, after the military coup, "they are forbidding people to say that there is corruption among businessmen, and to speak against the new regime. ... The government is now putting a protest law in place to force everyone to agree with what they are doing and do what they want. ... There will come a time when people will not accept this anymore" (EGY8).

Protest event analysis provides some systematic support to these observations on contentious politics. If we look at the evolution of protest in a long-term perspective (Figures 9.1 and 9.2), we note that, after the peak in 2010–2011, contentious politics remained well alive in the following years when, also here, there was some stabilization of protest. The map reporting territorial distribution of protest events (Figure 9.3) shows that, although a predominantly urban phenomenon with high concentration in Cairo and Alexandria, contestation spread all over the country, especially along the Nile.[2]

---

[2] Intensity is measured as the aggregate sum of events taking place in a certain location. On the map, the dots indicate volume of protests and range from light to dark gray.

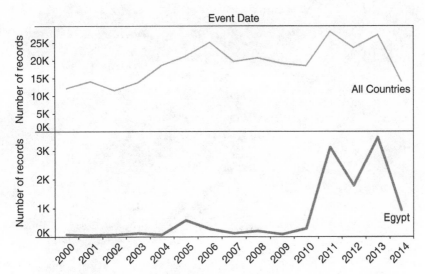

FIGURE 9.1 Evolution of Recorded Protests: Egypt versus All Countries (ICEWS)
Source: Data collected and analyzed for this project by Hugo Leal.

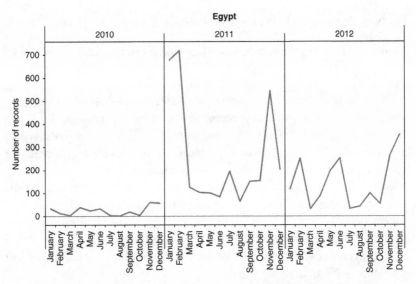

FIGURE 9.2 Number of Reported Protests (graph line and table: ICEWS)

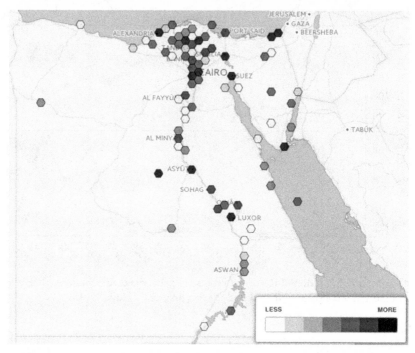

FIGURE 9.3 Geographic Distribution of Protest Events in Egypt (2010–2012), GDELT
Source: Data collected and analyzed for this project by Hugo Leal.

If we look at the protest forms (see Table 9.1),[3] demonstrations and rallies comprise about 70 percent of the reported protests in Egypt between 2010 and 2012, with some reduced presence of strikes, which are however the second-most reported form of collective action in the covered period. Protests also often took the form of roadblocks or railway blocks. While hunger strikes are rare, there is a relevant presence of riots and violent protests, either intentional or as the unintentional outcome of other unconventional actions such as demonstrations. Significantly, these forms of contention also remain highly present in 2012. One-fifth of all protest events covered in Egypt between 2010 and 2012 included violent incidents, with an increase since 2011.

[3] Each one on the protest forms corresponds to a coded variable in the CAMEO event code scheme. The root code 14 for Protest is subdivided in Demonstrate or rally, Conduct hunger strike, Conduct strike or boycott, Obstruct passage/block, Protest violently/riot (Schrodt 2012, 136).

TABLE 9.1 *Protest Forms in Egypt by Year (source ICEWS)*

Protest form	2010	%	2011	%	2012	%	Total
Demonstration	176	60.07	2078	66.56	1254	70.10	3508
Hunger strike	4	1.37	3	0.10	10	0.56	17
Strike	45	15.36	47	1.51	98	5.48	190
Blockade	6	2.05	67	2.15	14	0.78	87
Riot	62	21.16	927	29.69	413	23.09	1402
Total	293		3122		1789		

Source: Data collected and analyzed for this project by Hugo Leal.

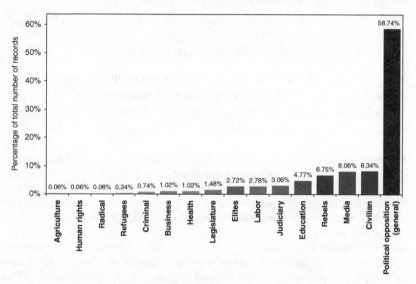

FIGURE 9.4 Protest Actors in Egypt (GDELT)
Source: Data collected and analyzed for this project by Hugo Leal.

Looking at protest actors (see Figure 9.4),[4] the political opposition emerges as the most cited actor of protest events (60 percent of the recorded protests). Very active are individuals and organizations linked to platforms

[4] CAMEO's actor-dictionary has three layers for actors: the first, more aggregated, reflects the generic status of a category of actors (e.g., opposition, government); the second, more detailed, refers to the area of activity or stratum of the identified actors (e.g., education); and the third covers the orientation of the actor (either moderate or radical). The three levels are not merely sequential, but ordinal, following a coding hierarchy; they are nevertheless not necessarily mutually exclusive (Schrodt 2012, 94). The GDELT coding scheme introduces small changes to this logic allowing concurrent coding, that is, the

of mass communication, including journalists and bloggers, which were particularly relevant before the fall of Mubarak's regime. Rebels – a category used for violent opposition groups – are also quite present, with almost 7 percent of the recorded protests. Important are students, teachers, judges and lawyers, and workers and their organizations (coded as "elites").

In sum, while protests increased slowly in the first decade of the twenty-first century, the year 2011 saw a very quick intensification of the mobilization, which brought together on and about Tahrir the various streams of oppositions to the regime. After the ousting of the dictator, protests increased rather than decreased, pushed by mechanisms of emulation and competition over the ownership of the revolution.

Protesting for Democracy in Tunisia

In Tunisia, as well, mobilization against the authoritarian regime of Ben Ali had increased gradually before 2011. In the beginning, a strongly authoritarian regime repressed any opposition. In the words of an activist, a leader of the center-left secular party CPR (Congress for the Republic),

For more or less 20 years, under the rule of Ben Ali, there were no social movements, because Ben Ali ruled the country with an iron fist. He forbade society to express itself, he forbade the people to express themselves, it was absolutely forbidden to protest – apart from protests that had been approved by the ruling party in a few big events: for instance with the Gulf War. . . . [But] there were social movements in the area of Siliana, at the start of Ben Ali's rule, but the regime repressed these movements and jailed many people. . . . The moment opened and closed, and we were left waiting for about twenty years for a true uprising of youngsters that want to express opposition to the ruling regime. (TU3)

The few existing protests tended in fact to be co-opted by those in power, as was the case in 2000 on the occasion of the al-Aqsa uprising, and of the protests in support of the Iraqi people during the 2003 invasion. As the regime party, the Democratic Constitutional Rally (RCD) "heard that a protest would take place at a certain place, they sent some people with pictures of Ben Ali and they entered these places. . . . Every time, the same thing would happen. There would be a protest at the Avenue Bourguiba, in support of Palestine, and then there would be pictures of Ben Ali" (TU1).

introduction of up to three types (or roles) per actor. All three levels appear spread along the Actor1type1 dimension.

Here as well, however, during the 2000s, protests grew in numbers and became more and more politicized. As reforms pushed for by the World Bank had increased unemployment, protests not only by unemployed but also by employed or precarious workers multiplied. In 2008, protests developed in the Gafsa area in the southwest. In the reconstruction of an activist, "The people of Gafsa made the regime tremble in 2008. It was a true uprising, the regime repressed it with full force and killed a number of activists and jailed a number of leaders of this movement" (TU3). In 2010, strong protests spread from the southwest to the southeast, in the agricultural area of Sidi Bouzid and other regions, against regional disparity in development. The unemployed coordinated via informal friendship networks, and the unionists through pre-existing militant networks (Mersal 2011).

Young people also protested. Important for the development of online protest groups were the World Summit on the Information Society in November 2005 and the October 18 Movement for Rights and Freedom, with participation of leftists, liberals, and Islamists, and hunger strikes against the Anti-terrorist Law of 2003. While the protestors did not succeed in mobilizing beyond the middle class, interactions among different groups increased later on. In 2008, a wave of strikes was accompanied by student protests. At the university, student representative bodies also mobilized, and pupils from high schools also took part in the protests. So, "The initial uprising built on youngsters that had already graduated, but did not enter professional life – with high youth unemployment a considerable group in Tunisia. Therefore they generally did not belong to college or university life" (Ayeb 2011). Collective protests targeted rampant nepotism and corruption asking for human rights (Perkins 2004, 165).

Also the subaltern classes, from street vendors to unemployed, mobilized. Fights with police were carried out by unemployed and precarious youth, networks of friends who followed a ritual script. Young people organized quick attacks against the police in various places, while indiscriminate repression favored solidarization (Allal 2012, 837). As in Egypt, politicization of soccer supporters happened as

the most active social movement in the last years during Ben Ali's rule took place during sports events. More or less every week, there were true uprisings within stadiums. There were fierce battles, and violence within stadiums between citizens and security. At the start, there were sport related slogans, but later they politicized. With time passing, there were clear political signs aimed at the regime, aimed at some symbols of the regime, etc. ... I see here the beginning of the end of Ben Ali's regime. Because it was clear that youth went to the field, to the stadiums, to express their rejection of the regime. (TU3)

What is more, movement organizations networked, bridging specific, material concerns with political discourse about their potential solution. Annual conferences, such as the Arab Technies collective in Cairo in 2008, the Arab blogger summits in Beirut in 2008 and 2009, and the Re:pubblica Digital media conference in Berlin, provided occasions for the activists to meet (Tufekci and Wilson 2012).

Even if these protests were heavily repressed, they also contributed to the accumulation of skills for collective action. As a member of Ennahda stated, "I see the revolution as a by-product of this kind of social protest-ing against the regime. ... The streets were very angry at that time. It started as social and political mobilization, in the inner cities – in Jendouba, in Kasserine, in Sidi Bouzid. And then ... it transformed from social mobilization to what might be called a revolution" (TU2).

These experiences were indeed important as the Jasmine Revolution started on December 17, 2010, in the peripheral region of Sidi Bouzid, while protests intensified after the suicide of Mohammad Bouazizi, who had set himself on fire in protest against the regime. After activists, including friends and relatives of the victim, called a sit-in in front of the regional government headquarters, police repression triggered escalation (Ayeb 2011). Self-immolations in protest against social inequalities and lack of freedom contributed to further mobilization, which radicalized and politicized after two demonstrators were killed by the police in Menzel Bouzaienne on December 24. Two days later, the protest spread in Kasserine and other cities. Between January 8 and 12, as many as fifty demonstrators were killed by police, while half a dozen citizens killed themselves in protest. On the 10th, "demonstrations reach the city of greater Tunis through neighbourhoods such as Ettadhamoun, Intilaka and Ibn Khaldoun, where most of the inhabitants, generally of modest means, come from poor or marginalised regions" (Ayeb 2011, 474). Afterward, between the 11th and 14th, several demonstrators were killed during violent fights in Tunis. On January 14, 2011, a huge crowd gathered on Bourguiba Avenue, receiving there the news that Ben Ali had left the country.

As in Egypt, during the uprisings, the protest campaign moved into the popular neighborhoods of the large cities, where practices of everyday resistance had developed against cuts in social services and increasing unemployment, as well as against police harassment. Protest and repression spiraled. As a student activist pointed out, this was a conscious move by the opposition, as

According to us, the popular neighborhoods had to mobilize, because if the lower-class areas mobilized, the Ben Ali regime could not repress them. ... So we agreed at the end of December that organization-wise, every organization would go to a lower-class neighborhood, hold a general meeting there, and mobilize citizens to go to the street. After these meetings, immediately everyone was arrested. ... they arrested them and interrogated them, using violence, torture: "what were you conspiring, what were you planning?" They, and Ben Ali, were really very afraid of this movement. We, at that moment, at the end of December, thought that the regime would stay. ... There was nobody who thought that Ben Ali would go. We had only one thought: we will follow mobilization through until the very end, whatever the costs. There was no chance to retreat. Because there had been martyrs, there had been bullets fired ... we arrived to more than 200 martyrs [in the end]. There were pictures going round on Facebook ... they were ... of huge influence. (TU11)

The Tunisian success in ousting the dictator and even in taking some steps toward democracy has been linked to a slow but steady increase in organizational resources that happened during the mobilization itself. So, in Tunisia, the presence of these resources is praised as a main reason for the success of the uprising. An activist talked, in fact, of the presence of a "quasi-leadership." If those who mobilized succeeded in toppling Ben Ali, this is linked to the fact that, according to an Ennahda supporter,

From the start, they were organized. They were not spontaneous as the press was calling it. ... Because social organizations, and the student organizations, in addition to the UGTT and political activists from a number of parties, *they* were the leaders of this movement. At a local level, at a regional level, up to the national level: there was a coordination between currents, there was shared coordination between the leadership of various movements. ... From the start there was a quasi-leadership. (TU10)

Additionally, in comparison with Egypt, there was a broader experience of cooperation within protest between Islamic and secular forces. The emergence of sustained, cross-class, geographically widespread, mass demonstrations was facilitated by the moderation of Islamic actors and the dialogue between secularist and Islamist groups within the opposition. As Angrist (2013) noted,

In the 2000s, Tunisia's secular opposition actors concluded that President Ben 'Ali was a bigger threat to their interests than were the potential consequences of allowing Tunisian Islamists to hold or share power in a post-Ben 'Ali environment. This development was facilitated by apparent Islamist moderation concurrent with the unrelenting intensification of Ben 'Ali's dictatorship. Second, political dialogue and bridge-building between secularists and Islamists within Tunisia's opposition community during the 2000s laid the foundation for collaboration during (and after) the revolution.

Similarly, ideological divisions among Tunisian cyber-activists were overcome, given the need to coalesce against the common experience of censorship; so, "over time, activists came to share a very generally democratic orientation and advocated a shared common aspiration for basic political liberties online as well as off-line, rather than any specific political agenda" (Angrist 2013, 559). The quest for dignity constituted the common bases of different social groups, from the poor to the middle class (Willis 2016).

In Tunisia as in Egypt, protests continued after the dictator left the country, at least partly out of an emulative dynamic. As Teije Donker (2012) noted,

> After the exit of Ben Ali a mobilization wave rolled over the country. This wave was highly fragmented: all kinds of specific groups mobilized around (material) grievances: the police wanted increases in their pay, journalists demanded improved media, people protested around the country in front of regional state offices to claim their right to work, (wildcat) strikes demanded higher wages for factory workers, etc. They would continue well into the consolidation phase, after the elections of 23 October 2011.

Emulative protests took place on social issues, with sometimes specific, sometimes politicized, frames. First of all, as was noted by several activists, protest created a taste for further mobilization, empowering citizens, as

> Tunisians had been barred from protesting. They discovered this with surprise right after the revolution, and there were – you know when someone loses something and then finds it, there is an exaggeration in its use. ... as a result of discovering freedoms, as a result of acting out freedoms that were inaccessible for more than fifty years – there were social movements and daily protests at Avenue Bourguiba and other places. (TU3)

In fact, "specific groups of people sometimes led by trade unions, sometimes not, started to ask for their rights ... teachers, doctors, and people continued to demonstrate" (TU8). This increased as pressures were perceived to have been somewhat successful, as an Islamist supporter noted, while "[The protesters] block the roads, they block the trains that carried phosphates, they block the railroads." The Union Générale Tunisienne du Travail (UGTT, General Tunisian Workers' Union) then influenced the choice of the new government: "They chose the government and they said 'ok, we will help you: there will be no strikes, etc.'" (TU9).

Emulative protests often took the form of strikes – according to some interviewees, used as a means of pressuring the government out of power – brought about by dissatisfaction with social inequality and bolstered by the hope that the uprising had provided. As an Ennahda supporter critically noted, "37,000 strikes ... this is a record number. It can defeat a country that is rich and has resources. ... Most of these strikes were politicized. ... The majority of the communist party were from the UGTT. It was obvious" (TU10).

Even economic protests escalated then, as they were considered a resource of the Left against the Islamists. Especially when, after the first elections, the Islamist Ennahda party came into power, labor protests pressured the governments toward more social policies, as – in a young activist's perception – "the only solution to protect themselves was to return to where they came from: to the protection of the UGTT. And this was what the strategy was like ... 'We lost the elections, but those that won the elections won't rule the country.' So they went to the UGTT, they strengthened the Union, and started organizing protests, strikes and blockages" (TU1). The situation then escalated, as Ennahda reacted by stating that, in the words of an interviewee, "the union is not necessary for safeguarding trust. We are the most powerful force in the country and, in government, we are doing what the people have tasked us to do" (TU1). Fights also transferred on the street:

The "day of purging the Union" came, or the "day of fighting the union." The protests started, and the police was not there. The union were calling people to protect the building ... they were attacked. ... The UGTT were shocked, because the Muhammad Ali square [the square where its headquarters are] for the UGTT is sacred: for them it is almost a shrine – a sacred place. And then these people came in. ... The reaction of the Union was clear: protests in Siliana, protests I don't know where – everywhere, and really violent protests. (TU1)

First and foremost, during the installation of the new regime, protests and counterprotests tended in fact to be fueled, as in Egypt, by moments of competition between the once-oppositional forces – both taking to the street to assess their strength and determination through what an activist describes as a "street split," with "protests of the opposition, and protests of the Troyka parties." Experiences of cooperation between secularists and Islamists did not preclude competitive protests. The struggle is described, here as well, as oriented to assess "who owned the revolution" (TU1).

The tensions between secularists and fundamentalists were also visible here, as the Islamist groups were perceived as disrupting the unity of the people by trying to impose their religious values. As a young activist recalled,

There was here, at this place, a person shouting "Democracy!" And everyone behind him "Apostate! Human Rights! Apostate!" [Kafirr, Huquq Insan! Kafir!] [Laughter] Really! Here, in this place ... there was this guy – well, with a beard – he had gone to Iraq. And [he was saying] that it wasn't normal, that there were girls and boys together, drinking alcohol. ... Really, these [fundamentalist] youngsters can be on drugs, alcohol, I don't know what, and at the same time they say "God is great." (TU1)

Similarly, another activist noted an exacerbation of the cleavage between secularists and Islamists: "If you see the situation on the television ... the leftists, the Islamists. First there is a dialogue, and they talk ... and then: 'you are a radical!,' 'You are a terrorist!'" (TU1). Divisions in the oppositional elites then played out in the street, both for the government and for the opposition as, an Ennahda leader recalled: "The political elites are no longer unified after the revolution. They are split in their demands. ... And they have a social basis ... the government also had the capability to mobilize the street" (TU2).

Protests also continued after the end of the regime, even increasing in number. There is in fact a widespread perception that "the revolution has not achieved its aims yet. It is true that Ben Ali fled, but the system of Ben Ali was still present. So, the street mobilized to implement the revolutionary agenda" (TU3). In several moments during the constitutional process, throughout 2011, camps were set up on several occasions at the Kasbah and in Bardo Square (in front of the constitutional assembly) in order to steer, in one direction or the other, the institutional decision making. This happened in the beginning against the remnants of the authoritarian regime, and later on against the Islamists in power. So a young, secular activist described the evolution of the aims of the protests:

At the Kasbah there were no long-term demands: "we want the end of the RCD, now." "We want the end of the Ghannouchi government, now." Kasbah II had more long-term demands: "We want a Constituent Assembly." ... The demands were more political than at the Kasbah I. At the Kasbah I there was one direction: "No against remaining injustice." ... between Kasbah I and II, society became split and changed: the radical left emerged, radical Islamists emerged, the "moderates" emerged. It became a mosaic. (TU1)

Protests were therefore considered as "a reaction from political groups that had lost the elections. They therefore put pressure on the Constituent

Assembly, they expressed their objection to the National Constituent Assembly, to send the message that the street rejects the electoral results, or rejects the government that was formed as a result [of the elections]" (TU3).

Here, as in Egypt, mobilization continued to be high, given competition over the ownership of the revolution. Mobilizations and countermobilizations pitted especially Islamists against secularists, both endowed with large capacity for mass mobilization. In the recollection of a young activist,

Ennahda mobilized 200 or 300,000 at the Kasbah. And the opposition 200,000 at Bardo. And this for about a month: during Ramadan. ... Their organization is incredibly solid. Trucks were coming from the governorates. And at that square there was a big truck with sandwiches, because people were hungry: many came from other governorates, and had fasted from the morning onward. Food and tea, and everything was there. ... So they were every night at Bardo, and Ennahda every night at the Kasbah. ... Because of course during Ramadan everything happens from night to morning. So during Ramadan it was really a crowd ... between the two [camps] and the different days maybe a million Tunisians participated. (TU1)

As the Egyptian events played a symbolic role, the Tunisians also organized a *tamarod* [rebel] movement; after the Egyptian model, supporters of the Islamist party Ennahda carried pictures of Mursi (TU1).

Protest after the end of Ben Ali's regime was indeed first and foremost aimed at continuing the revolution and achieving its aims, with a process of increasing structuration of the conflict. This is presented by a critical young former member of Ennahda:

The primary demands at the Kasbah were for the constitutive assembly, the dissolution of the RCD, and a new constitution. ... This was Kasbah I ... [Afterwards] we left the Kasbah, [but] then we returned again [to Kasbah II]. It became more organized: there was a press council, there were speeches, etc. There was a real atmosphere, it was very beautiful. I will never forget. (TU10)

As in Egypt, a dynamic of protests and counterprotests developed in Tunisia. In a young secularist blogger's account,

We have big demonstrations in front of the constituent assembly, because people were afraid, as we have Islamists in power. And we started to see the demonstration and the counter-demonstrations. ... whenever there is a demonstration against Islamists, there is a counter-demonstration. And we also started to see demonstrations by Salafists asking for sharia and all this ... we had big demonstrations, with hundreds of thousands of people. And they were asking for the dissolution of the constituent assembly, for the departure of the Ennahda party, or the Troyka. (TU8)

Competitive protests reemerged vigorously after the assassinations of two oppositional leaders, Choukri Belaid and Mohamed Brahmi, which were attributed to fundamentalists, protected by the government.

The pressures from the street then continued, reinvigorating themselves at each important turn of the events. A student activist's account points at this continuous mobilization, which sometimes even had some influence, as after the assassination of Muhamed Brahmi, when

all the opposition parties created an alliance, with a group of the civil society and organizations and associations, in a front: the Salvation Front. ... And the main demand of this front was the dissolution of the government *and* the dissolution of the Constituent Assembly. ... Then, related, [we demanded] the formation of an independent government that is linked to a clear program, for a limited period of time, and that would form a council of experts to write the constitution. Ennahda rejected this suggestion and they just wanted to go forward. Despite the social movements, the protests, everything. (TU11)

But then, thanks to the mobilization, "The UGTT entered the national center, the political center, and generally became central to the Tunisian scene. The UGTT entered and made a proposition through this route, they refused the Ennahda government, and the Troyka generally. All the other organizations and parties trusted it, and then they pressured the Ennahda party to accept [the UGTT's] plan" (TU11).

The division between seculars and Islamists is considered as fueling a radicalization process that interrupted a more positive trend of empowerment. So, as a human rights activist noted, "After the revolution, Tunisian citizens and civil society started to talk in absolute freedom. We have the freedom to express our opinion. ... And then an up-take in the Tunisian feelings emerged. They started to talk with power and fierceness" (TU6). However, the escalation into a civil war is seen as (fortunately) interrupted, as "thank god: now the constitution is finished and its agreement/ratification is done. All sides in Tunisia have agreed on it: it is a consensus constitution. And even though there are people that are opposed to it, the country is now going somehow better" (TU6).

In fact, competitive mobilizations were supported by frequent experiences of success – again in the words of a militant of the center-left, secular CPR bloc in the Constitutional Assembly,

The Constituent Assembly was the result of a social movement; it was the result of the sit-ins of Kasbah I and Kasbah II. This pressured the authorities into concessions and allowed for elections for the National Constituent Assembly to prepare for constitutional changes. And also at the beginning, after the revolution, there was the attempt to create a government with members of the RCD party. But street protests forced the government to fall, and this government only lasted for a week or ten days and fell. And after that there has not been any government with members of RCD in it. This is because of social movements, because of the street, because of pressure from organizations, parties, etc. (TU3)

There is therefore the belief that, even after the ousting of the dictator, protests were fundamental in moving in a democratic direction. Pressures were particularly important during the constitutional process as, here as in Egypt, Islamist groups pushed toward a higher public recognition of religion and secularist ones instead for a more lay asset. During this period, the mobilizations from below were often successful – or at least, perceived as such. A student union activist thus assessed:

We demanded the creation of the Assembly to make a constitution. The Ennahda government had the majority in the Constituent Assembly and they wanted to pass their project. But pressure from the people and pressure from the streets deterred the Ennahda government into retreating on some decisions that they had made. If we take a look at the first version of the constitution [for instance], Ennahda wanted the Sharia as the basis of the constitution, to appoint a number of judges, and to decrease the [social] position of wives [versus their husbands] etc. Freedoms were not included in the constitution. This was in the first version. ... They retreated under pressure: it was not in their interest to retreat. (TU11)

Protest event analysis helps systematizing these observations also for the Tunisian case. Based on the GDELT database, Figure 9.5 presents the normalized number of (monthly) episodes of protests and coercion in Tunisia from 1979 until the end of 2014. After the peak in late 2010 to early 2011, the number of protest events did decline, although remaining at a higher level than in the period before the Jasmine Revolution. Based on protest event analysis drawn from the LexisNexis databases, we can note that not only the number of events but also the number of partici-pants followed a similar trend (Figure 9.6).

Not only did the number of protests normalize, so did, to a certain extent at least, the protest forms (see Figure 9.7). While self-destructive forms of action such as hunger strikes (especially by political prisoners and their relatives) were widespread before the upheavals, they sharply declined afterward. Moreover, although violence was present in 2011, especially during the days of the most intensive mobilization against the authoritarian regime, it also declined sharply in 2012, while political opportunities opened up for demonstrative forms of protest such as public

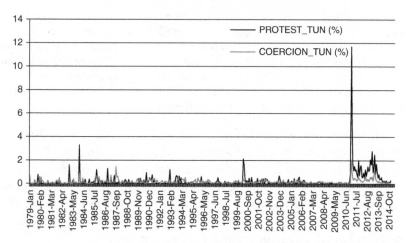

FIGURE 9.5 Normalized Number of Protests and Coercion in Tunisia by Month–Year in Percentages, 1979–2014 (GDELT)
Source: Data collected and analyzed for this project by Kivanc Atak.

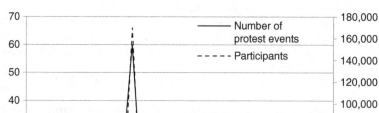

FIGURE 9.6 Number and Size of Protest Events in Tunisia by Month (2010–2012)
Source: Data collected and analyzed for this project by Kivanc Atak

meetings and marches; in Tunisia today, "protests have become a regular mode of political expression" (Chomiak 2011, 74).

Protests targeted the political regime, calling not only for freedom but also for economic improvements. As Figure 9.8 shows, protest was most

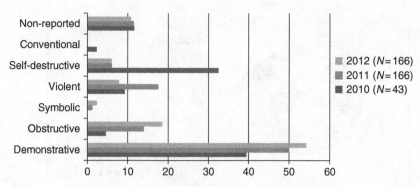

FIGURE 9.7 Forms of Protest in Tunisia per Year (%)
Source: Data collected and analyzed for this project by Kivanc Atak

widespread in the capital area, but also in the poor areas in the midwestern and southern governorates of Gafsa and Sidi Bouzid (Boughzala and Tlili Hamdi 2014).

Attention to economic issues is confirmed if we look at the protest claims (see Table 9.2). In 2010, more than half of the protest addressed corruption, unemployment, and poverty, while protest against state repression was widespread, addressing the conditions of political prisoners and Internet censorship. From mid-January 2011, mass protestors took a clear anti-regime stance, demanding the resignation of Ben Ali. After he left the country, they continued unabashed with massive demonstrations at the end of February against the interim government of acting prime minister Mohamed Ghannouchi, which led indeed to its resignation on the 27th. Contentious politics remained relevant throughout 2011, with demands of justice for the victims of the revolution as well as the banning of the elites from the previous regime, the institution of the rule of law, and judicial reform. Already in February, however, pro-Islamist claims started to be put forward by protestors. In 2012, however, protests tended to address a more varied range of issues, confirming a sort of normalization of contentious politics. Contentious events targeted persisting unemployment, poverty, and corruption, but also local administration (e.g., governor appointments) and urban infrastructural problems (e.g., water cuts). While Salafi groups called for Sharia, civil rights groups demonstrated for freedom of expression and assembly, press, and religion.

While the vast majority of the observations mention generic categories such as "Tunisians," "citizens," "residents," or simply "protestors,"

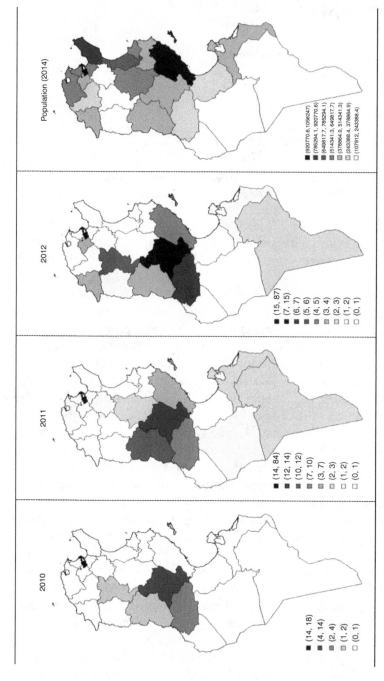

FIGURE 9.8 Provincial Distribution of Protests (2010–2012) and the Population (2014) in Tunisia
Source: Data collected and analyzed for this project by Kivanc Atak.

TABLE 9.2 *List of Categorical Issues of Protest in Tunisia by Year (%)*

	2010 (N=43)	2011 (N=166)	2012 (N=166)
Anti-transnational union/alter-globalist	–	1.2 (2)	–
Civil rights: government repression & political prosecutions	30.3	8.5 (14)	7.2 (12)
Civil rights: prisoners' rights and conditions	16.3	–	1.2 (2)
Civil rights: freedom of expression and assembly	–	1.2 (2)	1.2 (2)
Civil rights: press freedom and media	2.3	–	5.4 (9)
Civil rights: freedom of religion	–	–	1.8 (3)
Civil rights: issues of other minorities	–	–	0.6 (1)
Conservative social values – pro-Islamist claims	–	5.4 (9)	9.6 (16)
Economic policies and activities	2.3	1.2	4.6
Environment & ecology	–	1.2	0.6
Feminist struggle/women's movement	–	0.6	2.4
International human and civil rights/ democratization	7.0	5.4	3.6
Labor and syndical issues	4.6	4.2	10.2
National pride and secular Tunisian identity	–	3.0	1.2
Peace movement/anti-violence	–	1.8	2.4
Political regime/rule of law and jurisprudence	–	32.1	5.4
Pro-government	2.3	1.2	1.8
Sports	–	–	0.6
Urban policies and problems	–	1.8	7.2
Various social issues	51.1	27.9	25.3
Non-reported	–	2.4	2.4
TOTAL No.	43	166	166
TOTAL %	100.0	100.0	100.0

Numbers in brackets represent reported number of protests.
Source: Data collected and analyzed for this project by Kivanc Atak.

notable is a relatively frequent reference to occupational categories (especially of professionals, but also unemployed) in 2011 and 2012 and an (even if modest) increase of religiously oriented groups in the short-term post-revolutionary context (Figures 9.9 and 9.10). Labor unions and (to a much lesser extent) professional associations (especially judges and lawyers) are most present in the protest arena covering around two-thirds of the coded events, while one-third is covered by advocacy

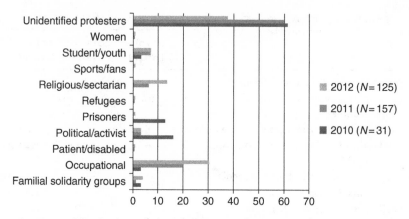

FIGURE 9.9 Mentioning of Social Groups of Protest (when organizational affiliation is not reported) per Year in Tunisia (%)
Source: Data collected and analyzed for this project by Kivanc Atak.

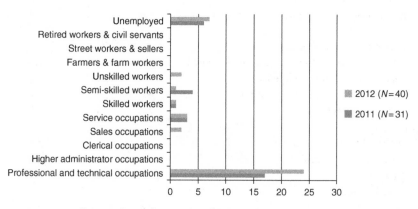

FIGURE 9.10 Occupational Categories of Protest Groups per Year in Tunisia (%)
Source: Data collected and analyzed for this project by Kivanc Atak.

associations, civil rights associations, civic associations, students' and youth groups, political parties, and other political groups.

Summarizing, here as well, we found a slow growth of protest throughout the 2000s, with a sudden peak in 2011, followed by a multiplication of mobilization on both social and political issues spread through mechanisms of emulation and contestation. Violence was also present here, even if at a lower level than in Egypt.

CONCEPTIONS OF DEMOCRACY IN THE ARAB SPRING

In the MENA region as in the CEE cases, the evolution of protest is connected to processes at the cognitive, emotional, and relational levels. From the cognitive point of view, the progressive movement activists refer to a horizontal conception of democracy, developed in action, which then entered in tension with the transformed conditions after the ousting of the dictators.

The Arab Spring movements stressed a participatory and deliberative vision of democracy. Rather than the (Western) model of representative institutions, those who promoted the mobilization against the dictator pushed for "real," direct democracy, against corruption and crony capitalism (Nigam 2012). The (apparently sudden) upheavals that brought about the fall of dictators in Tunisia and Egypt have been defined as moved by "post-national, post-ideological, civil and democratic" popular movements in a post-Islamist period (Bayat 2012). These protests were praised for their similarity not only to those in 1989 but also to the ones in 1968 in their emphasis on horizontality, participation, and nonviolence (Wallerstein 2011), rejecting "the idea of an absolute moral order that could create a golden age in any fashion" (Khosrokhavar 2012, 19). Democratization movements in the MENA region have in fact been described as leaderless, fragmented, and atomized, relying on new media for coordination. This vision included attention to deliberation, as

Continuous and seemingly limitless dialogue was the revolution's means of discovering not just its own goals, but also of acquainting itself with the vast magnitude of energy unseen before. ... This dialogue did not presuppose the necessity of arriving at any particular conclusion. Rather, the very existence of a comprehensive interactive environment meant acting out the capacities of the self, discovering talents of the other and practicing the dialectics of ideas. (Bamyeh 2012, 37)

In *Egypt*, protestors called for direct democracy, with opportunities for participation in all fields of political life. During the struggle against the authoritarian regime, organizational models privileged coordination amidst spontaneity (Chalcraft 2012), with horizontal structures presented as facilitating a learning together. The model of organization has been presented as "rhizomatic" – as rhizome roots, linking together underground, are difficult to eradicate: "If you rupture one area, it just picks up in another area" (ibid.). During the opposition to the authoritarian regime, activists were then socialized within groups characterized by "decentralized and segmented organizational structures, diffuse boundaries and dependence" (Abdelrahman 2013, 569), stressing spontaneity against the perceived oligarchy of the old political organizations. These types of structures were typical for the human rights groups – as a Kefaya activist observed, "We celebrated Kefaya for its new 'form' – horizontal, non-hierarchical, loose, and flexible – because it was everything that traditional political parties were not" (cit. in Abdelrahman 2013, 576). In fact, since the very beginning, Kefaya saw political parties as part of the problem rather than the solution (Shorbagy 2007). Similarly, the protests of several social groups – "from taxi and tuk tuk drivers to street vendors, and from small farmers to shanty town dwellers and housewives demonstrating against rising food prices and rapidly deteriorating living conditions" (Abdelrahman 2013, 579) – were characterized by their small size, horizontal structure, and quick eruption and decline. As the Egyptian activist Ghonim declared in an interview, "A revolution is like Wikipedia, okay? Everyone is contributing content, [but] you do not know the name of the people contributing it. . . . There is no hero in that picture" (cit. in Khosrokhavar 2012, 192).

This organizational vision, however, while successful in avoiding repression, seemed unfit for the production of long-term mobilization. As a Kefaya activist recalled, "The problem . . . is that Kefaya does not exist beyond the event. In other words, Kefaya is very successful at organizing a rally or a demonstration; it attracts people, emotions rise high. However, once the event (demonstration) is over, there is nothing left. Those newly mobilized, especially the youth, who are so inspired, full of energy and desire to do something, really have nothing to do" (cit. in Abdelrahman 2013, 576). While the organizational model favored mobilization under repressive conditions, a reduced capacity to adapt to the political transformation has been related to the very organizational structure of the mobilization, as "the loose organizational structures of the pro-democracy movement and labour activism meant that they could not provide an institution capable of bringing the dispersed struggles together under a broadly-based coalition" (Abdelrahman 2013, 580). For a long time, given strong state control,

despite intersecting paths, cross-fertilisation, demonstrable effects and interchangeable membership, the different struggles by all these groups were insufficiently connected. This was evidenced by the absence of initiatives to build broadly based coalitions which could bring together and coordinate the efforts of all protestors. . . . The loose organisational structure and the absence of leadership were the trademarks of these protest networks and were, indeed, among their major rallying points in mobilisation against the regime and set them apart from stale, traditional political organisations. However, these characteristics meant that the different groups lacked a robust base from which to reach out and attempt coordination let alone create a broad coalition. (Abdelrahman 2012, 618)

Only in the new millennium did labor and human rights groups start to develop some new organizational formats, including through the politicization of labor protests, as claims for better working conditions and labor rights bridged with those against repressive laws and the regime. Also emerging was an economic basis for the political protest of the middle classes, who suffered increasingly from the rapid deterioration of their living conditions (Abdelrahman 2012). A good example of coalition building is the Revolutionary Youth Coalition, which formed during the days of the revolt. In the account of an interviewee from MB,

There were different protest movements led by youth groups. Different youth groups had formed in Tahrir, but back then, all movements were in harmony. Not in unity, but in harmony. They were creating pressure through their demonstrations and protests against the regime. And I think that was the magic point and the point of strength in 2011. The most important one was the Revolutionary Youth Coalition. ... It was between youth from leftist and communist and Islamist and liberal backgrounds. (EGY12)

During the intense time of the transition, new organizational structures emerged, in some cases filling voids left by the retreating regime. Tahrir Square and the other "liberated zones" developed into quasi-utopian communities nurturing norms of solidarity, care, respect for others – they were described as a sort of "safe haven, virtually free of any sort of discrimination or aggression" (Holmes 2012, 406). Intercommunal prayers were organized to reduce the risk of inter-sectarian tensions between Muslims and Christians (Holmes 2012). In order to fill the vacuum left behind by the falling regime, "at least twenty-five popular committees were organized in neighborhoods throughout Cairo. In addition to replacing the police force, which had disappeared, they created a bridge between activists who were occupying Tahrir and those who remained in their neighborhoods. They also served to spread information and counterbalance the state propaganda" (Holmes 2012, 405).

While coordinator committees were formed during the days of the revolts, the organizational forms seemed unfit to keep the momentum of the revolution going. In fact, the various initiatives such as the launching of the Protection of the Revolution, the campaigns "Let's Write Our Constitution" or "No to the World Bank and IMF Loans" were not sufficient to develop new organizational structures. Moreover, being internally very heterogeneous, structures for coordination became very conflict prone, as "the cross-ideological coalitions which served activists' needs during the Mubarak era were beleaguered with challenges including deep ideological rifts and difficulties of coordination" (Abdelrahman 2013, 581). As activists on the Left observed, the weakness of the organization of the protest contributed to the mistake of stopping the mobilization before it had achieved its main goals – to the fact that

there was no political force that was organized and sizable that was clear in understanding the reality of the SCAF and the need to continue the popular revolution. ... The grassroots were calling for change, but we were not organized or centralized. We did not even, as in other revolutions, develop centers from below. Instead, the movement from below was amorphous and not organized or politically conscious. This made it more dependent on the organized political forces in society. (EGY9)

The claimed democracy also went beyond the idea of "free elections and freedom for people, freedom of speech, and the periodical elections from time to time where you chose your president, human rights" (EGY2). This institutional conception emerged indeed as too limited – as an April 6 activist rhetorically asked,

How can I call what happened in Egypt: if there are only free elections, already a democracy? This is not a democracy, and if we consider only free elections a democracy we will lose our revolutionary goals. What about freedom of speech? Freedom for everybody to express their point of view? Where is the freedom of anyone to be elected? What about media that concentrates in one man only? That is not democracy but a dictatorship. Elections were not actually the crucial point for the January 25 revolution. We went to the streets for many things, not just elections. (EGY2)

After the ousting of the dictator, moreover, the opposition split on the meta issue of the conception of democracy. While the MB did promote protest at times, in general it tended to push for a demobilization, while the secular groups tried to "reappropriate" a revolution they perceived as stolen. In the words of an interviewee,

On the liberal side there was an increased feeling of an unfinished business. People felt that the revolution had been stolen from them, by both the military and Islamists. ... They perceived the Muslim Brotherhood's desire for early elections as a desire to steal the revolutionary gains and try to reveal themselves as the rightful owner of the revolution. They perceived the Muslim Brotherhood as a threat to their goals and not as a positive force of change. So the goals of the liberal protest movement began to change. They began to protest against the Muslim Brotherhood, as well as the SCAF. Especially after the first elections, they started to organize protest against the Muslim Brotherhood-dominated parliament, because they perceived it as not being legitimate. (EGY1)

On the other side, the Islamist groups

looked at the transitional period as a democratic project and were willing to play along with what the military was going to do, provided that the democratic course was appropriate and no serious transgressions were committed. Other than that, they viewed protesting almost as a waste of time, and even counter-productive. For them more protests meant more instability, and the likelihood that elections would be put off. Of course they did not want that. They believed that free and fair elections were the only way to shore up legitimacy and a new democratic system. (EGY1)

The MB in fact promoted a very electoral definition of democracy. According to a former member of MB, they claimed, "We were elected, so you have to listen to us and accept whatever we are doing"; while on the other side, secular citizens started to think that "democracy was a bad thing. And that's the majority of society now. They think that as long as democracy will bring Islamists to power, it is bad" (EGY12). As a socialist activist noted, for the Muslim Brotherhood,

The revolution had achieved victory by ousting Mubarak, and was therefore over now. ... And because the SCAF was in power, their proposition was easy: now that we got rid of the dictator, we should sit together with the army to discuss how the transition should be steered. First of all, we should demobilize the street movement, because there is no role for street mobilization in the transition. Their role ended because we achieved what we wanted, it was a happy ending. So they sat down with the SCAF. (EGY9)

Instead, a large part of the secular activists, especially the young ones, defended a different conception of democracy, contesting the very foundation for the political regime that they perceived the West as wanting to impose. In the words of a women's rights activist,

I don't follow the idea of democracy imposed by the West. For me democracy can be defined in different ways. I don't believe that there is one definition of democracy that has to be imposed on every society. In the U.S., for example, ... you are either conservative or liberal. If your whole existence is trapped between two choices, then you don't really have a choice. If the U.S. preaches democracy, they don't present a good model. (EGY5)

A minimalistic conception of democracy is therefore considered as characterizing the MB, as – a member of the Al-Dustor party noted – "the Muslim Brotherhood have never played democracy; they just had elections, electoral boxes. Boxocracy we call it. But democracy is not just about going to electoral committees and casting your ballot. Democracy is supposed to be more" (EGY11).

A "democracy of the voting booths" is all the less compelling, given the uncompromising attitudes of the MB members in power. In the account of a women's rights activist, while "democracy entails not just elections but inclusiveness," an electoral conception is exclusivist, as "when the Muslim Brotherhood won, they thought people voted for them, but that's not a right to do whatever. ... They excluded everyone else from the dialog, started speaking a different language in parliament and in the media, they weren't inclusive of women and minorities. ... They were brutal in their discourse against others" (EGY5). The electoral democracy is thus considered as far from satisfying, especially in situations in which trust needs to be built and elections, also used by the previous regime, do not have a reputation for fairness. In the words of a student activist,

Democracy in a basic definition is that everyone is free to say his point of view and be part of the community, no matter his beliefs and religions, we are all equal. But elections are not enough for that. To only write your opinion on a piece of paper is not enough because not all people can go to elections. The percentage of people that participated was like 60 percent or less; and the people were only choosing from the options that they were put up to. ... People here in Egypt are all the time running to get bread because life is getting harder. And then you come to tell them to vote, but they haven't read any of the programs for who they are electing. (EGY10)

Similarly, in this reading of the situation by a socialist: "bourgeois representative democracy is failing," as

when you go to the ballot box, you are then surprised by filthy people being elected because the army just gets rid of the results and does what it wants anyway. ... After the 30th of June 2013 people were saying "but Mursi was elected and you should only challenge Mursi through another ballot box." Others were saying Mursi was given the opportunity for elections because millions of people moved through the streets, so why would we have to wait for other ballot box? (EGY9)

So, the experience with Mursi's election delegitimized what activists called "boxocracy," as "after Mursi, many people said they didn't believe in democracy anymore. People here in Egypt think that these people should not be treated in a democratic way" (EGY10).

International actors are consequently criticized for imposing old ideas of democracy and democratization processes that are unfit for Egypt ("they should change their ideas about what kind of democratic transition Egypt needs," EGY4) as well as for failing to take into account that, as a MB supporter noted, "the revolution was about national independence and this is a real demand for the Egyptian people. I think they should understand carefully what happened in Egypt, and they should be doing this without the think tanks in Washington. They should come to Egypt and see for themselves carefully. They should not try to fit Egypt into the models of democratic transitions they are supporting" (EGY4).

The promoted conception of democracy was, instead, for several activists a social, participatory and deliberative one. As stated by a socialist activist, "Democracy should not become another absolute, like other dogmas. It should be understood relatively and socially, then you would understand the difference between formal and procedural democracy and democracy from below that has a relation to class forces" (EGY9). This view is linked to the search for a different path of democratization from the one that is seen as typical for other regions. A critique is expressed of electoral democracy in the name of participation and social justice, as "we want what we could call a social democracy, we want to engage a lot of Egyptian people in the political process, we want to support decentralization in Egypt" (EGY10). In this vision, the military intervention on June 30, 2013,

was about the failure of the idea of democratic transitions and the idea that Egypt should follow the model of Eastern Europe or Latin America. . . . You can go for an idea of democracy where you have elections every five years, and otherwise want people to stay away from political life, and this didn't work. We have a real socio-economic conflict in Egypt, and normal elections will not solve it. We have a civil-military conflict and elections will not solve it. Egypt now doesn't just need normal elections, but it needs to learn about how to engage normal people more in political life. . . . We need social participatory democracy. (EGY4)

Participatory conceptions of democracy were said to be particularly widespread among the young people, while the older are perceived as looking for security: "The age level from like 16 to 25, these are radical and they still see democracy as something that we should all participate in" (EGY10).

The failure to achieve the revolutionary aim is also attributed to an early demobilization, which is linked to the lack of leadership. As a human rights activist observed,

We come from a generation that had no democratic culture, so it was easy for the previous regime to hijack the revolution, for the Muslim Brotherhood to hijack it. . . . Now we are learning. If another uprising happens, people would have learned from their mistakes. Getting a leader for a start. One of the reasons why revolutionaries did not rule so far is because we do not have a leader. . . . Many revolutionaries say our biggest mistake was leaving the square and not staying until power was properly handed over. We should have remained there. (EGY3)

Lack of continuity in mobilization is in general considered as a main problem – as a young former MB supporter self-critically noted, "We should have focused more on the regime, and tried to somewhat keep pressure on the regime in the street and combine it with another path of political pacts with other opposition movements and parties and alliances. But until now all of Egypt's youth has been divided between the political path and the revolutionary path" (EGY12).

We can observe a partly similar evolution in terms of conception of democracy in the *Tunisian* case, although previous experiences of interactions between secular and religious oppositions reduced the degree of polarization.

Regarding the organizational model, here as well, while the more loosely structured groups were better able to survive repression under the dictatorship, they were perceived as more problematic after transition. Organizational resources and conceptions developed in action, during the sporadic waves of protest. Already in 1984, with the bread uprisings, as well as in the union movement and the student union, a unionist noted, "Civil society organizations were defending the interests of the poor and especially the marginalized, against the logic of social injustice" (TU5). This created an "accumulation where society developed a political consciousness to stop the dictatorship" (TU5). Thus, social movements "crystallized as a result of harsh social situations perceived by people through their personal experiences. They gradually gained a more collective identity: they developed from personal experiences to a communitarian one" (TU5).

While before the uprising the organizational structure of the protest is described as mainly "spontaneous," some more organized presence emerged at the peak of the mobilization. According to an interviewee from the CPR bloc,

Before the revolution, all the uprisings that took place were spontaneous uprisings. Civil society organizations supported them, but they did not initiate them. Thus, [they were] spontaneous uprisings, non-organized, and they lacked framing. Therefore in many instances the regime was successful in attacking these movements and uprisings. ... But in the final stages of the revolution, when revolutionary slogans came up, and it became clear that Ben Ali's regime would fall, these organizations and associations started to participate in the uprising – especially January 14th and the days before; at least the important leaders of parties and associations were attending. (TU3)

Also in Tunisia, the uprising opened up some free spaces. Experiences with self-management of spaces vacated by the regime happened within the Leagues for the Protection of the Revolution, formed by "the revolutionary forces, meaning: the Communist workers party, the Movement for the Liberation of the Nation, and the Ennahda movement. But at the basis it was the left that founded it, and the others participated with them. ... Originally they were in every neighborhood, with youth that were from this neighborhood" (TU1).

The extent to which organization balanced spontaneity is open to debate. The narrative of a leaderless revolution is in fact challenged by several activists. As a militant of Ennahda stated,

Concerning the Tunisian revolution, they say that there was no leadership. This is not correct. Maybe there is no central leadership that we know of. The dominant narration, the narrative of revolutions is that the accomplishment of the French revolution, of the Bolshevik revolution, was [because of] a central leadership that led social mobilization. This was not available in the Tunisian revolution or in the other revolutions of the Arab Spring, for one main reason: repression. (TU2)

In this situation, however, a flexible and field-based leadership was able to mobilize as, even after Ben Ali left, "there was anger and social, economic and political protests worked together. Surely, in the new regime the social and economic situation did not change that much – but what changed was the political climate. What resulted from this [change] was social mobilization: the emergence of an extreme protest tendency. [This] political climate enabled a context of [social] freedom" (TU2).

Here as well, some former oppositors of the regime, especially in the religious camp, supported an electoral conception of democracy according to which

in a democratic climate it should not happen that the government is brought down through other means than the ballot box. ... This is the difference between a democratic regime and a dictatorship: because a democracy has channels to absorb protests. For those who are angry with or reject the government, they can change the government through the ballot box. We were saying to people: anybody that wants to change the government: welcome. You can change it through elections. You can go to the ballot box. (TU2)

Instead, the secular part of the opposition to the authoritarian regime considered protest as necessary to push forward the very aim of the protests. In fact, only the street is seen as able to reappropriate the revolution. In the words of a young activist,

Even the national constituent Assembly was a result of a big sit-in at Kasbah. That is what we can call an achievement: because of this sit-in, we got a constitution. Even if that costs too much and too many years, it is something positive. There is also the protesters in the streets after the assassination of Choukri Belaid. The mobilization just revived the [idea] that the revolution is not something to be taken for granted. Never take it for granted! It was the first time we had a politician murdered. So there was just like a slap: wake up! That was why the funeral was something historic. The aim of this mobilization was: "hey, people, don't take it for granted. He can get back. You always have the corrupt people. You have the bad people. You have the ones that do not want this country to go through a democratization and get good results. You have people who are going to take it back." ... After the Choukri Belaid assassination there was this big event mobilization and awareness ... they were just taking naps: and then [suddenly] they woke up ... after the assassination of Choukri Belaid there was this: "Hey people, wake up." So the deputies woke up and worked hard for the first draft of the constitution. So we got the first constitution draft. ... People who assassinated Choukri Belaid, who were the direct reason for assassinating him, they weren't pleased by this rising awareness. So they needed something else: the assassination of Brahmi. Because that time, we were just too close to having a constitution. (TU4)

Divisions are lamented here as well since, while the struggle against a strong dictator had unified the opposition, as an Ennahda leader noted,

After the revolution the situation changed. Social movements were no longer unified. Because with Ben Ali's repression, they had a common enemy: he started with the Islamists, then attempted progressively to hit the other political forces [as well]. All this provided on the ground for differing ideological and political movements to oppose the Ben Ali regime. After the revolution the situation became more complex and diverse. (TU2)

Differently from Egypt, however, the Tunisian case was marked by "the encounter or coalition between the moderate Islamists and the moderate seculars" (TU2).

The implementation of democracy is thus perceived as a process that requires trials and errors, and must be adapted to different circumstances. So, in the words of a secular young activist, "The understanding of democracy in Tunisia is under construction," as "democracy is a tricky word" that "is not applicable the same way in every country in the world. Each country creates its definition of democracy" (TU12). This opens up some positive expectations for the future as, in the words of the same activist, "I believe in the future, it will be like: everybody will admit we are different, but we have to live together. Because it starts from the family itself. So this co-habitation is a must" (TU12).

Concluding, in both countries a horizontal conception of democracy arose and spread during the waves of protest around democracy, through a mechanism of framing in action. In both, the implementation of a minimalistic, procedural vision of democracy after the ousting of the dictators was at odds with the type of participatory, deliberative, and socially sensitive political conceptions that progressive activists had come to adopt, as frames emerging during the upheaval consolidated. The fight over the very meaning of democracy was particularly harsh in Egypt, where the members of the MB aimed at demobilizing protest, developing (unstable) pacts with the military.

EMOTIONAL SHIFTS

Emotional shifts accompanied, in both Egypt and Tunisia, the evolution of the protest. Even more than in the CEE cases, during the Arab Spring emotions were proudly displayed, among other ways, in slogans and symbols. Here as well, the waves and cycles of protests included several steps, in which different emotional work emerged as most relevant and specific emotions dominated.

First of all, as much as, or even more than in the CEE countries, emotional work was oriented to transform fear into moral shock. While in the four countries analyzed for 1989 no protestor lost his/her life during the events, many people died in both Egypt and Tunisia, before, during, and even after the mobilizations to oust the dictators. The main symbols of both uprisings then became the martyrs of repression and police harassment. As a Tunisian demonstrator recalled, empowerment developed out of moral shock: "I was standing here [hundred meters from the ministry] and saw it happening: they were just aiming and shooting straight into the protesters. This is when you realize you can die at any moment. The strange thing is, at a day like that, you just don't care" (cit. in Donker 2012).

In fact, conflict with police had escalated, especially in some milieus where reciprocal hatred had fueled everyday battles. So, in Egypt, "Football 'ultras' – fans of popular clubs like Zamalek and el-Ahly – hated the police because of the frequent clashes after matches. Microbus drivers hated them for being constantly targeted with arbitrary road fines, with which officers were topping up their miserly salaries. Young people resented them because of random searches and harassment" (Gerbaudo 2012, 59). In Cairo, conflicts escalated between the most marginalized groups and the police, especially in areas of urban renewal and tourist development (Ismail 2013). In 2010, during the campaign against the police torture and killing of Khaled Said, the mobilization grew with outrage at a repression that was portrayed as affecting all citizens – as "People were angry and frustrated. Khaled Said focused this because he looked like anyone else, he was just a very peaceful and average Egyptian young man. This mobilized a lot of people because it gave them something to have a link with" (EGY5).

Confrontation with police brutality affected individuals personally, changing their order of preferences or, even more, their self-definition. This is well expressed, for instance, by an Egyptian woman who told us:

Khaled Said affected me tremendously. I wanted to join an organized peaceful stand by the Corniche that asked people to dress in black and to face with their backs to the street ... the risk and the amount of security that the police deployed scared me. But, through that, I realized how much we were imprisoned, that I wasn't going to protest because of that, even though protesting at that moment wasn't political for me but humanitarian. When I realized that even mourning at the Corniche wasn't an option, then I became politicized. (EGY5)

In Egypt, as in Tunisia, various devices were used in order to overcome fear. Through their rituals, the ultras contributed to transform fear into anger. As Dorsey observed, "The ultras' street-battle experience helped other protesters break down barriers of fear that had kept them from confronting the regime in the past." In the words of one of them, "We were in the front line. When the police attacked we encouraged people. We told them not to run or be afraid. We started firing flares. People took courage and joined us, they know that we understand injustice and liked the fact that we fight the devil." Another noted, "The ultras killed my fear. I learnt the meaning of brotherhood and got the courage of the stadium" (Dorsey 2012, 414).

Similarly, the participation of the marginalized was also considered as important, as they were perceived as fearless, having nothing to lose. A Tunisian former Islamist noted, "The revolution would not succeed if it did not reach the capital, and specifically the popular neighborhoods in the capital, because the lower-class neighborhoods have a demographic weight. And the youngsters [there] do not have fear in their hearts. It is like they died already, the neighborhood died. There are no services, there is no cultural level [of development], there is nothing" (TU10).

So, at the peak of the mobilization, brutal repression produced and reproduced moral shocks, as indignation was fueled by the indiscriminate and brutal use of force. In Tunisia, activists, including those from the Islamist side, remembered the indignation at the brutal repression in Kasserine, in the very early days of the upheavals. Kasserine is in fact considered as a "point of no return":

Because in Sidi Bouzid there were no killings ... but in Kasserine the bloodletting and killing started. And really, it is like they say: If blood is spilled ... the people will rise up. This is a historical truth. And really, the issue for us youth [was], how can they kill youngsters that are demanding freedom, dignity and social justice? ... using live ammunition. Not even tear gas or rubber bullets – they are using live ammunition. Also they were hitting particular areas [of the body]: aiming to kill people not to hurt them. They were hitting the head and the heart. (TU10)

The events in Kasserine helped indeed in overcoming fear – as an activist remembered, "The wall of fear was still there. We needed to break the wall of fear. So we started to call: 'no fear after today'" (TU10). Bravery then fueled positive feelings, as "the events picked up speed ... in the three days up to the 14th of January. ... We were so happy" (TU10).

Also in Egypt, during the days of the upheaval, the use of tear gas, rubber bullets, and even live ammunition (as well as stones, when other weapons were no longer available) by the police produced moral shocks. Perceived as addressing "us," the brutality shocked the citizens; but rather than scaring them, it produced a "sudden prominence of bravery – the ineffably but potentially influential desire to engage in risky protest" (Kurzman 2012, 377). Appeals to demonstrate pointed in fact at the need to "be brave," and bravery became a mobilizing disposition. As repression during this exceptional time resonated with the everyday experience of harassment, the police were finally "rendered inefficient by the dynamism and stamina of exceptionally diverse crowds, each with their own know-how in the art of interfacing with gendarmes" (El-Ghobashy 2011).

Emotionally, protest appeals needed to overcome despair ("I had lost all trust in this country," said an activist) as well as anti-political senti-ments ("Myself, politics ... no thanks ... those habits, full of police around, and then, end. That told me nothing," [cit. in El Chazli 2012, 857]). They did succeed, as protest started to be perceived as a happy moment. In a participant's words, "It was one of the most profound moments of my life. The sight of the square filled with tens of thousands heralded the long-awaited dawn. As we entered the square, the crowds installed there cheered the coming of a new battalion, greeting us with joy. I wept" (cit. in El-Ghobashy 2011).

Hope then sustained the intense days of the uprising. The mobilization for democracy is widely praised as empowering: it produced a "capacity to dream." In Egypt, "It gave a lot of hope to a hopeless generation, my generation and younger. It gave hope that their voice matters, and that change could happen and to be dreamy. Even if it's too optimistic, but we like to dream" (EGY5). About Tahrir, an activist remembered "walking down the streets shouting chants. It was really a good day because for once in my life I felt free to say what I wanted, free to hope and to dream for something better" (EGY1). The eighteen days, after the protest started on January 25, were defined as characterized by "a huge positive energy . . . . People started to feel that they belonged to this land" (EGY12).

Here as well, demobilization was fueled by sustained frustration and search for emotional adaptation, even if a higher level of dissatisfaction as compared with CEE also brought about the belief in the need to continue the struggle. Disillusionment with the outcomes of the uprising was particularly strong in Egypt, where the impression was widespread that, as a women's rights supporter observed, "The revolution never ruled: we as young people were never in power; we never achieved our ideas" (EGY5). The frustration of expectations developed during the upheavals was particularly demoting, as the perception of a disempowerment of the revolution spread, especially among the young people who had participated in it. One of them remembered, in fact, in 2012, many people lost hope in the face of "our friends dying and us going to the morgue and burying them, while all those coming to the throne to rule never look down to us for our opinion, and then us going back to the streets, it made many people especially in the youth very frustrated" (EGY10). In particular, the situation under the military regime was then considered as proof of the failure of the revolution, which ended up "in a cold civil war where people are killed in the street and we have bombings, and a lot of strife and division in Upper Egypt" (EGY7). Frustration was particularly felt by the young, as "Al Sisi supporters are mainly from an older generation, while most of my generation is just getting too disappointed to do anything" (EGY11).

The very use of a term like "revolution" is considered as dangerous, raising hope that cannot be fulfilled. In Egypt, in the assessment of a student activist,

the way the regime fell down gave people too much hope. . . . People that were going to protests were very brave, and we were not used to so many brave people going to the streets. So after the revolution people were filled with hope, they had seen that small actions may make big changes. But this hope made the transition phase harder. When you think that a small action can make big changes, you have high expectations, and if those expectations do not match reality, people start losing hope again. (EGY10)

In Tunisia, as well, high levels of frustration were connected to the high expectations during the upheaval, as people imagined, according to an Ennahda leader, that "after the fall of the previous regime, after its quick fall in three or four weeks, their economic and social situation would very quickly change" (TU2).

At moments, however, hope still seemed to emerge, as a long-lasting sentiment, with a growing trust in what people learn during the uprising. There is hope, in particular, that the experience of an episode of democracy will leave behind a taste for freedom – as, an April 6 movement activist observed, "There is a saying in Egypt that the one who tried freedom once has to try freedom again. That is what we are doing in Egypt now, we are trying freedom once more and more even if we risk. That is what is keeping us going on fighting" (EGY8). Overcoming fear to voice claims in public is therefore considered as a permanent transformation, as

the main achievement is for people to be able to tell what they want and to really understand the value of participating in the political process, and to be able to speak out and act against the government. Because of this, they will achieve whatever they want. ... The revolution showed everyone that, if you go to streets and ask for your rights, people will hear you. (EGY8)

Another interviewee concurred that a culture of protest had developed, so that people are now ready to go into the streets when they think the circumstances require it:

There were a lot of people who were frustrated during and after the revolution for economic and political reasons. ... A lot of people again were facing economic problems after the revolution, so they could not continue to support protests. Or they did not see the benefits of going to the streets still. But on the 30th of June 2013, all of these people again went down to the streets as they did during the revolution ... now people are no longer afraid to say what they think. (EGY3)

The mobilization for democracy is thus credited for having socialized to politics large groups of citizens, as "Before the revolution you could not find 50,000 people participating in politics. ... After the revolution a lot of people start to be interested in politics and be part of movements and the revolution." Even if "a lot of people think the revolution is over and that it has failed," a culture of protest is still expected to bring people back into the street, as

> The culture of protesting is now in every place in Egypt, in every town; if something happens, people start protesting, it's now a part of the culture. ... The biggest achievement is that the culture has changed. Before January 25, 2011, the normal culture of the Egyptian people was that we shouldn't criticize the President. ... now people started to think that we are part of the whole and to think that we have rights and that we need to work to solve our problems. (EGY7)

As another interviewee observed, empowerment was long-lasting, as the upheaval fed a culture of protest: "Tahrir was a spectacle at the time, so many people were drawn to it that were not overtly political. ... Also a lot of people romanticized the revolution too much. ... Many of these people had completely unrealistic expectations of what would happen after the revolution. ... Especially during Mursi's presidency, there was almost something like a culture of protest, every Friday people would go to the streets because of a sense that nothing had been achieved" (EGY1).

In both countries, then, the development of protest, initially hindered by widespread fear in light of brutal repression, was then fueled through the working up of moral shock, up to a feeling of empowerment. At the peak of the mobilization, participation was no longer felt as a cost – instead eliciting hope, fun, and happiness. As the excitement for the ousting of the dictators sobered, however, given the difficulties in implementing the ambitious aims of the revolution, disappointment (particularly strong in Egypt) fueled some demobilization, but also re-mobilized at times. So, emotional prefiguration gave way to emotional adaptation.

CHANGING TIMES

Also in the Arab Spring, the perception of time, and with it the relations among people, intensified with the rhythms of the protest, relaxing afterward. Similar to the CEE region, the organizational and material resources accumulated first slowly, then quickly, with an alternance of disruptive moments in quiet times that eventually peaked in the intense, revolutionary periods. Here as well, the intense time is considered as inevitably short, ending in time normalization.

Surprise about the uprising is often cited in both countries as breaking the expectation developed in normal times. Surprise is mentioned in Tunisia, where a young activist so recalled his personal experience, just before the mass demonstration:

We were watching [and discussing] in the neighborhood [among friends] that *maybe* after five years – maybe – it will spread outside the regional context and it *might* reach Tunis. ... And less than a year later [see what happens]! When it started in Sidi Bouzid, we were thinking that maybe after five years it will reach the capital. And that we would be very happy if this had happened [within the five years]. And then suddenly ... everyone went out to the streets. Everything that had been repressed for a period of fifty years started to mobilize spontaneously. (TU1, emphasis added)

Egyptian activists concurred: "Nobody was prepared, even those who thought this might be a revolution ... the 25th of January turned out to be much bigger than anybody thought. ... The 28th was the day of the revolution when everything changed" (EGY9); "It was a surprise on the 25th" (EGY4).

The intensity of the perceived time was mentioned when talking of the street battles and camps in the squares, which emerged as an "'exceptional episode' of the revolution's long life-course." As Bayat (2013, 594) noted, exceptional episodes involve

a swift transformation of consciousness, utopia and euphoria. It is this extraordinary moment (with its unique spatial, temporal and cognitive elements) that espouses awe, inspiration and the promise of a new world. Revolutionaries become the master of the streets at these transitory times. Their unremitting initiatives, bravery and sacrifices appear as if they signal the coming of a new historical order. This represents the street politics of the revolutionary times.

A revolutionary euphoria is also mentioned by our interviewees. In Tunisia, not only the intense time of the upheaval but also the time after it are recalled as extraordinary as, according to a young blogger,

everyone was on the streets demonstrating: women, men, the young, old people. ... Everyone was willing to change the situation. ... We continued to have big mobilizations in the first months after the departure of Ben Ali. There is this revolutionary euphoria. So people were happy: we succeeded in getting rid of Ben Ali and we have to get rid of his system and of the people that used to work for him. (TU8)

A slogan in Tunisia read, "Nothing will be as before" (Allal 2012). Also for Egypt, the events were presented as part of a moment of epiphany: as a "truly historical moment," a "revolutionary moment" – as "everybody understood that it was, in fact, a moment" (Nigam 2012, 54).

After the revolution, however, the perception of time changed again. Time normalization has been cited in other research. As Bayat noted, "While the 'exceptional episode,' the insurrection, echoes the mastery of revolutionaries, 'post-revolution' times are the occasion of the 'free riders.' The free riders – those non-participants, the well-wishers, the benign and the watchers of events, if not opportunists – assume immediate power the day after the dictators relinquish power." Extraordinary moments in fact "are precisely that – *extra-ordinary*, which in ordinary times reveal their limitations; they cannot be sustained for a long span of time, for they would be costly, while their routinization would diminish their clout and effectivity. Ironically, these spectacular and extra-ordinary street showdowns are too feeble to carry on for long" (Bayat 2013, 595).

Egyptian and Tunisian activists also described fatigue with being permanently on the street as a factor in the declining phase of the mobilization – with a changing perception of time. Tunisian activists indeed often talk of a perceived desire to return to a normal time. In the words of a young activist, there was the need to "go back to our lives," as "after the election, . . . citizens [thought], ok we vote for you: take the job. We have to get back to our lives, so it is your job to control the country, to do whatever you have to do. What we voted for. After the elections, we just have this illusion that we do not have to protest again. We do not have to go to the streets again, now that we have democracy and it is being constructed" (TU4). A widespread desire for a return to order is voiced by an Ennahda leader, as "people are tired. . . . this is what most people think. They have had enough of protests, they have had enough of strikes, they have had enough of political instability" (TU3). This desire for normality leads to frustration, so producing demobilization – as a young, secular activist recalled, "if I am stressed and frustrated, I will retreat into myself. I don't want to talk about politics. There are people, friends, they participated in the revolution – at the Kasbah they were very influential. Now, they never talk about politics. They broke off from politics . . . even on Facebook – their profile is completely apolitical. They do not want anything political" (TU1).

In Egypt, as well, a change of time was noted, as "asking people to be active for so long, for months, was a lot . . . a lot of people were fed up with protests, a lot of people also left the revolutionary movement and started their own lives" (EGY5). From the surprise of the revolution, expected as a short and powerful moment, activists move to a longer-term vision. An Egyptian socialist activist thus stated,

For me and many people the revolution did not end on February 11, 2011. The word revolution for us is not defined by the eighteen days of protest. In fact, the revolution might have only started there. After the 11th of February, of course, things started to develop. In the eighteen days we were all taken by surprise, and they were very tough, but in some way also easy. After that, mobilization and activities developed. People started to organize parties and there were million-strong events on a weekly basis. (EGY9)

The process is then imagined as a long-lasting one in which

many people died and will die. More blood will be shed, and pain and instability will continue. But all these pressures and fights possibly will leave a different configuration of forces and way of doing things. ... what happened is that you have burst this open and the cockroaches are moving all around. They were under control before, but now they are moving. This is the only way to kill them, if they are out in the open. The revolution romantics thought that it is easy: just eighteen days and everybody would be nice to everybody, but now they have learned the hard way that it is not only Mubarak, but it is vested interests, it is classes, it is clusters of people, people who have millions and are totally corrupt. (EGY9)

The revolution is reframed then as a long-lasting battle against a powerful enemy, a durable process, rather than a short breaking event. As an Egyptian socialist observed,

Revolutions develop in a certain tempo, they develop in a process of failed aspirations that push maybe for more radicalization. The masses think it is enough to oust Mubarak and they have to learn it is not ... a profound revolution is a process, not an event. A deep revolution means that the metabolism of society exploded in a way. ... It is not replaced quickly by another metabolism but in a painful and long process of struggle between the rulers, and between the rulers and the ruled, until in time there is something new. (EGY9)

So, a member of the liberal Al Dustour party concurred, "The effect of ousting Mubarak through the street was the direct empowerment of the people. ... Egyptians now feel much more effective. ... people felt that they could do something. That was something new" (EGY11).

The role of the eventful protest in creating a long-lasting consciousness is similarly stressed in Tunisia. As an activist of the Union of Unemployed Graduate argued,

Most people call it – and it is a big word – but [they call it] a "spontaneous" revolution. But the mentality [of these movements] was activated inside these people's associations that were present in Tunisia [long before], and it is this mentality/consciousness that was nurtured into a revolutionary, political consciousness. And so this process, from 17 December until 14 January, the development of the consciousness of the Tunisian street from a mentality aimed at direct demands – in relation to work, in relation to dignity, in relation to development of the peripheries, in relation to justice of the peripheries ... then it developed into a more general consciousness, a complete political consciousness: that demanded the fall of the regime, that demanded the fall of the government, that demanded the exit of Ben Ali, that demanded the end of politics of starving and the politics of marginalization. And so it continued. (TU5)

The risk of a new, and more violent, upheaval is also pointed at in Tunisia, as an Islamist activist noted, "if the revolution is stolen from the people that made it, maybe there will be a second revolution and people will take to the gallows" (TU9). In sum, in both countries, after the slow pace of the building of an opposition, the extraordinary times of the days and weeks that brought about a regime change represented a long-lasting turning point – as "nothing will be as before." An intensification of relations was linked to the short moments of the upheavals, with an opening of the range of possibility. After the end of the dictatorship, however, some of that enthusiasm left space for a search for normalization, as new routines were built but also a new vision spread of the revolution as a process rather than a moment.

CONCLUDING REMARKS

Protests increased in the MENA region, as they had in the CEE region, in the decade before the uprisings. Those uprisings in fact grew upon those previous developments, as spin-off mobilizations. Differently from the CEE regions, protests involved however more multiform actors here. Besides the human rights groups, which had dominated in the CEE countries, in the Arab Spring we found a strong mobilization of labor, precarious workers, and poor people, as well as ultras and religious groups. The social component was more structured in Tunisia – where the local branches of the official union had often organized against the center – but also visible in Egypt. General strikes contributed to the breakdown of the regime. All of these streams of protest had interacted only very loosely before the upheaval, although with some increasing trends in coordination – somewhat more so in Tunisia than in Egypt. Contacts grew rapidly during the mobilization, with a higher degree of radicalization in the forms of action during the Arab Spring than in 1989.

After the ousting of the dictator, in contrast to the CEE region, protests continued unabated. First, given sudden freedom, social groups multiplied their demands through emulative mechanisms. Second, an interoppositional competitive struggle emerged over the ownership of the revolution. Third, there was still an escalation between social movements and the state and protestors and police. Much differently than in the CEE, and more in Egypt than in Tunisia, violence was present both in the days of the upheaval and after it, both in street battles with the state apparatuses and in interactions between progressive movements and religious fundamentalists.

At the cognitive level, here as in the CEE region, conceptions of democracy that developed during the incubation of protest praised horizontality and lack of leadership, among others as ways to limit the disruptive effects of repression. Through mechanisms of framing in action, participation and deliberation were very much emphasized as conditions for high-quality democracy against the minimalistic visions of electoral accountability. Here as in the CEE region, however, a conception of democracy that had emerged as appropriate during the dictatorship, and had allowed for networking during the upheavals, showed its limitations after the ousting of the dictators. Given electoralization but also repression, internal divisions interacted with the declining capacity to mobilize the normal citizens, with a perception of inadequacy to the new times but also difficulties in devising a new, more apt, formula. Low-quality elections and weak parties were criticized, especially in Egypt, as incapable of addressing the needs of freedom and dialogue of divided societies. The "boxocracy" (or the myth of the electoral booths), promoted by the West, was more explicitly criticized here than in Eastern Europe, as electoral, majoritarian conceptions of democracy appeared to fuel conflicts rather than appeasing them. Those consolidated frames of participatory and deliberative democracy remained persistent, however, continuing to fuel waves of protests.

Emotional dynamics were very relevant here as well throughout the protest cycles, changing in type and intensity in a similar way to the CEE region, through mechanisms of emotional prefiguration and emotional adaptation. Given much stronger forms of repression, moral shock was even more explicitly referred to here than in the CEE region; outrage at regime brutality ensued, changing the very predispositions of Egyptians and Tunisians. Even more than in Czechoslovakia or German Democratic Republic, the very use of the term "revolution" was charged with emotional feelings of hope and happiness, as well as pride in belonging to the "people," whose capacity to oust the hated dictator produced long-lasting feelings of empowerment. However, frustration was even more bitter than in the CEE area, as the perception spread of having been unable to really change the regime. Continuous repression spiraled in continuous moral shocks, and hopes for rapid change were disillusioned.

Emotional mechanisms interacted with shifting relations, and perceptions thereof, with the changing speed of the lived experience through mechanisms of time intensification and, then, time normalization. As in the CEE area, there was a slow accumulation of material and symbolic resources for the mobilizations, followed at the peak of the protest by a perception of a rapid (and surprising) intensification of time as well as of interactions. Eventually, however, these left space for a demobilization, explained – at least in part – by the search for a return to quiet, normal times, after the excitement of the revolution. Among those who remained mobilized, the conception of the revolution also changed – from a moment to a process.

Arab Spring

Which Democratic Qualities in Egypt and Tunisia?

The state is breaking [freedom] every day, the text about human rights was never put into action, people are arrested for trivial reasons, like for walking by a demonstration. One of my brother's colleagues was arrested for having an electrical circuit on the subway. He was carrying a backpack full of school stuff when police stopped and searched him. They found just school stuff, like a notebook, a computer, and a small electron circuit for a project he was doing. He was arrested because they claimed he was planning a bombing to support the Muslim Brotherhood, even though he is Christian. He was put in custody for three days. .... And we are just expected to live this, and take sides either with the state or the Muslim Brotherhood. We are living our worst nightmare. (EGY11)

The Arab Spring has been defined as an uprising for freedom, but also for social justice, in an institutional context perceived as deteriorating on all the various aspects of citizens' rights (della Porta 2014a). Activists tend, however, to point at the persistence of human rights abuse. In order to account for this difference in the outcome in the Middle East and North Africa (MENA) region if compared with Central Eastern Europe (CEE), we have to look at the changing relations between different actors during the struggle for democracy.

In the MENA region in the 1970s and 1980s, a degradation of social conditions had followed economic liberalization, breaking the social compromise of the national populist regimes (Amin 2012). While former leaders, even if authoritarian, tended in fact to support a Third World project of non-aligned movements involving promises of peace, bread, and justice, the debt crisis of 1980s was then a turning point, with dramatic cuts in welfare and public education (Prashad 2012). The first decade of the 2000s was thus characterized by an increase in the number of people living below the poverty line, growing unemployment rates, and increases in food prices (Joffé 2011; Salt 2012). Demographic pressures and lack of housing spread dissatisfaction, contributing to youth mobilization. With the destabilizing impact of neoliberal policies, the prevalence of inequalities, clientelism, corruption, and emigration of qualified people remained high (Mouhoud 2011–2012). Market liberalization went hand in hand with political deliberalization. In explaining the survival of authoritarian regimes in the MENA region, Eva Bellin (2004, 140) talked in fact of their "robust authoritarianism" and "robust coercive apparatus." Others have also pointed at a strategy of *divide et impera* on the part of the liberalized autocracy (e.g., Cavatorta 2007).

The Arab Spring had raised optimistic assumptions about (yet another) wave of democratization, which was all the more important as it was taking place in a world region where authoritarian regimes had been considered as resilient. Dictators seemed to fall one after another in Tunisia, then Egypt, and then Libya and Yemen. However, quite soon the expectations changed as it became evident that the protest cascade had not brought about a regime change cascade, let alone a revolutionary one. The majority of the MENA dictators were still in power, and, what is more, the fall of the dictator did not automatically bring about democracy. Assessing the quality of democracy even in the two apparently more successful cases is a sobering task as, in comparison with the four CEE countries we analyzed, civic, political, and social rights emerged as much weaker in Tunisia and, even more so, in Egypt.

The mobilizations of 2011 criticized both economic liberalization and political deliberalization, claiming freedom and justice. However, the results in terms of civil and political rights remained limited, particularly for social rights. While the evolution of the new regimes is still open, with some more hope for a democratic transformation in Tunisia than in Egypt, some relational dynamics of the mobilization for democracy might contribute to explaining both successes and failures. Legalization and legitimation of citizens' rights emerged as weaker than in the CEE area and more subject to quick reversal.

CIVIL RIGHTS AND THE CIVIL SOCIETY AFTER THE ARAB SPRING

In the Arab Spring as in 1989, those who mobilized claimed civil rights, primarily in terms of the development of civic freedoms and a civil society. Not by chance, freedom of speech and association was often mentioned in the activists' conceptions of democracy. Interviewees stressed civic rights such as those related to freedoms as a fundamental aspect of democracy that was still lacking. As an Ennahda supporter stressed, in Tunisia,

those that are in the movement: firstly they demand freedom. What is freedom? I am Muslim. I go to pray, I go to the mosque .... The state should ensure these freedoms in the constitution. What does it mean to ensure freedoms? If I think religious duties are important, nobody would forbid me to [do these things]. And the leftists, in what they do, should also not be forbidden by anyone. Respect me, and I respect you. And I do not impose my opinion on you, and you don't impose your opinion on me. ... We all live as brothers, and we all live in a country that takes care of all, without exception, without differentiating, and without preferences. (TU7)

As we will see in what follows, even though the changes of regime did have an effect in terms of the enrichment of associational life, repression of the civic and political participation of the citizens is an issue – especially in Egypt, but also in Tunisia.

Empowering Civil Society?

It is expected that democratic institutions, in granting freedom of speech and association, will empower civil society organizations, through the legalization as well as the legitimation of civil rights. However, this increase in civil rights happened only to a limited extent in Tunisia, and was even reversed in Egypt.

In Tunisia, civil society organizations are seen as proliferating in various forms during and after transition. Before the transition, they were described as controlled by the regime party: "You had to show your support for Ben Ali, and you had to glorify him" (TU1). After the ousting of the dictator, however, the development of civil society, or at least of various types of voluntary associations, is indeed seen as a positive process since, according to several interviewees, a "good thing was that in every neighborhood, new associations were created" (TU1). In fact, civil society organizations developed quickly after the transition – as an Islamist activist noted: "before the revolution there were three thousand associations; from the revolution to today, 17,000 associations: so 14,000 associations have been newly founded" (TU9). Associational life also became more plural throughout the upheaval and afterward, as a socialist observed, "before the revolution, there was just one type of organization or association: the charity," while "during the revolution there was really the start of all kinds of associations" (TU4). The legitimation of civil society is perceived as increasing, as "in the period since the revolution until now, whereas the reputations of politicians and politics is decreasing, [the reputation of] NGOs is increasing. People are trusting NGOs, but not parties, since there was an election, there were promises – and [these promises] were not kept. So people [stopped having] faith in political parties, while considering NGOs as hard working" (TU4).

In Egypt, as well, associational life was enriched after the end of the regime, and this is linked to the mobilization for democracy. Particularly on gender issues, notwithstanding a strong cultural and institutional bias against women's rights, "women have increasingly pushed the boundaries of what is socially acceptable when joining the protests and making their own gender-specific demands, in addition to joining in the wider calls for reforms, democratization, an end to corruption, political transparency and human rights" (Al-Ali 2012, 28). As noted by a founder of the social movement organization Women for Change, participation in Tahrir in fact sensitized activists to various issues of freedom and emancipation through specific experiences, which had long-lasting consequences:

I always had a passion for women's rights, and I saw so many women in Tahrir, and I realized that many of them actually came from far away and had left their families behind just to be in Tahrir. So I felt a social obligation to explain to them what was going on, what the situation was. ... I started talking to them, and asking them what they were doing, where they came from and in what ideas they believed. What I realized was that they had put their lives on hold to be there. This started my passion for women's rights, I wanted to give back what I had learned during the revolution and start sharing my experiences. So we started to have this free spirited group that we called Women for Change. (EGY5)

After the ousting of the dictators, legislative changes favored this development, with some more recognition of civil rights in Tunisia than in Egypt. In the former, after January 14, both political and nonpolitical organizations flourished with what a unionist defined as

the stage of freedom of organization, freedom of gathering, freedom of doing political work, freedom of expression, etc. Anyone who wanted, could just make an association ... associations that were started from a political idea, that were started from a political agenda. ... Charitable associations that do social work with the aim to soften the social situation in [lower-class] neighborhoods ... associations with a cultural background, especially those that focus on youth and do cultural work in Tunisia. ... organizations that were fighting corruption. (TU5)

Legal provisions are seen here as facilitating the development of an open civil society, by facilitating the foundation of associations. In fact, in the assessment of an Ennahda leader,

After the revolution, those types of restraints did not return. So the space for movements became very wide ... more liberal. ... There is only a limited [set of] conditions to meet in order to found an association, a social, economic, educational, or other type of organization. So the texture of civil society widened a lot. ... The protest spaces are now not the only channel [for expressing views], because there are now new spaces and other channels for expression. The only channel for expression that was available for changing a situation [before] was protesting, going to the streets. After the revolution it became possible to change situations through other means: through civil work, through work within associations, in unions, student activism. (TU2)

In this view, with the fall of the dictator, "the political landscape changed. There was no extreme pressure anymore, no threat of political repression for social and political movements. And so the society expresses itself more freely. ... There are freedoms: freedom of expression, freedom of organizations, and freedom of gathering. They did not give the chance to return to repression as it was during the rule of Ben Ali" (TU2).

Besides more liberal legislation, the cultural climate also emerged as legitimating the development of civil society, as "People's understanding of Tunisian society did change. The majority thought that Tunisian society was sleeping and frozen. But during the revolution it became clear that the Tunisian society is mobilized and dynamic. And there is a lot of anger and protest" (TU2). The revolution is in fact praised as a school of democracy, with some long-lasting positive consequences in terms of political socialization and the construction of a civil society infrastructure.

In sum, even if with some limits and selectivity, Tunisian civil society was perceived as growing in strength and pluralism after the transition, as well as being capable of pushing forward more inclusive visions.

In Egypt, too, an empowering of civic society was noted, although much more contested here than in Tunisia. The revolution is perceived to have allowed for the development of a more participatory culture. As an activist observed,

Now we have young people around my age that believe in democracy, they believe in revolution and change, they believe that Egypt is better than before. A lot of NGOs and movements developed since the revolution 'til now. Politics happened. Lots of people went to the public, to be social actors and to think about the political problems of the country. Egypt's young people now think about how to improve political life, and Egypt. This wasn't there before the revolution. ... Now all the young people are interested in politics and believe in change. This is a great improvement. (EGY4)

So, some improvements were also noted in Egypt, where some (at least subjective) empowerment of civil society was singled out as one of the outcomes of the mobilization for democracy.

Repressing Civil Society

These improvements notwithstanding, the picture is far from rosy. First, the legitimacy of some groups and claims produced during the mobilization was challenged afterward. If the revolutions certainly empowered groups working on civil issues, after the ousting of the dictator women are again marginalized in male-dominated institutions, and obstacles to women's rights are strengthened by the discourses against Western culture (Elsadda 2011). Legitimation is therefore selected and contested.

Divisions in civil society between secularists and Islamists are also criticized as partly responsible for a selective inclusion of rights, with a civil society divided between Islamist associations and independent ones (TU4). International donors' programs are also considered as selective, as "they are used in support of particular political efforts. They are used with the aim of aiding people with a particular outlook. They don't distribute throughout civil society unless it is to people that are from their approach" (TU9). In addition, a criticized effect of donors' intervention is some lack of authenticity in the civil society – as a young activist said, "The goals of these associations: 'Liberate Tunisia,' 'Liberate the planet,' 'Liberate the world.' ... Everything: 'protecting mice' – everything and everyone got their association. But many of them were empty [shells]. ... And a number of people entered associations, quit after a while, and took all the money that they could get" (TU1).

The situation is similar, from this point of view, in Egypt, where the superficiality and selectivity of foreign donors is also criticized. As an activist observed,

They should support the real NGOs of Egypt. In Egypt we have people that are making money out of founding an NGO, but for the society this does nothing. Normal Egyptian people are away from political life, so they cannot use any of these funds in their normal life. ... The international community should be down to the normal Egyptian people, supporting Egyptians in Upper Egypt, and talking to them directly, asking them about their demands. ... They just give money to NGOs and run away to their countries. (EGY4)

Also in more general terms, the legal protection of civil rights is still limited. Together with freedom, the rule of law is considered as a fundamental guarantee for democracy that is largely underdeveloped in Tunisia, as in Egypt. Activists complain in fact about the lack of legal equality since, as a Tunisian Islamist activist expressed, "We are scared now that the state is not a state based on the rule of law. The Interior Ministry does what it wants and gets away with it" (TU9). Even worse in Egypt, the weakness of civil society is also related with the weakness of civil rights – as "We do not have enough freedom, said a human rights activist, we do not have proper elections ... we do not have social equality" (EGY3). With several hundred demonstrators killed in 2011 and 2012, the Muslim Brotherhood (MB) in power was accused of having postponed the approval of a law on freedom of association, and the preoccupation with the violation of human rights even increased after the military intervention in 2013. Even secular people are afraid that hatred against the MB can bring about a justification of human rights violations against them – as one of them recalled during the interview, "Yesterday a court sentenced over 530 Muslim Brotherhood members to death, which is catastrophic. ... There are a lot of people supporting these decisions" (EGY3).

Particularly striking when compared with the CEE countries are in fact the memories of brutal waves of repression even after the regime change, testifying to a low recognition of protest rights. This was particularly the case in *Egypt* given the power the military maintained after Mubarak left the country. Repression had been particularly brutal here during the dictatorship and during the eventful protests in January 2011, with notable (especially, victorious) fights with the police. In particular, activists identified January 28 a critical juncture, as it was "not only the day that protesters captured Tahrir, but, even more significantly, it was the day the people defeated the despised police force. All across Egypt, hundreds of police stations and an estimated 3,000 police vehicles were burned to the ground" (Holmes 2012, 405). Similar effects emerged from the fights against the regime's use of thugs during the so-called Battle of the Camel on February 2.

What is more, repression remained strong after the formal end of Mubarak's regime.

Data on Egypt show a high use of different forms of repression (see Figure 10.1) which does not decline after the ousting of the dictator. Peaks are related with moments of intensification of protest such as in 2011, in March during the constitutional referendum; in October, on the occasion of the peaceful demonstration in Maspero against the Supreme Council of

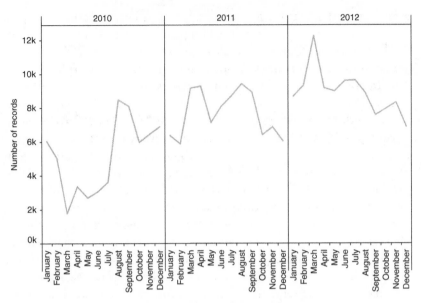

FIGURE 10.1 Repression by Months in Egypt (Gdelt data)
Source: Data collected and analyzed for this project by Hugo Leal.

the Armed Forces (SCAF); in November, on the occasion of the protests in Mohamed Mahmoud street; and on February 1, 2012, in Port Said (with 74 people killed and about 500 injured). Repression included different forms (see Figure 10.2), being particularly intense during the period in which the SCAF was in power, declining after Mursi's accession to power in terms of brutal interventions in the streets but also of detentions and trials.[1]

Exclusive attitudes are visible in the legislation that restricted the rights to protest. A law on thuggery was passed in 2011 to increase, up to death sentences, the penalties for disturbing the peace. Permission was required before writing articles critical of the military forces as well as for NGOs to receive funds from abroad; military prosecutors and military courts were used against dissidents. According to a report by Amnesty International, some of these measures

reinforced long-standing patterns of serious human rights violations, while others – such as subjecting women protesters to forced "virginity tests" – represented disturbing new forms of abuse. From the end of February onwards,

---

[1] We used Cameo event code base 18 (Assault), 20 (Use Unconventional Mass Violence), and 19 (Fight: Fight with small arms and light weapons and Fight with artillery and tanks) when civilians are the target of the action. All measures are aggregated.

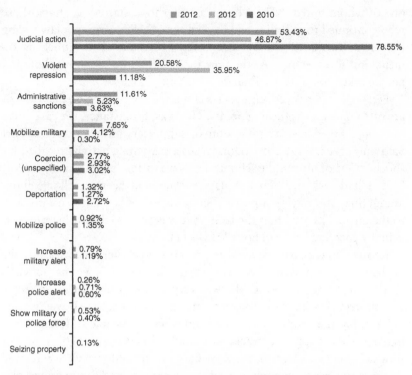

FIGURE 10.2 Reported Repression in Egypt by Year (ICEWS)
Source: Data collected and analyzed for this project by Hugo Leal.

the armed forces used violence to forcibly disperse protesters on several occasions. They used tear gas and rubber bullets and fired into the air with live ammunition and accused those they detained of looting or damaging public or private property or other crimes. (Amnesty International 2012, 12–13)

After the military coup d'état on July 3, 2013, demonstrations were heavily repressed, protestors arrested and often tortured, the security forces perpetrated high levels of state violence (for instance on January 25, 2014, 49 persons were killed and 247 injured during a commemoration of the third anniversary of the beginning of the uprising against the Mubarak regime), and judicial repressions included the death penalty (as the 183 pronounced against MB activists on June 21, 2014) (Bassiouni 2016). In 2013 and 2014, new laws criminalized protest and opposition.

Both the military and the Islamists were considered as responsible for the restriction in civil rights, at least in the assessment of secular activists, one of whom noted, "The Muslim Brotherhood started to attack those who continued to mobilize and backed the SCAF in issuing a law saying that demonstrations are forbidden. The SCAF started to attack movements in the streets. ... At the time there were around twelve thousand people taken to military tribunals" (EGY9).

Personal experiences with repression after the ousting of the dictator are often narrated as turning points. This was, for instance, the case when the police killed seventy-four football supporters after a match in Port Said on February 12, 2012 (Dorsey 2012). A young activist recalled his shock: "One of my middle school friends was attending the match in Port Said. I had just met him five days earlier, and he was talking about graduating, and having a party afterwards. ... When I was on my way to the airport I heard that the train that was supposed to bring him was actually carrying his dead body" (EGY11).

Repression is also considered as a reaction to earlier successes, and the challenges they presented to conservative actors. In a young activist's perception, in 2011, the SCAF "was very aware of the power of people and protests," with "a consistent pattern where the SCAF was issuing decrees that the people did not like and when the people started protesting, the SCAF would backtrack. So, initially, they recognized the power of protest" (EGY1). Later on, tough reactions by the military were perceived by the activists as a consequence of the awareness by those in power that "the fear of people has been broken and that protest could actually bring about change" (EGY1).

Repression then continued to produce moral shocks that brought people into the streets again and again, against the "atrocities committed by the SCAF" (see also Chapter 9). As a women's rights activist noted, "The crimes they were committing were horrific and they were unprecedented. We never had virginity tests conducted over women by the police or the army" (EGY5). During competitive protests, repression fueled mobilization, especially during the "very turbulent" eighteen months from February 2011 to the first presidential elections in June 2012 – with "many actions like the dispersal of the July 8 sit-in of the families of the revolutionary martyrs in Tahrir, the clashes between the army and Christians in Maspiro, the Mohammed Mahmoud battles in 2011, the cabinet battle, we had all of these continuous actions during these eighteen months until the elections in 2012" (EGY6).

The situation further escalated when violence at demonstrations was perceived as coming also from the Islamists themselves. Remobilization happened in fact after the MB, in power, sent its militants against protestors, for instance after the clashes at the presidential palace in 2012. There, said a student activist, "we saw too many friends being beaten by the Muslim Brotherhood again. So some people who had lost hope came back for the sake of their friends" (EGY10). In fact, the perception of an alliance between MB and SCAF against protest rights outraged the activists, who believed, as did this member of the April 6 movement, that

Through the agreement between the Muslim Brotherhood and the SCAF, the SCAF committed a lot of crimes against the revolution on many levels. Those crimes like the Mohammed Mahmoud massacre, and Port Said stadium, Maspiro and Abassaya massacres, showed us the ugly face of the SCAF and their corruption. It showed us that they will not leave Egypt because they control its economic and social life. We discovered the ugly face of Muslim Brotherhood as well, which was leaving the revolution and making agreements only to reach their own goals, the throne of Egypt, and making agreements against us. (EGY2)

Repression is in fact perceived by the activists as aiming at protecting continuities with the old regime. Through the alliance with the MB, the SCAF was considered as attempting to control the streets in the name of the preservation of Mubarak's elites. Their initial favoring of the Muslim Brotherhood over other parties and groups is read by a student activist as

a simple calculation: the military said to itself now that Mubarak was ousted, this was the only way to preserve ourselves and the established way of doing things. In order to control things, we have to operate with the political force that can control the streets, and this is not the liberals, because they are very small. So the SCAF oriented themselves towards the Muslim Brotherhood because, for the old regime, this was the only way to control things. (EGY9)

Through repression, a member of the liberal party Dostour concurred, "the SCAF was fighting to recollect the old regime, just with different approaches and different people at the top. They tried to contain the youth movement, and tried to make deals with the heads of the political parties, and deals with the Muslim Brotherhood" (EGY6).

Repression is then perceived as even more on the rise after the military coup of July 3, 2013, led by General Al Sisi. Since then, an April 6th movement supporter noted,

the military committed great crimes against people in the Al Raba'a sit-in. They killed thousands of people, and a lot of blood was in the streets. They brought activists under detention, nearly 30,000 activists. They made a protest law that says it is not legal to protest. Therefore in the constitutional referendum it was not permitted for any activist to call on the people to say NO against the constitution. This constitution allows for military trials against civilians, and legalizes bringing activists into prison without any reason. Now the state of Egypt is very bad. Under the allegation of terrorism, the military brought activists under detention, and with that limited the revolution in the streets. They recorded phone conversations, and carried out torture in police stations. (EGY2)

Repression is thus perceived as high and even growing, notwithstanding promises of democracy that did not materialize in legal protection of civil rights. Among the secular activists, everyday experiences strengthened the perception of a new authoritarianism.

In sum, in the Egyptian case a polarization of social and political conflicts was addressed by the military through a return of the brutal repressive methods of the past regime, including the killing of protestors, arrests and long detentions, even mass death penalties.

In *Tunisia*, as well, under Ben Ali there had been moments of serious repression that produced escalation, with radicalization around religious identities especially after the Terrorism Law was implemented in 2003. As a result, an Islamist complained, "youngsters were taken to prison, and they were saying: 'you are thinking about going to Iraq, you have that intention'" (TU9). The repression of religious beliefs is perceived as eventually fueling religious identification. In the words of a human rights blogger, during Ben Ali's dictatorship, to the one who "believed in Ennahda, they would take him, his mother, his wife, children and everything. My father [at the time] had some books, he made a hole in the garden and he put the books in there – because if they found these books or cassettes, they would arrest him" (TU8).

Here as well, repression continued after the regime change in 2011. In 2012, a secularist activist recalled, "There were strikes in Siliana and the police were really savage and using arms, the kind we use for hunting. It caused something horrible for young students: many of them lost their eyes because of this" (TU12). Repression was denounced as especially strong against the national mobilization of unemployed citizens – "it was the same kind of repression as Ben Ali's. They didn't care that they were the unemployed and were demanding work" (TU11). As an activist of the unemployed graduate union lamented, "Some people were arrested, some of those were tortured. They even took people from the national bureau of the union of graduates" (TU5). Repression is thus considered as a challenge after transition too, as, according to an activist, "for us maybe the most dangerous thing that is now happening is repression" (TU5).

Additionally, attempts at repression involved the use of private militias, and Ennahda is accused of having protected radical Salafists against protest. As an activist of a union of unemployed graduates recalled,

"There were attempts to attack any protest movement from militias, even from the Salafists. We would be at a sit-in or protest, and it would be 'an attack on religion, and a deviation on religion'" (TU5). The alliance between moderate and radical Islamists is indeed criticized as, according to secularist activists,

it was the Ennahda movement that was sending them. ... There was a type of alliance between the Ennahda movement, the Salafists and others. I saw them with my own eyes, they were sitting at a café [with one another]. There was the Ennahda regional office, where they would always have meetings with the Salafists of the neighborhood. And every neighborhood would be attacked on blasphemy and apostasy. And so this Salafists craziness was directed at the opposition, and at the civil society that was not aligned to the government of Larayedh and Jebali. (TU5)

An especially outraged reaction was produced by the assassinations of two leaders of the opposition, which were attributed to Islamic fundamentalists. In particular, on the day when Choukri Belaid was buried, "1,400,000 citizens took part in the funeral. They were demanding the Jebali government to resign" (TU11).

Repression of ideas is also seen as a continued challenge to the establishment of democracy in Tunisia – and this in the perceptions of both Islamist and secular activists. Thus, an Islamist noted an increase in control and legal repression: "It starts bit by bit. They pick up people who talk and bring them to court. People who were sharing things on Facebook have been taken [to court]. ... It is therefore necessary for all to speak out against repression. Not just that they are barred just because they have a beard. Today they take you because you have a beard, tomorrow because you have an idea" (TU9). Repression is indeed still considered as a main limitation on freedom, also by secular activists – as one of them said, "It is true that we have new newspapers, new TV and new radio channels and all this. This is true. But I don't think that [press freedom with this] is defended. ... And when it comes to freedom of speech in general: it is true that today we can say whatever we want. But we have to expect trials, intimidation, threats ... many peaceful demonstrations have been repressed by the police" (TU8). In this respect, Western countries are also accused, as "they don't seem to understand that repression is what threatens their interests [as well]. Really, I don't get it: does Europe want Arab countries to become democracies or not?" (TU9). A return of authoritarianism is then feared, even in the democratic system – that "the police state is coming back" (TU9).

Still, the assessment of the success and failure of the revolution in terms of civil rights is more mixed in the Tunisian than in the Egyptian case.

Here, while some of the claims of the revolution are considered as acquired, others are not – as a unionist lamented, "civil political democracy has been achieved, up to a certain point. Still, a number of changes are pending: concerning freedom of the press, freedom of expression, freedom of conscience, civil laws in general." However, there is the hope that "these are positive issues: there is the ability to change the majority of this state of affairs in Tunisia" (TU5).

In sum, especially in comparison with Egypt, even though repression reemerged, often in brutal forms, a more tolerant and inclusive attitude toward protest developed within the institutions.

POLITICAL RIGHTS AFTER THE ARAB SPRING

> We lack an understanding of how a country is run, of which demands are achievable. ... We should have paid more attention to building political support, to having political figures from our generation playing the role of politicians. We needed politicians of our own age who could lobby for us and do both, the revolution in the streets and the politics in the parliament. ... We needed to have a stronger struggle in parliament, but instead we just abandoned elections and went to the Mohamed Mahmoud clashes. ... Now we live as outcasts. ... We needed politics since day one, and we needed politicians who believed in the revolution, who could understand when to go to the streets and when to the parliament, when to lobby and when to push. We were naïve youngsters. (EGY11)

Civil rights are strictly linked to political ones, and these are related to the quality of formal rights but also to their practical implementation. Some similarities and some differences can be noted, here as well, both cross-areas and infra-area, in order to explain the pessimistic narrative that a young Egyptian activist presents in the citation above.

First of all, similarly to the CEE countries we analyzed, transition to the new regimes brought about a shift in the power of different actors. As power moved away from the streets, actors other than those who had mobilized for democracy acquired more influence.

This was observed about the *Egyptian* struggle for democracy after the ousting of Hosni Mubarak in February 2011, with particular reference to the crucial issue of the power of the military. While the SCAF took power and the MB exploited the opening of opportunities, "activists who had bravely challenged an increasingly repressive regime for the years leading up to the 25 January uprising, who had occupied Egypt's main squares for eighteen days, sacrificed their lives and taken the brunt of brutal state violence, found themselves on the margins of this power struggle"

(Abdelrahman 2013, 569). Besides the MB and SCAF, the Salafists also acquired unexpected influence, as "after decades of shunning politics and rejecting the existing political system, ... since the downfall of the Mubarak regime in February 2011, Salafis have ardently participated in the political process" (Anani and Maszlee 2013). While classical Salafists avoided politics, the change in political opportunities pushed some of them to contest elections, relying on well-rooted social networks to raise support for their candidates (ibid.).

The electoral failure of the oppositional secular forces is a main source of frustration. At the first elections, in fact, the Islamist parties won a sound majority, with the Salafist political parties al-Nour (Light), al-Asala (Authenticity), and al-Fadhila (Virtue) obtaining together 20 percent of the votes, with 41 percent for the MB. As a secularist activist recalled, "we had already lost the elections in the first phase at the end of 2011/beginning of 2012. ... We lost the second phase and we started to feel totally lost" (EGY11). As the citation in the incipit of this part indicates, similarly to the CEE region, the lack of experience in electoral politics, together with some disdain for it, are considered as responsible for the failure.

Electoral politics is also accused of producing a misfit between the organizational forms that had developed during the struggle for democracy and those required after the ousting of the dictator. In fact, it was noted that "the combination of the closure of political systems and socioeconomic distress led to the emergence of a new set of political movements which were, in large part, leaderless, relying on non-traditional forms of organisation and communication, and focused on broad demands of regime change and political reform" (Durac 2013, 176). As mentioned in the previous chapter, "these characteristics meant that the new movements more easily escaped the control and repressive apparatus of the state than the older, formal political organisations to which state control had previously been directed. However, the novel, somewhat disorganised, leaderless character of these movements also limited their potential to take advantage of the political openings which followed the demise of autocratic rulers" (Durac 2013, 176). The experiences within protest seemed, here as in the CEE area, to prove at odds with a normalization of political participation, leaving people longing for more protest action and despising institutional politics. In fact, some activists self-critically observed that their dismissive attitude toward electoral politics limited the chances for the secular forces to transform their strength in mobilizing in the street into institutional strength. So, according to an Egyptian interviewee, the excitement of protest politics discouraged investment in institutional politics, with some negative effects in terms of citizens' rights:

In 2012 the secular and liberal protest movements could have played by the rules of democracy, organized themselves into an electoral machine and taken a majority of seats in parliament. When there were finally parliamentary elections, they actually had more popularity than Mursi. They had a chance to compete for the majority of seats in parliament. If they had done that, they could have revised the constitution, they could have had a say on the prime minister, they could have even impeached Mursi himself. But procedural democracy all seems very boring to these people ... being in Tahrir during the revolution had also given some people an unrivaled rush, a feeling that they had never experienced before, and that they did not want to let die. So they longed for another Tahrir regardless of what happened on the ground. They enjoyed this rush. (EGY1)

As mentioned in the previous chapter, in the oppositional participatory conception of democracy, party politics has in fact little appeal as, a founder of the liberal Dostour party lamented, "the youth, they have this stigma, that the political party is not a proper thing and a cool and revolutionary thing; that being a party member means that you are reformist and they are revolutionist" (EGY6). The focus on parties as core actors in electoral politics is considered, by April 6th supporters, as all the more problematic given their nature in Egypt – not "real parties," but rather "cartoons in the hands of the regime" (EGY2).

Moreover, particularly by young and secular activists, party politics is considered divisive. Among other factors, the lack of a common ground beyond the shared goal of democratization pushed the youth coalition to keep a strong preference for protest over election (Hasanen and Nuruzzaman 2013). Moreover, divisions are particularly critiqued among the secularist political parties that "could have made changes if they had just overcome their conflicts" (EGY10). MB supporters also blamed divisions within the secular opposition for having jeopardized the possibility to challenge the military and pursue democratization: "What happened through three years of transition was that political actors and forces were interested more in the conflict between them as political actors and therefore stayed away from the conflict between them and the regime" (EGY4). Responsible for the failures of the revolution is, in the secular vision, the presence of "a billion fronts, each one attacking the other and blaming the other. The Islamists, in contrast, were unified, and that's why they won the elections" (EGY5). As a socialist activist summarized, splits within those who mobilized for democracy eventually slowed down the revolution, as "if the revolutionary forces had succeeded in joining together instead of fighting on small things ... this could have given more space to political alternatives in society that were different from the miserable present political alternatives" (EGY9).

In sum, notwithstanding some alliances between Islamist and secularist forces in the past, reciprocal mistrust remained high in Egypt, pushing the MB toward an active role in the demobilization of the protest and unstable pacts with the military against those who wanted to continue the revolution. On their side, mistrustful of the MB and of the military, the opposition continued to prefer the streets to the ballot booth, considering only protest as an efficient means to oppose the unholy alliance. This strongly impinged upon the development of political rights in terms of both institutional rules and practices – legislation and legitimation.

Also in *Tunisia*, a sort of political normalization through the creation of political parties is considered by many activists as an (unwanted) outcome of the electoralization of politics. While here as well Islamist parties won the first elections (with the Islamist Ennahda achieving 41 percent of the 217 seats in the Constituent Assembly), the very creation of parties is seen by young movement participants as jeopardizing protest – for example, as a young activist noted, after Essebsi became head of government in February 2011, "there was a big protest every month, but when he called for the elections, the level of tension declined, and the organizational stage started: associations and parties were created" (TU1).

In Tunisia, too, party politics itself is seen as leading to divisions and, therefore, fragmentation, particularly on secularism or religion. After the upheavals, an Ennahda supporter noted,

Everyone moved to this and that party. And so there was a fragmentation of the youth revolutionary movement. There had been a clear plan, a plan of the youth, of all sides – I mean communists, liberals – we had set ideas: this is why we had a revolution; this and this is what we have to do. Afterwards, we entered the political game. And every person went to a political party. ... And so there was the first demonstration – and I don't know who organized it ... – in April or March, [with the slogan:] "Tunisia for you, Tunisia for me, Tunisia is a secular country." Who posed this problem? Tunisia is a Muslim country, and the civil nature of the state is [safeguarded] within it. This problem just does not exist – never. ... The struggle went from some social demands and freedom, [to a phase where] ideological struggles were revealed. ... This ideological struggle preceded the elections. Maybe this actually ensured the electoral victory of Ennahda. Because the people, in their basis, they have an Islamic identity. So even if the people are far away from religion (they drink alcohol, etc.), there is this basis that they love Islam. (TU10)

The shift from claims of dignity and freedom to the issues of religion and its position in the state is in fact perceived as a factor that fueled division. A blogger thus recalled: "I have been traveling from one area to another during the revolution, or the uprising, but I didn't hear people talking about identity or religion. I heard people talking about unemployment, about freedom, about corruption, about nepotism" (TU8). Talking about religion is considered, from this point of view, as particularly dangerous, as – a unionist criticized – "using religion divides and fractures. The far right in Germany uses religion. In Ukraine, they use religion. In Tunisia, there are parties that use religion. In Saudi Arabia, they use religion. And the Zionist entity [Israel], the same thing: it uses religion. . . . Using religion: we are against it. Because when religion is used, rights and justice disappear: equality and civility disappear" (TU5).

In sum, the secular/religious cleavage also emerged as very divisive in Tunisia, with a similar mistrust of the secular opposition in electoral and party politics. But if this cleavage divided, in a similar way, the political systems in Egypt and Tunisia, the comparatively broader polarization of those conflicts in the former is explained by the different position occupied by the military. In both countries, the corruption of the regime centered around the dictators' families, and the exclusive attitudes of the regimes had also alienated groups that had previously participated in the dominant coalitions.

Other similarities, but also differences, emerge on the actors struggling for power in the new regimes. In both countries, the dictators had alienated potential supporters even within their own parties. In Tunisia, Ben Ali had gradually dismantled the state apparatus inherited from Habib Bourguiba, centering power and money in the hands of his own family, enlarged to include his wife, Leila Trabelsi, and her relatives. Privatization was orchestrated to enrich the Ben Ali and Trabelsi families: "If a company was profitable, they took a cut of the profit. On foreign investments, they took commissions or a cut of the profits. They also served as intermediaries for the award of public contracts. The Trabelsi network controlled customs and smuggling operation" (Durac 2013, 182; see also Anderson 2011). In this evolution, not only was the business class only selectively integrated, but the regime party lost power. While Bourguiba had ruled through the RCD (Rassemblement Constitutionel Démocratique), Ben Ali progressively reduced its influence, creating resentment on the part of many RCD notables. In the name of "a silent RCD majority," they signed a declaration criticizing Ben Ali (Angrist 2013). Similar signs of dissatisfaction emerged in the main union, the UGTT (Union Générale Tunisienne du Travail), especially at the periphery. In Egypt, as well, an exclusivist tendency had grown since the early

2000s, with rising influence of a business elite strongly linked to Mubarak's family, which had greatly profited from the privatization and deregulation policies imposed by international financial organizations (Hassabo 2005; Collombier 2007). Especially discussed was the growing power of the dictator's son.

While the exclusive and corrupt development of political institutions was similar in the two dictatorships, the military – both during the authoritarian regime and after Mubarak's departure – maintained a much more powerful position in Egypt than in Tunisia, with derailing effects on the transition to democracy. In Tunisia, in fact, the military had been weakened by Ben Ali and remained weak: "Although its refusal to support Ben Ali's regime contributed to the country's revolution, the military has not participated meaningfully in managing the transition period and is unlikely to shape the ultimate outcome in any significant way" (Anderson 2011, 3). Tunisian members of the military were said to have followed their interests when defecting from the regime, as "the decision to refrain from using force against the Tunisian protesters ... occurred in a context in which the military had little to lose (and potentially some to gain) from abandoning Ben Ali, while protecting him would have introduced significant costs to the military" (Brooks 2013, 207). Following the position of his predecessor, Habib Bourguiba, Ben Ali had relied in fact on the police and the security services, keeping "the military small and poor" (Brooks 2013). Additionally, there were suspicions that Ben Ali had been involved in a helicopter crash in which a general in chief and twelve senior officers and personnel were killed in 2002. Given the size of the uprising, the military feared that "mass repression of the kind required in mid-January to quash the protests was likely to be viewed as a threat to the integrity of the organization and engender a loss of prestige and social esteem" (ibid., 208). After the army commander, General Rachid Ammar, refused to fire on the protestors on January 9 and neutralized the presidential guards, it was stated that "the national army guarantees the revolution" (ibid.). Following the ousting of Ben Ali on March 7, 2011, however, the military never took power, while the political police was abolished.

In Egypt, instead, a strong army quickly took control of the situation after Mubarak's departure as, on February 13, 2011, the SCAF dissolved the parliament, suspending the 1971 constitution. Traditionally, the military had been deeply intertwined with the political and economic elites, with the Egyptian army controlling between 25 percent and 40 percent of the country's economy (Blades 2008, 2; Abdul-Magd 2011). After transition, the role of the military establishment in the economy remains one of the major taboos in Egyptian politics. ... The military's economic interests encompass a diverse range of revenue-generating activities, including the selling and buying of real estate on behalf of the government, domestic cleaning services, running cafeterias, managing gas stations, farming livestock, producing food products, and manufacturing plastic table covers. (Abdul-Magd 2011)

During the most acute days of the struggle for democracy, the army kept an ambivalent position, declaring very late its support for the "legitimate demands of the people." While initially sustaining the police's effort in the repression, on January 31, addressing the "great people of Egypt," the army promised that "your armed forces, acknowledging the legitimate rights of the people ... have not and will not use force against the Egyptian people" (Holmes 2012, 399). However, it did not prevent aggression against the protestors, allowing pro-Mubarak thugs to enter Tahrir Square on their camels and horses, killing at least a dozen people. Additionally, "the revolutionaries were not supported by any dissident junior officers, and certainly had no allies among the generals" (Holmes 2012, 399; see also Anderson 2011). If the Egyptian army did not shoot, a main reason has been in fact singled out in the exclusion of its rank-and-file members by patronage protection under Mubarak, rather than intrinsic support for democracy (Bou Nassif 2012).

While taking a secondary role in the consolidation of the new Tunisian regime, in Egypt, by contrast, the military was considered as a main challenge to democracy, as the "difference in the military-civilian balance in the two states in turn explains the political neutrality of the Tunisian army in contrast to the deep involvement of the Egyptian army in constitutional negotiations" (Arjomand 2013, 303). In the words of an Egyptian MB activist, in fact,

the real need of Egypt is now to improve civil-military relations and to make the military stay away from politics. They are controlling about 30 percent of the economy; so the problem is how to get this back and how to improve socioeconomic relations and restructuring the socioeconomic process to make Egypt's economy one for poor people and those people that deserve subsidies. ... This is the most important issue for Egypt. Without this ... we cannot consider this transition as democratic. (EGY4)

The different roles of the military also had dramatic consequences for the process of constitution making, where we also saw very relevant differences between Tunisia and Egypt in the previous chapter. As we had noted for the CEE countries, the characteristics of the constitutional process seem to have played an important role here as well. The different timing of constitution making seems in fact very influential in producing a successful process in Tunisia, but a messy one in Egypt.

The constitutional process was in fact an arena where several cleavages emerged – first of all, on the role of religion within the state. Stressing the compatibility between Islam and democracy, Arjomand (2013) pointed at the difference between the Shi`ite counter-constitutionalism of the Islamic Republic of Iran – which legitimizes government by religious jurists, with no judicialization of political contestation – and the position of the MB in Egypt, as well as of Ennahda, and even of the Salafist al-Nour Party in Tunisia, for which "the shari'a as a, or the source of law should be a limitation on legislation rather than the basis of the political regime" (ibid., 302). The reference to the Sharia became however a very contentious issue in both countries, with a stronger polarization in Egypt where MB, in contrast to Ennahda in Tunisia, refused any compromise.

As for the constitutional process, the Tunisian interim government created a Higher Commission for Political Reform, led by a former judge of the Constitutional Court. This group had to be dissolved after the election of a constituent assembly with the tasks of writing a new constitution, setting up interim governing structures, and forming a new government. In March 2011, a Higher Authority for Implementing the Objectives of the Revolution, Political Reform, and Democratic Transition was set up, with up to 155 members. The October 2011 election for the National Constituent Assembly, with a very high turnout and fair implementation, resulted in a relative majority for Ennahda, with eighty-nine seats, followed by the liberal Congress pour la Republique (twenty-nine seats) and the socialist Democratic Forum for Labour and Liberties (Ettakol) (twenty seats). The power was then shared between parties, as the National Constituent Assembly elected as president of the republic the leader of the Congress for the Republic, Moncef Marzouki, who appointed Ennahda's Hamadi Jebali as prime minister. The leader of Ettakol, Ben Jafar, became the speaker of the assembly.

A tendency to compromise thus emerged in the Tunisian case, notwithstanding deep divisions between secularist and Islamist parties on issues such as the reference to the Sharia, the development of women's rights, and the criminalization of blasphemy. As Ennahda was amenable to compromise, these divisions in fact slowed down, but did not interrupt the work of the assembly. After having proposed the mention of Sharia as a source for legislation, in March 2012 Ennahda officially withdrew that proposal. A compromise was subsequently developed based on the first article of the

1959 constitution, which declared Tunisia an Arab and Muslim state, although without reference to Sharia. A few months later, it also renounced declaring as an offense the harming of sacred values. In May 2013, a compromise was reached on another controversial issue: the division of powers between the head of state and head of government. Additionally, responding to pressures by secular forces, Ennahda agreed to renounce controlling the ministries of the interior, defense, and foreign affairs, while also adopting a less lenient attitude toward violent Salafists. After the assassination of Mohamed Brahmi, a MP from the Left, and the ensuing protests demanding the resignation of the Ennahda-led government as well as the dissolution of the Constituent Assembly, in 2013 Ennahda's leader Rachid Ghannouchi was able to build some new compromises with the opposition (Arjomand 2013).

Constitution making in Egypt followed a very different path, as an alliance of the military and Islamists dominated the first period of the transition. After assuming control, the SCAF appointed a Constitutional Reform Committee, with strong presence of the MB, with the task of amending some provisions of the constitution in order to guarantee fair presidential and parliamentary elections (Bernard-Maugiron 2011). The proposed constitutional amendments introduced some new requirements for eligibility to run for presidential elections, among them that the president had to be Egyptian, to be born of Egyptian parents, and to have held no other nationality (Bernard-Maugiron 2011). The requests by secular and left-wing groups to have a constitution before the election and to have more time to organize for the parliamentary election were rejected as, with the agreement of the MB, the SCAF allowed for elections to be held before a constitution was passed.

Conflicts developed on the electoral law. In March 2011, the SCAF had suggested amending the Assembly Law toward a mixed electoral system, with one-third of the seats elected through a proportional party list system and the rest on a two-round individual candidacy system – eliminating an existing quota that, since 2007, had allocated sixty-four parliamentary seats to female candidates. Secular and liberal groups asked instead for proportional representation with a party list system, considering the individual candidacy system as facilitating vote-buying practices and favoring candidates with strong local family and clan connections. Eventually, the law assigned half of the seats to list-based candidates and half to individual candidacy systems.

Under the new rules, parliamentary elections were held in late 2011, with a very low electoral turnout. The results gave a clear victory to

Islamist parties, with the Democratic Alliance for Egypt, led by the MB, winning 235 seats and the Islamist Bloc, led by the Salafi Al-Nour Party, adding 127 to the Islamists' large majority. In contrast, the secular Wafd Party obtained only forty-one seats and the Revolution Continues coalition only seven. With 61 percent of the votes going to the Islamists, the assembly built a constitutional committee that reflected those electoral proportions, with a majority set at 57 percent on second reading (Awad 2013). With strong protests targeting the SCAF and MB, over a quarter of the non-Islamist members of the constitutional drafting committee refused to take their seats. Eventually, the transitional constitutional order was based on the constitutional declaration of March 30, 2011, which relied on the 1971 constitution as amended by the March 19 referendum: "The ostensible justification of these principles was that they amounted to a bill of rights, but in fact, they also included the confirmation of the shari'a as the main source of legislation in the Egyptian 'civic democratic state'" (Arjomand 2013).

The referendum on the constitution had a very polarizing effect. In the words of a former member of the MB's youth organization,

The right direction would have been to avoid polarization, like in the referendum of March 19, 2011. This referendum caused huge polarization, like who is for the Sharia, who is against the Sharia, although there was nothing about the Sharia in the referendum. . . . We should have been focused on the regime, because it is still the same regime. Control is in the army's hands and it is still the same regime. People considered the end of the regime when they got Mubarak out, but he was just the face. . . . When polarization started, I realized that we had lost. (EGY12)

The situation became more polarized after the 2012 presidential elections. As the two candidates who passed to the second stage were the MB's Muhammad Mursi and Mubarak's former prime minister Ahmad Shafiq, "Egyptians were faced with choosing between a stalwart of the authoritarian regimes that had ruled the country since 1952 and a conservative leader of the Islamist movement that had served as the dominant opposition force in the country since its foundation in 1928" (Durac 2013, 189). Afterward, tensions also developed in the relations between the secular opposition and the MB because of the latter's alleged betrayal of agreements made on the occasion of the second round of presidential elections, in exchange for supporting Mursi. As an interviewee from the April 6th movement observed,

For our support, we bargained some conditions for the Muslim Brotherhood to make a safe transition and to achieve equality, to face the corruption of the country and to participate with each other in controlling the country. But they broke these conditions and wanted to control all of Egypt by themselves, thinking they could control it alone without support from revolutionists. ... With the SCAF they thought they could control them alone and deceive them. They even brought some activists under detention because activists were a threat to their throne. (EGY2)

As the presidential elections approached, Egypt was living a constitutional crisis, "with the SCAF in control of the administration and the police, the Muslim Brothers in control of parliament and the constitutional assembly, and the administrative courts and Supreme Constitutional Court as the arbiters, who were approached by every party" (Arjomand 2013, 305). The fights between secularists, Islamists, and the SCAF continued, also involving the judiciary. After Mursi won the second round, "the electoral commission refused to declare the winner, while SCAF, following up on the SSC judicial coup, unabashedly carried out its own constitutional coup" (ibid., 306). The parliament was dissolved; 100 new members were co-opted for the drafting commission; and the powers of the president were reduced. In this struggle, the parliament resisted the SCAF's decision and "President-Elect Mohammad Morsi was brought on board before he was declared President, turning the constitutional coup into a tacit tripartite deal. ... He asserted his authority by issuing an executive order on July 8 that convened Parliament, cancelling SCAF's earlier order that had dissolved it, but taking pains to state that it was not intended against the ruling of the SCC" (ibid.).

The conflicts between the various institutional powers continued, until on November 22, 2012, President Mursi issued a "constitutional declaration," which gave immunity from judicial review to his own law decrees and decisions and to those of the constitutional assembly. A few days later, he called for a national referendum on the final draft of the constitution. It has been noted that protests were a means to influence this institutional struggle between the president and the Supreme Constitutional Court as well as the judiciary more in general, which objected to the constitutional declaration issued by Mursi on November 22. At that time,

disparate groups in the secular opposition had discovered that their voice had been much better heard in the Tahrir and other massive demonstrations than through the ballot box. Massive demonstrations comparable to those of the "Eighteen Days" that had toppled Mubarak took place nation-wide but this time against the Muslim Brothers and the elected President. The demonstrations turned violent, with several people killed in street fights and the offices of the Muslim

Brotherhood ransacked in at least two dozen cities. Particularly damaging was President Morsi's televised speech asserting that prosecutors had obtained confessions from hired thugs paid with black money to thwart the revolution. It turned out that it was the Muslim Brother thugs who had taken 49 captives and tried to extract confessions by beating them. (Arjomand 2013, 307)

A further step in polarization was taken as President Mursi proceeded with the referendum, which resulted in 64 percent approving the constitution (with a very low turnout of 33 percent of eligible voters). In sum, the public debate in the constitutional assembly has been defined as "raucous but intermittent and inconclusive ... marred by constant wrangling and repeated boycotts and threats of resignation by its non-Islamist members" (ibid.). Given these difficulties, the new constitution was an amended version of the 1971 constitution. A presidential and exclusive institutional system was maintained, "contrary to the revolution's cry against dictatorship and vociferous demand for a parliamentary regime" (ibid.). The military also kept strong power, while Article 2 of the 2012 constitution declared Islam as the state religion, Arabic as the official language, and the Islamic Sharia as the main source of legislation.[2] Laws on parties remained quite exclusive, demanding at least 5,000 founding members plus the publication of materials in at least daily newspapers with high circulation, at quite high costs (ibid.).

Given the institutional conflict, the opposition then perceived a choice between two evils, neither of them representing a step toward democracy: the army and the MB. The situation escalated particularly when, in 2012, Mursi issued the constitutional declaration and, in reaction, Mohamed Al Baradei and Hamdeen Sabahi established the Salvation Front. In a socialist interviewee's narration, the Salvation Front however tended to ally with the right wing, and

bluntly told people to cooperate with the army and the police because Mursi was the number one danger. ... 60 percent of the revolutionary youth rallied with the Salvation Front saying that the army is the solution to Mursi. ... Because of that choice and their mobilization of people in this direction, they created a colossal movement against Mursi, but in the direction of uniting with the old Mubarak state, and counter revolutionary forces. The ordinary masses who voted for Mursi

[2] Amendments to the constitution reduced the presidential term to four years, with a two-term limit, and reinstated judicial supervision of elections and referendums. Also established was a policy mandating that the president could no longer proclaim a state of emergency without the approval of the People's Assembly, and for not more than six months. As for electoral rules, the requirements for becoming a candidate in elections were set quite high and allowed for individual candidatures.

and Muslim Brotherhood in elections, just after Mursi came to power started to hate him and say that they were wrong in giving him their votes because Mursi did not respond to their expectations. ... The Salvation Front channeled that hatred into the counter-revolution. This was responsible for what happened on the 30th of June 2013, when the military took over. ... The street movements were politically paralyzed. With the conflict between Mursi and the opposition, all of the revolutionary youth and the demonstrations were attacking the headquarters of the Muslim Brotherhood; they were fighting against them and were politically directed towards the goal "let's unite with the army." (EGY9)

In sum, the political developments were much more complex in the MENA region than in the CEE countries, with intra-institutional and extra-institutional conflicts particularly disruptive in Egypt.

SOCIAL RIGHTS AFTER THE ARAB SPRING

We were seeking economic change; free elections were only a small part of the revolution. We mobilized people for economic change, for dignity and social equality, for freedom of speech, and not only for free elections. Egypt's revolution was not only a political revolution but an economic one, and one for human beings to feel human in their country. (EGY2)

As one of our secularist Egyptian interviewees stated, more explicitly than in the CEE area, social rights were central claims during the Arab Spring, whose main slogans combined references to freedom, dignity, democracy, and justice. Social conditions were indeed considered in both countries as increasingly unjust, given growing inequalities and declining welfare services. In this perspective, social justice and political freedom have been bridged in 2011 and after as:

On the whole, democratic movements in the Arab world have changed the subjective framework of society, creating new expectations and demands in terms of social justice (blue-collar workers ask for better wages and more favorable working conditions in the name of a regained dignity, building on a relative absence of power) and political freedom (the reign of charismatic strongmen is over). They have also endowed citizens with a desire to be politically relevant, not marginalized and excluded, as it was in the past. These dimensions – social justice and political democracy – have become the major manifestation of the sense of reconquered dignity through a new definition of the individual. (Khosrokhavar 2012, 113)

Social claims have been well visible in Tunisia where, as mentioned, protests started in the poor periphery, on claims of dignity, and the trade unions played an important role before, during, and after the uprising. Notwithstanding some expansion of government expenditures in social provisions, the country was characterized by unequal economic growth and increasing inequality. In particular, unemployment had been on the rise among young people, especially among university graduates (from 8.6 percent in 1999 to 44.4 percent in 2009). As income inequalities grew and economic and political business increasingly overlapped, labor organizations gained support. While the north and northwestern regions were economically more successful, poverty remained at high levels in the south and southwest.

Similarly in Egypt, social insecurity increased in 1991 with the adoption of neoliberal economic policies through agreements signed with the IMF and the World Bank (Durac 2013). In the 1990s, pushed by the IMF, the government launched a plan of structural economic reform, with a first wave of privatization. Per capita income declined, then, from among the highest among Arab countries (second only to Lebanon) to among the lowest (Amin 2012, 161). The middle class – which had grown under Nasser, thanks to expansion of education and employment in the public sector – remained a victim of neoliberal policies, between the pauperization of the many and the enrichment of the few.

During the upheavals, in Tunisia the demands of the protestors prominently included opposition to unemployment, underemployment, low wages, growing inequality, and corruption of elites (Shahshahani and Mullin 2012, 87). Protestors denounced increasing inequalities in welfare and insecurity among young people, as well as a 19 percent rate of unemployment in the population overall – twice as much for young people, even with high educations (Shahshahani and Mullin 2012). Following a series of wildcat strikes in the industrial and tourist sectors, demonstrations in 2011 called for "bread," as synonymous for jobs (Hibou 2011, xv). A main slogan was, in fact, "freedom, justice and national dignity" as "the protest movement, with its broad extent and its deeprootedness in society, was also and perhaps above all born of the sense of injustice and humiliation" (Hibou 2011, xvi).

The Egyptian events were also framed as aiming at re-establishing a lost dignity – as activists stated, "This is not a political revolution. This is not a religious revolution. This is an all Egyptians revolution. This is the dignity and freedom revolution" (cit. in Nigam 2012, 7). The uprising was carried out "in the name of my brother's dignity" (Nigam 2012, 7). The protest converged on calls for social justice and political inclusion, opposing the effects of the liberalizing reforms of the past. Requests included a minimum and a maximum wage, land redistribution, and renegotiation of the "odious debt" of Mubarak's regime. Main slogans were not only "the people want the downfall of the regime" but also "bread, freedom, social justice" (Teti and Gervasio 2012).

Claims on social rights were in fact important in the different moments of the transition, producing disappointment as the new regimes proved unwilling to implement economic reform. In Egypt, there is a shared belief that the struggle had an important social dimension. As social rights had in fact become a fundamental component of the activists' conceptions of democracy, after the ousting of the dictator, the stagnating economic situation was perceived by the protestors on the Left as producing frustration with democracy – especially among those who had mobilized but "did not see improvements in their daily lives. ... A lot of people soured when they saw that salaries had not increased and lives had not changed, that there was still unemployment, still high inflation. And so they thought that democracy was not as good as people were claiming" (EGY1). Another concurred, "a big motive for the mobilization before the revolution was topics like social justice, police violence, the failure of the state. These are the same topics, they didn't change, but now we have in addition the military and the killing of people in the streets, and people in jail" (EGY7). The social situation is considered, also by an Al-Dostour member, as responsible for the frustration of people who felt "desperate, and because of that, lost faith in change. I know many people who are leaving Egypt. I know students who are now out of political movements in general, and activists who have stopped because they recognized our failure" (EGY6). An activist lamented that "we couldn't get a president who could represent the true values of the Egyptian revolution of freedom and social equality and bread. These were the main slogans and we couldn't achieve them" (EGY6). Persisting social inequalities are also criticized by a former member of the MB's youth organization as responsible for the failures of electoral accountability: "successful control cannot happen before real social justice is established, because otherwise the country would be run for the benefit of rich people. Once we eliminate the poor layer and the ultra-rich layer of society and increase the normal or above medium layer, this would be healthy for a democratic society" (EGY12). The feeling is therefore of lack of achievements on social rights – as "the problems after the revolution were the same problems as before" (EGY7).

Similarly in Tunisia, protests in 2011 and after were perceived as claiming a social change that was never implemented, with consequent frustration with the socioeconomic situation. In the narration of a member of the graduate unemployed union, protests crystallized as a result of harsh social situations perceived by people through their personal experiences. They gradually gained a more collective identity: they developed from personal experiences to a communitarian one. [From this] in Tunisia many social movements emerged that [focus their] demands at a fundamental level. ... First, there is the question of marginalization – and especially the marginalization of the periphery. In Tunisia there is a vast difference in the level of development on the side of the coastal regions and on the side of the interior ones. And even among the coastal regions there is a deep rift between the rich and the lower class areas. ... This social split was present before in Tunisia and has developed especially since 1970 ... since the Tunisian market was opened to capitalism and was opened to global incursions. This opened up [the economy] for investments on the levels of employment and building infrastructure ... then there was another side where you had food crises especially concerning the interior regions: in Sidi Bouzid, Kasserine and Gafsa. Despite their richness on the level of natural resources and agricultural resources, [these cities] did poorly: they were marginalized in infrastructural terms, in the means that the state provided them in covering the needs of inhabitants concerning education – and this is a fundamental need – media, health networks, networks of water purification, and other things. (TU5)

Given these premises, interviewees often mentioned a broad dissatisfaction with the lack of achievement in terms of social rights, as "citizens don't want to have inflation: they want to eat and have a good salary. It's the economic and social rights that are most important for them. So the one who is fighting for [these things] is the one who is on their side" (TU4). Democracy was then perceived as a way to implement freedom, but also justice. In the words of an activist, democracy will fail if it "doesn't touch society and poor people ... [then] there will be no democracy. Just words" (TU4). Frustration is therefore high as no improvement is seen in the socioeconomic situation of the country. A widespread perception is in fact that:

The economic and social state of affairs has not changed a bit: still the same social state of affairs, the same type of distribution of benefits, the same kind of national strategy in Tunisia, the same dependencies, even the [state financial] budget of 2014, in its specificities. They just took over the budget of Ben Ali. We saw it, we compared it. For us, it was the main reason behind the uprising ... injustice and poverty and absence of dignity. To stop all this, they wanted a dignified country and respectful society. But these things have not been achieved yet ... there are politicians that go to the stage and they say we had a revolution of dignity, not for bread. ... But the issue of dignity is linked to social justice, which in turn is linked to social equality. ... The revolution for instance, it demanded work, freedom and national dignity. It was one of the most important slogans. But the constitution does not say anything about the right to work. So marginalization continues. (TU5)

The post-transition governments are therefore considered, in terms of social justice, as bad as ever. Referring to the power sharing among the main three parties, a unionist activist said:

they promised some similar things as Ben Ali. Even in the electoral campaign, they promised to create jobs for 400,000 citizens, that they would realize the goals of the revolution, and to fight corruption: "we will do this, and this and this." But they did not realize anything of what they promised. And the main proof of this is that the protests were continuing during the Troyka government. The central slogan of the revolution was "Work, Freedom, National Dignity." The [government] was failing on this, even more so than [was the case during] the previous period. Because, the Troyka, what did they do? the Ben Ali regime returned, but in an improved version. Concerning employment, the Troyka government was assigning jobs to relatives, and members from their party. ... There was similar corruption, with the same old logic but in a new shape. ... In reality nothing changed. Second, the Troyka government, the first thing they did was to keep the same social and economic policies of the Ben Ali government ... raising prices and the cost of living. What will increase [in the end] is unemployment and poverty rates. Social justice is gone. (TU11)

Even today, unaddressed socioeconomic inequalities are perceived as motives for protests. So, a union representative predicted,

You just need a spark. There are no [specific] tools, not at the economic level nor at the social one, for these governments to seriously address problems that exist in the periphery, or those concerning general issues. And when there were movements [about these problems] then people started to listen. ... These movements were under the auspices of the UGTT, or there were movements that were organized by the Union for the Relatives of Martyrs or by the unemployed. Then you have movements that were organized by the students. And then there are spontaneous movements. People mobilize spontaneously around a specific demand. (TU5)

Also among the youth, social issues kept its momentum as major claims for protestors. According to a student activist,

The protests were continuing on a daily basis, especially among students. Their financial state of affairs and social situation did not change at all [after the revolution]. From their [point of view] it might seem that the revolution has not entered the universities at all. There are no reforms in grants, not in educational organization, not to strengthen the departments of the universities ... the same situation now, today. ... What was Ennahda's approach? To sell things ... to neglect the public sector. (TU11)

Indeed, activists lamented the lack of achievements on social issues, as no step forward is perceived with the new regime. "What we didn't achieve? – said a socialist member – social equality. It is something that is so hard to achieve: it takes time. But there are no signs forward, that in the future there will be something better" (TU12). Frustration developed with the impression that what people got was much less than what they had asked for: "Claiming things, not getting anything in return ... you have the feeling that things are changing, but eventually no: it is more or less the same thing" (TU6). In this regard, the foreign lending programs are blamed for failing to solve the socioeconomic problems, as "They are the ones that are directing the government of Mehdi Jomaa. The World Bank is the one that directs this government through its dictations. It's like I give you a coffee, but then you have to do this and this. They did this with Ben Ali. And as they did with him, they now have the same intentions. They specialize on public institutions, on foreign resources" (TU5). The impression is indeed that, with the economic crisis, "people were demanding things and politicians were debating other things. So there was a rupture between the people and the politicians. I think at that point people started losing hope" (TU6), as, if "from 17th of December to 14th January and even after, people were demanding social justice, work and everything. Then just before the elections and all the debates started to talk about the Islamic state and religion and everything" (TU6). Rising dissatisfaction with the economic situation contributes to politicized frames and economic protest, given that the

economy is going down, because no one, none of the governments is trying to find solutions. We have been talking about polygamy. ... It is so funny: people are hungry and we are talking about polygamy. ... Life here is more and more expensive. The rate of unemployment went up, instead of going down. ... People see that they are demonstrating for nothing. We are here on the streets, and there is no result. (TU8)

Nevertheless, the assessment of the developments in Tunisia remains somewhat more optimistic than in Egypt. As a secularist young activist said, "I think it is a process. We did things, we missed others, and we still have the time. I am an optimist" (TU6). There is in fact still hope in the sense that the process will take a positive turn as, in the words of another young activist, "we are having a training. And one day, I don't know when, [laughs] things will change" (TU8).

Concluding, in both countries, social rights were considered as a fundamental claim of those who mobilized for democracy, which the new groups in power did not address.

CONCLUDING REMARKS

Eventful protests appeared in the CEE region to have produced higher quality democracy than did participated pacts. Egypt and Tunisia are both cases of eventful democratization but with much lower democratic quality in terms of civil, political, and social rights than in the CEE countries. Legalization and legitimation mechanisms of citizenship rights have been weak and discontinuous. More in general, the analysis of the achievements in terms of development of the democratization process of the new regimes testifies to relevant cross-area differences – so much so that while Egypt is increasingly considered as a failed case of democratization, with a transition from a hybrid to another hybrid regime, Tunisia seems the only successful case in the region, after the wave of mobilization for democracy in 2011 had raised hopes for a new wave of democratization.

From the point of view of civic rights, in both countries mobilization for democracy led to an increase in autonomous civil society organizations, as well as in their plurality in terms of issues covered, organizational forms, and cultural leanings. While criticism of the inauthenticity of some civil society organizations and selectivity by donors emerged here as well, there were several narratives stressing the empowering capacity of the "revolutionary" moments on the creation of a lively civil society, among others on gender issues, women's rights, social equality, and the like. The quality of the legislation on civil rights and freedoms still appears low, however – particularly in Egypt. In addition, in both countries, but more strongly in Egypt, brutal state repression is still addressed to a civil society, sharply divided between secular and religious groups, the Left, and the conservatives.

Similarly, from the point of view of political rights, the achieved quality is low – even lower in Egypt than in Tunisia. In particular, political institutions are perceived as still very distant from the people, more in continuity with the old regime than representing the revolution in its claims. In fact, more explicitly than in the CEE areas, activists express the widespread belief that they still need to be in the street in order to push for those changes – with, in Tunisia, but less so in Egypt, the impression of having been often effective in doing so. Fundamental differences between Tunisia and Egypt emerge in the constitutional process, its timing, and its outcomes. While in Tunisia, the claims of the secular forces of a constitution before the parliamentary elections had facilitated a more consensual (or at least pragmatic) process, in Egypt the choice to go for elections first complicated the constitutional process, which was characterized by continuous tensions not only between Islamists and secularists but also between the parliament, the president, the military, and the judiciary. The result was a low-quality constitution that was an amended version of the old one. It maintained a quite exclusive representative system and a recognition of Sharia, as well as a powerful military, in a process that ended in a military coup d'état.

Finally, the situation in terms of social rights was perceived as not at all improved by the changes. Different from the CEE countries, which saw a move from real socialism to neoliberalism with deterioration of several social rights, during the Arab Spring, the protest had addressed capitalism as well as dictatorship. More explicitly than in Eastern Europe, the claims had indeed been for justice and dignity, after decades of neoliberalist policies, perceived as a breaking of the social pact under which the first nationalist leaders had governed after the victories against colonialism. In the face of growing inequalities and unemployment, as well as corruption, under conditionalities imposed by international financial institutions, the social struggles had converged and been fueled by the activists' strong disappointment in the lack of advancement on social rights.

The lower quality of democracy in Egypt than in Tunisia can be explained, at least in part, by the dynamics of the transition, particularly the relationship inside the coalition that mobilized against the authoritarian regimes as well as the position the different actors acquired during the regimes' installation. In Egypt, the failure of the transition to democracy could in fact be linked to the ambivalent participation of the MB during the first days of the protest, which did not allow for the building of a revolutionary legitimacy (Ketchely forthcoming). Lack of reciprocal trust brought about the failure of any attempt at compromise, with the MB choosing to ally with the military against the protestors. In Egypt even more than in Tunisia, the rapidity of the changes did not allow for a gradual and consensual building of strategies for civil, political, and social change, instead leaving open spaces for alliances between some moderates of the regime and some moderates in the protest not for, but against, democracy. In turn, institutional evolutions tended to confirm the belief that the power was in the street, often with spirals of emulative and competitive types of protests.

During the contentious months and years that followed the ousting of the dictators, the contingent need to read each other's behavior based on loose hints rather than structured expectations also gave strong emotional and cognitive impact to some specific eventful protests – for example, on Muhammad Mahmud Street, where the MB was accused of standing by the army that had not only killed many protestors, but also showed maximum disrespect in their disposal of the bodies. Besides protests, institutional events, such as the constitutional referendum on March 18, had long-lasting polarizing effects.

Where Did the Revolution Go? Some Conclusions

In this volume, I singled out some mechanisms that convey the effects of social movements' participation in regime transition on some democratic qualities of the ensuing regime. Departing from the puzzling observation that social movements tend to disappear from our radar after the troubling events that bring about a new regime are over, I have addressed two connected questions: how does demobilization happen? And what are the effects of the mobilization in terms of the democratic qualities of the ensuing regime? In doing so, I built my theoretical model in consideration of the relational dynamics embedded in the interactions of contentious actors before, during, and after the regime change, although without overlooking the importance of long-lasting structures or of the contingent choices of some relevant actors. In this sense, I tried to build upon theoretical reflections and empirical knowledge already accumulated in the cognate fields of research on democratization, revolution, and social movements.

In sum, the research aimed at making the following contributions. First of all, it took up a puzzle – Where did the revolution go? – that has not been previously addressed in such a systematic and broadly comparative way within a comparative perspective and based on empirical fieldwork. Second, I have read democratization through the lenses of social movement studies, which is a very rare exercise in the literature in both fields. The cognitive, affective, and relational mechanisms I single out have not been much covered in the democratization literature (which focused either at the macro level, or on elites, or just assumed rational individuals). Third, while research on transitions had pointed at the resurgence of party politics and the decline of movement politics, my research provides a more nuanced analysis, not only by singling out various mechanisms (including but not limited to co-optation) but also by looking at ways in which civil society and social movements remain important in the new regimes. I also believe there is added value in the analysis of emotions and time intensification – which, while building upon existing work, introduces original elements connected with the "eventful" approach – as well as in the analysis of activists' conceptions of democracy, which I contrast with the liberal version. My message indeed is not that the revolution is gone, but rather that it has complex paths of resilience. Also new is the attempt at analyzing specific developments of civil, political, and social rights in relation to social movements (and their activists' perceptions). Last but not least, while memories of those times do exist, there has been no comparative research project that uses in-depth, oral history interviews with activists. These testimonies have high added value per se, presenting a point of view that had not been much considered in previous analysis. In this concluding chapter, I want to link the empirical evidence presented in the rest of the volume's research in the three mentioned fields, singling out some innovative results.

A main assumption considered in this research is that social movements in times of transition contribute to produce critical junctures that transform relations in broad fields of action. In eventful democratization, resources, visions, and opportunities are constructed and reconstructed in the intense days of the transitions through mechanisms of resource mobilization, collective framing, and appropriation of opportunities (McAdam, Tarrow, and Tilly 2001; della Porta 2014a). In these moments, big changes are expected and promoted by actions that challenge existing structures. In the changed context that follows those big changes, those very contentious actors who had appeared as so visible and audible seem to vanish. Nevertheless, the empowering effects of those transformative effects tend to be resilient.

These assumptions build upon social movement studies that have linked movements' outcomes to the intense moments of protest that create changes in action (Fantasia 1988). These studies suggest some mechanisms through which movements created long-term transformations. At the micro level, deep-rooted consequences of participation in social movements have been identified in research on the biographical consequences of activism, which has confirmed the persistent effects of socialization in social movements in terms of individuals' values and norms (Downton and Wehr 1997). Not only are former activists likely to remobilize at each new wave of protest, but their choices in lifestyles as well as in work and politics tend to remain coherent with those first intense experiences of social and political commitment (for a review, see Giugni 2004).

Second, eventful protests create mobilizing structures that tend to persist beyond each wave of protest. At the meso level, movements are expected to have effects on each other. First and foremost, movements inherit some frames from their predecessors (Whittier 2004). In cycles of protest, spin-off movements follow early risers, adapting ideas to their own preferences and changing circumstances. Moreover, social movements do influence each other – both within and without social movement families, domestically and transnationally – through direct and indirect channels of communication. Tactical and cultural repertoires spread from one movement to the next, fueled by perceptions of their success but also as a sign of identification (ibid., 539; also della Porta and Mattoni 2014).

Third, success is linked to movements' capacity to build new identities or cultures of solidarity, but also to their influence on cultural changes, community building, and personal politics (Polletta and Jasper 2001). What one movement conquers in terms of recognition for particular issues and for protest rights affects the options of its successors. In this way, social movements produce long-lasting normative changes (Gamson 1990). Social movements are in fact brokers of new ideas, which develop in small intellectual circles and then spread to the society at large (Rochon 1998). Memories of transformative events contribute to the consolidation of collective identities as they are transmitted by veterans of previous waves of protest, or by consolidated narratives (Zamponi 2015). Movements function indeed as mnemonic entrepreneurs, promoting their own visions of the past (Bernhard and Kubik 2014a).

Vis-à-vis traditional research on the effects of social movements, which has mainly addressed gradual changes as explained by structural conditions, the focus on large and rapid changes is innovative. Rather than incremental changes in "normal" time, I have in this research addressed broad and rapid transformations. In fact, it was during the search for inspiration on understanding big changes that I looked at the social science literature on democratization and revolution, which considered breaks rather than continuity. While studies of democratization have focused on elites' strategic choices, research on revolution has taken into account the mobilization from below – seeing the masses not as an aggregate of individuals but as an incarnation of the people. As we will see in these concluding remarks, in different ways, studies of democratization and revolutions as critical junctures help us in understanding deep and sudden change. Studies of democratization do so by pointing at the presence of some moments in which old structures break down, and with them old orders. This leaves space to people's choice, strengthening the impact of individual agency, especially of elites' norms and preferences. Studies on revolutions (violent and nonviolent) also bridged attention to structural conditions with attention to the capacity of the masses to defy resilient power (Selbin 2010).

By referring to social movement, democratization, and revolution studies, my aim has been to develop a theoretical model that is constructed, reflecting on the importance of the cognitive understanding of a context; emergent, in considering the transformative capacity of emotionally intense events; and dynamic, in its attention to the relational nature of contentious politics.

ON THE RISE AND FALL OF MOBILIZATION

In addressing the first question concerning the apparent disappearance of street politics after transitions, I have looked not only at the rise and fall of protest actions but also at the developments of the cognitive, affective, and relational mechanisms that accompany them. Without taking a methodologically individualist turn, I have analyzed some micro-dynamics of mobilization and demobilization. Rather than considering protest events as an aggregate of acts, to be counted on the assumption that the larger and more disruptive the event, the more threatening for the incumbents, I was mainly interested in the ways in which participation transformed the cognitive, emotional, and relational world of those who mobilized, as it is through these changes that the rapid increase in commitment first, and its transformation later on, can be understood.

Some useful reflections on how to address these questions came from democratization studies that – although they often underestimated the role of social movements in favor of elites – did take into account the strategic choices of the different actors, linking them to their preferences and interests. The inconsistent results of the structuralist approaches first used to explain democratization have in fact moved scholars away from the search for general theory aimed at discovering identical conditions for the presence or absence of democratic regimes, and toward instead an analysis of "a variety of actors with different followings, preferences, calculations, resources, and time horizons" (Karl 1990, 5–6). My research has taken up from democratization studies this interest in strategic choices in times of uncertainty. While democratization studies focused on elites, however, my interest has been in the ways in which contentious actors perceive and feel their environments – a topic sometimes addressed by research on revolutions. In addressing these issues, I referred to research on individual strategic choices, which singles out how a change in the type of game implies a transformed availability to express existing preferences. I however took some distance from this interpretation, by suggesting that what really changes is much more than preferences – rather, those very identities that precede preferences are built.

Additionally, rather than focusing on individual choices, I was interested in collective dynamics. While much research on social movement outcomes has singled out some endogenous as well as exogenous characteristics of protest (their opportunities, size, disruptiveness, and so on) as causes of their capacity to affect policies, I have looked inside contentious events, paying attention to the ways in which they affected the collective visions of politics and democracy, the widespread emotional moods, and the forms of relations within a process of time intensification. After the ascending phase, I also looked at the descending one and at how conceptions of politics and democracy, emotional climate, and relational forms changed again in the new context.

At the *cognitive* level, I singled out mechanisms of framing in action and framing consolidation. Conceptions and practices of democracy evolved in the different moments of the democratization process. In all of our cases, the democratic opposition to the authoritarian regimes criticized liberal conceptions of democracy, instead building upon participatory and deliberative visions, which understood politics as grassroots and consensual (see also Olivo 2001; Joppke 1995). These conceptions developed in action as protest events (such as the Monday prayers) worked as schools of democracy, encouraging dialogue and participation. Local roundtables and citizens' committees grew as free spaces in which citizens were socialized into politics, conceived as the realm of self-government by an autonomous civic society. Equality, inclusiveness, and transparency became widespread participatory values, bridged as they were with deliberative values, including consensual decision making.

The achievements in terms of liberal, representative democracy tended then to disappoint many activists who saw elections, parliaments, and parties as neither participatory nor deliberative. Especially in cases of eventful democratization, after experiences with horizontal forms of participation, activists became disillusioned about delegation, party politics, and electoral accountability – all the more so in the German Democratic

Republic (GDR), where the impression was widespread of an (far from democratic) annexation to the West. While participatory and deliberative conceptions and practices of democracy were apt to survive repression and motivate dissenters, they were less capable of sustaining mobilization after the transition to liberal democracy, which focused on elected elites, denying the political role of the civil society. Supporters of an idealistic conception of politics, activists were often demotivated to participate in the institutions that instead followed a (minimalistic) representative vision, for which they had neither experience nor taste.

At the *emotional* level, I singled out mechanisms of emotional prefiguration and emotional adaptation. Social movements are embedded in passionate politics – and this is all the more true in events that aim at, and bring about, broad changes. Considering in particular "high order" emotions (Jasper 1997; Reed 2004, 668), I looked at the sequences of moral outrage, hope, and frustration that accompanied mobilization for democracy. Cycles of protest also implied intense emotional work, which accompanied the different steps of mobilization, developing in context (Goodwin, Jasper, and Polletta 2001), linked as they were to cognitive assessment of the context, opportunities, and constraints. At the beginning of the mobilization, activists experimented with ways of overcoming fear, transforming it into anger. Moral shocks were produced by episodes of repression that were considered as grossly inappropriate and unjust. Mobilization grew together with the shift from negative emotions linked to repression as traumas fueled what Whittier (2001) defined as emotions of resistance, such as outrage and hope. Emotionally intense, especially in eventful democratization, the peak of the mobilization testifies to a spread of sentiments of hope and happiness, which contributed to the rapid increase in participation in protest – considered no longer as a cost, but rather as a pleasurable, exciting experience. Emotions were rooted at the collective level in the changing relations produced by protests, with an empowerment of the citizens.

As exciting moments cannot last forever, intense emotions then tended to be reabsorbed, with the emergence of exhaustion, often linked to frustration based on a negative (or only partially positive) assessment of the outcomes of the protest. The spreading of moral shocks required a broad identification with those who protested and were repressed. Various devices were used to generate positive feelings for collective action (della Porta and Giugni 2009), up to a pride in rebelling against injustice (Wood 2004). This did not imply, however, that emotions could easily be manipulated, as they were embedded in collective moods, rooted in the widespread appreciation of the situation: with "revolutionary catharsis" but also disenchantment. Linked to the assessment of the achievements of mobilization, emotional feelings remained more positive where activists could claim, at least for a while, to have kept ownership of the revolution – as was the case in Czechoslovakia. As Bernhard and Kubik (2014a, 2014c) recently noted, the type of transition also had an effect on the collective memory of the past. The cases of participated pacts were characterized by a fractured memory of the past: in Hungary, Fidesz worked as a mnemonic warrior (Seleny 2014), promoting a single and unidirectional type of memory; similar attempts were also made from the center-right in Poland (Bernhard and Kubik 2014b). In the Czech Republic, instead, with a plural vision of the past dominating at the institutional level, the memory of 1989 was revived from below, with civil society organizations claiming an ownership of the Velvet Revolution, against the claimed betrayal by those in power (O'Dwyer 2014), while 1989 tended to be absorbed in a shared collective memory of the past in Germany (Art 2014).

At the *relational* level, I suggested the working of mechanisms of time intensification and time normalization. The type of time perception is a relevant dimension of the broader context, as different times not only are perceived in different ways but also work differently in terms of the relational forms they harbor. As times of change are, above all, times in which routines no longer work and, additionally, assessments are made in a hurry, actors' preferences change, new identities are formed, and old assumptions then become outdated. As the power of structures declines, the role of contingency increases, allowing changes to happen. Events are underdetermined (O'Donnell and Schmitter 1986, 363; Di Palma 1990). Once again, perceptions of time are also changing: after an intensification linked to the perception of time as extraordinary comes a normalization, as new structures acquire consistency and stabilize.

These mechanisms contribute to explaining the dynamics of mobilization and demobilization in moments of large and rapid changes. At the micro level, sudden growths in collective mobilization have been analyzed through threshold models, according to which an increase in the number of participants decreases the risk of repression (as it is more difficult for police to deal with large demonstrations, but there are also fewer people available to participate in repression). Meanwhile, there is an increase in the expected advantages of mobilization (in terms of self-esteem, reputation among peers, and ensuing expectations of success). The size of protest is seen here as a signal of the spread of dissatisfaction with the regime – a way through which private preferences become public (Kuran 1991), thus starting an information cascade. Given the awareness of reciprocal inter-dependency, the unthinkable is therefore suddenly transformed into the unavoidable (Biggs 2003). At the meso level, the perception of intense time transforms relations as it brings about the emergence of new actors, with the formation of new identities. Not only is there a shift in the ability to express preferences in public but the very preferences and interests are transformed in action as previously established collective entities dissolve, routines are broken, and power vacuums are filled by the activation of new groups. As strategizing can no longer be based upon routine, by making predictions unreliable, contingency opens up new possibilities, which then develop in action. The very speed of the changes breaks those fixed identities on which the assessment of long-term benefits is usually made (Pizzorno 1993), as well as jeopardizing the chances for collecting information, reflecting, and deliberating, making them resemble betting. We also noted, however, that intense times do not last forever; rather, they are bound to dissolve as new institutions are created, identities estab-lished, and routines formed. After a break, a reconsolidation follows, while actors split in their assessment of aims and strategies.

ON FURTHER PROTEST AND DEMOCRATIC QUALITIES

The decline of mobilization does not imply, however, that the collec-tive energies invested in the struggle are lost. On its second main question, the long-term effects of social movements during democratic transitions, the research has in fact pointed at some mechanisms that link the paths of contention during the episodes of mobilization for democracy to some qualities of the ensuing regime, in terms of civil, political, and social rights. The comparison of Poland's participated pact and the eventful democratization in Czechoslovakia and then in the Czech Republic confirm many insights coming from previous com-parisons of Spain and Portugal (Fishman 2011, 2013; Fernandes 2013) as well as other countries (Schmitter 1984; Casper and Taylor 1996; Munck and Leff 1997). In eventful democratization, in fact, specific mechanisms fuel some democratic qualities in terms of both formal institutional characteristics and cultural practices. In this perspective, I have in particular looked at what I defined as legitimation (as cultural acceptance) and legalization (as legal norms) of civil, political, and social rights. By adding other two cases in the Central Eastern Europe (CEE) region (Hungary and the former GDR), as well as two cases during the Arab Spring (Egypt and Tunisia), my aim was not just to confirm the robustness of some causal mechanisms, but also to reflect on how they are affected by varying contexts. Once again, I do not pretend to build a parsimonious and powerful explanation, including all main causes, but rather to reflect on the ways in which causal mechanisms work, keeping in mind the complex relations that are constructed in action.

In terms of *civil rights*, the importance of social movements in the falling of the regime gives legitimacy to civil society and protest, which are recognized in laws that are more inclusive in terms of rights to political participation and more supportive of their associations. As democracy is meant to rest on civil rights, these are of course expected to increase with episodes of democratization. With growing freedoms, civil society organizations are supposed to bloom, in different fields, given symbolic and material support for them. This proved true in our CEE cases, to an even larger degree in the cases of eventful democratization. In particular, when former activists entered governments and administrations, this translated into inclusive attitudes and behaviors toward various types of associations, which were seen as in continuity with the logic of the civil society that had mobilized for democracy. Formal and informal associations, thus, increased in number.

However, much literature has converged in indicating some weakness in civil society, which in CEE countries has been defined as generally poor in terms of members and volunteers as well as trust in public opinion, dependent on donors, rather bureaucratic in its structures, and tame in its discourses, sometimes instrumentalized by party interests. If this is in part true, I also noted that the civil society did not disappear or homogenously institutionalize, instead undergoing a process of normalization. Informal groups remained very present, often bridging lobbying, protest, service provision, and information campaigns. Many organizations and activists kept being loyal to a conception of civil society as self-organization of the citizens, rooted in their experience of struggles for democracy along with support for horizontal forms of organizations. Social movement action and organizational strategies continued to be present also after the democratic transformations, even if in various degrees and forms in different areas and on different issues – with environmental groups emerging as quite successful, and unions (at least initially) as the most unsuccessful. Cross-country variation in the CEE area is linked to the legacy of the struggles for democracy, with eventful democratization (especially) reflected in a larger degree of institutional inclusiveness, with more freedom for and more resources invested in the civil society as well as in more institutional channels and a more supportive general culture for civic participation.

Also in terms of *political rights*, social movement pressure is usually reflected in a more inclusive political system, where actors from below find their way, both outside and inside political institutions. If elections and electorally accountable institutions are considered as the sign of a successful mobilization for democracy, they are often resented by the activists as biased against their ideas of politics and democracy. Privileging delegation to political parties, electoral politics is in fact perceived as disempowering the civil society. This is all the more the case as parties and elections fail to achieve strong legitimacy in the public opinion, given broad patronage ties and low loyalties. While adapting to a new situation proves difficult, powerful external actors are perceived as appropriating the results of the mobilization. Skepticism prevails, in fact, in the assessment of institutional politics as corrupted, especially when evaluated against the high moral standards of the former dissidents. However, there is also a process of co-optation of former dissidents into political institutions – both in elective bodies and in public administration – bringing with them some of the revolutionary claims and frames. Cross-nationally different, however, are the movements' capacities to affect the changes – with a larger capacity to enter institutions in cases of eventful democratization. The political inclusivity is here higher, given the (institutional and cultural) imprinting by those civic society activists who entered political and administrative institutions in large numbers.

In terms of *social rights*, in eventful democratization the broader range of social groups that can claim ownership of the revolution is reflected in a larger investment in social protections. Social rights are an important part of democratic quality, even if, as mentioned, they do not necessarily improve with democracy. In double transitions to liberal democracy and to free market, social rights are indeed perceived as declining, as specific forms of neoliberalism tend to dominate (Bohle and Greskovits 2013), with only some residual social protection. The deceptive "software" of the 1989 transitions (Offe 1996), steered under neoliberal hegemony, was reflected in the implementation of economic policies of privatization, liberalization, and deregulation that brought about unemployment, poverty, and insecurity. Dissatisfaction ensued in the public opinion at large but also, and even more, among former activists who had in general combined a quest for freedom with a quest for social justice, rooted in the traditions of a dissidence, which under "real socialism" had developed on the Left. Indeed, the new economic regime met bitter criticism by former activists, being considered as particularly immoral. If their high expectations for change can explain some of the frustration, activists also point at direct experiences with social injustice, perceived as violating deep-rooted values. While similarly assessing the socioeconomic developments in their countries as frustrating, however, activists varied in their degree of disappointment, with Czech activists mentioning a better welfare system as an effect of their empowerment in the first few years after transition.

In sum, as in the Iberian Peninsula (Fishman 2011; 2013), also in the CEE area a higher level of participation of social movements during the transition was reflected in their higher influence during consolidation. Several indicators but also perceptions of some qualities of democracy therefore emerged as stronger in Czechoslovakia than in Poland, but protests were more frequent in the latter than in the former. [These results confirm the assumption that, as episodes of democratization represent critical junctures that affect democratic development and therefore the quality of citizenship rights, the degree and forms of social movements' participation in them have long-lasting consequences. Even if the activists who had led the mobilization for democracy no longer enjoyed public visibility, even if their organizations were dissolved, and even if they were therefore disappointed by the results of their action, we can still find sustained and long-lasting traces of their existence.]

This does not mean that openness is reflected in more contentions, but rather in the different ways in which civic, political, and social rights are fostered. Not only did better qualities of democracy produce less dissatisfaction but, even more, eventful democratization built multiple institutions for channeling and addressing demands coming from the civil society. Protest after the authoritarian regime collapsed was influenced by the paths of transition, although not in a linear manner (see also Ekiert and Kubik 1998). In addition to the magnitude of protests, however, I noted that cyclical dynamics could be found in the eventful paths, showing a growth in generality and in politicization during the ascending phase and moderating forms and depoliticizing claims in the declining phase. My analysis also confirmed that the more rapid the economic transformation, the more protests grew, given higher suffering and consequent higher dissatisfaction (see also ibid.). Protests were also more disruptive in those cases – even if they generally tended to remain more moderate in the CEE experience than in Latin America, where neoliberalism had been most brutal (Greskovits 1998, 56). While transition literature tends to predict a decline in mobilization in the street after democratization, we noted in the comparison of East Germany with West Germany a normalization of protest, with Easterners remaining quite contentious. When protests temporarily declined, some radicalization happened in the declining phase, as those who were dissatisfied returned from time to time to protest, using traditional as well as new forms. In the CEE area, it is especially on social rights that protest tends to peak periodically, while other social movements also built their organizational resources.

As is usually the case in comparative analysis, additional cases help to specify theoretical assumptions. Hungary, as a second case of participated pacts, tended to confirm what we had learned for Poland. Similar in their development as eventful democratization, the GDR and Czechoslovakia/ Czech Republic varied, however, in the effects mobilizations from below had on the qualities of democracy. Besides the capacity to mobilize, the opportunity to occupy political institutions at the moment of the installation of the new regime appeared to have played a most influential role. In fact, while in Czechoslovakia and then in the Czech Republic some of the most visible activists of the mobilization for democracy formed the first democratic government, in the former GDR activists stigmatized what they saw as colonization by the West. Even in unified Germany, however, former dissidents were well represented in local and state politics as well as in civil society.

COMPARING 1989 AND 2011

Comparing eventful democratization with participated pacts, I have shown that the mobilization of social movements during transitions as well as their positions during the installation of the regime influence the qualities of the ensuing regime. When looking at civil, political, and social rights, a main observation was that they do not always vary together, nor do they follow the traditional path from civic to political and then to social. Rather, their interaction is messy, as for instance in the CEE area, where civil and political rights were perceived as increasing during democratic consolidation, while social rights were seen at times as declining. Similarly in the Arab Spring, civil and political rights improved, even if temporarily, but social rights did not. With the first elections installing Islamist governments, in the Middle East and North Africa (MENA) region political rights are even perceived as potentially jeopardizing civil rights.

Both of the episodes of eventful democratization in the MENA region have shown significant differences in comparison with Czechoslovakia and GDR. First and foremost, protest did decline, but keeping an intense pace and disruptive forms. In particular, following mechanisms of emulation and competition, protestors frequently filled the streets and the squares, claiming social, civil, and political rights. The competition was especially intense on the very ownership of the revolution, with frequent escalations of fights between police and protestors, but also movements and countermovements. What kept people in the street, even if with short waves of mobilization and demobilization, was indeed the very low perceived quality of the achievements of the new regime.

As in the CEE area, protest also increased in numbers and strength in the MENA region – initially slowly, but accelerating its pace in 2011. The mobilization here involved a more plural spectrum of actors: from human rights associations to ultras' clubs, religious groups and labor unions, but also movements of precarious workers and poor people's resistance. These groups had started to loosely coordinate before the upheaval, with some better structuration in Tunisia than in Egypt; contacts then increased quickly at the peak of the protests, with people meeting in free spaces such as Tahrir or Kasbah. This happened especially as social groups multiplied their demands through mechanisms of social emulation, of competition between former oppositional groups (especially progressive secularists and religious fundamentalists), and of escalations between protestors and police, and movements and countermovements.

Again as in the CEE region, also in the MENA region conceptions of democracy developed in action, promoting horizontal, rhizomatic structures that, during the dictatorship, were apt to increase commitment and reduce the effects of repression. While participation and deliberation were considered as important democratic qualities that countered the minimalistic vision of electoral democracy (which activists defined as "boxocracy"), here, as in the CEE region, this conception of democracy seemed difficult to adapt to the changed context after the ousting of the dictator. Given the electoralization of politics but also quite heavy repression (especially, but not only, in Egypt), internal divisions increased with high frustration about the results of the revolution. Low-quality elections and weak parties were considered as not only corrupt and corrupting but also as incapable of addressing the need for dialogue in divided societies. Rooted in action, however, horizontal conceptions of democracy contributed to fueling the struggle for ownership of the revolution, which was indeed in several post-revolutionary moments of fundamental importance in pushing for citizens' rights.

Emotional dynamics were similar to those in the CEE region, changing in type and intensity throughout the cycle. The very use of the term "revolution" testifies to the intense feelings of hope, pride, and happiness, as well as a robust sense of empowerment that transformed fear into outrage. Against expectations for ambitious change, the uncertainty and even the failures of the transition produced bitter disappointment, while brutal episodes of repression continued to fuel moral shocks and related mobilization.

The perception of time also changed, with a fast acceleration into extraordinary time at the peak of the protests. After the ousting of the dictators, however, a slowing down into more normal (although not totally normal) times ensued. The conception of the revolution shifted from a focus on a revolutionary *moment* into attention to the revolution as a *process*, in which the upheavals were perceived as important catalysts for further struggles.

The importance of the dynamics of installation also emerges from the analysis of Tunisia and Egypt, which helps in specifying the conditions under which eventful democratization succeeds or fails. Indeed, in both cases the mobilization from below was huge and certainly eventful in its capacity to trigger mechanisms of resource mobilization, collective framing, and appropriation of opportunities. Even if the massive protests of the few weeks preceding the ousting of the dictators had an impressive capacity to change structures and relations, the civil, political, and social qualities of the new regimes remained rather low in comparison with the CEE region – even more so in Egypt than in Tunisia.

From the point of view of *civic rights*, there was after transitions a growth of an autonomous and plural civil society, which often took on social movement characteristics. Notwithstanding a low quality of legislation on civil society and citizens' freedom (especially but not only in Egypt), the activists' narratives stressed the persistent empowering effects of the upheavals. Even in the new regimes, state repression however hits hard upon a civil society, which emerges (especially in Egypt) as bitterly divided between secular and religious groups, and progressive and conservative forces. If this division was perceived at times as disappointing, however, it also fueled new mobilizations.

From the point of view of *political rights*, as well, the democratic qualities achieved in the new regimes are, at best, low – especially in Egypt. Not only are political institutions perceived as extremely distant from the people but the continuity with the old regime is often stressed. Taking to the street is in fact still considered by activists as the one and only means to influence the political decision making. While in Tunisia the constitutional process was tense but eventually open to consensual solutions, in Egypt the democratic development was jeopardized by strong conflicts, not only between secularists and Islamists but also between the military and both actors, as well as with the judiciary and the presidency. This resulted in a low-quality constitution, and eventually a military coup d'état.

Finally, the quality of *social rights* did not improve. Poverty, unemployment, social insecurity, and inequality remained high, much more so than in the CEE region where previous welfare showed some resilience. Notwithstanding strong claims for social justice, the old neoliberal policies survived – as activists lamented – unchanged, with only some limited capacities of the Tunisian unions to exert pressure on the coalition in power. Given high levels of social inequalities and lack of employment, social struggles indeed continued after the ousting of the dictators in order to reappropriate the revolution and change society.

In sum, comparing 1989 and 2011, democratization appeared as much more difficult in the latter than in the former period, and even more challenging in Egypt, where rather than a transition from authoritarianism to democracy there was a transition from one hybrid regime to another hybrid regime. How to explain these cross-area and infra-area differences? Addressing this question, we can broaden the reflections on the context in which causal mechanisms thrive.

A first set of answers could be given if we go back to some of the structuralist explanations developed in the three sets of literature we have analyzed. The research results in fact indicated the role of critical junctures, but also the need to locate them within longer time dynamics that also influence the power struggle after transition. As mentioned, democratization studies as well as studies on revolutions have considered the cultural and social aspects of modernization as relevant preconditions – with modernization favoring democratization, and dysfunctions in modernization processes fueling revolutions instead. Moreover, both of them, as well as social movement studies, paid attention to political conditions, particularly the characteristics of the state.

While socioeconomic conditions were certainly more backward in the MENA region (where dependent economies had developed in the periphery) than in the "second world" CEE, they appeared especially influential when looking at their interaction with the political environment.

Consolidation is said to be easier when there is a simple transition: that is, a straightforward process of political democratization, rather than one that overlaps with a transition in the relations between state and market and/or the (re)emergence of issues related to state sovereignty (Linz and Stepan 1996). The comparison of the CEE and MENA regions, however, does not unequivocally confirm these expectations. Rather, it seems that what counts more in our cases is the claims of those who mobilized, particularly the fact that social questions were at the core of protests in Egypt and Tunisia, producing a strong backlash in a situation in which the power of the previous regime's elites was challenged but not destroyed – as indicated, specifically, by the persistent power of the military in Egypt but also the electoral success of politicians from former regimes in both Egypt and Tunisia.

Literature on revolutions also suggests that different types of revolutions might be expected to have different potential outcomes. According to Goldstone (2014; also 2001), social revolutions, aiming at social redistributions in favor of the previously excluded, raise more counterrevolutionary pressures and therefore require a centralized, authoritarian state to consolidate gains in order to avoid civil war. In the Arab Spring, if some of the middle class had supported claims for freedom, the economic elites were clearly resilient and effective in their struggle against protestors' claims for more social rights. The continuous tensions after the ousting of the dictators confirm "a further lesson from history," which is that "we should not expect most revolutions to suddenly create stable democracies. Revolutions create new dilemmas and unleash new struggles for power" (ibid., 133).

A more class-issue-oriented mobilization in the MENA than in the CEE region is reflected in the narrative of the events. Looking at the power of narratives for social change developing in revolutions, Selbin distinguished a civilizing (Western) notion that is at the basis of a democratizing narrative within a liberal, elites' tale, in which "central tropes here are of civilization, progress, democratization and, somewhat ironically, nobility" (2010, 96).[1] This has been the narrative of the upheavals during the so called third wave of democratization, which have been located in continuity with the American, French, and British revolutions as well as 1848, as springtimes of the people. In contrast, social revolutions (from Russia to Cuba) are narrated as class-based revolts that aim at

---

[1] As he noted, "People choose to resist and rebel and people make revolutions. They do this in no small measure by making stories, stories that also make them people" (ibid., 185).

transforming the world (ibid., 120), a story of mobilization of small heroic groups, but also of masses of the oppressed. While the former narrative characterized 1989, the latter narrative was present in the visions of the 2011 events.

Social and cultural differences meant higher degrees of repression before, during, and after the upheavals, with persistent mobilization, as repression further justified resistance – yet another piece of evidence that "popularly supported insurgencies have persisted when and where the armed forces of weak states have committed massive and indiscriminate abuses against civilians suspected of collaborating with the insurgents" (Goodwin 2001, 33). During the Arab Spring, mobilizations indeed developed around the many martyrs of the revolution and the period afterward (Olesen 2015). Already, the narrative around Bouazizi and Saeed had resonated with a broader culture of "virtual reliquaries," as "the *combination* of culturally resonant, historically constructed narratives that speak to a shared heritage and desire to resolve past moral, ethical, and nationalist crises, along with the wide communication opportunities provided by social media, produced the necessary bonds, as well as the shared political imaginary, amongst protesters and disaffected citizens to transform them into revolutionaries" (Halverson, Ruston, and Trethewy 2013, 313). Later on, as well, other martyrs were created as the police killed many among those who protested against the new (supposedly democratic) governments, often asking for justice for previous martyrs.

State violence thus fueled violent protest, with also potentially risky conditions for democratization. In fact, according to the literature on nonviolent resistance, rulers are undermined if citizens devise strategies of noncooperation by refusing to acknowledge the rulers as legitimate, contesting the mentality/ideology of obedience, failing to obey laws and cooperate with the regime, withdrawing material resources by refusing to use their skills to support the regime activities, or undermining the state's sanctioning power (in particular, by persuading soldiers and police to side with the citizens) (Nepstad 2011). Nonviolence, predominant in our CEE cases, is seen as more likely to produce democratic development; violence – which often exploded during the Arab Spring – could indeed have favored escalation.

Explanations for the more disruptive nature of the Arab Spring versus the CEE experience could also be linked to the tensions between radicals and moderates that were stressed, in a mirrored way, by literature on democratization to invoke moderation and by literature on revolutions to stress the need for a radical turn, at least in some specific sociopolitical regimes (Wood 2000, but also Moore 1966). Focusing on a sort of natural history of revolutions, several scholars have in particular distinguished specific steps after the taking of power by the revolutionaries: conflicts within the revolutionary coalition, with initial victories by moderates, followed by radicalization with seizing of power by the radical wing once moderates fail. Radicals then impose coercion and military leaders often emerge, until moderates again win control (see Goldstone 1991). Playing on ideological purity and moderates' failure, the radical wing often displaces the moderate one; however, with time, processes of institutionalization bring about either the defeat or the moderation of the (once) radical groups, although with the possibility of new radical attempts at returning to revolutionary purity.

If we compare Egypt with Tunisia, the democratic qualities (or lack thereof) of the post-2011 regimes can certainly be linked to institutional conditions – first and foremost the power of the military – but also to some characteristics of the civil society. In particular, the lower quality of democracy in Egypt than in Tunisia is related to the (different) degree of mistrust between secularist and Islamic groups, which pushed the MB to actively attempt to demobilize the protest through a tense alliance with the military. In 2011, higher repression in Egypt was in fact combined with the military in power and the presence of multiple social cleavages as well as intra-institutional struggles – with a particular conflict between the MB and secularist activists, the MB and the military, the military and secularist activists – eventually also involving the judiciary, the presidency, and the parliament.

The research also supported some other insights from social movement studies that have stressed the importance of cultural changes. The main outcome of the Arab Spring seems to be, in fact, primarily cultural: citizens' empowerment as readiness to take the street, defying fear of repression, but also acquiring a consciousness of one's own rights. These feelings are strengthened when experiences confirm that the struggles pay off – even that victory is more easily achieved by mobilizing in the street than by engaging in electoral politics.

Finally, international interventions were, in general, criticized as inconsistent during the Arab Spring. Reference is often made to the then secretary of state Hillary Clinton voicing support for the regime, declaring that "the Egyptian government is stable and is looking for ways to respond to the legitimate needs and interests of the Egyptian people" – only a few days later confirming that "there is no discussion as of this time about cutting off any aid" (cit. in Holmes 2012, 409). Thus, activists complained that international support went in Egypt to the SCAF and/or the MB, as "despite their preaching for democracy, we found that the Western community is silent now" (EGY2).

Concluding, the cases of Tunisia and Egypt testified to the difficulties in neatly defining successes and failures, positive and negative cases, as sometimes found in literature on both democratization and revolution. As social movement studies have often demonstrated, the effects of protests are in fact complex to assess and always challenged, requiring constant mobilization, even if with different intensity and in different forms. In both countries, in fact, I noted a semantic shift in the meaning of the revolution: from a sudden break, to a long-lasting process. Similarly, far from being achieved in the moment of the first elections, democratization is perceived as a long-term endeavor.

Bibliography

Abbott, Andrew 1992. "From Causes to Events: Notes on Narrative Positivism," *Sociological Methods and Research* 20(24): 428–55.

Abbott, Andrew 2001. *Time Matters: On Theory and Method*. Chicago: University of Chicago Press.

Abdelrahman, Maha 2011. "The Transnational and the Local: Egyptian Activists and Transnational Protest Networks," *British Journal of Middle Eastern Studies* 38(3): 407–24.

Abdelrahman, Maha 2012. "A Hierarchy of Struggles? The Economic and the Political in Egypt's Revolution," *Review of African Political Economy* 39(134): 614–28.

Abdelrahman, Maha 2013. "In Praise of Organization: Egypt between Activism and Revolution," *Development and Change* 44(3): 569–85.

Abdul-Magad, Zeinab 2011. "The Army and the Economy in Egypt," *Jadaliyya*, www.jadaliyya.com/pages/index/3732/the-army-and-the-economy-in-egypt (accessed April 14, 2013).

Adely, Fida 2012. "The Emergence of a New Labor Movement in Jordan," *Middle East Report* 264: 34–7.

Agh, Attila 2013. "Progress Report of the New Member States. 20 Years of Social and Political Developments," *Budapest College of Communication and Business, Together for Europe Series* No.17.

Aksartova, Sada 2006. "Why NGOs? How American Donors Embrace Civil Society after the Cold War," *The International Journal of Non-for-Profit Law* 8(3): 15–20.

Al-Ali, Najda 2012. "Gendering the Arab Spring," *Middle East Journal of Culture and Communication* 5(1): 26–31.

Allahyari, Rebecca Anna 2001. "The Felt Politics of Charity: Serving the 'Ambassadors of God' and Saving the 'Sinking Classes,'" in Jeffrey Goodwin, James J. Jasper, and Francesca Polletta (eds.), *Passionate Politics. Emotions and Social Movements*. Chicago: University of Chicago Press, pp. 195–211.

Allal, Amin 2012. "Trajectoires 'révolutionnaires' en Tunisie. Processus de radicalizations politiques 2007–2011," *Revue Française de Science Politique* 62(5): 821–41.

Amin, Samir 2012. "The Arab Revolutions: A Year After," *Interface: A Journal for and about Social Movements* 4(1): 33–42.

Amnesty International 2012. *Year of Rebellion: The State of Human Rights in the Middle East and North Africa*. London: Amnesty International.

Anani, Khalil and Maszlee Malik 2013. "Pious Way to Politics: The Rise of Political Salafism in Post-Mubarak Egypt," *Digest of Middle East Politics* 22(1): 57–73.

Anderson, Jeremy 2013. "Intersecting Arcs of Mobilization: The Transnational Trajectories of Egyptian Dockers' Unions," *European Urban and Regional Studies* 20(1): 128–33.

Anderson, Leslie E. 2010. *Social Capital in Developing Democracies. Nicaragua and Argentina Compared*. Cambridge: Cambridge University Press.

Anderson, Lisa 2011. "Demystifying the Arab Spring: Parsing the Differences between Tunisia, Egypt, and Libya," *Foreign Affairs* 90(3): 2–7.

Angrist, Michelle P. 2013. "Understanding the Success of Mass Civic Protest in Tunisia," *Middle East Journal* 67(4): 547–64.

Anheier, Helmut K., Eckhard Priller, and Annette Zimmer 2000. "Civil Society in Transition: The East German Third Sector Ten Years after Unification," *East European Politics & Societies* 15(1): 139–56.

Anheier, Helmut and Wolfgang Seibel 1998. "The Nonprofit Sector and the Transformation of Societies: A Comparative Analysis of East German, Poland, and Hungary," in Walter W. Powell and Elisabeth S. Clemens (eds.), *Private Action and the Public Good*. New Haven and London: Yale University Press, pp. 177–91.

Arjomand, Said Amir 2013. "The Islam and Democracy Debate after 2011," *Constellations* 20(2): 297–311.

Arnstein, Sherry R. 1969. "A Ladder of Citizen Participation," *Journal of the American Institute of Planners* 35(4): 216–24.

Art, David 2014. "Making Room for November 9, 1989? The Fall of the Berliner Wall in German Politics and Memory," in Michael Bernhard and Jan Kubik (eds.), *Twenty Years after Communism: The Politics of Memory and Commemoration*. Oxford: Oxford University Press, pp. 195–212.

Awad, Ibrahim 2013. "Breaking Out of Authoritarianism: 18 Months of Political Transition in Egypt," *Constellation* 20(2): 275–92.

Ayeb, Habib 2011. "Social and Political Geography of the Tunisian Revolution," *Review of African Political Economy* 38(129): 467–79.

Ayoub, Phillip M. 2013. "Cooperative Transnationalism in Contemporary Europe: Europeanization and Political Opportunities for LGBT Mobilization in the European Union," *European Political Science Review* (EPSR) 5(2): 279–310.

Baker, Gideon 1999. "The Taming Idea of Civil Society," *Democratization* 6(3): 1–29.

Balan, Jorge and Elisabeth Jeilin 1980. "La structure sociale dans la biographie personelle," *Cahiers Internationaux de Sociologie* 69: 269–89.

Bamyeh, Mohammed 2012. "Anarchist Philosophy, Civic Traditions and the Culture of the Arab Revolutions," *Middle East Journal of Culture and Communication* 5(1): 32–41.

Barker, Colin 2001. "Fear, Laughter, and Collective Power: The Making of Solidarity at the Lenin Shipyard in Gdansk, Poland, August 1980," in Jeffrey Goodwin, James J. Jasper, and Francesca Polletta (eds.), *Passionate Politics. Emotions and Social Movements*. Chicago: University of Chicago Press, pp. 175–94.

Barkin, Kenneth D. 1976. "Autobiography and History," *Societas* 6: 83–108.

Bassiouni, M. Cherif 2016. "Egypt's Unfinished Revolution," in Adam Roberts, Michael J. Willis, Rory McCarthy, and Timothy Garton Ash (eds.), *Civil Resistance in the Arab Spring: Triumphs and Disasters*. Oxford: Oxford University Press, pp. 53–87.

Bayat, Asef 2012. "The 'Arab Street,'" in Jeannie Sowers and Chris Toensing (eds.), *The Journey to Tahrir: Revolution, Protest, and Social Change in Egypt*. London: Verso, pp. 73–84.

Bayat, Asef 2013. "The Arab Spring and Its Surprises," *Development and Change* 44(3): 587–601.

Beckmann, Andreas 1999. "From Puppet Master to Listless Puppet," *Central European Review* 1(25), www.ce-review.org/99/25/beckmann25.html.

Beichelt, Timm and Wolfgang Merkel 2014. "Democracy Promotion and Civil Society: Regime Types, Transition Modes and Effects," in Timm Beichelt, Irene Hahn-Fuhr, Frank Schimmelfennig, and Susann Worschech (eds.), *Civil Society and Democratic Promotion*. London: Palgrave, pp. 42–65.

Beinin, Joel 2011. "A Workers' Social Movement on the Margin of the Global Neoliberal Order, Egypt 2004–2009," in Joel Benin and Frédéric Vairel (eds.), *Social Movements, Mobilization and Contestation in the Middle East and North Africa*. Stanford, CA: Stanford University Press, pp. 181–201.

Beinin, Joel 2012. "Egyptian Workers and January 25: A Social Movement in Historical Context," *Social Research* 79(2): 323–50.

Beissinger, Mark R. 2002. *Nationalist Mobilization and the Collapse of the Soviet State*. Cambridge: Cambridge University Press.

Beissinger, Mark R. 2007. "Structure and Example in Modular Political Phenomena: The Diffusion of Bulldozer/Rose/Orange/Tulip Revolutions," *Perspectives on Politics* 5(2): 259–76.

Bellin, Eva 2004. "Why Have the Middle East and North Africa Remained so Singularly Resistant to Democratization," *Comparative Politics* 36(2): 139–58.

Bermeo, Nancy 1986. *The Revolution within the Revolution: Workers' Control in Rural Portugal*. Princeton, NJ: Princeton University Press.

Bermeo, Nancy 1990. "Rethinking Regime Change" (review article): "Transitions from Authoritarian Rule: Southern Europe" by Guillermo O'Donnell, Philippe C. Schmitter, and Laurence Whitehead; "Transitions from Authoritarian Rule: Latin America" by Guillermo O'Donnell, Philippe C. Schmitter, and Laurence Whitehead; "Transitions from Authoritarian Rule: Comparative Perspectives" by Guillermo O'Donnell, Philippe C. Schmitter, and Laurence Whitehead; "Transitions from Authoritarian Rule: Tentative

Conclusions about Uncertain Democracies," by Guillermo O'Donnell and Philippe C. Schmitter, *Comparative Politics*, 22(3): 359–77.

Bermeo, Nancy 1997. "Myths of Moderation: Confrontation and Conflict during Democratic Transition," *Comparative Politics* 29(2): 205–322.

Bernard-Maugiron, Nathalie 2011. "Egypt's Path to Transition: Democratic Challenges in the Constitution Reform Process," *Middle East Law and Governance* 3: 43–59.

Bernhagen, Patrick and Michael, Marsh 2007. "Voting and Protesting: Explaining Citizen Participation in Old and New European Democracies," *Democratization* 14(1): 44–72.

Bernhard, Michael 1996. "Civil Society after the First Transition: Dilemmas of Post-Communist Democratization in Poland and Beyond," *Communist and Post-Communist Studies* 29(3): 309–30.

Bernhard, Michael and Ekrem Karakoç 2007. "Civil Society and the Legacies of Dictatorship," *World Politics* 59(4): 539–67.

Bernhard, Michael and Jan Kubik 2014a. "A Theory of the Politics of Memory," in Michael Bernhard and Jan Kubik (eds.), *Twenty Years after Communism: The Politics of Memory and Commemoration*. Oxford: Oxford University Press, pp. 7–36.

Bernhard, Michael and Jan Kubik 2014b. "Round Table Discord: The Contested Memory of 1989 in Poland," in Michael Bernhard and Jan Kubik (eds.), *Twenty Years after Communism: The Politics of Memory and Commemoration*. Oxford: Oxford University Press, pp. 60–84.

Bernhard, Michael and Jan Kubik 2014c. "The Politics and Culture of Memory Regimes: A Comparative Analysis," in Michael Bernhard and Jan Kubik (eds.), *Twenty Years after Communism: The Politics of Memory and Commemoration*. Oxford: Oxford University Press, pp. 261–96.

Bertaux, Daniel 1980. "L'approche biographique: sa validité en sociologie, ses potentialités," *Cahiers internationaux de sociologie* 69: 198–225.

Biezen, Ingrid van 2003. *Political Parties in New Democracies: Party Organization in Southern and East-Central Europe*. Basingstoke: Palgrave Macmillan.

Biggs, Michael 2003. "Positive Feedback in Collective Mobilization: The American Strike Wave of 1886," *Theory and Society* 32(2): 217–54.

Biggs, Michael 2014. "Size Matters: The Perils of Counting Protest Events," working paper, Department of Sociology, University of Oxford.

Binnie, Jon and Christian Klesse 2013. "'Like a Bomb in the Gasoline Station': East-West Migration and Transnational Activism around Lesbian, Gay, Bisexual, Transgender and Queer Politics in Poland," *Journal of Ethnic & Migration Studies* 39(7): 1107–24.

Blades, Lisa 2008. "Authoritarian Elections and Elite Management: The Case of Egypt," Paper prepared for delivery at the Princeton University Conference on Dictatorships, April.

Bohle, Dorothee and Béla Greskovits 2013. *Capitalist Diversity on Europe's Periphery*. Ithaca: Cornell University Press.

Bohle, Dorothee and Gisela Neunhoeffer 2009. "Why Is There No Third Way? The Role of Neoliberal Ideology, Networks and Think Tanks in Combating

Market Socialism and Shaping Transformation in Politics," in Dariusz Aleksandrowicz, Stefanie Sonntag, and Jan Wielgohs (eds.), *The Polish Solidarity Movement in Retrospective.* Berlin: GSFP, pp. 66–87.

Bosi, Lorenzo and Herbert Reiter 2014. "Historical Methodologies: Archival Research and Oral History in Social Movement Research," in Donatella della Porta (ed.), *Methodological Practices in Social Movement Research.* Oxford: Oxford University Press, pp. 117–44.

Botcheva, Liliana 1996. "Focus and Effectiveness of Environmental Activism in Eastern Europe: A Comparative Study of Environmental Movements in Bulgaria, Hungary, Slovakia, and Romania," *Journal of Environment and Development* 5(3): 292–308.

Boughzala, Mongi and Mohamed Tlili Hamdi 2014. "Promoting Inclusive Growth in Arab Countries: Rural and Regional Development and Inequality in Tunisia." Global Economy & Development Working Paper 71. Washington: Brookings.

Bou Nassif, Hicham 2012. "Why the Egyptian Army Didn't Shoot," *Middle East Report* 42: 625.

Branco, Rui and Tiago Fernandes 2013. "Civil Society and the Quality of Democracy: Portugal 1974–2010," paper presented at the Council for European Studies (CES) Conference, June 25.

Branford, Sue and Jan Rocha 2002. *Cutting the Wire: The Story of the Landless Movement in Brazil.* London: Latin American Bureau.

Bratton, Michael and Nicolas van de Walle 1997. *Democratic Experiments in Africa: Regime Transition in Comparative Perspective.* Cambridge: Cambridge University Press.

Brooks, Risa 2013. "Abandoned at the Palace: Why the Tunisian Military Defected from the Ben Ali Regime in January 2011," *Journal of Strategic Studies* 36(2): 205–20.

Bruszt, Laszlo, Nauro F. Campos, Jan Fidrmuc, and Gerald Roland 2010. "Civil Society, Institutional Change and the Politics of reform, United Nations University," working paper, World Institute for Development Economics Research.

Buhle, Paul 1981. "Radicalism: The Oral History Contribution," *International Journal of Oral History* 2(3): 205–15.

Bunce, Valerie and Sharon Wolchik 2010. "Transnational Networks, Diffusion Dynamics and Electoral Change in Post-Communist World," in Rebecca Kolins Givan, Kenneth M. Roberts, and Sarah A. Soule (eds.), *The Diffusion of Social Movements.* Cambridge: Cambridge University Press, pp. 140–62.

Burdick, John 2004. *Legacies of Liberation: The Progressive Catholic Church in Brazil at the Start of a New Millennium.* Aldershot: Ashgate.

Calhoun, Craig 2001. "Putting Emotions in Their Place," in Jeffrey Goodwin, James J. Jasper, and Francesca Polletta (eds.), *Passionate Politics. Emotions and Social Movements.* Chicago: University of Chicago Press, pp. 45–58.

Capoccia, Giovanni and Kelemen, R. Daniel 2007. "The Study of Critical Junctures: Theory, Narrative and Counterfactuals in Historical Institutionalism," *World Politics* 59(3): 341–69.

Carmin, JoAnn and Barbara Hicks 2002. "International Triggering Events, Transnational Networks, and the Development of Czech and Polish Environmental Movements," *Mobilization: An International Quarterly* 7(3): 305–24.

Carmin, JoAnn and Stacy D. VanDeveer 2004. "Enlarging EU Environments: Central and Eastern Europe from Transition to Accession," *Environmental Politics* 13(1): 3–24.

Casper, Gretchen and Michelle M. Taylor 1996. *Negotiating Democracy: Transitions from Authoritarian Rule.* Pittsburgh: University of Pittsburgh Press.

Castles, Francis G., 2006. "The Welfare State and Democracy: On the Development of Social Security in Southern Europe, 1960–90," in Richard Gunther, P. Nikiforos Diamandouros, and Dimitri A. Sotiropoulos (eds.), *Democracy and the State in the New Southern Europe.* Oxford: Oxford University Press, pp. 42–86.

Cavatorta, Francesco 2007. "More than Repression: The Significance of Divide et Impera in the Middle East and North Africa – The Case of Morocco," *Journal of Contemporary African Studies* 25(2): 187–203.

Chalcraft, John 2012. "Horizontalism in the Egyptian Revolutionary Process," *Middle East Report* 262: 6–11.

Chenoweth, Erica and Maria J. Stephan 2011. *Why Civil Resistance Works: The Strategic Logic of Nonviolent Conflict.* New York: Columbia University Press.

Chomiak, Laryssa 2011. "The Making of a Revolution in Tunisia." *Middle East Law and Governance* 3(1–2): 68–83.

Chong, Dennis 1991. *Collective Action and the Civil Rights Movement.* Chicago: University of Chicago Press.

Císar, Ondrej 2010. "Externally Sponsored Contentions: The Channeling of Environmental Organizations in the Czech Republic after Communism," *Environmental Politics* 19(5): 736–55.

Císar, Ondrej 2014. "At the Ballot Boxes or in the Streets: Contentious Politics in the Visegrad Group and Its Europeanization," paper presented at the Cosmos Talks, European University Institute, Florence, September.

Císar, Ondrej and Martin Koubek 2012. "Include 'Em All? Culture, Politics and a Local Hardcore/Punk Scene in the Czech Republic," *Poetics: Journal of Empirical Research on Culture, the Media and the Arts* 40(1): 1–21.

Císar, Ondrej and Kateřina Vráblíková 2010. "The Europeanization of Social Movements in the Czech Republic: The EU and Local Women's Groups," *Communist and Post-Communist Studies* 43(2): 209–19.

Clark, Culpepper E., Michael J. Hyde, and Eva M. McMahan 1980. "Communication in Oral History Interview: Investigating Problems of Interpreting Oral Data," *International Journal of Oral History* 1: 28–40.

Cohen, Jean 1989. "Deliberation and Democratic Legitimacy," in Alan Hamlin and Philip Pettit (eds.), *The Good Polity.* Oxford: Blackwell, pp. 17–34.

Collier, Ruth Berins 1999. *Paths toward Democracy: The Working Class and Elites in Western Europe and South America.* New York: Cambridge University Press.

Collier, Ruth Berins and Sebastián Mazzuca 2008. "Does History Repeat?," in Robert E. Goodwin and Charles Tilly (eds.), *The Oxford Handbook of Contextual Political Analysis*. Oxford: Oxford University Press, pp. 472–89.

Collins, Randall 2001. "Social Movements and the Focus of Emotional Attention," in Jeffrey Goodwin, James J. Jasper, and Francesca Polletta (eds.), *Passionate Politics: Emotions and Social Movements*. Chicago: University of Chicago Press, pp. 27–44.

Collombier, Virginie 2007. "The Internal Stakes of the 2005 Elections: The Struggle for Influence in Egypt's National Democratic Party," *Middle East Journal* 61(1): 95–111.

Corrigall-Brown, Catherine and Mabel Ho 2013. "Life History Research and Social Movements," in David Snow, Donatella della Porta, Bert Klandermans, and Doug McAdam (eds.), *Blackwell Encyclopaedia of Social Movements*. Oxford: Blackwell, pp. 678–81.

Crowley, Stephen 2004. "Explaining Labor Weakness in Post-Communist Europe: Historical Legacies and Comparative Perspective," *East European Politics and Societies* 18(3): 394–429.

Crowley, Stephen and David Ost 2001. *Workers after Workers States: Labour and Politics in Post-communist Eastern Europe*. Lanham: Rowman and Littlefield.

Dale, Gareth 2005. *Popular Protest in East Germany, 1945–1989*. London: Routledge.

Davis, Steven M. 2004. "Building a Movement from Scratch: Environmental Groups in the Czech Republic," *Social Science Journal* 41(3): 375–92.

della Porta, Donatella 1992. "Life Histories in the Analysis of Social Movement Activists," in Mario Diani and Ron Eyerman (eds.), *Studying Collective Action*. London: Sage, pp. 168–93.

della Porta, Donatella 1995. *Social Movements, Political Violence and the State*. Cambridge/New York: Cambridge University Press.

della Porta, Donatella 2004. "Multiple Belongings, Tolerant Identities and the Construction of Another Politics: Between the European Social Forum and the Local Social Fora," in Donatella della Porta and Sidney Tarrow (eds.), *Transnational Protest and Global Activism*. Lanham: Rowman and Littlefield, pp. 175–202.

della Porta, Donatella 2008. "Comparative Analysis: Case-Oriented versus Variable-Oriented Research," in D. della Porta and Michael Keating (eds.), *Approaches and Methodologies in the Social Sciences*. Cambridge: Cambridge University Press, pp. 198–222.

della Porta, Donatella (ed.) 2009a. *Another Europe. Conceptions and Practices of Democracy in the European Social Forums*. London: Routledge.

della Porta, Donatella (ed.) 2009b. *Democracy in Social Movements*. Houndsmill: Palgrave.

della Porta, Donatella 2013a. *Can Democracy Be Saved? Participation, Deliberation and Social Movements*. Oxford: Polity.

della Porta, Donatella 2013b. *Clandestine Political Violence*. Cambridge: Cambridge University Press.

della Porta, Donatella 2014a. *Mobilizing for Democracy*. Oxford: Oxford University Press.

della Porta, Donatella 2014b. "Life Histories," in Donatella della Porta (ed.), *Methodological Practices in Social Movement Research*. Oxford: Oxford University Press, pp. 262–88.

della Porta, Donatella 2015. *Social Movements in Times of Austerity. Bringing Capitalism Back into the Study of Protest*. Cambridge: Cambridge University Press.

della Porta, Donatella and Marco Giugni 2009. "Emotions in Movements," in Donatella della Porta and Dieter Rucht (eds.), *Meeting Democracy*. Cambridge: Cambridge University Press, pp. 123–51.

della Porta, Donatella and Alice Mattoni (eds.) 2014. *Spreading Protest*. Essex: ECPR Press.

della Porta, Donatella and Dieter Rucht (eds.) 2013. *Meeting Democracy: Power and Deliberation in Global Justice Movements*. Cambridge: Cambridge University Press.

della Porta, Donatella and Sidney Tarrow 1987. "Unwanted Children: Political Violence and the Cycle of Protest in Italy, 1966–1973," *European Journal of Political Research* 14: 607–32.

de Nardo, James 1985. *Power in Numbers: The Political Strategy of Protest and Rebellion*. Princeton, NJ: Princeton University Press.

Diamond, Larry and Juan Linz 1989. "Introduction: Politics, Society and Democracy in Latin America," in Larry Diamond, Juan Linz, and Seymour Martin Lipset (eds.), *Democracy in Developing Countries: Latin America*. Boulder, CO: Lynne Rienner, pp. 1–70.

di Palma, Giuseppe 1990. *To Craft Democracy*. Berkeley: University of California Press.

di Palma, Giuseppe 1991. "Legitimation from the Top to Civil Society: Politico-Cultural Change in Eastern Europe," *World Politics* 44(1): 49–80.

Dobbin, Frank 2001. "The Business of Social Movements," in Jeffrey Goodwin, James J. Jasper, and Francesca Polletta (eds.), *Passionate Politics: Emotions and Social Movements*. Chicago: University of Chicago Press, pp. 74–82.

Donker, Teije H. 2012. "Tunisia amid Surprise: Change and Continuity," working paper, http://cosmos.eui.eu/Documents/Publications/WorkingPapers/2012WP12COSMOS.pdf.

Dorsey, James 2012. "Pitched Battles: The Role of Ultra Soccer Fans in the Arab Spring," *Mobilization* 17(4): 411–18.

Downton, James and Paul, Wehr 1997. *The Persistent Activist: How Peace Commitment Develops and Survives*. Boulder, CO: Westview Press.

Dryzek, John S. 2000. *Deliberative Democracy and Beyond: Liberals, Critics, Contestations*. New York: Oxford University Press.

Dryzek, John S. and Leslie Holmes 2000. "The Real World of Civic Republicanism: Making Democracy Work in Poland and the Czech Republic," *Europe-Asia Studies* 52(6): 1043–68.

Duboc, Marie 2011. "Egyptian Leftwing Intellectuals' Activism from the Margins," in Joel Benin and Frédéric Vairel (eds.), *Social Movements, Mobilization and Contestation in the Middle East and North Africa*. Stanford, CA: Stanford University Press, pp. 61–79.

Durac, Vincent 2013. "Protest Movements and Political Change: An Analysis of the 'Arab Uprisings' of 2011," *Journal of Contemporary African Affairs* 31(2): 175–93.

Eckstein, Susan (ed.) 2001. *Power and Popular Protest: Latin American Social Movements* (2nd edn.). Berkeley: University of California Press.

Einhorn, Barbara 1991. "Where Have All the Women Gone? Women and the Women's Movement in East Central Europe," *Feminist Review* 39: 16–36.

Ekiert, Grzegorz 1996. *The State against Society: Political Crises and Their Aftermath in East Central Europe*. Princeton, NJ: Princeton University Press.

Ekiert, Grzegorz and Roberto Foa 2011. "Civil Society Weakness in Post Communist Europe: A Preliminary Assessment," *Carlo Alberto Notebooks* No. 198.

Ekiert, Grzegorz and Jan Kubik 1998. "Contentious Politics in New Democracies: East Germany, Hungary, Poland, and Slovakia, 1989–1994," *World Politics* 50: 547–81.

Ekiert, Grzegorz and Jan Kubik 1999. *Rebellious Civil Society: Popular Protest and Democratic Consolidation in Poland, 1989–1993*. Ann Arbor: Michigan University Press.

El-Chazli, Youssef 2012. "Sur les sentiers de la revolution," *Revue francaise de science politique* 62(5): 843–65.

El-Chazli, Youssef and Chaymaa Hassabo 2013. "Sociohistoire d'un processus révolutionnaire," in Amin Allal and Thomas Pierret (eds.), *Au coeur des révoltes arabes. Devenir révolutionnaires*. Paris: Armand Colin, pp. 185–212.

El-Ghobashy, Mona 2011. "The Praxis of the Egyptian Revolution," *Middle East Report* 258: 2–13.

Elsadda, Hoda 2011. "Women's Rights Activism in Post-Jan25 Egypt: Combating the Shadow of the First Lady Syndrome in the Arab World," *Middle East Law and Governance* 3: 84–93.

Elster, Jon 1997. "The Market and the Forum: Three Varieties of Political Theory," in James Bohman and William Rehg (eds.), *Deliberative Democracy: Essays on Reason and Politics*. Cambridge: MIT Press, pp. 3–33.

Elster, Jon 1998. "Deliberation and Constitution Making," in Jon Elster (ed.), *Deliberative Democracy*. Cambridge: Cambridge University Press, pp. 97–122.

Eyal, Gil 2003. *The Origins of Postcommunist Elites: From Prague Spring to the Breakup of Czechoslovakia*. Minneapolis: University of Minnesota Press.

Fabian, Katalin 2006. "Against Domestic Violence: The Interaction of Global Networks with Local Activism in Central Europe," *Contemporary Studies in Economic and Financial Analysis* 88: 111–52.

Fagan, Adam 2005. "Taking Stock of Civil-Society Development in Post-Communist Europe: Evidence from the Czech Republic," *Democratization* 12(4): 528–47.

Fagin, Adam 2000. "Environmental Protest in the Czech Republic: Three Stages of Post-Communist Development," *Czech Sociological Review* 8(2): 139–56.

Fantasia, Rick 1988. *Cultures of Solidarity: Consciousness, Action, and Contemporary American Workers*. Berkeley/Los Angeles: University of California Press.

Faris, David E. 1980. "Narrative Form and Oral History: Some Problems and Possibilities," *International Journal of Oral History* 1(3): 159–80.

Fehr, Helmut 1995. "Von der Dissidenz zum Gegen-Elite. Ein Vergleich der politische Opposition in Polen, der Tschechoslowakei, Ungarn und der DDR (1976 bis 1989)," in Ulrike Poppe, Rainer Eckert, and Ilko-Sascha Kowlczuk (eds.), *Zwischen Selbstbehauptung und Anpassung. Formen des Widerstandes und der Opposition in der DDR*. Berlin: Ch.Links Verlag, pp. 301–34.

Ferber, Marianne A. and Phyllis Hutton Raabe 2003. "Women in the Czech Republic: Feminism, Czech Style," *International Journal of Politics, Culture, and Society* 16(3): 407–30.

Fernandes, Tiago 2013. "Rethinking Pathways to Democracy: Civil Society in Portugal and Spain, 1960s–2000s," paper presented in Luso-American Foundation for Development (FLAD) Workshop Inequality, *Civil Society and Democracy: Cross-Regional Comparisons, 1970s–2000s*, Lisbon, June 7–8.

Ferree, Myra Marx 1995. "Patriarchies and Feminisms: The Two Women's Movements of Post-Unification Germany," *Social Politics: International Studies in Gender, State and Society* 2(1): 10–24.

Fillieule, Olivier and Manuel Jiménez 2003. "Appendix A: The Methodology of Protest Event Analysis and the Media Politics of Reporting Environmental Protest Events," in Christopher Rootes (ed.), *Environmental Protest in Western Europe*. Oxford: Oxford University Press, pp. 258–79.

Fish, Stephen and Jason Wittenberg 2009. "Failed Democratization," in Christian W. Haerpfer, Patrick Bernhagen, Ronald F. Inglehart, and Christian Welzel (eds.), *Democratization*. Oxford: Oxford University Press, pp. 249–67.

Fishman, Robert M. 1990. *Working Class Organizations and the Return of Democracy in Spain*. Ithaca, NY: Cornell University Press.

Fishman, Robert M. 2011. "Democratic Practice after the Revolution: The Case of Portugal and Beyond," *Politics and Society* 39(2): 233–67.

Fishman, Robert M. 2013. "How Civil Society Matters in Democratization: Theorizing the Iberian Divergence," paper presented at the Conference of CES, Amsterdam, June 25–27.

Fishman, Robert M. and Omar Lizardo 2013. "How Macro-Historical Change Shapes Cultural Taste: Legacies of Democratization in Spain and Portugal," *American Sociological Review* 78: 213–39.

Flam, Helena 2001. *Pink, Purple, Green: Women's, Religious, Environmental and Gay/Lesbian Movements in Central Europe Today*. New York: Columbia University Press.

Foran, John 2005. *Taking Power: On the Origins of Third World Revolutions*. Cambridge: Cambridge University Press.

Foran, John and Jeff Goodwin 1993. "Revolutionary Outcomes in Iran and Nicaragua: Coalition Fragmentation, War, and the Limits of Social Transformation," *Theory and Society* 22(2): 209–47.

Francisco, Ronald A. 2005. "The Dictator's Dilemma," in Christian Davenport, Hank Johnston, and Carol Mueller (eds.), *Repression and Mobilization*. Minneapolis: University of Minnesota Press.

Fric, Pavol, Rochdi Goulli, Stefan Toepler, and Lester M. Salamon 1999. "The Czech Republic," in Lester M. Salamon, Helmut K. Anheier,

Regina List, Stefan Toepler, Wojciech S. Sokolowski, and Associates (eds.), *Global Civil Society: Dimensions of the Nonprofit Sector*. Baltimore, MD: Johns Hopkins Center for Civil Society Studies, pp. 285–303.

Gabor, Tomasz 2013. *Explaining Divergence in Patterns of Inter-organisational Collaboration among Non-profit Organisations in Poland and Czech Republic*, PhD Thesis, European University Institute, Department of Political and Social Sciences.

Gagnon, Nicole 1980. "Données autobiographiques et praxis culturelle," *Cahiers internationaux de sociologie* 27(69): 291–304.

Gamson, William 1990. *The Strategy of Social Protest* (2nd edn.). Belmont, CA: Wadsworth.

Garcia, Marisol and Neovi Karakatsanis 2006. "Social Policy, Democracy and Citizenship in Southern Europe," in Richard Gunther, P. Nikiforos Diamandouros, and Dimitri A. Sotiropoulos (eds.), *Democracy and the State in the New Southern Europe*. Oxford: OUP, pp. 87–137.

Gardawski, Juliusz, Adam Mrozowicki, and Jan Czarzasty 2012. "History and Current Developments of Trade Unionism in Poland," *Warsaw Forum of Economic Sociology* 5(3): 9–50.

Gasior-Niemiec, Anna 2010. "Lost in the System? Civil Society and Regional Development Policy in Poland," *Acta Politica* 45(1–2): 90–111.

Gerbaudo, Paolo 2012. *Tweets and the Streets*. London: Verso.

Giugni, Marco 2004. *Social Protest and Policy Change*. Lanham: Rowman and Littlefield.

Giugni, Marco, Lorenzo Bosi, and Katrin Uba 2013. *Outcomes of Social Movements and Protest Activities*. In Oxford Bibliographies Online: Political Science, www.oxfordbibliographies.com/view/document/obo-9780199756223/obo-9780199756223-0037.xml.

Glenn, John K. 2001. *Framing Democracy: Civil Society and Civic Movements in Eastern Europe*. Stanford, CA: Stanford University Press.

Glenn, John K. 2003. "Contentious Politics and Democratization: Comparing the Impact of Social Movements on the Fall of Communism in Eastern Europe," *Political Studies* 51: 103–20.

Gliński, Piotr 1994. "Environmentalism among Polish Youth: A Maturing Social Movement?," *Communist and Post-Communist Studies* 27(2): 145–59.

Gliński, Piotr 2006. "The Third Sector in Poland. Dilemmas of Development," in Dariusz Gawin and Piotr Gliński (eds.), *Civil Society in the Making*. Warsaw: IFis Publishers, pp. 265–88.

Goldstone, Jack 1991. *Revolution and Rebellion in the Early Modern World*. Berkeley/Los Angeles: University of California Press.

Goldstone, Jack 2001. "Toward a Fourth Generation of Revolutionary Theory," *Annual Review of Political Science* 4: 139–87.

Goldstone, Jack 2014. *Revolutions: A Very Short Introduction*. Oxford: Oxford University Press.

Goldstone, Jack and Charles Tilly 2001. "Threat (and Opportunity): Popular Action and State Response in the Dynamics of Contentious Action," in Ron Aminzade (ed.), *Silence and Voice in the Study of Contentious Politics*. Cambridge: Cambridge University Press.

Goodwin, James, James J. Jasper and Francesca Polletta (eds.) 2001. *Passionate Politics: Emotions and Social Movements*. Chicago: University of Chicago Press.

Goodwin, Jeff 2001. *No Other Way Out: States and Revolutionary Movements, 1945–1991*. Cambridge: Cambridge University Press.

Goodwin, Jeff and Steven Pfaff 2001. "Emotion Work in High-Risk Social Movements: Managing Fear in the U.S. and East German Civil Rights Movements," in Jeffrey Goodwin, James J. Jasper, and Francesca Polletta (eds.), *Passionate Politics: Emotions and Social Movements*. Chicago: University of Chicago Press, pp. 282–302.

Gould, Deborah 2001. "Rock the Boat, Don't Rock the Boat, Baby: Ambivalence and the Emergence of Militant AIDS activism," in Jeffrey Goodwin, James J. Jasper, and Francesca Polletta (eds.), *Passionate Politics: Emotions and Social Movements*, Chicago: University of Chicago Press, pp. 135–57.

Gould, Deborah 2004. "Passionate Political Processes: Bringing Emotions Back into the Study of Social Movements," in Jeff Goodwin and James J. Jasper (eds.), *Rethinking Social Movements*. Lanham, MD: Rowman and Littlefield, pp. 155–75.

Granovetter, Mark 1978. "Threshold Models of Collective Behavior," *American Journal of Sociology* 83: 1420–43.

Green, Andrew T. 1999. "Nonprofits and Democratic Development: Lessons from the Czech Republic," *Voluntas: International Journal of Voluntary and Nonprofit Organizations* 10(3): 217–35.

Grele, Ronald J. 1975. "A Surmisable Variety: Interdisciplinarity and Oral Testimony," *American Quarterly* 27(3): 275–95.

Grele, Ronald J. 1979. "Listen to Their Voices: Two Case Studies of the Interpretation of Oral History Interview," *Oral History* 7(1): 33–42.

Greskovits, Béla 1998. *The Political Economy of Protest and Patience: East European and Latin American Transformations Compared*. Budapest: Central European University Press.

Gruszczynska, Anna. 2009. "Sowing the Seeds of Solidarity in Public Space: Case Study of the Poznan March of Equality." *Sexualities* 12(3): 312–33.

Grzymala-Busse, Anna M. 2002. *Redeeming the Communist Past: The Regeneration of Communist Parties in East Central Europe*. Cambridge: Cambridge University Press.

Habermas, Juergen 1981. *Theorie des kommunikativen Handeln*. Frankfurt am Main: Suhrkamp.

Habermas, Juergen 1996. *Between Facts and Norms: Contribution to a Discursive Theory of Law and Democracy*. Cambridge: MIT Press.

Hahn-Fuhr, Irene and Susann Worschech 2014. "External Democracy Promotion and Divided Civil Society – The Missing Link," in Timm Beichelt, Irene Hahn-Fuhr, Frank Schimmelfennig, and Susann Worschech (eds.), *Civil Society and Democratic Promotion*. London: Palgrave, pp. 11–41.

Hall, Peter 2003. "Aligning Ontology and Methodology in Comparative Research," in James Mahoney and Dietrich Rueschemeyer (eds.), *Comparative Historical Research*. Cambridge: Cambridge University Press, pp. 373–404.

Halverson, Jeffry, Scott Ruston and Angela Trethewy 2013. "Mediated Martyrs of the Arab Spring: New Media, Civil Religion, and Narrative in Tunisia and Egypt," *Journal of Communication* 63(2): 312–32.

Hankiss, Agnes 1981. "Ontologies of the Self: On the Mythological Rearranging of One's Life History," in Daniel Bertaux (ed.), *Biography and Society. The Life History Approach to Social Sciences*. London: Sage, pp. 203–09.

Harper, Krista 1999. "Citizens or Consumers?: Environmentalism and the Public Sphere in Postsocialist Hungary," *Radical History Review* 74: 96–111.

Hasanen, Mohammed M. and Mohammed Nuruzzaman 2013. "The New Egypt: Socio-Political Dynamics and the Prospects of the Transition to Democracy," *Mediterranean Journal of the Social Sciences* 4(4): 137–45.

Hassabo, Chaymaa 2005. "Gamal Moubarak au centre du pouvoir: une succession achevée?," *Centre d'Études et de Documentation Économiques, Juridiques et Sociales*, www.cedej.org.eg/article.php3?id_article=258&var_recherche=hassabo.

Haufe, Gerda and Karl Bruckmeier (eds.) 1993. *Die Bürgerbewegungen in der DDR und in den ostdeutschen Bundesländern*. Opladen: Westdeutscher Verlag.

Hedstrom, Peter and Peter Bearman 2009. "What Is Analytic Sociology All About? An Introductory Essay," in Peter Hedstrom and Peter Bearman (eds.), *The Oxford Handbook of Analytic Sociology*. Oxford: Oxford University Press, pp. 3–15.

Henderson, Sarah L. 2002. "Selling Civil Society: Western Aids and the Nongovernmental Organization Sector in Russia," *Comparative Political Studies* 35: 139–67.

Herrschel, Tassilo and Timothy Forsyth 2001. "Constructing a New Understanding of the Environment under Post-Socialism," *Environment and Planning A* 33(4): 573–88.

Hibou, Béatrice 2011. *The Force of Obedience: The Political Economy of Repression in Tunisia*. Oxford: Polity Press.

Hicks, Barbara 2004. "Setting Agendas and Shaping Activism: EU Influence on Central and Eastern European Environmental Movements," *Environmental Politics* 13(1): 216–33.

Higley, John and Richard Gunther 1992. *Elites and Democratic Consolidation in Latin America and Southern Europe*. New York: Cambridge University Press.

Hipsher, Patricia L. 1998. "Democratic Transitions and Social Movements Outcomes: The Chilean Shantytown Dwellers' Movement in Comparative Perspective," in Mario Giugni, Doug McAdam, and Charles Tilly (eds.), *From Contention to Democracy*. Lanham, MD: Rowman and Littlefield, pp. 149–67.

Hirschman, Albert 1982. *Shifting Involvements: Private Interests and Public Action*. Princeton, NJ: Princeton University Press.

Holmes, Amy Austin 2012. "There Are Weeks When Decades Happen: Structure and Strategy in the Egyptian Revolution," *Mobilization* 17(4): 391–410.

Holzhacker, Ronald 2012. "National and Transnational Strategies of LGBT Civil Society Organizations in Different Political Environments: Modes of Interaction in Western and Eastern Europe for Equality," *Comparative European Politics* 10(1): 23–47.

Huntington, Samuel 1991. "How Countries Democratize," *Political Science Quarterly* 106(4): 579–616.

Hutter, Swen 2014. "Protest Event Analysis and Its Offspring," in Donatella della Porta (ed.), *Methodological Practices in Social Movement Research*. Oxford: Oxford University press.

Innes, Abby 2001. *Czechoslovakia: The Long Goodbye*. New Haven, CT: Yale University Press.

Ismail, Salwa 2013. "Urban Subalterns in the Arab Revolutions: Cairo and Damascus in Comparative Perspective," *Comparative Studies in Society and History* 55(4): 865–94.

Jancar-Webster, Barbara 1998. "Environmental Movement and Social Change in the Transitional Countries," in Susan Baker and Petr Jehlicka (eds.), *Dilemmas of Transition: The Environment, Democracy and Economic Reform in East Central Europe*. New York: Frank Cass, pp. 113–28.

Jasper, James 1997. *The Art of Moral Protest: Culture, Biography, and Creativity in Social Movements*. Chicago: University of Chicago Press.

Jasper, James 2004. "A Strategic Approach to Collective Action: Looking for Agency in Social Movement Choices," *Mobilization* 9(1): 1–16.

Jelin, Elizabeth (ed.) 1987. *Movimientos Sociales y Democracia Emergente* (2 vols.). Buenos Aires: Centro Editor de América Latina.

Jessen, Ralph 2009. "Massenprotest und zivilgesellschaftliche Selbstorganisation in the Buergerbewegung von 1989/90," in Kalis-Dietmar Henke (ed.), *Revolution und Vereinigung 1989/90. Also in Deutschland dir Realitatet die Phantasie Ueberholte*. Munich: Deutscher Taschenbuch Verlag, pp. 163–77.

Joffé, George 2011. "The Arab Spring in North Africa. Origins and Prospects," *The Journal of North African Studies* 16(4): 507–32.

Joppke, Christian 1995. *East German Dissidents and the Revolution of 1989: Social Movement in a Leninist Regime*. New York: New York University Press.

Kaldor, Mary and Ivan Vejvoda 1999. "Democratization in Central and Eastern Europe: An Overview," in Mary Kaldor and Ivan Vejvoda (eds.), *Democratization in Central and Eastern Europe*. London: Pinter, pp. 1–24.

Kane, Anne 2001. "Finding Emotions in Social Movement Processes: Irish Land Movement Metaphors and Narratives," in Jeffrey Goodwin, James J. Jasper, and Francesca Polletta (eds.), *Passionate Politics. Emotions and Social Movements*. Chicago: University of Chicago Press, pp. 251–66.

Karatnycky, Adrian and Peter Ackerman, 2005. *How Freedom Is Won: From Civic Resistance to Durable Democracy*. New York: Freedom House.

Karl, Terry Lynn 1990. "Dilemmas of Democratization in Latin America," *Comparative Politics* 23(1): 1–21.

Keck, Margaret E. and Kathryn Sikkink, 1998. *Activists Beyond Borders: Advocacy Networks in International Politics*. Ithaca: Cornell University Press.

Kemper, Theodore 2001. "A Structural Approach to Social Movement Emotions," in Jeffrey Goodwin, James J. Jasper, and Francesca Polletta (eds.), *Passionate Politics. Emotions and Social Movements*. Chicago: University of Chicago Press, pp. 58–73.

Ketchely, Neill, Forthcoming. *Electoralization of Contention*. Manuscript.

Khamis, Sahar, Paul B. Gold, and Katherine Vaughn 2012. "Beyond Egypt's 'Facebook Revolution' and Syria's 'YouTube Uprising': Comparing Political Contexts, Actors and Communication Strategies," *Arab Media and Society* 15.

Khosrokhavar, Farhad 2012. *The New Arab Revolutions That Shook the World.* Boulder, CO: Paradigm Publishers.

Kitschelt, Herbert 1986. "Political Opportunity Structures and Political Protest: Anti-Nuclear Movements in Four Democracies," *British Journal of Political Science* 16: 57–85.

Kitschelt, Herbert 1993. "Comparative Historical Research and Rational Choice Theory: The Case of Transitions to Democracy," *Theory and Society* 22(3): 413–42.

Kitschelt, Herbert, Zdenka Mansfeldova, Radoslaw Markoswski, and Gabor Toka 1999. *Postcommunist Party Systems.* Cambridge: Cambridge University Press.

Koopmans, Ruud and Dieter Rucht 2002. "Protest Event Analysis," in Bert Klandermans and Suzanne Staggenborg (eds.), *Methods of Social Movement Research.* Minneapolis: University of Minnesota Press, pp. 231–59.

Korolczuk, Elżbieta 2013. "Promoting Civil Society in Contemporary Poland: Gendered Results of Institutional Changes," *Voluntas: International Journal of Voluntary and Nonprofit Organizations* 25(4): 949–67.

Kostadinova, Tatiana 2003. "Voter Turnout Dynamics in Post-Communist Europe," *European Journal of Political Research* 42(6): 741–59.

Kostadinova, Tatiana 2009. "Abstain or Rebel: Corruption Perceptions and Voting in East European Elections," *Politics and Policy* 37(4): 691–714.

Kramer, Mark 2002. "Collective Protests and Democratization in Poland 1989–1993: Was Civil Society Really 'Rebellious'?," *Communist and Post-Communist Studies* 35(2): 213–22.

Kriesi, Hanspeter 1991. *The Political Opportunity Structure of New Social Movements,* Discussion Paper FS III: 91–103. Berlin: Wissenschaftszentrum.

Kriesi, Hanspeter, Koopmans, Ruud, Duyvendak, Jan-Willem, and Giugni, Marco 1995. *New Social Movements in Western Europe.* Minneapolis/London: University of Minnesota Press/UCL Press.

Krzywdzinski, Martin 2012. "Trade Unions in Poland: Between Stagnation and Innovation," *Management Revenue* 23(1): 66–82.

Kuran, Timur 1991. "Now Out of Never: The Element of Surprise in the East European Revolution of 1989," *World Politics* 44(1): 7–48.

Kurzman, Charles 2012. "The Arab Spring Uncoiled," *Mobilization* 17(4): 377–90.

Leetaru, Kalev and Philip A. Schrodt 2013. "GDELT: Global Data on Events, Location, and Tone, 1979–2012," Paper presented at the ISA Annual Convention (Vol. 2, p. 4). Retrieved from http://eventdata.psu.edu/presenta tions.dir/Schrodt.Leetaru.GDELT.Presentation.pdf.

Lemke, Christiane 2013. "Protestverhalten in Transformationsgesellschaften," *Politische Vierteljahresschrift* 38(1): 50–78.

Lindekilde, Lasse 2014. "Frame Analysis and Discourse Analysis," in Donatella della Porta (ed.), *Methodological Practices in Social Movement Research.* Oxford: Oxford University Press.

Linz, Juan and Alfred Stepan 1996. *Problems of Democratic Transition and Consolidation: Southern Europe, South America, and post-Communist Europe.* Baltimore: The Johns Hopkins University Press.

Lohmann, Susanne 1993. "A Signaling Model of Informative and Manipulative Political Action," *American Political Science Review* 87: 319–33.

Lohmann, Susanne 1994. "The Dynamics of Informational Cascades: The Monday Demonstrations in Leipzig, 1989–91," *World Politics* 47(42): 102.

Long, Michael 1996. *Making History. Czech Voices of Dissent and the Revolution of 1989.* Lanham, MD: Rowman and Littlefield.

Mackell, Austin 2012. "Weaving Revolution," *Interface: A Journal for and about Social Movements* 4(1): 17–32.

Mahoney, James 2003. "Tentative Answers to Questions about Causal Mechanisms," paper presented at American Political Science Association Meetings, Philadelphia, August 29–September 1.

Mahoney, James and Goertz, Gary 2004. "The Possibility Principle: Choosing Negative Cases in Comparative Research," *American Political Science Review* 98(4): 653–69.

Mahoney, James and Gary Goertz 2006. "A Tale of Two Cultures: Contrasting Quantitative and Qualitative Research," *Political Analysis* 14(3): 227–49.

Mahoney, James and Daniel Schensul 2006. "Historical Context and Path Dependence," in Robert E. Goodwin and Charles Tilly (eds.), *Oxford Handbook of Contextual Political Analysis.* Oxford: Oxford University Press.

Malinowska, Ewa 2001. "'Kobiety i Feministki' ('Women and Feminists'), Kultura i Spoleczenstwo," *Culture and Society* 45(2): 21–38.

Mann, Michael 1973. *Consciousness and Action among the Western Working Class.* London: Palgrave.

Marshall, Thomas Humphrey 1992. "Citizenship and Social Class," in Thomas Humphrey Marshall and Thomas Bottomore (eds.), *Citizenship and Social Class.* London: Pluto Press, pp. 3–51.

Marwell, Gerald and Pamela Oliver 1993. *The Critical Mass in Collective Action: A Micro-Social Theory.* Cambridge/New York: Cambridge University Press.

Matějů, Petr 1996. "Winners and Losers in the Post-Communist Transformation: The Czech Republic in Comparative Perspective," *Innovation: The European Journal of Social Sciences* 9(3): 371–90.

Mayntz, Renate 2004. "Mechanisms in the Analysis of Social Macro-Phenomena," *Philosophy of the Social Sciences* 34(2): 237–59.

McAdam, Doug 1982. *Political Process and the Development of Black Insurgency 1930–1970.* Chicago: University of Chicago Press.

McAdam, Doug and William H. Sewell 2001. "It's About Time: Temporality in the Study of Social Movements and Revolutions," in Ronald R. Aminzade, Jack A. Goldstone, Doug McAdam, Elizabeth J. Perry, William H. Sewell Jr., Sidney Tarrow and Charles Tilly (eds.), *Silence and Voice in the Study of Contentious Politics.* New York: Cambridge University Press, pp. 89–125.

McAdam, Doug, Sidney Tarrow, and Charles Tilly 2001. *Dynamics of Contention.* Cambridge: Cambridge University Press.

McAllister Groves, Julian 2001. "Animal Rights and the Politics of Emotions: Folk Constructions of Emotions in the Animal Rights Movement," in

Jeffrey Goodwin, James J. Jasper, and Francesca Polletta (eds.), *Passionate Politics. Emotions and Social Movements*. Chicago: University of Chicago Press, pp. 212–31.

McCarthy, John D. and Zald, Mayer N. 1977. "Resource Mobilization and Social Movements: A Partial Theory," *American Journal of Sociology* 82: 1212–41.

McCarthy, John, Clark McPhail, and Jackie Smith 1996. "Images of Protest: Dimensions of Selection Bias in Media Coverage of Washington Demonstrations, 1982 and 1991," *American Sociological Review* 61: 478–99.

Meardi, Guglielmo 2005. "The Legacy of 'Solidarity': Class, Democracy, Culture and Subjectivity in the Polish Social Movement," *Social Movement Studies* 12: 261–80.

Mendelson, Sarah and John K. Glenn 2002. *The Power and Limits of NGOs*. New York: Columbia University Press.

Mentzel, Peter C. 2012. "Nationalism, Civil Society, and the Revolution of 1989," *Nations and Nationalism* 18(4): 624–42.

Mersal, Iman 2011. "Revolutionary Humor," *Globalizations* 8(5): 669–74.

Mishler, William and Richard Rose, 1997. "Trust, Distrust and Skepticism: Popular Evaluations of Civil and Political Institutions in Post-Communist Societies," *The Journal of Politics* 59(2): 418–51.

Mishler, William and Richard Rose 2001. "What Are the Origins of Political Trust? Testing Institutional and Cultural Theories in Post-Communist Societies," *Comparative Political Studies* 34(1): 30–62.

Moore, Barrington 1966. *Social Origins of Dictatorship and Democracy: Lord and Peasant in the Making of the Modern World*. Boston, MA: Beacon Press.

Morlino, Leonardo 1998. *Democracy between Consolidation and Crisis. Parties, Groups and Citizens in Southern Europe*. Oxford: Oxford University Press.

Morlino, Leonardo 2012. *Changing for Democracy*. Oxford: Oxford University Press.

Mouhoud, El Mouhoub 2011–2012. "Economie politique des révolutions arabes: analyse et perspectives," *Maghreb-Machrek* 210: 35–47.

Mueller, Carol 1999. "Claim 'Radicalization'? The 1989 Protest Cycle in the GDR," *Social Problems* 46: 528–47.

Munck, Gerardo L. and Carol Skalnik Leff 1997. "Modes of Transition and Democratization: South America and Eastern Europe in Comparative Perspective," *Comparative Politics* 29(3): 343–62.

Myant, Martin 2005. "Klaus Havel and the Debate over Civil Society in the Czech Republic," *Journal of Communist Studies and Transition Politics* 21(2): 248–67.

Nelson, Daniel N. 1996. "Civil Society Endangered," *Social Research* 63(2): 345–68.

Nepstad, Sharon Erickson 2011. *Nonviolent Revolutions: Civil Resistance in the Late 20th Century*. New York: Oxford University Press.

Nigam, Aditya 2012. "The Arab Upsurge and the 'Viral' Revolutions of Our Times," *Interface: A Journal For and About Social Movements* 4(1): 165–77.

O'Donnell, Guillermo A. 1993. "On the State, Democratization and Some Conceptual Problems (A Latin American View with Glances at Some Post-Communist Countries)," *Working Paper Series No. 92*. Notre Dame:

The Helen Kellogg Institute for International Studies, University of Notre Dame.

O'Donnell, Guillermo A. 1994. "Delegative Democracy?," *Journal of Democracy* 5: 56–69.

O'Donnell, Guillermo A. and Philippe C. Schmitter 1986. *Transitions from Authoritarian Rule: Tentative Conclusions about Uncertain Democracies.* Baltimore: The Johns Hopkins University Press.

O'Dwyer, Conor 2012. "Does the EU Help or Hinder Gay-Rights Movements in Post-Communist Europe? The Case of Poland," *East European Politics* 28(4): 332–52.

O'Dwyer, Conor 2014. "Remembering, Not Commemorating, 1989: The Twenty-Year Anniversary of the Velvet Revolution," in Michael Bernhard and Jan Kubik (eds.), *Twenty Years after Communism: The Politics of Memory and Commemoration.* Oxford: Oxford University Press, pp. 171–93.

Offe, Claus 1996. *Varieties of Transition: The East European and East German Experience.* Oxford: Polity Press.

Olesen, Thomas 2015. *Global Injustice Symbols and Social Movements.* London: Ashgate.

Olivo, Christiane 2001. *Creating a Democratic Civil Society in Eastern Germany: The Case of the Citizen Movements and Alliance 90.* London: Palgrave.

Opp, Karl-Dieter 2004. "How Does Postcommunist Transformation Affect Political Protest? The Example of East Germany," *Mobilization: An International Quarterly* 9(2): 127–47.

Opp, Karl-Dieter, Peter Voss, and Christiane Gern 1995. *Origins of a Spontaneous Revolution: East Germany, 1989.* Ann Arbor, MI: University of Michigan Press.

Osa, Maryjane 1998. "Contention and Democracy: Labor Protest in Poland, 1989–1993," *Communist and Post-Communist Studies* 31(1): 29–42.

Ost, David 2000. "Illusory corporatism in Eastern Europe: Neoliberal Tripartism and Postcommunist Class Identities," *Politics and Society* 28(4): 503–30.

Ost, David 2001. "The Weakness of Symbolic Strength: Labour and Union Identity in Poland 1989–2000," in Stephen Crowley and David Ost (eds.), *Workers after Workers States: Labour and Politics in Post-communist Eastern Europe.* Lanham: Rowman and Littlefield.

Ost, David 2005. *The Defeat of Solidarity. Anger and Politics in Post-communist Europe,* Ithaca: Cornell University Press.

Pacek, Alexander C., Grigore Pop-Eleches, and Joshua A. Tucker 2009. "Disenchanted or Discerning: Voter Turnout in Post-Communist Countries," *Journal of Politics* 71(2): 473–91.

Padgett, Stephen 2000. *Organizing Democracy in Eastern Germany: Interest Groups in Post-Communist Societies.* Cambridge: Cambridge University Press.

Paige, Jeffery 1997. *Coffee and Power: Revolution and the Rise of Democracy in Central America.* Cambridge, MA: Harvard University Press.

Parsa, Misagh 2000. *States, Ideologies and Social Revolutions: A Comparative Analysis of Iran, Nicaragua and the Philippines.* Cambridge: Cambridge University Press.

Passerini, Luisa 1978. "Conoscenza storica e storia orale. Sull'utilità e il danno delle fonti orali per la storia," in Luisa Passerini (ed.), *Storia orale. Vita quotidiana e cultura materiale delle classi subaltern.* Torino: Rosenberg & Sellier, pp. VII–XLIII.

Passerini, Luisa 1981. "Sette punti sulla memoria per l'interpretazione delle fonti orali," *L'Italia Contemporanea* 33(143): 83–92.

Passerini, Luisa 1989. "Women's Personal Narratives: Myths, Experiences and Emotions," in Personal Narrative Group (ed.), *Interpreting Women's Lives: Feminist Theory and Personal Narrative.* Bloomington: Indiana University Press, pp. 189–97.

Pateman, Carole 1970. *Participation and Democratic Theory.* Cambridge: Cambridge University Press.

Perez Diaz, Victorio 1996. *Espana puesta a prueba 1976–1996.* Madrid: Alianza.

Perkins, Kenneth 2004. *A History of Modern Tunisia.* Cambridge: Cambridge University Press.

Perrot, Michelle 1974. *Les ouvriers en grève. France 1871–1890.* Paris: Mouton.

Petrova, Tsveta and Sidney Tarrow 2007. "Transactional and Participatory Activism in the Emerging European Polity: The Puzzle of East Central Europe," *Comparative Political Studies* 40(1): 74–94.

Pfaff, Steven 2006. *Exit-Voice Dynamics and the Collapse of East Germany: The Crisis of Leninism and the Revolution of 1989.* Durham, NC: Duke University Press.

Pfaff, Steven and Hyojoung Kim, 2003. "Exit-Voice Dynamics in Collective Action: An Analysis of Emigration and Protest in the East German Revolution," *American Journal of Sociology* 109(2): 401–44.

Pickvance, Katy 1997. "Social Movements in Hungary and Russia: The Case of Environmental Movements," *European Sociological Review* 13(1): 35–54.

Piotrowski, Grzegorz 2009. "Civil Society, Un-Civil Society and the Social Movements," *Interface: A Journal For and About Social Movements* 1(2): 166–89.

Piven, Frances F. and Richard Cloward 1977. *Poor People's Movements.* New York: Pantheon.

Pizzorno, Alessandro (ed.) 1993. *Le Radici della Politica Assoluta e Altri Saggi.* Milan: Feltrinelli.

Poirier, Jean and Simone Clapier-Vailadon 1980. "Le concept d'ethnobiographie et le récit de vie croisé," *Cahiers Internationaux de Sociologie* 27(69): 351–8.

Polanyi, Karl 1957. *The Great Transformation: The Political and Economic Origins of Our Time.* Boston: Beacon Press.

Pollert, Anna 1997. "The Transformation of Trade Unionism in the Capitalist and Democratic Restructuring of the Czech Republic," *European Journal of Industrial Relations* 3(2): 203–28.

Pollert, Anna 2001. "Labour and Trade Unions in the Czech Republic, 1989–2000," in Stephen Crowley and David Ost (eds.), *Workers after Workers' State: Labor and Politics in Post-Communist Eastern Europe.* Lanham, MD: Rowman and Littlefield, pp. 13–36.

Polletta, Francesca and Edwin Amenta, 2001. "Conclusion: Second That Emotion? Lessons from Once-Novel Concepts in Social Movement

Research," in Jeffrey Goodwin, James J. Jasper, and Francesca Polletta (eds.), *Passionate Politics: Emotions and Social Movements*. Chicago: University of Chicago Press, pp. 303–16.

Polletta, Francesca and James M. Jasper, 2001. "Collective Identity and Social Movements," *Annual Review of Sociology* 27: 283–305.

Poppe, Ulrike 1995. "'Der Weg is das Ziel.' Zum Selbstversaendnis und der politischen Rolle oppositioneller Gruppen der achtziger Jahre," in Ulrike Poppe, Rainer Eckert, and Ilko-Sascha Kowlczuk (eds.), *Zwischen Selbstbehauptung und Anpassung. Formen des Widerstandes und der Opposition in der DDR*. Berlin: Ch.Links Verlag, pp. 244–72.

Portelli, Alessandro 1991. *The Death of Luigi Trastulli and Other Stories: Form and Meaning in Oral History*. New York: SUNY Press.

Potůček, Martin 2000. "The Uneasy Birth of Czech Civil Society," *Voluntas: International Journal of Voluntary and Nonprofit Organizations* 11(2): 107–21.

Prashad, Vijay 2012. "Dream History of the Global South," *Interface: A Journal For and About Social Movements* 4(1): 43–53.

Preuss, Ulrich 1995. *Constitutional Revolution: The Link between Constitutionalism and Progress*. Atlantic Highlands, NJ: Humanities Press.

Reed, Jean-Pierre 2004. "Emotions in Context. Revolutionary Accelerators, Hope, Moral Outrage and Other Emotions in the Making of the Nicaragua Revolution," *Theory and Society* 33: 653–703.

Renwick, Alan 2006. "Anti-Political or Just Anti-Communist? Varieties of Dissidence in East-Central Europe and Their Implications for the Development of Political Society," *East European Politics and Societies* 20(2): 286–33.

Rink, Dieter 1999. "Mobilisierungsschwäche, Latenz, Transformation oder Auflösung? Bilanz und Perspektive der Entwicklung (neuer) sozialer Bewegungen in Ost-Deutschland," in Ansgar Klein, Hans-Josef Legrand, and Thomas Leif (eds.), *Neue soziale Bewegungen: Impulse, Bilanzen und Perspektiven*. Opladen: Westdeutscher Verlag, pp. 180–95.

Rink, Dieter 2001. "Institutionalization instead of Mobilization – The Environmental Movement in Eastern Germany," in Helena Flam (ed.), *Pink, Purple and Green: Women's, Religious, Environmental and Gay/Lesbian Movements in Central Europe Today*. New York: Columbia University Press.

Ritter, Daniel 2014. *The Iron Cage of Liberalism*. Oxford: Oxford University Press.

Roberts, Kenneth 2015. *Changing Courses*. Cambridge: Cambridge University Press.

Rochon, Thomas R. 1998. *Culture Moves: Ideas, Activism, and Changing Values*. Princeton, NJ: Princeton University Press.

Rootes, Christopher (ed.) 2003. *Environmental Protest in Western Europe*. Oxford: Oxford University Press.

Rosanvallon, Pierre 2006. *La contre-démocratie: La politique a l'age de la defiance*. Paris: Seuil.

Rucht, Dieter 1995. "The Impact of Anti-nuclear Power Movements in International Comparison," in Martin Bauer (ed.), *Resistance to New*

Technology. Nuclear Power, Information Technology and Biotechnology. Cambridge: Cambridge University Press, pp. 277–92.

Rucht, Dieter 1996. "The Impact of National Contexts on Social Movements Structure," in Doug McAdam, John McCarthy, and Mayer N. Zald (eds.), *Comparative Perspective on Social Movements: Political Opportunities, Mobilizing Structures, and Cultural Framing.* Cambridge/New York: Cambridge University Press, pp. 185–204.

Rucht, Dieter, Barbara Blattert, and Dieter Rink 1997. *Soziale Bewegungen auf den Weg zur Institutionalisierung. Zum Strukturwandel "alternativer" Gruppen in beiden Teilen Deutschlands.* Frankfurt/main: Campus Verlag.

Rucht, Dieter and Thomas Ohlemacher 1992. "Protest Event Data: Collection Uses and Perspectives," Ron Eyerman and Mario Diani (eds.), *Issues in Contemporary Social Movement Research.* London: Sage, pp. 76–106.

Salt, Jeremy 2012. "Containing the 'Arab Spring,'" *Interface: A Journal for and about Social Movements* 4(1): 54–66.

Santos, Boaventura de Sousa (ed.) 2005. *Democratizing Democracy: Beyond the Liberal Democratic Canon.* London: Verso.

Sarre, Philip and Petr Jehlička 2007. "Environmental Movements in Space-Time: The Czech and Slovak Republics from Stalinism to Post-Socialism," *Transactions of the Institute of British Geographers*, New Series 32(3): 346–62.

Saxonberg, Steven 2001. *The Fall: A Comparative Study of the End of Communism in Czechoslovakia, East Germany, Hungary and Poland.* Amsterdam: Harwood Academic Publishers.

Schimmelfenning, Frank 2014. "Conclusion," in Timm Beichelt, Irene Hahn-Fuhr, Frank Schimmelfennig, and Susann Worschech (eds.), *Civil Society and Democratic Promotion.* London: Palgrave, pp. 217–33.

Schmitter, Philippe 1984. "Patti e transizioni: Mezzi non-democratici a fini democratici?," *Rivista Italiana di Scienza Politica* 14(3): 363–82.

Schmitter, Philippe 2009. "The Nature and Future of Comparative Politics," *European Political Science Review* 1(1): 33–61.

Schnabel, Claus and Joachim Wagner 2003. "Trade Union Membership in Eastern and Western Germany: Convergence or Divergence?," IZA Discussion paper series No. 707, Bonn: Institute for the Study of Labour, available http://econpapers.repec.org/paper/izaizadps/dp707.htm.

Schneider, Cathy 1992. "Radical Opposition Parties and Squatter Movements in Pinochet's Chile," in Arturo Escobar and Sonia Alvarez (eds.), *The Making of Social Movements in Latin America. Identity, Strategy, and Democracy.* Boulder, CO: Westview Press, pp. 60–75.

Schneider, Cathy 1995. *Shantytown Protests in Pinochet's Chile.* Philadelphia: Temple University Press.

Schrodt, Philip A. 2012. *CAMEO: Conflict and Mediation Event Observations Event and Actor. Codebook.* Available at http://data.gdeltproject.org/documentation/CAMEO.Manual.1.1b3.pdf.

Selbin, Eric 2010. *Revolution, Rebellion, Resistance: The Power of Story.* New York: Zed Books.

Seleny, Anna 2014. "Revolutionary Road: 1956 and the Fracturing of the Hungarian Historical Memory," in Michael Bernhard and Jan Kubik (eds.), *Twenty Years after Communism: The Politics of Memory and Commemoration*. Oxford: Oxford University Press, pp. 37–59.

Sewell, William H. 1996. "Three Temporalities: Toward an Eventful Sociology," in Terence J. McDonald (ed.), *The Historic Turn in the Human Sciences*. Ann Arbor: University of Michigan Press, pp. 245–80.

Shahshahani, Azadeh and Corinna Mullin 2012. "The Legacy of US Intervention and the Tunisian Revolution: Promises and Challenges One Year On," *Interface: A Journal For and About Social Movements* 4(1): 67–101.

Shain, Yossi and Juan J. Linz 1995. *Between States: Interim Governments and Democratic Transitions*. Cambridge: Cambridge University Press.

Shorbagy, Manar 2007. "Understanding Kefaya: The New Politics in Egypt," *Arab Studies Quarterly* 29(1): 39–60.

Skocpol, Theda 1979. *States and Social Revolutions*. Cambridge: Cambridge University Press.

Smolar, Aleksander 1996. "Civil Society after Communism: From Opposition to Atomization," *Journal of Democracy* 7: 24–38.

Stark, David and Laszlo Bruszt 1998. *Postsocialist Pathways: Transforming Politics and Property in East Central Europe*. Cambridge: Cambridge University Press.

Stein, Arlene 2001. "Revenge of the Shamed: The Christian Right's Emotional Culture War," in Jeffrey Goodwin, James J. Jasper, and Francesca Polletta (eds.), *Passionate Politics. Emotions and Social Movements*. Chicago: University of Chicago Press, pp. 115–33.

Stork, Joe 2011. "Three Decades of Human Rights Activism in the Middle East and North Africa," in Joel Benin and Frédéric Vairel (eds.), *Social Movements, Mobilization and Contestation in the Middle East and North Africa*. Stanford, CA: Stanford University Press, pp. 83–106.

Sztompka, Piotr 1993. *The Sociology of Social Change*. Oxford: Basil Blackwell.

Tarrow, Sidney 1989. *Democracy and Disorder: Protest and Politics in Italy, 1965–1975*. Oxford: Oxford University Press.

Tarrow, Sidney 1994. *Power in Movement. Social Movements, Collective Action and Politics*. New York: Cambridge University Press.

Tarrow, Sidney 1995. "Mass Mobilization and Regime Change: Pacts, Reform and Popular Power in Italy (1918–1922) and Spain (1975–1978)," in Richard Gunther, Nikiforos Diamandouros, and Hans-Jürgen Puhle (eds.), *Democratic Consolidation in Southern Europe*. Baltimore: The Johns Hopkins University Press, pp. 204–30.

Teorell, Jan 2010. *Determinants of Democratization. Explaining Regime Change in the World, 1972–2006*. Cambridge: Cambridge University Press.

Teti, Andrea and Gennaro Gervasio 2012. "After Mubarak, before Transition: The Challenges for Egypt's Democratic Opposition," *Interface: A Journal for and about Social Movements* 4(1): 102–12.

Thompson, Edward Palmer 1978. *The Poverty of Theory and Other Essays*. London: Merlin Press.

Tilly, Charles 2001. "Mechanisms in Political Science," *Annual Review of Political Science* 4(1): 21–41.

Tilly, Charles 2004. *Social Movements, 1768–2004*. Boulder, CO: Paradigm.

Tilly, Charles 2006. *Regimes and Repertoires*. Chicago: University of Chicago Press.

Tocqueville, Alexis de 1955. *The Old Regime and the Revolution*. New York: Anchor Books.

Tufekci, Zeynep and Christopher Wilson 2012. "Social Media and the Decision to Participate in Political Protest: Observations from Tahrir Square," *Journal of Communication* 62(2): 363–79.

VanDeveer, Stacy D. and JoAnn Carmin 2004. "Assessing Conventional Wisdom: Environmental Challenges and Opportunities beyond Eastern Accession," *Environmental Politics* 13(1): 315–31.

Virchow, Fabian 2007. "'Capturing the Streets' – Marches as a Political Instrument of the Extreme Right in Contemporary Germany," in Matthias Reiss (ed.), *The Street as Stage: Protest Marches and Public Rallies since the Nineteenth Century*. Oxford: Oxford University Press, pp. 295–310.

Viterna, Jocelyn and Kathleen M. Fallon 2008. "Democratization, Women's Movements, and Gender-Equitable States: A Framework for Comparison," *American Sociological Review* 73: 668–89.

Waller, Michael 1995. "Adaptation of the Former Communist Parties of East-Central Europe: A Case of Social-Democratization?," *Party Politics* 1: 473–89.

Wallerstein, Immanuel 2011. "The Contradictions of the Arab Spring," www .aljazeera.com/indepth/opinion/2011/11/2011111111101711539134.html (accessed March 7, 2013).

Ward, Michael, Andreas Beger, Josh Cutler, Matthew Dickenson, Cassy Dorff, and Ben Radford. 2013. Comparing GDELT and ICEWS event data. Analysis, 21: 267–97.

Warkotsch, Jana 2012. "Bread, Freedom, Human Dignity: Tales of an Unfinished Revolution in Egypt," http://cosmos.eui.eu/Documents/Publications/Working Papers/2012WP14COSMOS.pdf.

Weiss, Hilde 2003. "A Cross-National Comparison of Nationalism in Austria, the Czech and Slovac Republics, Hungary, and Poland," *Political Psychology* 24(2): 377–401.

Whittier, Nancy 2001. "*Emotional Strategies: The Collective Reconstruction and Display of Oppositional Emotions in the Movement against Child Sexual Abuse*," in Jeffrey Goodwin, James J. Jasper, and Francesca Polletta (eds.), *Passionate Politics. Emotions and Social Movements*. Chicago: University of Chicago Press, pp. 233–50.

Whittier, Nancy 2004. "The Consequences of Social Movements for Each Other," in Davis A. Snow, Sarah H. Soule, and Hanspeter Kriesi (eds.), *The Blackwell Companion to Social Movements*. Oxford: Blackwell, pp. 531–51.

Williams, Dana M. and Matthew T. Lee 2012. "Aiming to Overthrow the State (without Using the State): Political Opportunities for Anarchist Movements," *Comparative Sociology* 11(4): 558–93.

Willis, Michael J. 2016. "Revolt for Dignity: Tunisia's Revolution and Civil Resistance," in Adam Roberts, Michael J. Willis, Rory McCarthy, and

Timothy Garton Ash (eds.), *Civil Resistance in the Arab Spring: Triumphs and Disasters*. Oxford: Oxford University Press, pp. 30–52.

Wolff, Jonas 2014. "From the Unity of Goodness to Conflicting Objectives; The Inherent Tensions in External Promotion of Democracy and Civil Society," in Timm Beichelt, Irene Hahn-Fuhr, Frank Schimmelfennig, and Susann Worschech (eds.), *Civil Society and Democratic Promotion*. London: Palgrave, pp. 67–85.

Wood, Elisabeth 2000. *Forging Democracy from Below. Insurgent Transitions in South Africa and El Salvador*. Cambridge: Cambridge University Press.

Wood, Elisabeth 2004. *Democratization from Below*. Cambridge: Cambridge University Press.

Yashar, Deborah J. 2005. *Contesting Citizenship in Latin America: The Rise of Indigenous Movements and the Postliberal Challenge*. New York: Cambridge University Press.

Zamponi, Lorenzo 2015. *Memories of Student Movements*. PhD Thesis, European University Institute, Department of Political and Social Sciences.

Ziblatt, Daniel F. 1998. "The Adaptation of Ex-Communist Parties to Post-Communist East Central Europe: A Comparative Study of the East German and Hungarian Ex-Communist Parties," *Communist and Post-Communist Studies* 31(2): 119–37.

Zolberg, Aristide R. 1972. "Moments of Madness," *Politics and Society* 2(2): 183–207.

LIST OF INTERVIEWEES

Czechoslovakia/Czech Republic

Interview CZ1. Before the revolution, an editor of a student newspaper that promoted actions against the regime, in 1989 was spokesperson for University Strike Committee and a founding member of the Civic Forum. After the year 1989, she was a member of the minister's private office and official spokesperson for the ministry.

Interview CZ2, 31.7.2013. Bishop, in 1977 he signed Charta 77 and, since 1979, was active in the Committee for the Defence of the Unjustly Persecuted. In 1981–1982 was also spokesman of Charta 77. He got involved in the events of November 1989 mainly as a moderator of various meetings and as a spokesman for the Civic Forum.

Interview CZ3, 13.9.2013. Signed Charta 77 in 1977 and in the year 1979 he became a member of the Committee for the Defence of the Unjustly Persecuted. He also participated in the Movement for Civic Freedom and was a founding member of Civic Forum. He served as deputy interior minister and later the minister of the interior.

Interview CZ4, 13.9.2013. Director of People in Need, in 1989 he founded the student movement organization STUHA. During the student protests in early November 1989, he was elected to the presidium of the Student Coordination Centre and also became a member of Civic forum. He also worked for Václav Havel's presidential administration as a foreign policy specialist.

Interview CZ5, 5.8.2013. Lyricist, poet, writer, journalist, and producer, in autumn 1989, he established a civic initiative called MOST (Bridge) that worked to form a platform for eventual talks between the communist government and dissidents. Later he became Civic Forum's spokesperson for foreign media. When Václav Havel was elected president, he resigned from the leadership of the Civic Forum.

Interview CZ6, 19.9.2013. Former dissident, he had focused on editorial and publishing work in samizdat (e.g. Revolver Revue) and on cooperation with opposition groups in Central and Eastern Europe (e.g. Polish-Czechoslovak Solidarity). He later signed Charta 77 and coauthored the petition "A Few Sentences." During the Velvet Revolution in November 1989, he participated in the foundation of the Civic Forum. After transition, he served as foreign policy advisor to President Vaclav Havel, Czech ambassador to the United States, and senator.

Interview CZ7, 12.9.2013. The son of one of the most active dissidents, he took part in the student movement and, in 1990, was elected to parliament. At the same time he was one of the founding members of the Christian Democratic Party.

Interview CZ8, 11.11.2013. A Czech playwright, writer, director, screenwriter, and actor, since 1978 he contributed to the opposition by signing petitions and, especially, through his theater activities. He was one of the key figures of the process of deciding about the strike of theaters during the first days of the revolution and later leader of the theater strike committee.

Interview CZ9, 9.10.2013. Participated on various dissident activities, mainly seminars and meetings.

Interview CZ10, 6.11.2013. A Czech composer, singer, and political activist, founder of MOST (Bridge). After November 17, he cofounded Civic Forum. Later he was elected MP. He then resigned from the parliament and returned to music. He was also Havel's external advisor and later became minister of human rights and minorities.

Interview CZ11, 22.7.2013. Industrial worker, during the Velvet Revolution, he organized the march of industrial workers on Wenceslas square on November 23. He became a member of Civic Forum and later minister of labour and social affairs.

Interview CZ12, a Czech playwright, his work was banned since 1972. In 1977 he signed Charta 77 and became a member of the Movement for Civic Freedom. During the revolution and shortly after it, he participated in Civic Forum. Later he became a member of Civic Democrats (ODS), serving as an MP and as a minister of culture.

Interview CZ13, 7.11.2013. A former member of Communist Party of Czechoslovakia since 1960, he left the party after the Prague Spring and started participating in anti-regime activities, signing the Charta 77 petition. During the Velvet Revolution, he was one of the leaders of Civic Forum and later served as an MP and prime minister.

Interview CZ14, 15.7.2014. She signed Charta 77, and served as Charta's spokesperson. Later she was one of the founders of the Committee for the Defence of the Unjustly Prosecuted. After the revolution she remained active in the field of protecting human rights.

Interviews GDR

Interview GDR1, 28.5.2013. Member of the opposition since 1982, within the Protestant Church cofounder of Independent Women's Association, represented it at the Round Table, member of the Bundestag via the same association as part of Bund 90/Greens.

Interview GDR2, 30.5.2013. Founder of Women for Peace since early 1980s, involved with Initiative Peace and Human Rights, and Peace Concrete, in 1989 cofounder of Democracy Now and representative at Round Table and member of Volkskammer (Bund 90).

Interview GDR3, 31.5.2013. Since 1984 active within the Protestant Church and founder of an environmental group, was later founder of the Green Party in the GDR, and then member of the Berlin city parliament.

Interview GDR4, 3.6.2013. Civil rights and environment activist already in the 1970s, was cofounder of the Environment Library and spokesperson of Green Party (GDR) for which he was at the Round Table and, then, served in the Berlin city parliament.

Interview GDR5, 7.6.2013. Expelled from SPD in 1983, after protests against nuclear missile stationing; founder of Peace Circle Pankow as well as members in Church from Below, and the Environment Library. For the Green Party of the GDR was member of the Volkskammer, and then member of Bundestag for the Greens and then the CDU.

Interview GDR6, 14.6.2013. Environmental activist before 1989, was later member of European parliament and state parliament for Bund 90/Greens.

Interview GDR7, 21.6.2013. Pastor at Thomas Church, Leipzig, he organized the peace prayers at that church.

Interview GDR8, 25.6.2013. Member of the Peace Circle in Samariter Church in Berlin, cofounder of Demokratischer Aufbruch (Democratic Beginning), after 1990 member of a borough parliament in Berlin.

Interview GDR9, 28.6.2013. In the late 1980s, founder and spokesperson of Democracy Now, represented it at the Round Table; member of the Volkskammer and later on of the Federal Parliament for Bund 90.

Interview GDR10, 2.7.2013. Founder of peace seminar at Immanuel Parish Berlin, with a focus on nuclear energy politics; cofounder of New Forum and its representative at the Round Table, minister without portfolio of the GDR government in 1990; later on member of the city parliament of Berlin (New Forum).

Interview GDR11, 19.7.2013. Organizer of oppositional activities with a focus on peace since 1977, he was pastor at the Thomas Church in Leipzig, where he initiated the peace prayers.

Interview GDR12, 5.6.2013. Active in oppositional circles since 1968, he is one of the initiators of the Initiative Peace and Human Rights and, in 1989 and 1990, its delegate to the Round Table; in 1990 minister without portfolio in the GDR government, party group leader in the Volkskammer and then member of Bundestag (Bund 90/Greens).

Interviews Egypt

Interview EGY1, 19.3.2014. Scholar and analyst, participated in the uprising in 2011.

Interview EGY2, 22.3.2014. Member of the April 6th movement, and the movement coalition Road to Revolution.

Interview EGY3, 25.3.2014. One of the founders of Shayfeen.com, an election monitoring and human rights organization.

Interview EGY4, 08.4.2014. Young MB since 2009, joining in 2011 the Strong Egypt party. He also participated in an NGO called Awareness, which aimed at bringing together Egyptians from different ideologies and religions.

Interview EGY5, 10.4.2014. A prominent women's rights activist during and after the uprising.

Interview EGY6, 10.4.2014. Activist and student leader, cofounder of Dostour (constitution) party in 2012, headed by Mohamed El Baradei.

Interview EGY7, 10.4.2014. Worked in the presidential campaign of Abdel Moneim Aboul Fotouh; program manager at the Egyptian Democratic Academy, a Cairo-based democracy development NGO.

Interview EGY8, 12.4.2014. One of the founders of the April 6th movement.

Interview EGY9, 12.4.2014. Member of the Socialist Renewal Current, revolutionary socialists who joined other forces to form a new party, in addition to the other leftist forces: the Popular Alliance Party.

Interview EGY10, 15.4.2014. Student at Cairo University, activist from 2011 to 2013.

Interview EGY11, 22.4.2014. A member of Al Dustour party, and a political activist in student politics since the uprising.

Interview EGY12, 26.4.2014. A former member of the Muslim Brotherhood youth, involved in the revolution, and actually a member of the Strong Egypt party.

Interviews Hungary

Interview HU1, 10.6.2013. A writer, teacher, and politician, he was active in the underground press, in the network of Free Initiatives, and the Hungarian Helsinki Committee. He founded the Alliance of Free Democrats and was a MP of the Alliance.

Interview HU2, 8.8.2013. He was a legal advisor for civil and environmental organisations in the late 1980s and among the founders of the environmentalist

Danube Circle. He was later one of the founders of the Hungarian Democratic Forum and represented that party in the Opposition Roundtable negotiations. Later on he was president of the Constitutional Court of Hungary and then President of Hungary.

Interview HU3, 2.7.2013. Former member of the Danube circle.

Interview HU4, 9.7.2013. After joining Fidesz during the transition to democracy, she was elected member of parliament in 1990. She left Fidesz in 1994 in critique to the party moving from liberal to conservative position and later joined the Together in 2014.

Interview HU5, 9.7.2013. Oppositional activist since the early 1980s, he cofounded the left-wing party Alliance of Free Democrat and then joined the Green Left.

Interview HU6, 15.7.2013. One of Fidesz founder and editor of *Magyar Narancs*.

Interview HU7, 1.8.2013. Founder of National Trade Union of Scientific Workers.

Interview HU8, 26.6.2013. Fidesz founder, and later member of the Alliance of Free Democrats. After the transition, she was a member of parliament and later leader of Free People for Hungary.

Interview HU9, 9.7.2013. Member of Fidesz from 1988 to 1993, he served as minister in the 2000s.

Interview HU10, 30.7.2013. Founder of Independent Lawyers' Forum, he later served as a minister in the national government.

Interview HU11, 25.6.2013. A Fidesz founder.

Interview HU12, 6.7.2013. One of the founders of Foundation for the Poor.

Interviews Poland

Interview PL1, 17.7.2013. Former dissident and publisher of an underground journal, now editor and publisher of a cultural journal.

Interview PL2, 18.7.2013. An oppositional activist, he was chairman of the board of the underground region of Solidarity and a member of the Provisional Coordinating Commission and for this was arrested and sentenced in 1982. Since December 1983, he participated in a hunger strike that lasted for 104 days. A member of the Civic Committee, he took part in the Round Table. Later, he was MP and minister.

Interview PL3, 25.7.2013. In 1980 he joined Solidarity, becoming a member of the National Coordination Committee, then the National Committee of the Union, and the chairman of the board of the Region Lower Silesia. In 1981–1982 he led the underground Regional Strike Committee of Lower Silesia. In the years 1982–1986, he was often imprisoned. In 1989, he took part in the Round Table sessions. He was chairman of the Freedom Union and the Democratic Party, and was a MP.

Interview PL4, 24.7.2013. An active member of the Linux community, he mobilized in 1989 with youth groups.

Interview PL5, 26.7.2013. In the 1980s, he was an activist in the movement Freedom and Peace. Later he cofounded the Anarchist Federation and is a coordinator of the National Trade Union of the Workers' Initiative, linked to the environment Poznan squat "Rozbrat."

Interview PL6, 26.7.2013. Theater actress, activist of the opposition with the Poznań's 8th Day Theatre.

Interview PL7, 5.8.2013. In the years 1980 to 1989 was an activist of Solidarity and, after the introduction of the martial law in Poland, a leader of underground Solidarity and chairman of the Steering Committee of Lower Silesia. He was repeatedly arrested and imprisoned. Also a promoter of the happenings of the Orange Alternative. He was later vice chairman of the Labour Union for Foreign Affairs and a member of parliament for the Group of European Socialists.

Interview PL8, 7.8.2013. In Solidarity since the early 1980s, interned after the imposition of the martial law and then in exile in Sweden, where he organized a Solidarity Support Committee.

Interview PL9, 7.8.2013. He was one of the initiators of the Orange Alternative movement.

Interview PL10, 16.10.2013. A member of the Polish Independence Alliance, during martial law he was interned for several days. Secretary of the Citizens' Committee with Lech Walesa, he was secretary of the Advisory Committee of the president. Member of center-party Civic Alliance, he was an MP and a minister.

Interview PL11, 16.10.2013. After the introduction of the martial law, she became part of the editorial team of the samizdat "TygodnikMazowsze" magazine edited by the underground Solidarity.

Interview PL12. 17.10.2013. A member of various organizations opposing the communist regime since the late 1970s. He promoted the Movement for Defense of Human and Civic Rights and the Confederation of Independent Poland as a right-wing party in the underground. In the Polish parliamentary elections of 1991, he became a member of the parliament.

Interview PL13, 15.1.2014. A prominent figure of the Polish anti-communist opposition, participating in the activity of the Workers' Defence Committee as well as editor of several underground newpapers. He was imprisoned, first, after the 1968 March Events, and then after the introduction of martial law in 1981. In 1988 he became an advisor of Lech Wałęsa's informal Coordination Committee, and later played a crucial role during the Polish Round Table Talks. He became a member of the Solidarity Citizens' Committee. After transition, he was a member of parliament and supported Prime Minister Tadeusz Mazowiecki's government and his candidature in the presidential election campaign against Lech Wałęsa in 1990.

Interview PL14. 30,1.2014. Oppositional student activist in the late 1960s, and in 1978–1979 he was in the Team of Citizens' Initiative. In May 1980 he was a participant of a hunger strike in St. Christopher church in protest against the detention in prison of opposition activists and from the autumn of 1981 advisor to Lech Walesa and during the martial law the editor of an underground magazine. In 1989, he participated in the Round Table on the team for political reform. He was minister in the government of Tadeusz Mazowiecki, and president of the Forum of the Democratic Right; later served in the Conservative Party and the Liberal Conservative Alliance.

Interviews Tunisia

Interview TU1, 8.3.2014. Two former activists in their early thirties. Were active in the 2010–2011 uprising, but demobilized in the year after. No organizational affiliation.

Interview TU2, 12.3.2014. Senior member of Ennahda and minister for the movement between 2011 and 2013.

Interview TU3, 12.3.2014. Member of the Congress for the Republic bloc in the Constituent Assembly.

Interview TU4, 12.3.2014. Female activist, mid-twenties, nonaligned but with an Ennahda background.

Interview TU5, 15.3. 2014. Male activist, mid-twenties, member of the Union of Unemployed Graduates.

Interview TU6, 17.3.2014. Secular human right activist, twenty years old, activist since 2011.

Interview TU7, 18.3.2014. Activist in one of the Councils for the Protection of the Revolution, in his late forties, currently focused on struggle against corruption; Ennahda supporter.

Interview TU8, 19.3.2014. Secular activist, thirty years old, became a well-known blogger during the 2010–2011 uprising.

Interview TU9, 21.3.2014. Salafist activist, mid-thirties, became publicly active since the revolution.

Interview TU10, 26.3.2014. Former Ennahda activist, mid-twenties, recently left the movement.

Interview TU11, 26.3.2014. Senior student activist at the student union.

Interview TU12, 30.3.2014. Secular activist, late twenties, active at an observatory for Tunisian elections.

Index

Books in the Series (continued from p. iii)